**o|s Ordnance Survey**

D0795353

# STREET ATLAS
# North
# Essex

## Contents

First colour edition published 1999

Ordnance Survey® and George Philip Ltd, a division of
Romsey Road Octopus Publishing Group Ltd
Maybush 2-4 Heron Quays
Southampton London
SO16 4GU E14 4JP

ISBN 0-540-07292 3 (pocket)

## Digital Data

The exceptionally high-quality mapping found in this book is available as digital data in TIFF format, which is easily convertible to other bit-mapped (raster) image formats.

The index is also available in digital form as a standard database table. It contains all the details found in the printed index together with the National Grid reference for the map square in which each entry is named and feature codes for places of interest in eight categories such as education and health.

For further information and to discuss your requirements, please contact the Ordnance Survey Solutions Centre on 01703 792929.

## Also available in various formats

- ◆ **Berkshire**
- ◆ **Birmingham and West Midlands**
- ◆ **Bristol and Avon**
- ◆ **Buckinghamshire**
- **Cannock, Lichfield Rugeley**
- ◆ **Cardiff, Swansea and Glamorgan**
- ◆ **Cheshire**
- ◆ **Derbyshire**
- **Derby and Belper**
- ◆ **Durham**
- ◆ **Edinburgh and East Central Scotland**

- ◆ **South Essex**
- ◆ **Glasgow and West Central Scotland**
- ◆ **Greater Manchester**
- ◆ **North Hampshire**
- ◆ **South Hampshire**
- ◆ **Hertfordshire**
- ◆ **East Kent**
- ◆ **West Kent**
- ◆ **Lancashire**
- ◆ **Merseyside**
- **Northwich, Winsford Middlewich**
- ◆ **Nottinghamshire**
- ◆ **Oxfordshire**

- **Peak District Towns**
- ◆ **Staffordshire**
- **Stafford, Stone Uttoxeter**
- ◆ **Surrey**
- ◆ **East Sussex**
- ◆ **West Sussex**
- ◆ **Tyne and Wear**
- **Warrington, Widnes Runcorn**
- ◆ **Warwickshire**
- ◆ **South Yorkshire**
- ◆ **West Yorkshire**

- ◆ Colour regional atlases (hardback, spiral, wire-o, pocket)  Colour local atlases (paperback)
- ◆ Black and white regional atlases (hardback, softback, pocket)

| | | | |
|---|---|---|---|
| | Motorway (with junction number) | | Railway station |
| | Primary route (dual carriageway and single) | | Private railway station |
| | A road (dual carriageway and single) | | Bus, coach station |
| | B road (dual carriageway and single) | | Ambulance station |
| | Minor road (dual carriageway and single) | | Coastguard station |
| | Other minor road (dual carriageway and single) | | Fire station |
| | Road under construction | | Police station |
| | Pedestrianised area | | Accident and Emergency entrance to hospital |
| DY7 | Postcode boundaries | H | Hospital |
| | County and Unitary Authority boundaries | + | Places of worship |
| | Railway | i | Information Centre (open all year) |
| | Tramway, miniature railway | P | Parking |
| | Rural track, private road or narrow road in urban area | P&R | Park and Ride |
| | Gate or obstruction to traffic (restrictions may not apply at all times or to all vehicles) | PO | Post Office |
| | Path, bridleway, byway open to all traffic, road used as a public path | | Camping site |
| | The representation in this atlas of a road, track or path is no evidence of the existence right of way | | Caravan |
| 126 | | | Golf course |
| 94 | Adjoining page indicators | | Picnic |
| | | Prim Sch | Important buildings, schools, colleges, universities and hospitals |
| | | River Medway | Water name |

**Walsall** (Railway station)

| | | | |
|---|---|---|---|
| Acad | **Academy** | Meml | **Memorial** |
| Crem | **Crematorium** | Mon | **Monument** |
| Cemy | **Cemetery** | Mus | **Museum** |
| C Ctr | **Civic Centre** | Obsv | **Observatory** |
| CH | **Club House** | Pal | **Royal Palace** |
| Coll | **College** | PH | **Public House** |
| Ent | **Enterprise** | Recn Gd | **Recreation Ground** |
| Ex H | **Exhibition Hall** | Resr | **Reservoir** |
| Ind Est | **Industrial Estate** | Ret Pk | **Retail Park** |
| Inst | **Institute** | Sch | **School** |
| Ct | **Law Court** | Sh Ctr | **Shopping Centre** |
| L Ctr | **Leisure Centre** | TH | **Town Hall/House** |
| LC | **Level Crossing** | Trad Est | **Trading Estate** |
| Liby | **Library** | Univ | **University** |
| Mkt | **Market** | YH | **Youth Hostel** |

|  |  |
|---|---|
| | Stream |
| | River or canal (minor and major) |
| | Water |
| | Tidal water |
| | Woods |
| | Houses |
| House | Non-Roman antiquity |
| VILLA | Roman antiquity |

■ The dark grey border on the inside edge of some pages indicates that the mapping does not continue onto the adjacent page

■ The small numbers around the edges of the maps identify 1 kilometre National Grid lines

**The scale of the maps is 3.92 cm to 1 km**
**(2½ inches to 1 mile)**

| 0 | ¼ | ½ | ¾ | 1 mile |
|---|---|---|---|---|
| 0 | 250m | 500m | 750m | 1 kilometre |

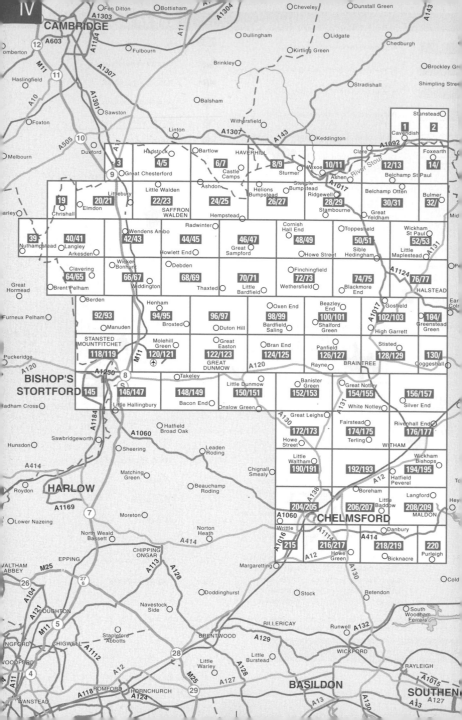

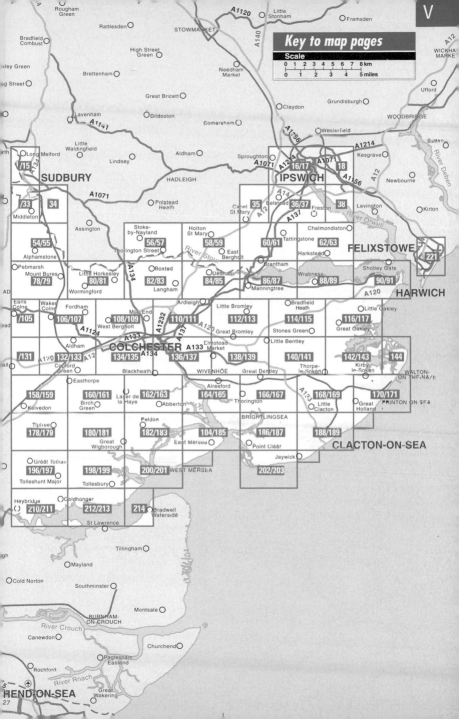

**Key to map pages**

Scale

| 0 | 1 | 2 | 3 | 4 | 5 | 6 | 7 | 8 km |
| 0 | 1 | 2 | 3 | 4 | 5 miles |

Rougham Green

Rattlesden○

STOWMARKET

○Little Stonham

○Framsden

Bradfield Combust○

A1120

A140

WICKHA MARKE

High Street Green

A12

xley Green

Brettenham

Needham Market

Grundisburgh○

Ufford○

g Street○

Great Bricett○

Claydon○

WOODBRIDGE

Westerfield○

A1214

Dutten

Lavenham

A1141

Bildeston○

Somersham○

A1156

Kesgrave○

River Deben

Long Melford○

Little Waldingfield○

Lindsey○

Aldham○

Sproughton○

A1214

16/17

18

Newbourne○

1/15

SUDBURY

HADLEIGH

A1071

A1071

IPSWICH

A1071

A1156

A12

Kirton○

7/33

34

Polstead Heath○

Canel St Mary○

35

Belstead

A14

36/37

Freston

38

Levington○

River Orwell

Middleton

Assington○

Stoke-by-Nayland○

Holton St Mary○

A12

A137

Chelmondiston○

FELIXSTOWE

54/55

56/57

58/59

East Bergholt○

60/61

Tattingstone○

62/63

Harkstead○

Shotley Gate○

221

Alphamstone

Thorington Street○

River Stour

Brantham○

90/91

Pebmarsh○ Mount Bures○

78/79

Little Horkesley○

80/81

Boxted○

82/83

Dedham○

84/85

86/87

Manningtree○

Wrabness○

88/89

A120

HARWICH

Wormingford

Langham

Earls Colne

Wakes Colne

Fordham○

Mile End

Ardleigh○

Little Bromley○

Bradfield Heath○

Little Oakley○

7/105

106/107

108/109

110/111

112/113

114/115

116/117

A1232

A137

A120

Great Bromley○

Stones Green○

Great Oakley○

Aldham○

A1124

West Bergholt○

COLCHESTER

A133

Elmstead Market○

138/139

140/141

142/143

144

/131

A120

132/133

A12

134/135

A134

136/137

Little Bentley○

Thorpe-le-Soken○

Kirby-le-Soken○

WALTON-ON-THE-NAZE

Copford Green○

Blackheath○

WIVENHOE

Great Bentley○

Easthorpe○

Alresford○

A133

168/169

170/171

158/159

160/161

162/163

164/165

166/167

Little Clacton○

Great Holland○

FRINTON ON SEA

Kelvedon○

Birch Green○

Abberton○

Thorington○

BRIGHTLINGSEA

Tiptree○

178/179

180/181

Peldon○

182/183

184/185

186/187

188/189

CLACTON-ON-SEA

Great Wigborough

East Mersea○

Point Clear○

Jaywick○

Great Totham○

196/197

198/199

200/201 WEST MERSEA

202/203

Tolleshunt Major○

Tollesbury○

Heybridge○

Goldhanger○

210/211

212/213

214

Bradwell Waterside○

St Lawrence○

Tillingham○

○Mayland

gh

○Cold Norton

Southminster○

Montsale○

BURNHAM-ON-CROUCH

River Crouch

Canewdon○

Churchend○

Paglesham Eastend○

Rochford○

River Roach

HEND-ON-SEA

Great Wakering○

27

5

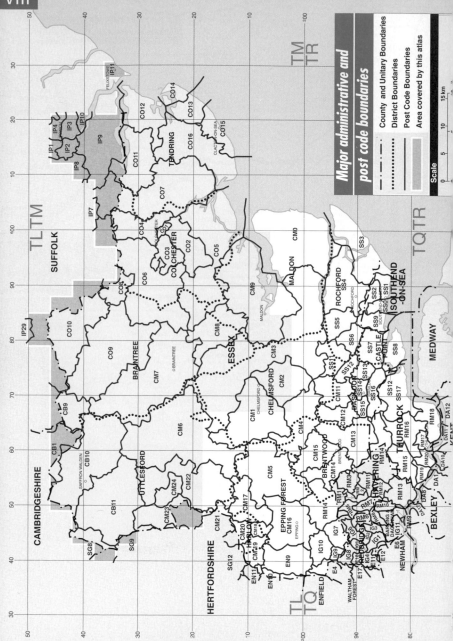

## Major administrative and post code boundaries

County and Unitary Boundaries

District Boundaries

Post Code Boundaries

Area covered by this atlas

Scale

0    5    10    15 km

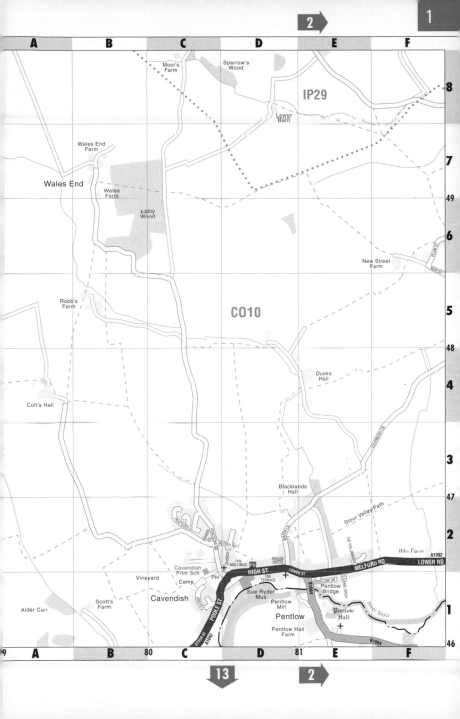

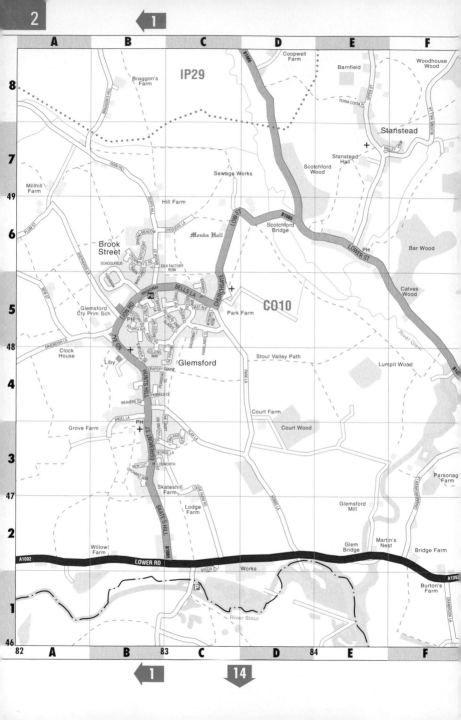

CB1

A  B  C  D  E  F

8

Hinxton

Field Farm

Field Farm
Cottages

Ford

DUXFORD RD

MILL LA

Hall
Farm

7

Field Farm
Cottages

Park Farm
Cottages

45

Red Lion
(PH)

CHURCH GN

Hinxton
Hall

÷CB2

The
Bungalow

Park Road
Farm

6

LC

A1301

A11

CB10

STUMP CROSS

Cemy

PARK RD

5

Sewage
Works

B1383

Dell's
Farm

44

4

Mill House
Farm

Ickleton

PH

NEWMARKET RD

WALDEN RD

Fairacre

3

JACKSON'S SQ
WAKEFIELD CL

Chesterford
House

COW LA

THE STACKYARD

43

Sch

PH
BARTHOLOMEW CL

Great
Chesterford

ROSE LA

2

LC

ICKLETON RD

GREAT
CHESTERFORD

Manor
Farm

Icknield Way
Path

LONDON RD

CHURCH ST
SOUTH ST

9

Smock Hill
House

Coploe
Hill

M11

Great
Chesterford

Highfield
House

Rectory
Farm

1

B184

B1383

42

A  B  50  C  D  51  E  F

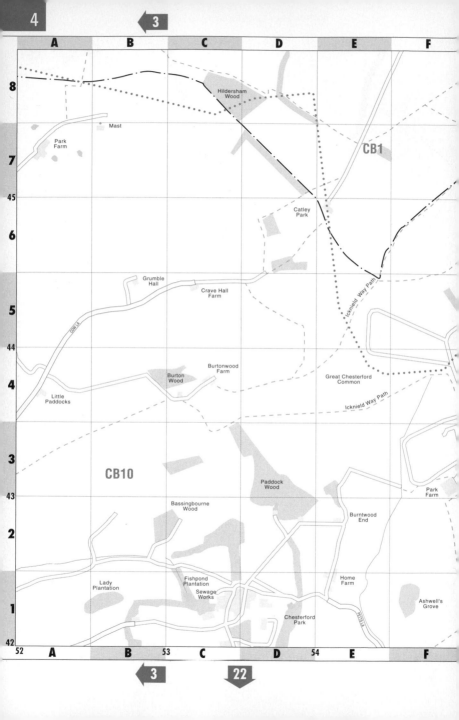

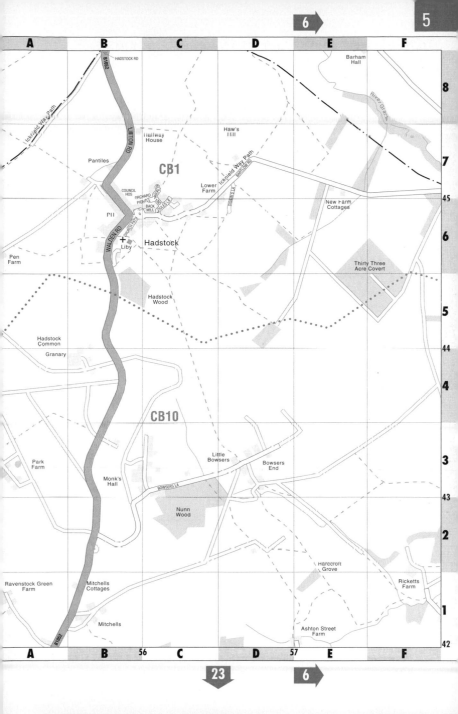

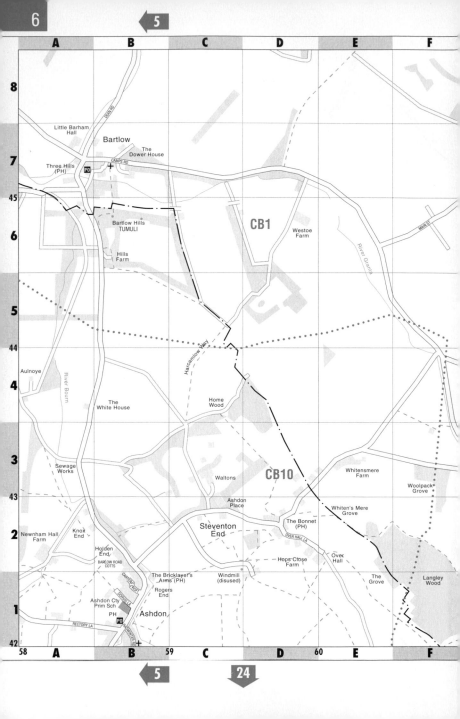

A B C D E F

8

Little Barham
Hall

Bartlow

The
Dower House

7

Three Hills
(PH)

PO

CAMPS RD

45

CB1

Bartlow Hills
TUMULI

Westoe
Farm

6

River Granta

Hills
Farm

MAIN ST

5

Harcamlow Way

River Bourn

44

Aulnoye

4

The
White House

Home
Wood

3

Sewage
Works

Waltons

CB10

Whitensmere
Farm

Woolpack
Grove

43

Ashdon
Place

Whiten's Mere
Grove

2

Newnham Hall
Farm

Knox
End

Steventon
End

The Bonnet
(PH)

OVER HALL LA

Over
Hall

Holden
End

BARLOW ROAD
COTTS

Hops Close
Farm

CAMPS CROFT

The Bricklayer's
Arms (PH)

Rogers
End

Windmill
(disused)

The Grove

Langley
Wood

1

Ashdon Cty
Prim Sch

PH

PO

Ashdon

RECTORY LA

42

58 A B 59 C D 60 E F

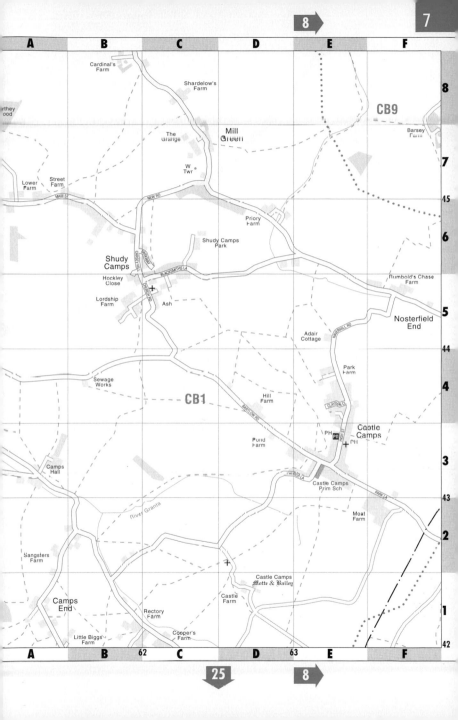

| A | B | C | D | E | F |

8

CB9

Cardinal's Farm

Shardelow's Farm

Barsey Farm

The Grange

Mill Green

7

W Twr

45

Lower Farm

Street Farm

MAIN ST

NEW RD

Priory Farm

6

Shudy Camps Park

GARRET HILL

SPARROW

Shudy Camps

BLACKSMITHS LA

Rumbold's Chase Farm

Hockley Close

CHURCH RD

Lordship Farm

Ash

Nosterfield End

5

Adair Cottage

HAVERHILL RD

44

Sewage Works

Park Farm

4

CB1

BARTLOW RD

Hill Farm

CLAYGATE CL

Castle Camps

HIGH ST

PH

PH

3

Pond Farm

Camps Hall

THURLOW LA

Castle Camps Prim Sch

PARK LA

43

River Granta

Moat Farm

2

Sangsters Farm

Castle Camps Motte & Bailey

Camps End

Castle Farm

1

Rectory Farm

Little Biggs Farm

Cooper's Farm

42

| A | B | 62 | C | D | 63 | E | F |

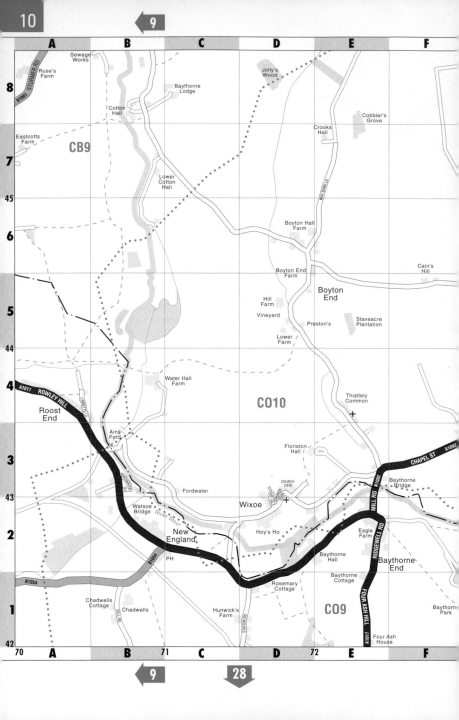

**A** **B** **C** **D** **E** **F**

8

Ruse's Farm

STURMER RD

B1061

Sewage Works

Baythorne Lodge

Jolly's Wood

Cotton Hall

Eastcotts Farm

7

**CB9**

Lower Cotton Hall

45

6

Cobbler's Grove

Crooks Hall

WAY BANK LA

Boyton Hall Farm

Cain's Hill

Boyton End Farm

**Boyton End**

5

Hill Farm

Vineyard

Preston's

Staveacre Plantation

44

Lower Farm

4

A1017 ROWLEY HILL

**Roost End**

Water Hall Farm

**CO10**

Thistley Common

Ains Ford

3

Floriston Hall

CHAPEL ST A1092

A1092

Baythorne Bridge

Fordwater

CHURCH VIEW

43

Watsoe Bridge

River Stour

Wixoe

STATION RD

MILL RD

2

**New England**

Hoy's Ho

Eagle Farm

RIDGEWELL RD

**Baythorne End**

B1054

PH

Baythorne Hall

Baythorne Cottage

B1054

Rosemary Cottage

FOUR ASH HILL A1017

1

Chadwells Cottage

Chadwells

FELL RD

Hunwick's Farm

**CO9**

Baythorne Park

Four Ash House

42

70 **A** **B** 71 **C** **D** 72 **E** **F**

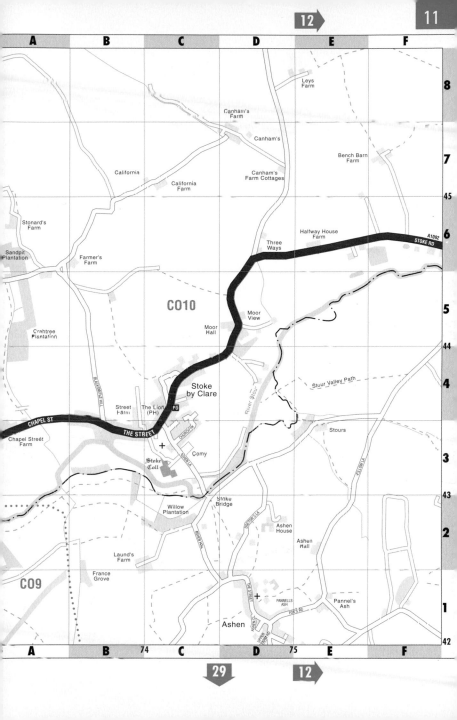

| | A | | B | | C | | D | | E | | F |

**8**

Upper Common

Lower Common

CLARENCE RD

Clare Camp

BRIDEWELL ST

ST BRIDEWELLS IND EST

Clare Cty Prim Sch

COMMON ST

GILBERT RD

GOSFORD CL

CALUS CT

Clare Mid Sch

Clare Hill Farm

A1092

Cemy

ST PETERS CT

Libry

B1063

Clare

PARK VIEW

CAVENDISH RD

Sewage Works

**7**

PASHLERS ALLEY
BUCKS LA
CHURCH LA
HALF MOON YARD

STONEHALL

NETHERGATE ST

WELL LA

PARK VIEW

STATION RD

MILL RD

HIGHFIELD

Clare Castle Country Park

The Mill House

River Stour

**45**

THE CHASE

New Cut

Priory (remains of)

**6**

A1092  STOKE RD

WESTFIELD

LOWES CL

STOUR VALE

STOUR LN

LOANEUM HOLT

CH

HICKFORD HILL

Hickford Hill

Lindsells Farm

**5**

Mill Farm

ASHEN RD

Claredown Farm

CO10

Mast

Langley Wood

**44**

**4**

Claret Farm

Bradleyhill Farm

Long Lane

**3**

**43**

**2**

Ovington Hall

Cutbush Farm

Donkey House

Butler's Farm

The Studio

BAKER'S RD

Lovelands Farm

**1**

Upper Farm

Ovington

ASHEN RD

Ovington Grange

Hall

CADE'S

**42**

Hole Farm

| 76 | A | | B | 77 | C | | D | 78 | E | | F |

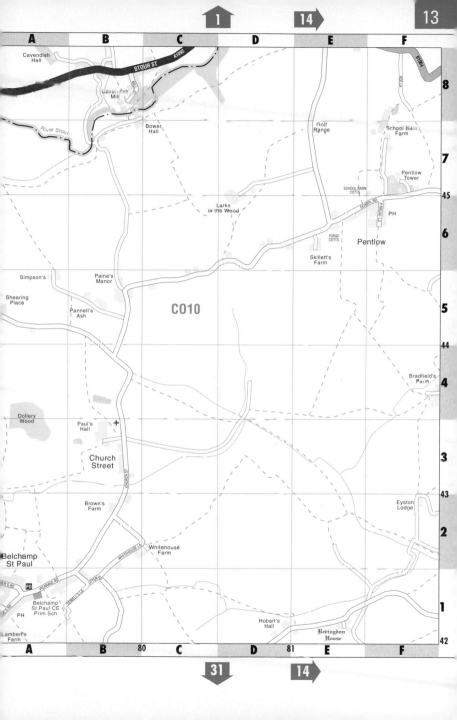

1 14

A B C D E F

**STOUR ST** A1092

Cavendish
Hall

8

Cavendish
Mill

River Stour

Bower
Hall

Golf
Range

TIDE LA

B1064

School Barn
Farm

7

Pentlow
Tower

SCHOOL BARN
COTTS

45

Larks in the Wood

SCOTTS RD

PH

PAINS LA

6

FORGE
COTTS

Pentlow

Skillett's
Farm

Simpson's

Paine's
Manor

CO10

Shearing
Place

5

Pannell's
Ash

44

Bradfield's
Farm

4

Dollery
Wood

Paul's
Hall

+

Church
Street

3

CHURCH ST

Brown's
Farm

43

Eyston
Lodge

Belchamp
St Paul

WHITEHOUSE LA

Whitehouse
Farm

2

OTTEN RD

PO

VICARAGE RD

SWILL'S LA

_____'S RD

Belchamp
St Paul CE
Prim Sch

PH

Hobart's
Hall

Bevingdon
House

1

Lambert's
Farm

42

A B C D E F

80 81

31 14

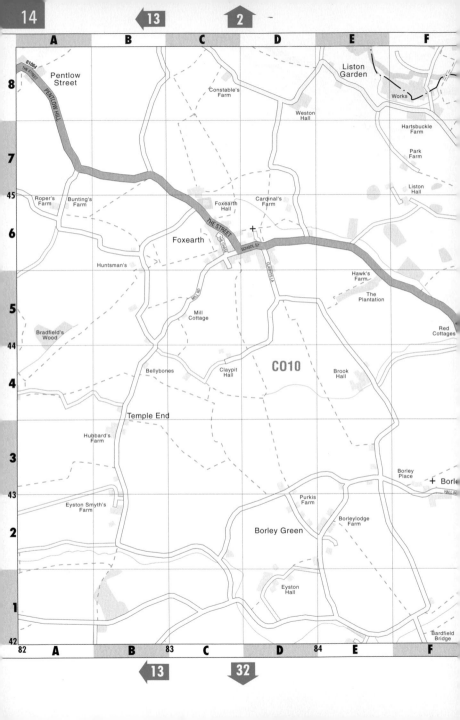

C2
1 BRAMBLEWOOD
2 LABURNUM CL
3 BROAD MEADOW
4 INNES END
5 PEACOCK CL
6 HALFORD CT
7 MERRION CL
8 MATLOCK CL
9 MOTTRAM CL

E1
1 DAWNBROOK CL
2 HILDABROOK CL
3 VINNICOMBE CT

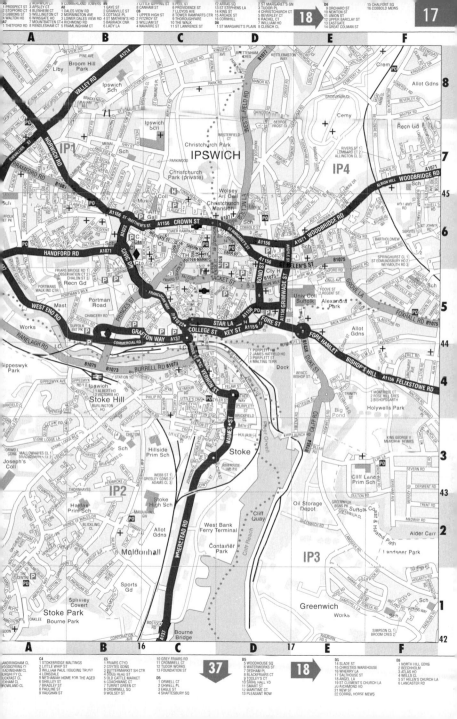

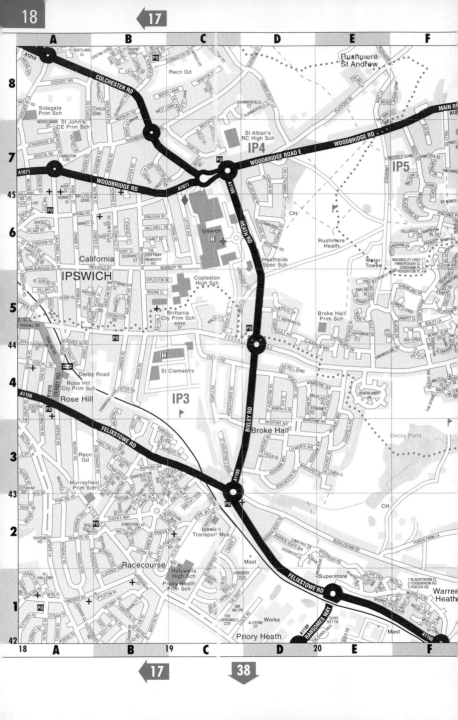

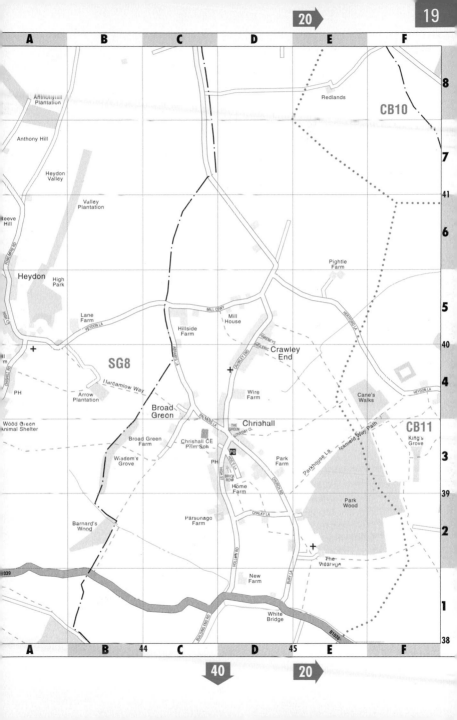

CB10

Valance Farm

Ickleton Old Grange

GRANGE RD

The Lodge

Ickleton

Welches Wood

8

Argers

7

41

Lodge Farm

ROYSTON LA

6

The Poplars

QUENDEN RD

5

Sewage Works

New Jersey Farm

40

Strethall Wood

Strethall Hall

Elmdonbury

Strethall Hall Farm

Strethall

ICKLETON RD

HORNDON CL

HEYDON LA

4

+

Elmdon

HOLLOW RD

Icknield Way

PH

Church Farm

Free Wood

FREEWOOD LA

Mill Hill

Felsted Croft Grove

Ann's Wood

ESSEX HILL

P'S DROVE

3

Freewood Farm

39

Bradley Grove

Bixett Wood

Lofts Hall

+

2

CB11

Littlebury Green

1

Lee Wood

Ash Grove

Gre Fa

Elmdon Lee

38

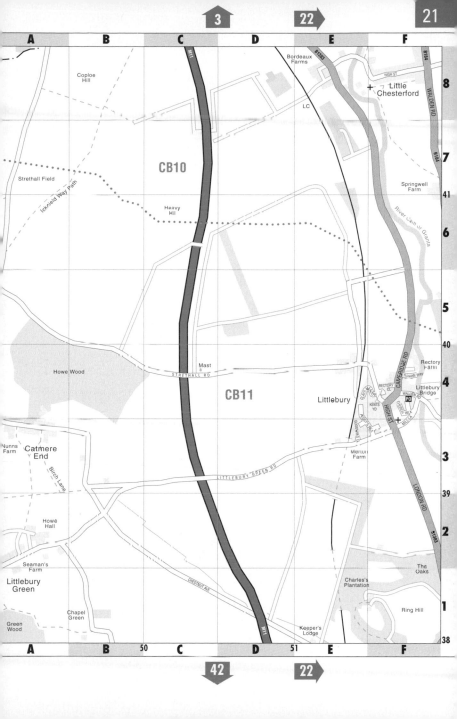

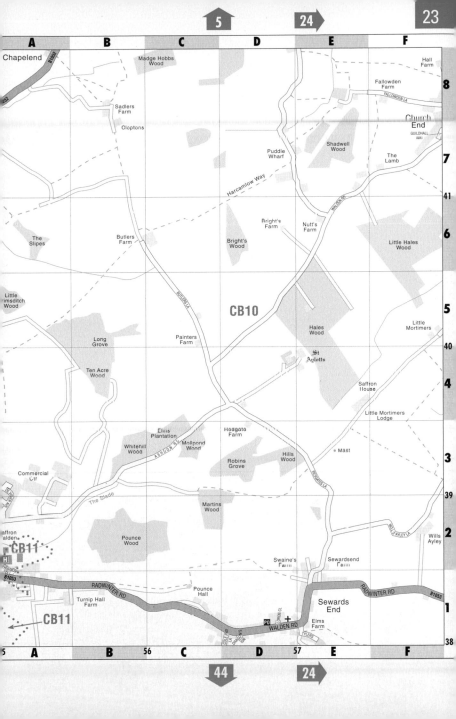

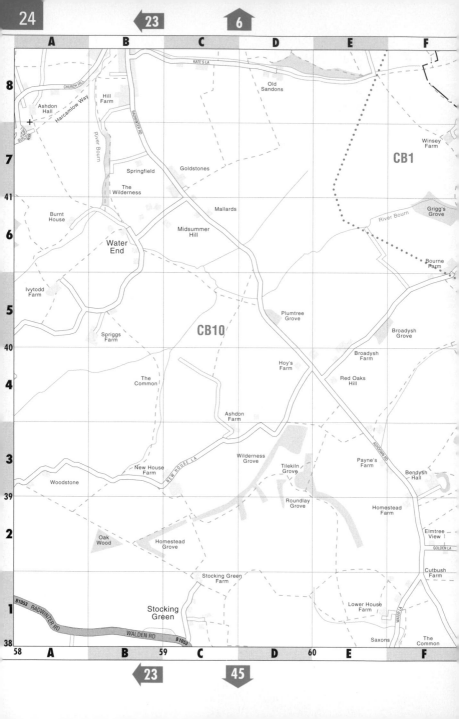

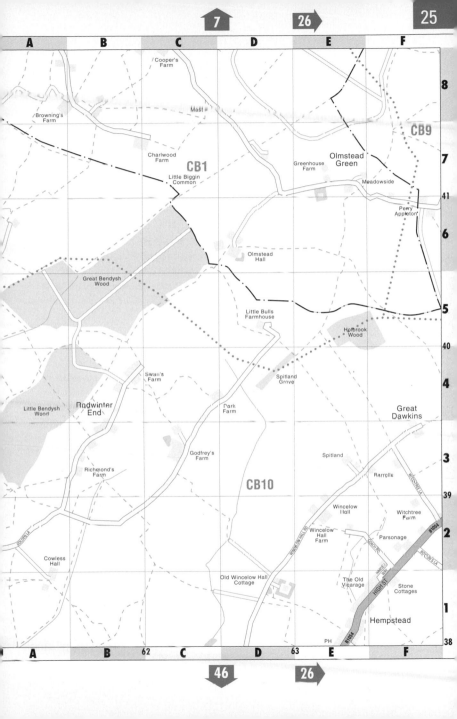

A   B   C   D   E   F

8

Monkhams   Sewage Works   Lowerhouse Farm   Ford   Broadgreen Hall

The Endway   LOIS RD   Broad Green

Steeple Bumpstead   Blois Farm

Devil's Grove

Hawk's Nest   7

41   Rookery Wood   Park Plantation

Freeze's Farm   CLAXWALL COTTS   OLD HALL CL   HOME CL   Moyn's Park   The Wildernes

LILLY CNR   Cemy   Stud Farm   6

CHURCHFIELDS   Recn Gd

Steeple Bumpstead Cty Prim Sch   Dock Plantation   Moyn's Park

Smith's Green   CB9   Bower Hall Farm   Arbour Grove   Maze Plantation   5

Smith's Green Cottages   Bushel Leys

Mill Farm   MILL CHASE   40

Old Hall   Coote's Farm   4

Latchley's Farm   Whitehouse Farm

Round Wood

Wilding's Farm   Oldhall Wood   Eggshell Cottage   CO9   3

Wakeland's Farm

39   2

Herkstead Green Farm   CM7   Martin's Farm   Prouds Farm

Messing's Farm

Herkstead Hall Farm   High Folly Cottages   Revels Farm   1

38

A   B   68   C   69   D   E   F

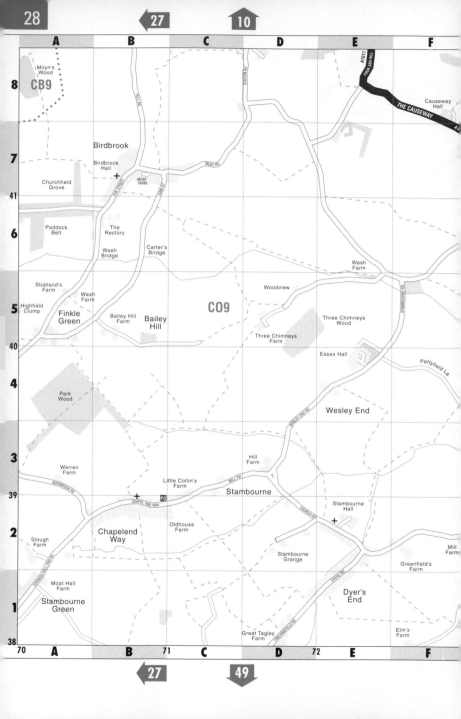

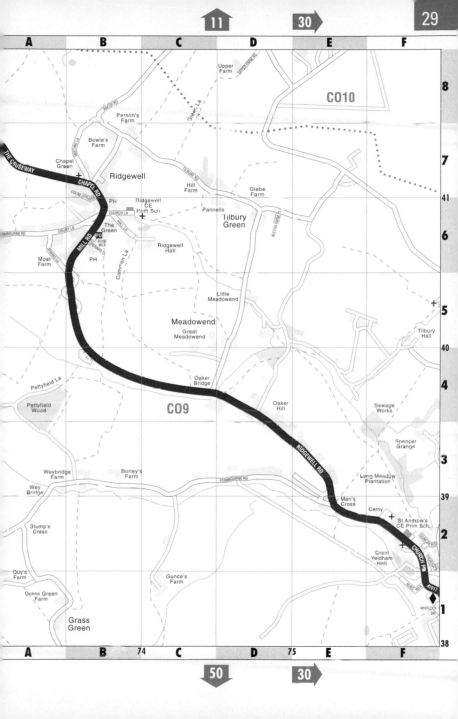

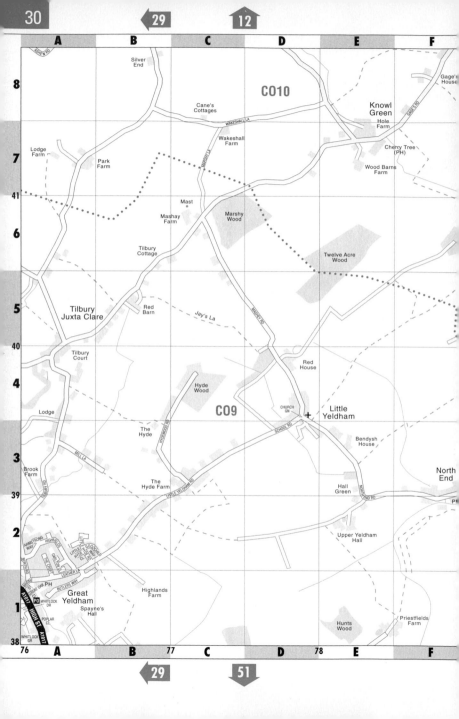

**CO10**

**CO9**

Silver End

Cane's Cottages

WAKESHALL LA

Wakeshall Farm

Knowl Green

Gage's House

Hole Farm

Cherry Tree (PH)

Wood Barns Farm

Lodge Farm

Park Farm

Mast

Mashay Farm

Marshy Wood

Tilbury Cottage

Twelve Acre Wood

Tilbury Juxta Clare

Red Barn

Jay's La

Tilbury Court

Red House

Hyde Wood

CHURCH GN

Little Yeldham

Lodge

The Hyde

Bendysh House

MILL LA

Brook Farm

The Hyde Farm

LITTLE YELDHAM RD

Hall Green

North End

PH

Upper Yeldham Hall

Highlands Farm

Great Yeldham

Spayne's Hall

Hunts Wood

Priestfields Farm

PO

WHITLOCK DR

HIGH ST

POPLAR CL

WHITLOCK GR

8
7
41
6
5
40
4
3
39
2
1
38

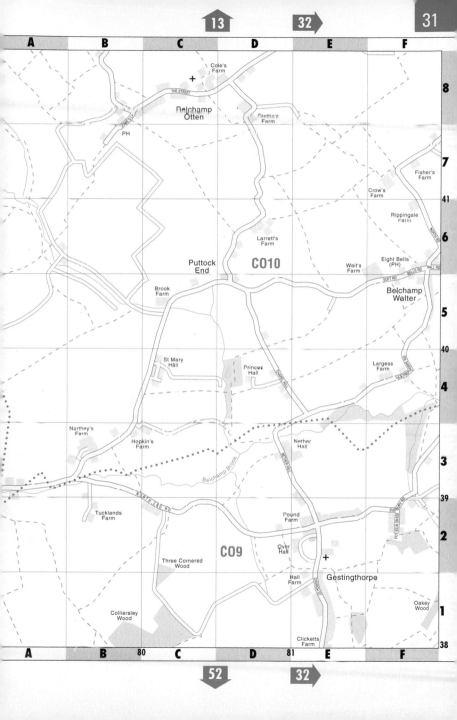

A   B   C   D   E   F

Cole's Farm

Belchamp Otten

THE STREET

Otettin's Farm

PH

8

Fisher's Farm

7

Crow's Farm

41

Rippingale Farm

SURREY RD

6

Larrett's Farm

CO10

Puttock End

Wait's Farm

Eight Bells (PH)

SOFT RD   BELLS RD   HALL RD

Brook Farm

Belchamp Walter

5

St Mary Hall

Princes Hall

CHAPEL HILL

40

Largess Farm

THE BRIDGE   GESTING

4

Northey's Farm

Hopkin's Farm

Nether Hall

NETHER HILL

Belchamp Brook

3

Tucklands Farm

NORTH END RD

Pound Farm

SUDBURY RD

39

POT KILN CHASE

CO9

Over Hall

2

Three Cornered Wood

Hall Farm

CHURCH ST

Gestingthorpe

Oakey Wood

1

Colliersley Wood

Clicketts Farm

38

A   B   80   C   D   81   E   F

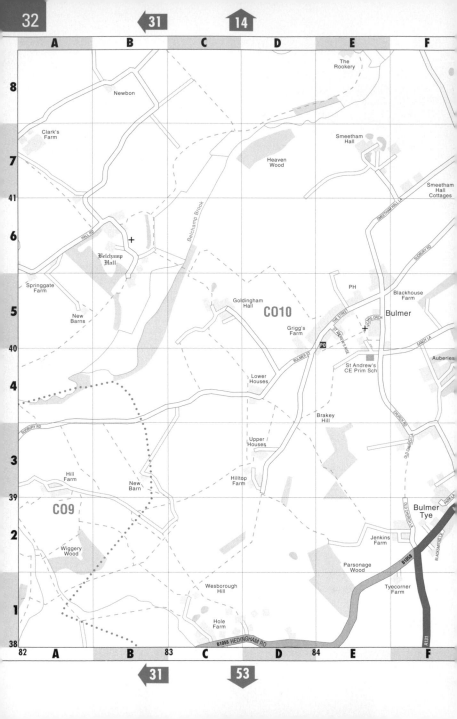

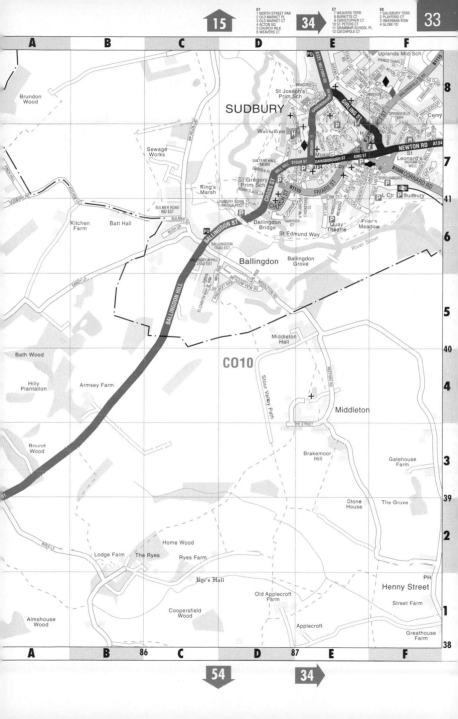

33

SUDBURY

Grange Farm

Cornard Tye

Valley Farm

The Elms

Lawn Farm

Water Tower

Tye Farm

Abbas Hall

Cemy
Pot Kiln
Cty Prim Sch

LANGUIDEC

CO10

Abbas Hall Wood

Great Cornard

Little Greys Farm

Wells Hall Cty Prim Sch

Great Cornard Upper Sch

Great Cornard Mid Sch

Great Cornard Country Park

Prospect Hill Farm

Greys Hall

Moor's Farm

Brook Farm

PH

Blackhouse Farm

Little Mere

Blackhouse Farm

Little Cornard

Nature Trail

Holly Lodge

Cornard Mere

Peacock Hall

Stone Farm

Sewage Works

LC

Shalford Meadow

Costens Hall

Casefields Farm

River Stour

Coles Green

Coles Green Farm

Washbrook

Fen Cottages

CHURCH LA

HOLLOW RD

DALES VIEW

FIELD RD

BACK LA

Westhill House

Copdock Cty Prim Sch

PHEASANT RISE

BRIDGE STREET

8

The Covey

Glenfield

CHATTISHAM RD

SMART LA

Copdock Hall

TOWN LA

Copdock

Mace Green

Daniels Farm

7

WENHAM RD

Hotel

Felcourt

THE AVENUE

ELM LA

41

Rookery Farm

Cottage Farm

Glebe Farm

OAKFIELD RD

The Grange Farm

Eight Elms Farm

LONDON RD

IP8

6

Elms Farm

A12

5

Apple Tree Farm

Orchard House

Redhouse Farm

Brockley Wood

40

Pippin Farm

FOLLY LA

Lane Farm

Bentley Old Hall

4

Clay Hall

NAUGHTON RD

:07

Bentley Long Wood

3

39

Station Farm

Ponder's Grove

Pond Hall

IP9

Bentley Park

2

Tare Grove

Fingery Grove

Capel St Mary

A1 STOCKMERS END
2 CHALKNERB CL
3 SAWYERS GR
4 LISLE GR
5 RED SLEEVE
6 LITTLE GULLS
7 DODMANS

B1 ROUNDRIDGE RD
2 JERMYNS CL
3 THE QUEECH
4 FARTHINGS WENT
5 THE SQUIRRELS

Motel

Pedlar's Grove

Pond Hall Lane Trk

Church Farm

Bentley Hall

1

Liby

Prim Sch

PO

PH

THE STREET

WHITE

MEADOWS

Capel Rig

Engry Wood

PINCH RD

38

A   B   10   C   D   11   E   F

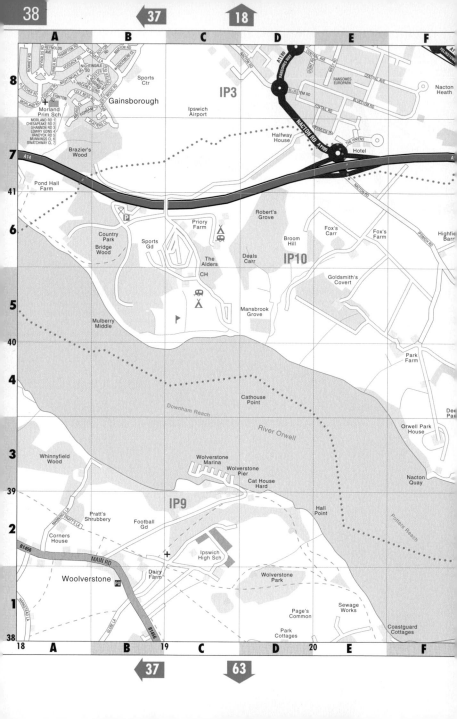

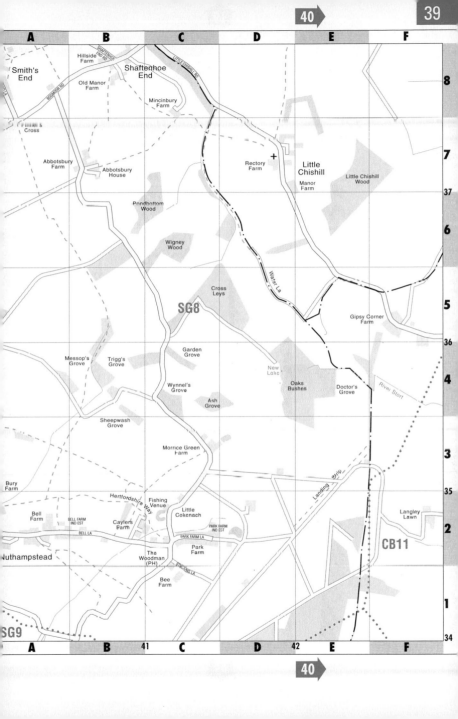

A B C D E F

8

7

37

6

5

36

4

3

35

2

1

34

Monkshole Wood

BUILDING END RD

Building End

Lower Farm

Upper Farm

BUILDING END RD

COMMON LA

SG8

Chiswick Hall

Lower Pond Street

B1039

B16

Hope Farm House

Mead Bushes Wood

Upper Pond Street

Harcamlow Way

Wicken Water

Duddenhoe End Farm

Hal

Common La

Pickerton Green

High Wood

Chrishall Common

Roughway Wood

Oldfield Grove

White Friar Farm

Killem's Green

Lorking's La

River Stort

PARK LA

Hall Grove

Church Farm

THE CAUSEWAY

The Hall

Duddenhoe Grange

CB11

Grange Farm

Harcamlow Way

Cosh Farm

Hall

Upper Green

BULL LA

THE KANGELS

LONG LEY

Langley

The Bull (PH)

HIGHFIELDS

Bury Farm

Lower Green

WATERING HILL

Ford

Roper's La

New Farm

43 A 44 C D 45 E F

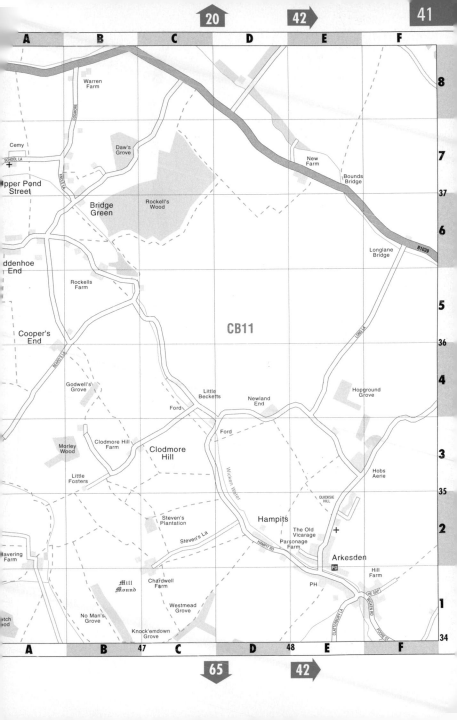

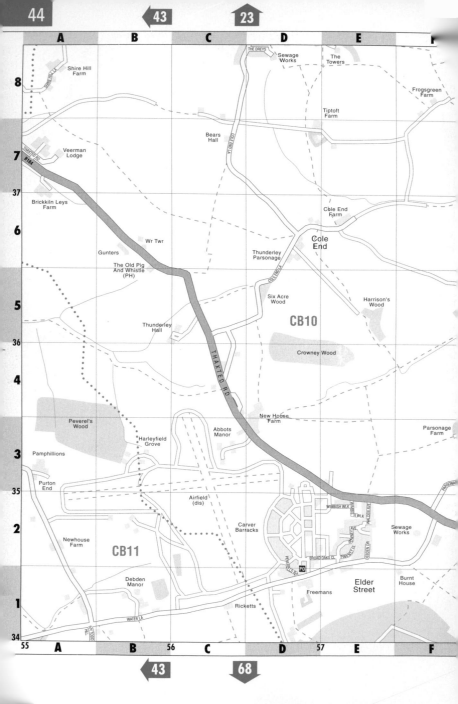

The Dreys
Sewage Works
The Towers
Shire Hill Farm
Frogsgreen Farm
Tiptoft Farm
Bears Hall
Veerman Lodge
Brickkiln Leys Farm
Cole End Farm
Wr Twr
Cole End
Gunters
Thunderley Parsonage
The Old Pig And Whistle (PH)
Six Acre Wood
Harrison's Wood
CB10
Thunderley Hall
Crowney Wood
Peverel's Wood
New House Farm
Parsonage Farm
Harleyfield Grove
Abbots Manor
Pamphillions
Purton End
Airfield (dis)
Newhouse Farm
CB11
Carver Barracks
Sewage Works
Broad Oaks Cl
Elder Street
Burnt House
Debden Manor
Freemans
Ricketts
Water La

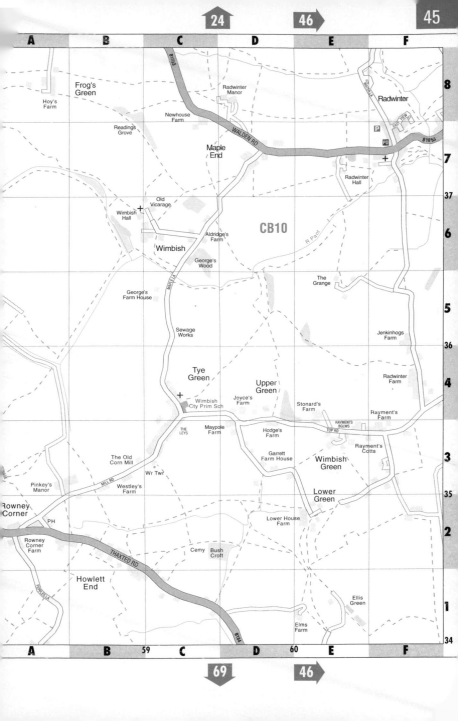

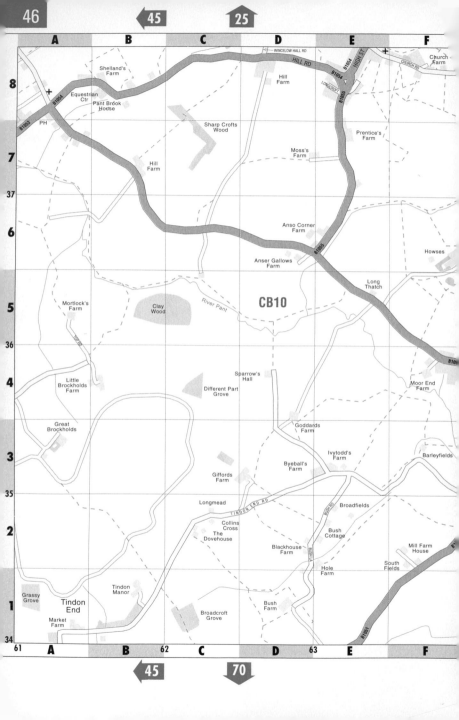

**A** **B** **C** **D** **E** **F**

CO9

Little
Nortons

Old Robin

Great
Nortons

8

Bushy Grove

Lopham's
Farm

Rockall's
Farm

Howsey
Wood

7

37

Springlette

Shore
Hall

The Grove

Sewage
Works

Rivett's Farm

White House
Farm

6

Briar Cottages

PH

Cornish Hall
End

Heard's
Farm

Heard's La

Whitleys

Hole Farm

5

CM7

36

Cornish Hall

Jekyll's Farm

4

Unwin's
Farm

Skyll's La

New
Cover

Hobtoe's
Farm

Mill La

3

35

Little London

Rook Hall

Yeldhams

Howe
Farm

Obourne's
Farm

2

Spainshall
Farm

Bumpstead
Lodge

Howe
Street

1

Spain's
Hall

Tridgate
Ley

34

67 **A** **B** 68 **C** **D** 69 **E** **F**

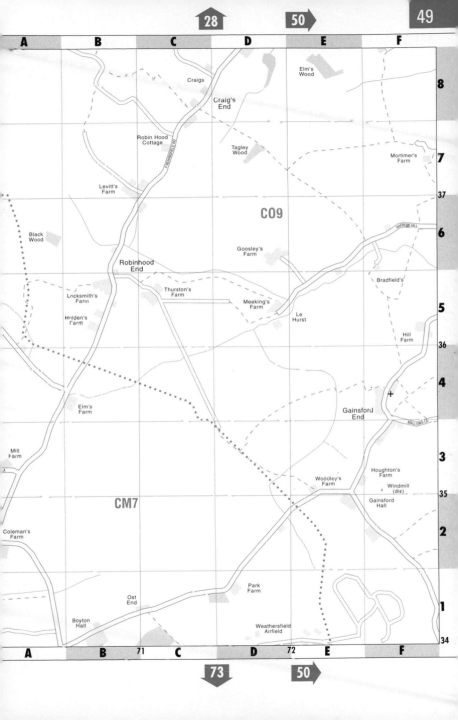

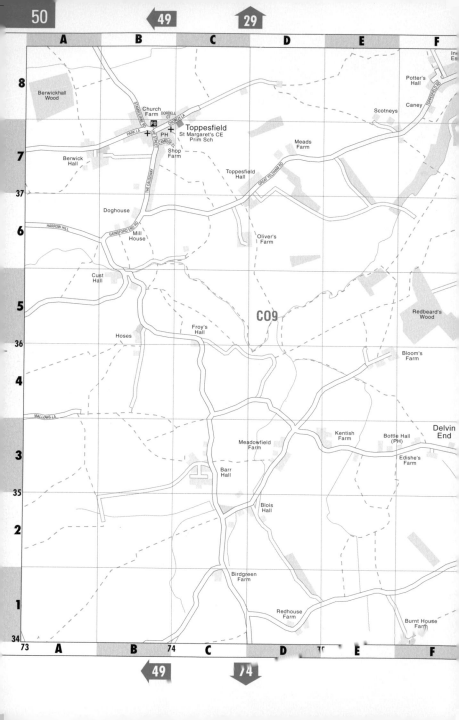

A B C D E F

8

Berwickhall
Wood

Potter's
Hall

Caney

Scotneys

Church
Farm

Toppesfield

DORDELL
CT

PO

7 Berwick
Hall

PH

St Margaret's CE
Prim Sch

Meads
Farm

Shop
Farm

Toppesfield
Hall

37

Doghouse

GREAT YELDHAM RD

6 HARROW HILL

Mill
House

Oliver's
Farm

Cust
Hall

5

Redbeard's
Wood

C09

Froy's
Hall

36 Hoses

Bloom's
Farm

4

Kentish
Farm

Bottle Hall
(PH)

Delvin
End

MALLOWS LA.

3

Meadowfield
Farm

Edishe's
Farm

Barr
Hall

35

Blois
Hall

2

Birdgreen
Farm

1

Redhouse
Farm

Burnt House
Farm

34

73 A B 74 C D E F

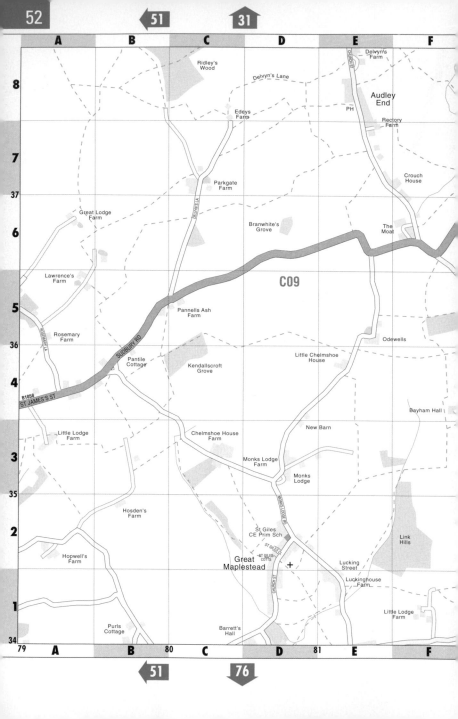

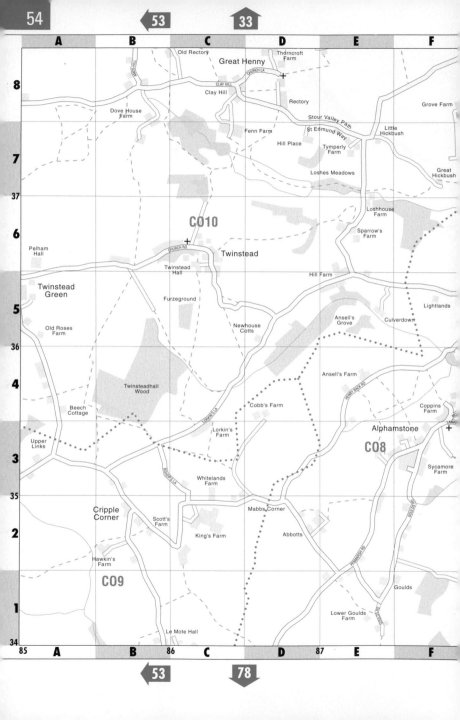

Old Rectory
Great Henny
Thorncroft Farm
CLAY HILL
CHURCH LA
Clay Hill
Rectory
Grove Farm
Dove House Farm
Stour Valley Path
Little Hickbush
Fenn Farm
St Edmund Way
Hill Place
Tymperly Farm
Great Hickbush
Loshes Meadows
Loshhouse Farm
CO10
Sparrow's Farm
Pelham Hall
Twinstead
CHURCH RD
Twinstead Hall
Hill Farm
Twinstead Green
Furzeground
Lightlands
Newhouse Cotts
Ansell's Grove
Culverdown
Old Roses Farm
Twinsteadhall Wood
Ansell's Farm
Coppins Farm
Beech Cottage
HENRY BACK RD
LOONS LA
Cobb's Farm
Alphamstone
Upper Links
Lorkin's Farm
CO8
Sycamore Farm
Whitelands Farm
Cripple Corner
BISHOPS LA
Scott's Farm
Mabbs Corner
King's Farm
Abbotts
Hawkin's Farm
CO9
PANNELLS RD
Goulds
Lower Goulds Farm
Le Mote Hall

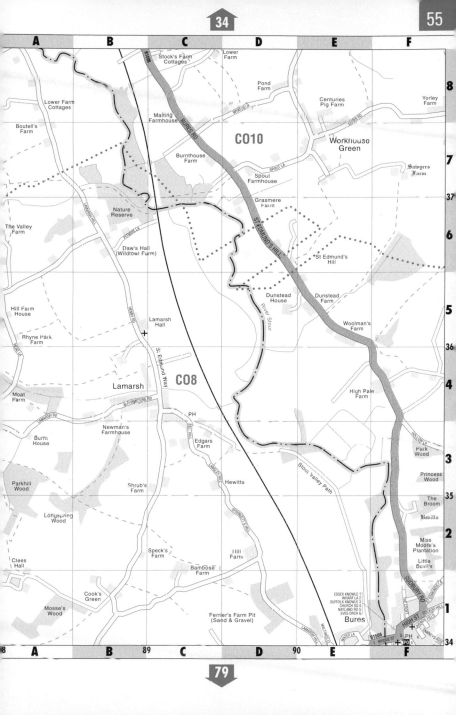

A  B  C  D  E  F

8

The Wades

Alder Carr

A137

Cragpit Farm

P

Lemons Hill Bridge

MILL HALL RD

7

Rookery Farm

Tattingstone

St Mary's  H

PH

THE CLOSE

37

Buxton Wood

Glebe Farm

CHURCH RD

GLEBE CL

Tattingstone CE Prim Sch

LEMONS HILL

GREEN LA

Alton Water (Resr) Nature Reserve

Tattingstone Place

Birchwood House

P

6

STATION RD

PH

BACK LA

Pond Hall Farm

Tattingstone Wonder

The Heath

/ Station Farm

The Heath

The Hollies

IP9

Tattingstone Wonder

Larch Wood

5

Morant

STUTTON LA

White House Farm

Argent Manor Farm

36

Folly Farm

Orchard Cottage

Furze Plantation

Argent Manor Belt

4

VALE LA

Vale Cottages

Holly Farm

Argent Manor Wood

Beckdale

VALE LA

Wallers Farm

Vale Farm

Roundwood Farm

LEISURE LA

WOODFIELD LA

3

Brantham Bridge

CATTS LA

POST OFFICE CNR

B1080

35

CO11

Alder Carr

Canhams Wood

MANNINGTREE RD

Stutton

Upper Street

PH

LEBER LA

FINDLEY CL

2

Hill Farm

STUTTON RD

B1080

THE STREET

PH

COURT FARM

Wolves Wood

Small Alder Carr

MARKS LA

Manor Farm

BONNALL LA

Brantham Court

Sutton Bridge

Crepping Hall

Lodge

Little Hall

1

34

A   B   C   D   E   F

8

Great Birch
Wood

The Dower House
Potash
Farm

The
Woodlands
Woodlands
Farm

B1080

7

Woodley
Wood

Little
Birch
Wood

Hale's
Grove

WOODLANDS RD
Redhouse
Farm

CLENCH RD

Freston
Grove

COUNCIL
HOS

Halesgrove
Cottage

Brown's
Farm

SAMFORD CL
Holbrook
High Sch

IPSWICH RD

6

Brook
Farm

Clifton
Wood

Holbrook
Prim Sch

HOLM OAK

THE STREET

GISFORD RD

COACHMAN'S PADDOCK

EAST
ROW

Park House

Holbrook
Gardens

Crag Hall
Covert

IP9

Walkgate
Cottages

Holbrook

FIREBRONDS RD

HARKSTEAD RD

RIVER

WHADS

PO

Fish
Pond

5

Old Alton Hall
Farm

Alton Hall
Cottages

Alton Hall
Cottages

FIVE
ACRES

MILL LA

WAINFLEET RD

CHURCH RD

FISHPONDS LA

FIR TREE LA

NEW RD

36

Alton Water
(Resr)
Nature Reserve

Sewage
Works

4

Draw off
Tower

Chestnut
Spinney

PRIMROSE HILL

Holbrook
Mill

Wall
Farm

BRICK
COTTS

Holbrook
Lodge

Park
Covert

Wall
Farm

HARKSTEAD RD

3

Visitors
Ctr
P

PO

H
Royal Hospl Sch

Lower
Holbrook

35

Sutton
CE Prim
Sch

LIMBOURNE RD

HOLBROOK RD

Wall Farm
Wharf

P

B1080
FINCLEY

Bay Tree
Farm

STUTTON RD

Alton
Wharf

The
Hermitage

2

HYAM'S LA

CROWE HALL LA

CHURCH

LOWER ST

STUTTON GN

Sutton
House

Markwell's
Farm

Lower
Street

Crowe
Hall

1

Crowe Hall
Farm

34

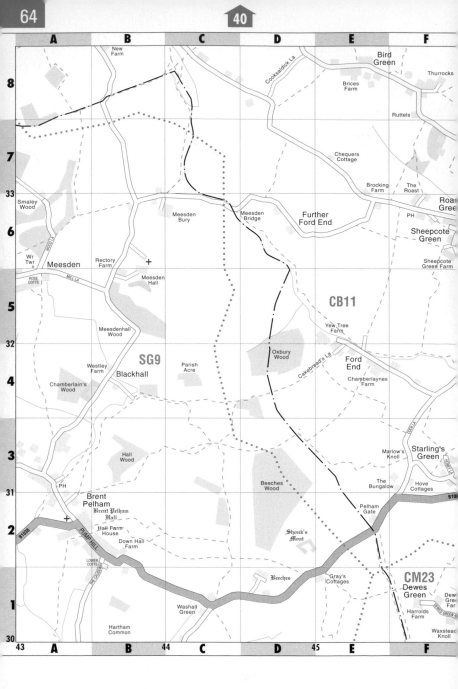

New Farm

Bird Green

Cooksaldick La

Thurrocks

Brices Farm

Ruttels

Chequers Cottage

Smaley Wood

Brocking Farm

The Roast

Roa Gree

Meesden Bury

Meesden Bridge

Further Ford End

PH

Sheepcote Green

Wr Twr

Meesden

Rectory Farm

Meesden Hall

Sheepcote Green Farm

ROSE COTTS

MILL LA

CB11

Meesdenhall Wood

Oxbury Wood

Yew Tree Farm

Westley Farm

SG9

Parish Acre

Cakebread's La

Ford End

Blackhall

Chamberlaynes Farm

Chamberlain's Wood

Hall Wood

Marlow's Knoll

Starling's Green

PH

Beeches Wood

The Bungalow

Hove Cottages

Brent Pelham

Pelham Gate

B10

Brent Pelham Hall

Hall Farm House

Shonk's Moat

Down Hall Farm

CM23

LOWER COTTS

Beeches

Gray's Cottages

Dewes Green

Dew Gre Far

Washall Green

Harrolds Farm

Hartham Common

Waxstead Knoll

43    A    B    44    C    D    45    E    F

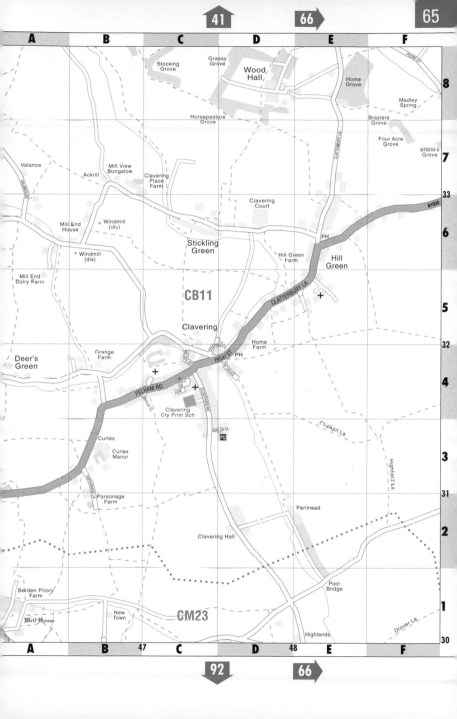

65
42

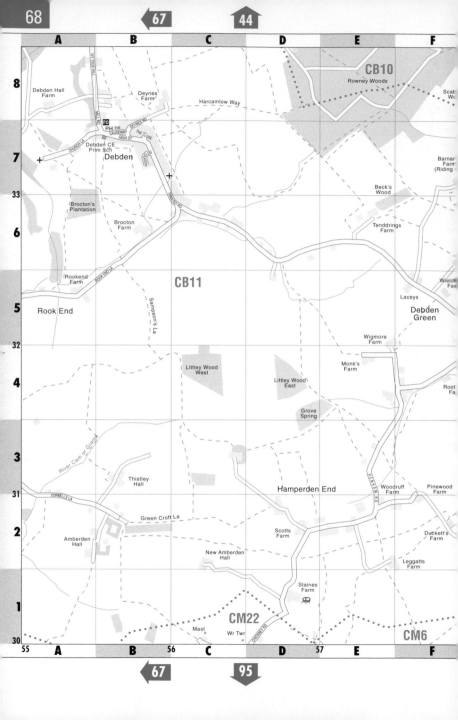

**A** **B** **C** **D** **E** **F**

**8**

Debden Hall
Farm

Deynes
Farm

Harcamlow Way

CB10

Rowney Woods

Scab
Wc

WY TOOT HILL

PO

PH THE
CAUSEWAY

Debden CE
Prim Sch

THE CLOSE

HIGH ST

**7**

**Debden**

DEYNES HILL

CHURCH LA

MILL RD

Barnar
Farm
(Riding

Beck's
Wood

**33**

Brocton's
Plantation

Brocton
Farm

THAXTED RD

Tenddrings
Farm

**6**

ROOK END LA

Rookend
Farm

**CB11**

Wield
Fa

Laceys

**5**

**Rook End**

Sampson's La

**Debden
Green**

**32**

Wigmore
Farm

Monk's
Farm

Littley Wood
West

Root
Fa

**4**

Littley Wood
East

Grove
Spring

**3**

River Cam or Granta

Thistley
Hall

Hamperden End

HERST RD

Woodruff
Farm

Pinewood
Farm

**31**

CORNELLS LA

Green Croft La

**2**

Amberden
Hall

Scotts
Farm

Duckett's
Farm

New Amberden
Hall

Leggatts
Farm

**1**

Staines
Farm

CROCKET RD

**CM22**

CM6

**30**

Mast

Wr Twr

**55** **A** **B** **56** **C** **D** **57** **E** **F**

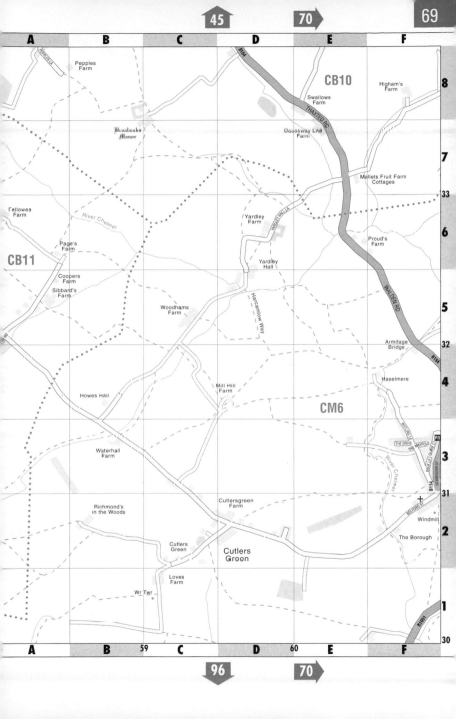

| A | B | C | D | E | F |
|---|---|---|---|---|---|

**8**

Pepples Farm

CB10

Swallows Farm

Higham's Farm

B184

THAXTED RD

**7**

Broaboaks Manor

Causeway Lne Farm

**33**

Mallets Fruit Farm Cottages

Tellowes Farm

River Chelmer

Yardley Farm

**6**

CB11

Page's Farm

Yardley Hall

Proud's Farm

WALDEN RD

Coopers Farm

Sibbard's Farm

Woodhams Farm

Harcamlow Way

**5**

Armitage Bridge

**32**

B184

Howes Hall

Mill Hill Farm

Haselmere

**4**

CM6

Waterhall Farm

THE DRIVE

MAYPOLE

**3**

BACK LA

River Chelmer

B184

**31**

Richmond's in the Woods

Cutlersgreen Farm

BOLFORD ST

Windmill

Cutlers Green

Cutlers Green

The Borough

**2**

Loves Farm

Wr Twr

B1051

**1**

**30**

| A | B | C | D | E | F |
|---|---|---|---|---|---|

59  60

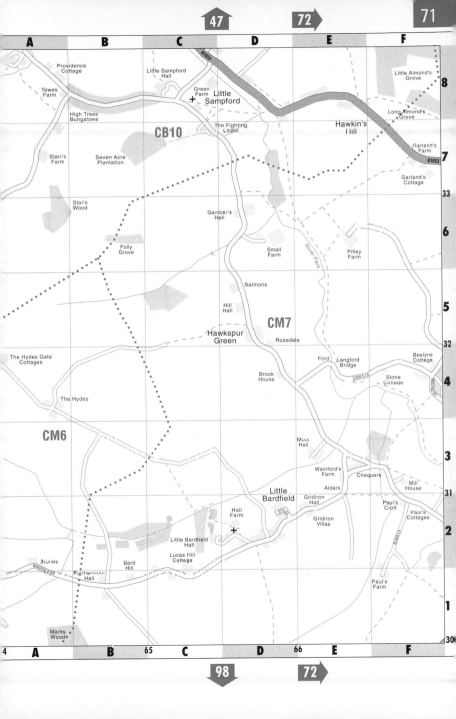

A  B  C  D  E  F

Providence
Cottage

Tewes
Farm

High Trees
Bungalows

Little Sampford
Hall

Green
Farm  Little
Sampford

Little Almond's
Grove

8

Long Almond's
Grove

Hawkin's
Hill

CB10

The Fighting
Cocks

Garland's
Farm

7

Starr's
Farm

Seven Acre
Plantation

B1053

Garland's
Cottage

33

Star's
Wood

Gamber's
Hall

6

Folly
Grove

Small
Farm

River Pant

Pitley
Farm

Salmons

5

Hill
Hall

CM7

Hawkspur
Green

Rosedale

32

The Hydes Gate
Cottages

Ford  Langford
Bridge

Beslyns
Cottage

Brook
House

COOK'S LN

Stone
Cottage

4

The Hydes

CM6

Moor
Hall

3

Wainford's
Farm

Chequers

Mill
House

Alders

Little
Bardfield

Gridiron
Hall

Paul's
Croft

Paul's
Cottages

31

Hall
Farm

Gridiron
Villas

2

Little Bardfield
Hall

Lucas Hill
Cottage

BLACK LA

Stones

Bard
Hill

Furthermoor
Hall

BARDFIELD RD

Paul's
Farm

1

Marks
Wood

30

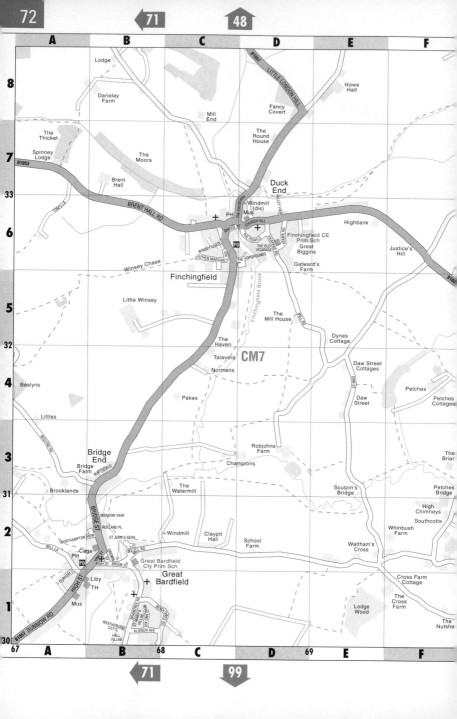

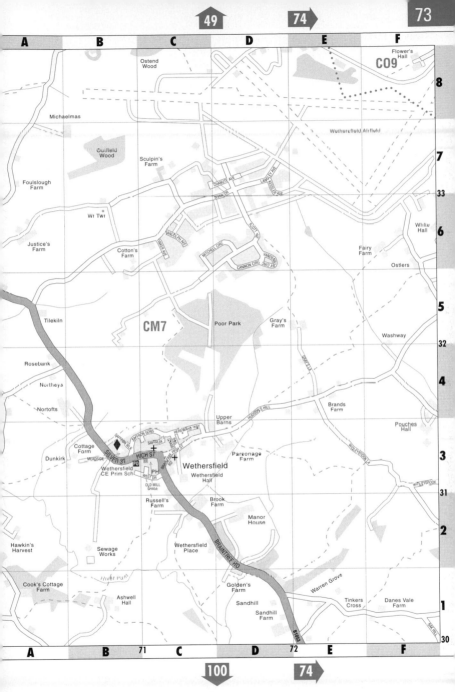

A   B   C   D   E   F

Ostend Wood

CO9

Flower's Hall

8

Michaelmas

Wethersfield Airfield

Outfield Wood

Sculpin's Farm

7

Foulslough Farm

33

CHANLITE AVE

LANCASTER AVE

Wt Twr

Willie Hall

6

Justice's Farm

Cotton's Farm

MITCHELL CIRC

Fairy Farm

Ostlers

CANNON CIRC

Tilekiln

CM7

Poor Park

Gray's Farm

Washway

5

32

Rosebank

Northeys

Nortofts

4

Brands Farm

Upper Barns

HUDSON'S HILL

Pouches Hall

3

Cottage Farm

MEADSIDE

SAFFRON GDNS

HEREWARD WAY

Parsonage Farm

Dunkirk

Wethersfield CE Prim Sch

HIGH ST

PH

OLD MILL CHASE

Wethersfield

Wethersfield Hall

31

Russell's Farm

Brook Farm

Manor House

2

Hawkin's Harvest

Sewage Works

BRAINTREE RD

Wethersfield Place

Cook's Cottage Farm

River Par

Ashwell Hall

Golden's Farm

Sandhill

Warren Grove

Tinkers Cross

Danes Vale Farm

1

Sandhill Farm

30

A   B   71   C   D   72   E   F

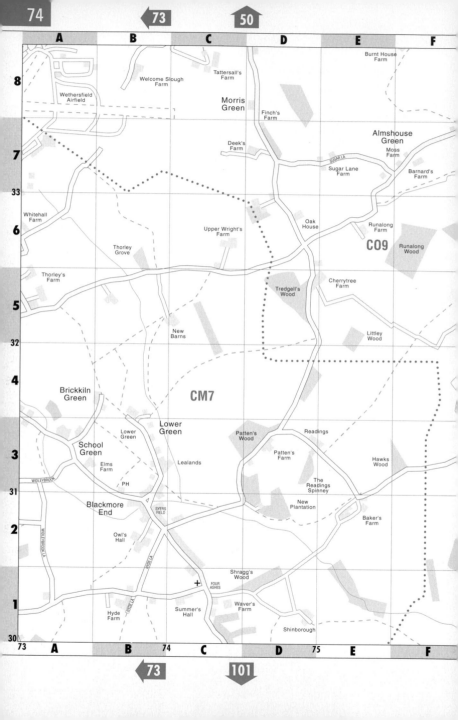

**A** **B** **C** **D** **E** **F**

Burnt House
Farm

8

Wethersfield
Airfield

Welcome Slough
Farm

Tattersall's
Farm

Morris
Green

Finch's
Farm

Almshouse
Green

Deek's
Farm

7

Moss
Farm

SUGAR LA

Sugar Lane
Farm

Barnard's
Farm

33

Whitehall
Farm

Upper Wright's
Farm

Oak
House

Runalong
Farm

6

**CO9**

Runalong
Wood

Thorley
Grove

Thorley's
Farm

Cherrytree
Farm

5

Tredgell's
Wood

New
Barns

Littley
Wood

32

4

Brickkiln
Green

**CM7**

Lower
Green

Lower
Green

Patten's
Wood

Readings

Hawks
Wood

School
Green

3

Elms
Farm

Lealands

Patten's
Farm

The
Readings
Spinney

WIDLEYBROOK

PH

31

Blackmore
End

SYERS
FIELD

New
Plantation

Baker's
Farm

2

Owl's
Hall

WIDLEYBROOK LA

Shragg's
Wood

1

FOUR
ASHES

Hyde
Farm

Summer's
Hall

Waver's
Farm

Shinborough

30

**A** **B** **C** **D** **E** **F**

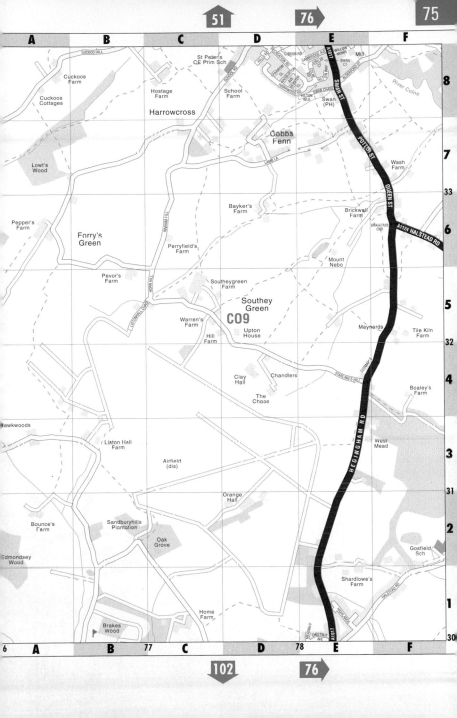

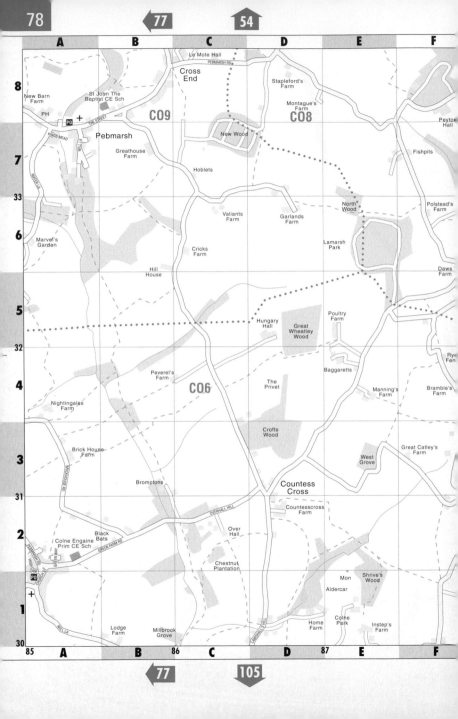

79

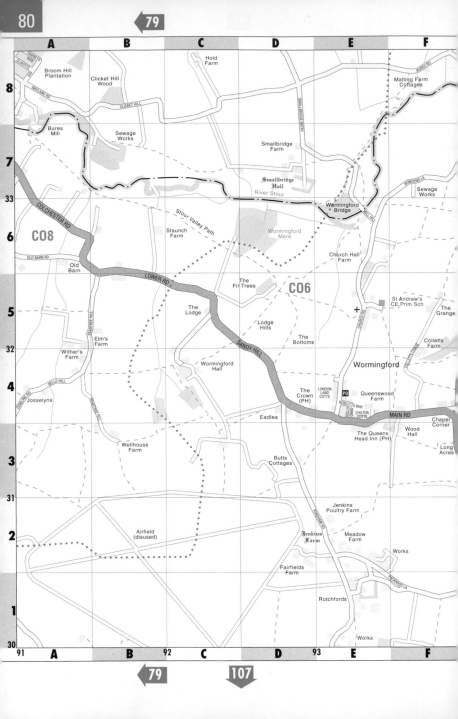

**8**

Broom Hill
Plantation

Clicket Hill
Wood

Hold
Farm

Malting Farm
Cottages

Bures
Mill

CLICKET HILL

Sewage
Works

Smallbridge
Farm

**7**

Smallbridge
Hall

Sewage
Works

**33**

River Stour

Wormingford
Bridge

COLCHESTER RD

Stour Valley Path

**6**

C08

Staunch
Farm

Wormingford
Mere

Church Hall
Farm

OLD BARN RD

Old
Barn

LOWER RD

The
Fir Trees

C06

St Andrew's
CE Prim Sch

**5**

The
Lodge

Lodge
Hills

The
Grange

Elm's
Farm

The
Bottoms

Colletts
Farm

**32**

Wither's
Farm

Wormingford
Hall

SANDY HILL

Wormingford

BELLS HILL

**4**

Josselyns

The Crown
(PH)

LONDON
LAND
COTTS

PO

Queenswood
Farm

CHILTON
COTTS

MAIN RD

Chapel
Corner

Eadlea

Wood
Hall

Long
Acres

**3**

Wellhouse
Farm

Butts
Cottages

The Queens
Head Inn (PH)

**31**

Jenkins
Poultry Farm

**2**

Airfield
(disused)

Jenkins
Farm

Meadow
Farm

Works

PACKARDS LA

Fairfields
Farm

**1**

Rotchfords

**30**

Works

79 107

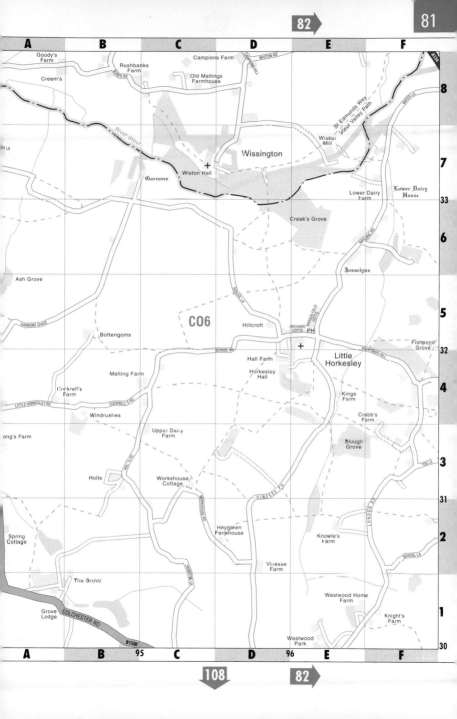

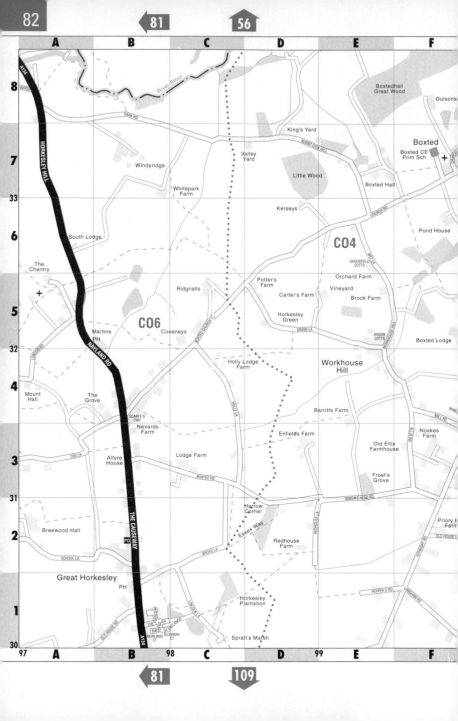

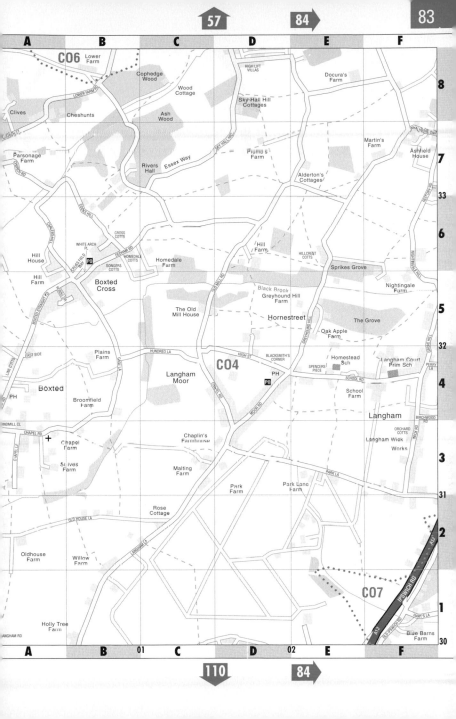

A  B  C  D  E  F

8

Clapper
Farm

Orvis
Farm

Gosnalls
Farm

Hogs La

Fen
Bridge

Sewage
Works

P

Hay
Barn

Bridge
Cottage

River Stour

Debham
Hall
Tara Breeds
Farm

Stour Valley Path
& St Edmund Way

Mus
Flatford
Mill

7

Flatford Mill
Field Ctr

Valley
Farm

Hallfields
Farm

33

Pound
Farm

Dedham Old River

CO7

Judas
Gap

6

MANNINGTREE RD

Dedham
CE Prim Sch

Lower Barn
Farm

5

OAKFRS
TERR

East
House

Castle
House

Heavy Horse
Ctr

The
Rookery

32

Cuckoo
Cottage

Stour
House

Lawford
Hall

DEDHAM RD

Lawford
Park

CO11

4

Hill
Farm

Shirburn
Mill

Broom
Knolls

Lufkins

Shir Burn

PH

WIGNALL ST
A137

3

Heath
Farm

Aldercar

Essex Way

Great Hickle
House

Bargate Lane
Farm

31

HARWICH RD

Glanfields

2

Foxash
Estate

Lower
Farm

Wisdom's
Farm

Grange
Farm

1

Oak Tree
Corner

30

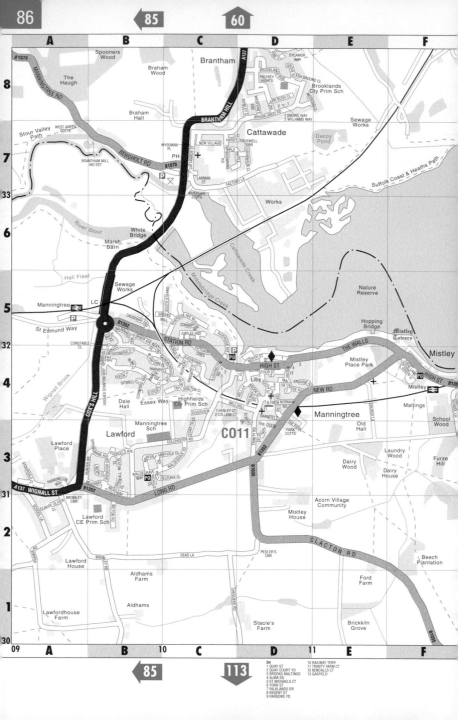

**IP9**

8

Backhouse
Ley

Holbrook Bay

Graham's
Wharf

7

33

Stutton
Ness

Dovehouse
Point

River Stour

6

Stone
Point

5

Wrabness
Point

Shore
Farm

PINE LA

32

Jacques Bay

Wrabness
Hall

Wrabness

CHURCH RD

4

Wrabness
Local Nature
Reserve

WALL LA

Cemy

Lower
Farm

P

P

STATION ROAD

Ragmarsh
Farm

WHEATSHEAF CL

3

Brakey
Grove

Dimbols
Farm

Jacques
Hall

SPINNEL'S LA

31

Gateways

Foxes
Farm

Domine
Farm

CO11

Lonbarn

PH

COOK'S
CORNER

2

B1352 HARWICH RD

LONBARN HILL

Lonbarn
Bridge

HARWICH RD

Priory
Farm

The
Firs

BUTLER'S LA

SPINNEL'S HILL

Butler's
Farm

Spinnel's
Farm

BERNER'S LA

1

Windmill

Pondhall
Wood

Bluehouse
Farm

30

A B C D E F

8

Nether
Hall
Sparrow
Hall
Beaumont
Hall
IP9

7

33

River Stour

6

5

32

West
Grove
East
Grove
Copperas Bay

Copperas Wood
Farm

4

Simpson's
Farm
Strandlands
Essex Way
L.C.

Nature
Reserve
Copperas
Wood

Wrabness
Rectory
Farm
Stour Wood
Nature Reserve
Coppetas

BLACKBOY LA

3

PII
CO11
W R A B N E S S   R D
CO12
BAY LA

Primrose
Hill
P
Home
Farm

RECTORY LA

31

HARWICH RD
White
Cross
Stourwood
Farm
Seagar's
Farm
FINNISH HILL B168

2

Primrose
Hall
Windmill

PRIMROSE LA
Ramsey
Roydon
Hall
Ramsey
Cty Prim
Sch
WINDMILL

WIX RD

1

Wash
Corner
TINKER ST
A120

30

89

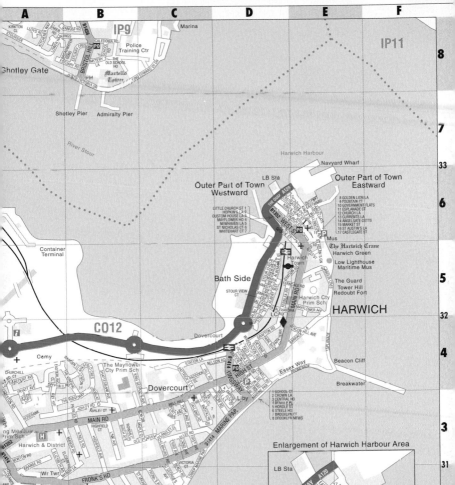

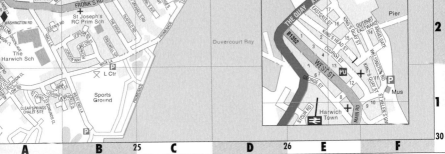

Enlargement of Harwich Harbour Area

91
65

| | A | B | C | D | E | F |
|---|---|---|---|---|---|---|

**8**

PIES GREEN RD.

White House Farm

BENNETT'S LA.

SPRING CL.

Berden

Highlands Farm

ST SCHOOL

CHURCH DR.

Berden Hall Farm

FIELD

THE STREET

Easingwell House

Coles Green

River Stort

Potash Farm

Berden Hall

Little London

CHAPEL LA.

**7**

Rooks Farm

The Byre

**29**

The Crump

**6**

Blakings La.

Peyton Hall

Park Green

Park Green

Brick House End

Brick House

**5**

Battle's Wood

**28**

**CM23**

**4**

Battles Hall

Maggotsend Farm

Mill Cottage

**SG9**

Maggots End

White House Corner

**3**

SHEPCOTT LA.

**27**

Mount Pleasant

BUTT LA.

Ford

THE STREET

STEWARTS WAY

MAGGOTS LA.

ANDERSON

Saucemeres

Mallows Green

**2**

MALLOWS GREEN RD.

Saucemeres Cottage

Manuden House

Applegarth

Ley Wood

Mallows Green Farmhouse

Manuden

DOUCHE LA.

Harcamlow Way

Uppend

Keeper's Cottage

Broome Cottage

**1**

Percy Wood

WATERY LA.

Little Croft

The Broome

MALLOWS GREEN RD.

Parsonage Farm

**26**

| 46 | A | B | 47 | C | D | 48 | E | F |
|---|---|---|---|---|---|---|---|---|

91
118

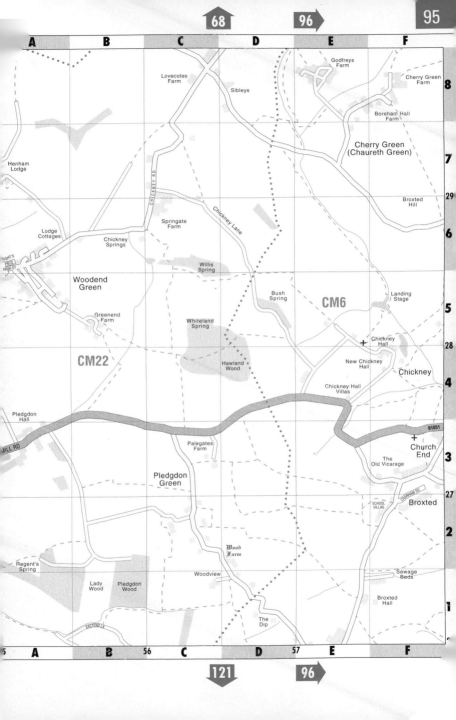

A   B   C   D   E   F

8

Brown's
Wood

Home
Wood

Stan Brook

Hill
Farm

B1051

Dairygreen
Farm

Warrens
Wood

Brickmead

Buckingham's
Farm

Stanbrook

Horham Hall

Armigers
Farm

7

29

Armigers

Hammer Hill
Farm

Hart's
Grove

Sharpes
Farm

FOLLY MILL LA.

The
Stepps

River Chelmer

Follymill

6

Su#ted
Green

Harcamlow Way

Delfits La

CM6

Broadfans
Farm

Chaureth Hall
Farm

5

28

Walters
Cottage

Brick House
Farm

Wolsey's
Farm

Broadwater
Bridge

Tingates

4

B1051

Hill
Pasture

Tilty Hill
Farm

Lower
Barn

Coldharbour
Farm

Duton
Hill

3

27

Coldharbour
Villas

Eseley
Wood

Dutonhill
Bridge

PH

PO

Duton Hill
Farm

Home
Wood

Mill

The
Maltings

Malting
Bridge

Tilty

2

The
Grange

1

Moor End
Farm

A   B   59   C   D   60   E   F

58

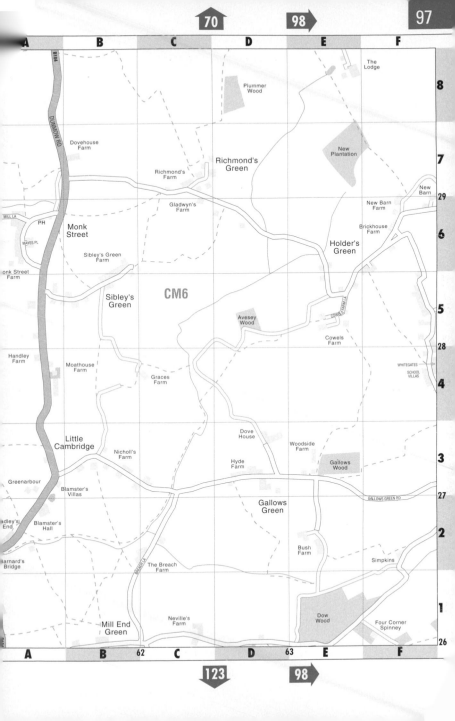

70
98

**A**   **B**   **C**   **D**   **E**   **F**

8

The Lodge

Plummer Wood

New Plantation

7

29

New Barn

DUNMOW RD

Dovehouse Farm

Richmond's Farm

Richmond's Green

New Barn Farm

Brickhouse Farm

MILL LA

PH

Monk Street

Gladwyn's Farm

MAYES PL

Holder's Green

6

Sibley's Green Farm

onk Street Farm

CM6

Sibley's Green

COWELS FARM LA

Avesey Wood

5

28

Handley Farm

Moathouse Farm

Cowels Farm

Graces Farm

WHITEGATES

SCHOOL VILLAS

4

Dove House

Little Cambridge

Nicholl's Farm

Woodside Farm

Gallows Wood

3

Hyde Farm

27

Greenarbour

Blamster's Villas

Gallows Green

GALLOWS GREEN RD

adley's End

Blamster's Hall

2

arnard's Bridge

Bush Farm

Simpkins

The Breach Farm

BREACH LA

Neville's Farm

Dow Wood

Four Corner Spinney

1

Mill End Green

26

**A**   **B**   62   **C**   **D**   63   **E**   **F**

123
98

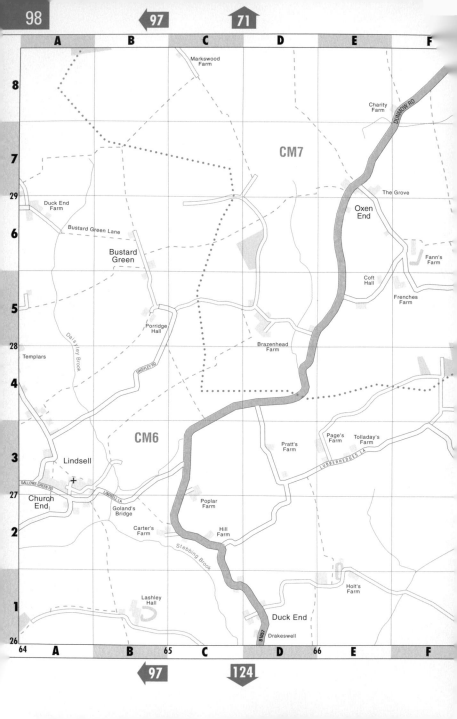

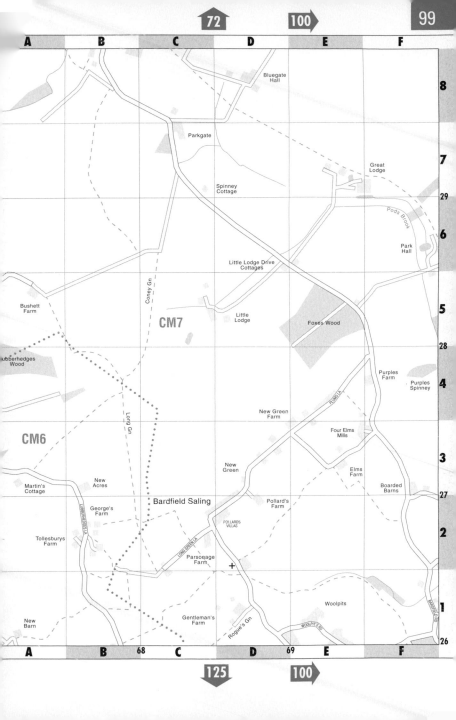

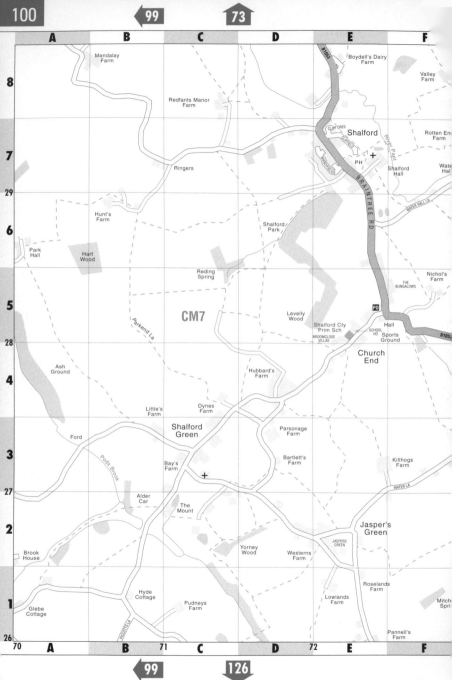

A B C D E F

8

Rotten End
House

Little
Woolmers

Beards Wood

CO9

Woolmers
Farm

Beardswood
Farm

Rotten End

PARKHALL RD

Beechley
Farm

7

29

Parkfields
Farm

Paddocks
Farm

+

Codham Little Park
Farm

PH

Fishers
Farm

Maid's Wood

Parkhall Wood

CODHAM LITTLE PARK DR

PARKGATE

Beazley End

6

Mast

Lone's Hole

Little Codham
Farm

Bovingdon Wood

5

Mill

Stone Cottages

28

an Office
Farm

Great Codham Hall

Beckwith's
Farm

INTREE RD

CM7

Bovingdon
Rows

FENNES RD

4

Abbot's
Hall

River Pant

Goldsticks
Farm

NTE LA

3

27

Bovingdon
Hall

Oak Wood

BOVINGDON RD

Sheering Hall

2

Hamblyn Wood

FENNES RD

1

B1053

26

A B C D E F

74

75

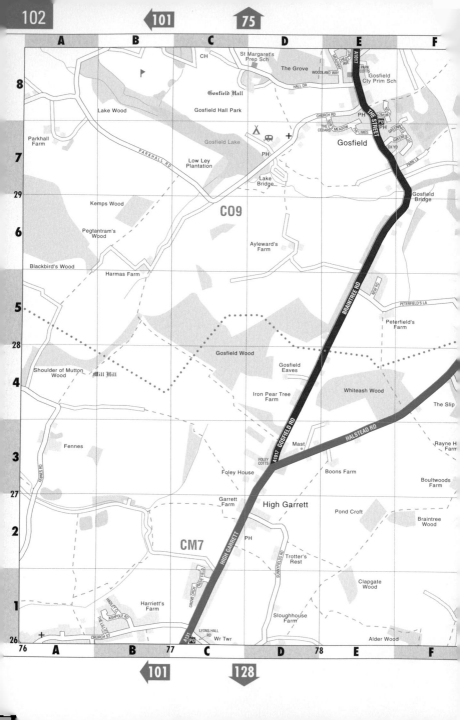

**A** **B** **C** **D** **E** **F**

RUSSELL'S RD

Highwoods
Farm

Attwoods

MOUNT HILL A131

SCHOOL CHASE
WEST YD

MEADOW
CL

**8**

Hobbs Wood

Wr Twr

Conies
Farm

Stone's
Farm

PO

**HALSTEAD**

Upper Beakley
Farm

Greenstead
Hall

**7**

Highwood's
Grove

Bourne
Farm

**29**

Sparrows
Pond

Bournebrook
Bridge

Bushey Leys

Letche's
Farm

BOURNEBRIDGE HILL

Aldercar Wood

**CO9**

Bourne Brook

**6**

Froyz Hall
Farm

Aylett's
Farm

ater Wood

Turnpike
Wood

Magpie Hall

PLAISTOW GREEN RD

Gladfen
Hall

**5**

Plaistow
Green

Gladfen Hall
Cotts

PETERFIELD'S
LA

Penny Pot

**28**

Rayne Hatch
Wood

Bee's Farm

Ward's Farm

Rivenshall
Farm

**4**

Highbarn
Hall

Leafy
Wood

Keeper's Cottage

Stable
Wood

Moat Farm

**3**

Moat Wood

**27**

**CM7**

Lower Wood

Belcher's
Wood

Lucas
Cottages

**2**

Mott Cottage

Church Farm

Brookes
Nature Reserve

P

Coppy Wood

LODGE LANE

Church's La

Broadfield
Wood

**1**

Brookes
Farm

entishes
Farm

Kentish
Cottages

Folly Green

Herbdell

**26**

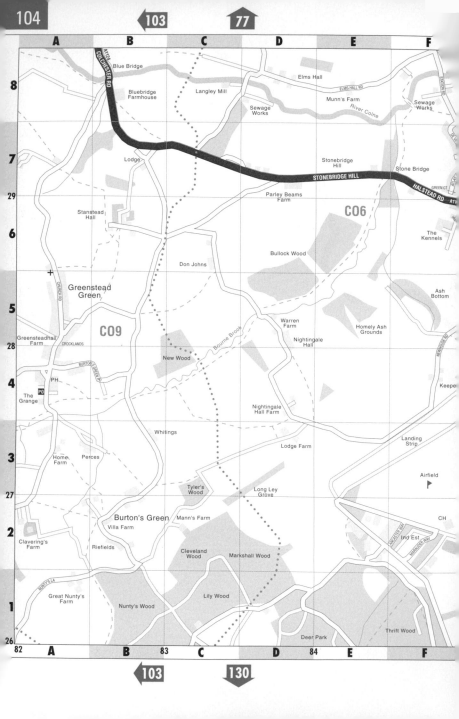

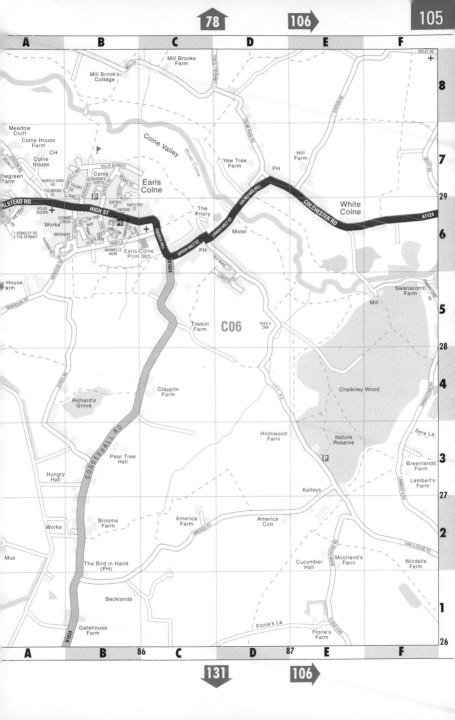

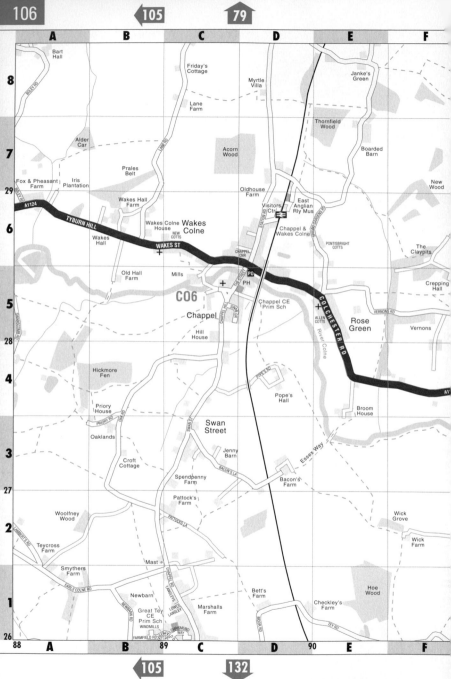

| | A | B | C | D | E | F |

**8** Bart Hall — Friday's Cottage — Lane Farm — Myrtle Villa — Janke's Green

**7** Alder Car — Prales Belt — Acorn Wood — Thornfield Wood — Boarded Barn — New Wood

Fox & Pheasant Farm — Iris Plantation — Wakes Hall Farm — Oldhouse Farm

**29** A1124 — TYBURN HILL

**6** Wakes Hall — Wakes Colne House — NEW COTTS — Wakes Colne — WAKES ST — Visitors Ctr — East Anglian Rly Mus — Chappel & Wakes Colne — PONTISBRIGHT COTTS — The Claypits

Old Hall Farm — Mills — CHAPPEL CNR — C06 — Chappel — PO — PH — Chappel CE Prim Sch — COLCHESTER RD — ALLEN'S COTTS — VERNONS RD — Crepping Hall

**5** Hill House — Rose Green — Vernons

**28** Hickmore Fen

**4** Priory House — Pope's Rd — Pope's Hall — Broom House — A1

**3** Oaklands — Croft Cottage — Swan Street — Jenny Barn — BACON'S LA — Bacon's Farm — Essex Way

**27** Spendpenny Farm — Pattock's Farm

**2** Woolfney Wood — PATTOCKS LA — Wick Grove — Wick Farm

Teycross Farm — Mast — Smythers Farm

**1** EARLS COLNE RD — Newbarn — LARGE'S RYS — LONGS LANGLEY — Marshalls Farm — Bett's Farm — Checkley's Farm — Hoe Wood

Great Tey CE Prim Sch — WINDMILLS — FARMFIELD RD — CHISBURY WAY — TEY RD

**26**

| 88 | A | B | 89 | C | D | 90 | E | F |

SWANSCOMB RD — BILEY RD — PRIORY RD — OAK RD — SWAN ST — CHAPPEL HILL — SWAN GN — SHRUB END RD — STATION RD — River Colne — LABELS RD — NEWBARN RD — CHAPPEL RD — BACON RD — MACON RD

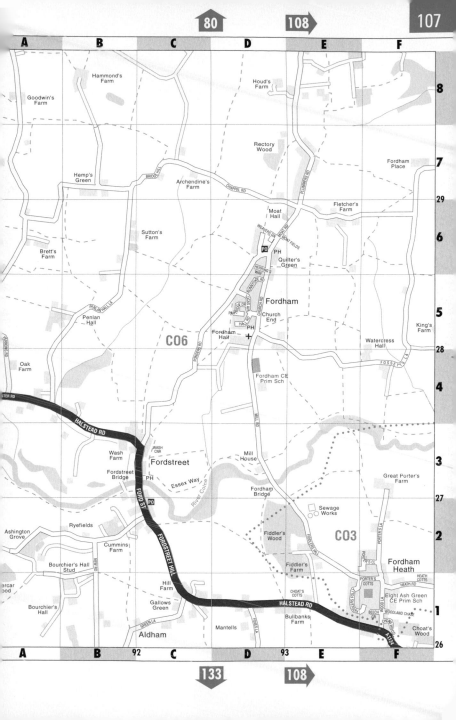

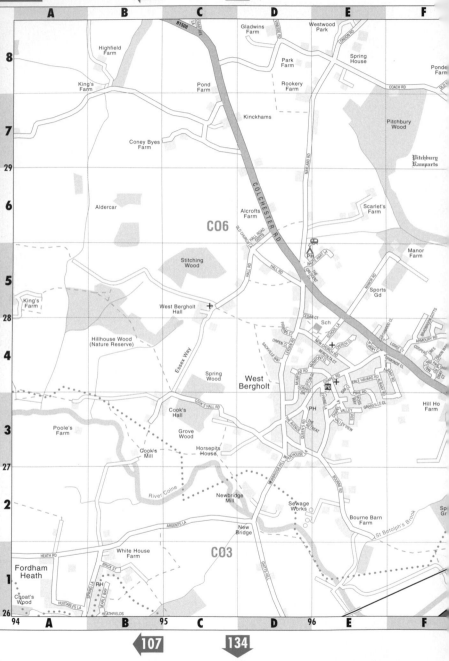

A    B    C    D    E    F

8

81508

Gladwins Farm

Westwood Park

Highfield Farm

Spring House

Ponde Farm

King's Farm

Pond Farm

Park Farm

Rookery Farm

COACH RD

7

Coney Byes Farm

Kinckhams

Pitchbury Wood

29

Pitchbury Ramparts

6

Aldercar

Alcrofts Farm

Scarlet's Farm

CO6

Manor Farm

5

Stitching Wood

PH

Sports Gd

28

West Bergholt Hall

Sch

King's Farm

Hillhouse Wood (Nature Reserve)

4

Essex Way

Spring Wood

West Bergholt

Hill Ho Farm

3

Poole's Farm

Cook's Hall

COOK'S HALL RD

Grove Wood

Cook's Mill

Horsepits House

PH

27

River Colne

Newbridge Mill

Sewage Works

2

ARGENTS LA

New Bridge

Bourne Barn Farm

St Botolph's Brook

Sp Gr

CO3

White House Farm

HEATH RD

Fordham Heath

BRICK ST

1

RH

Choat's Wood

HUXTABLES LA

SCARLE WAY

HEATHFIELDS

26

94    A    B    95    C    D    96    E    F

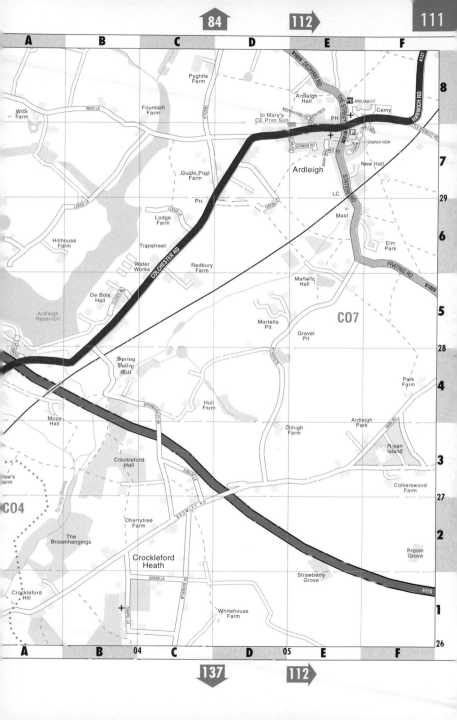

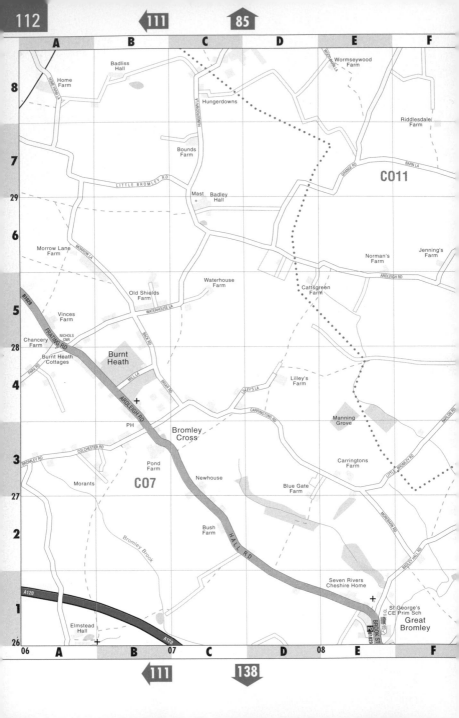

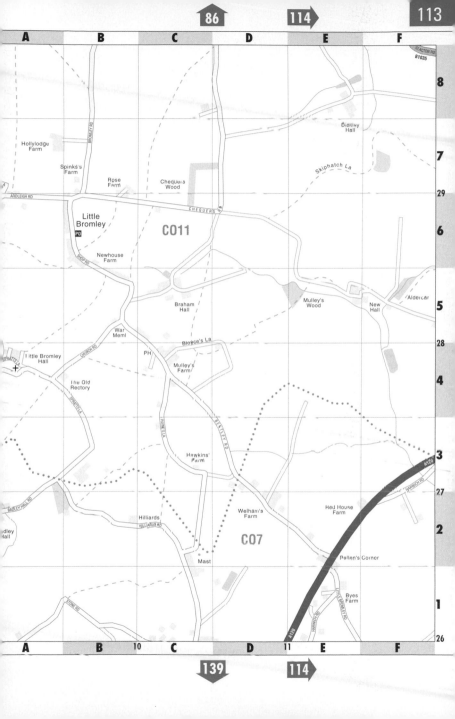

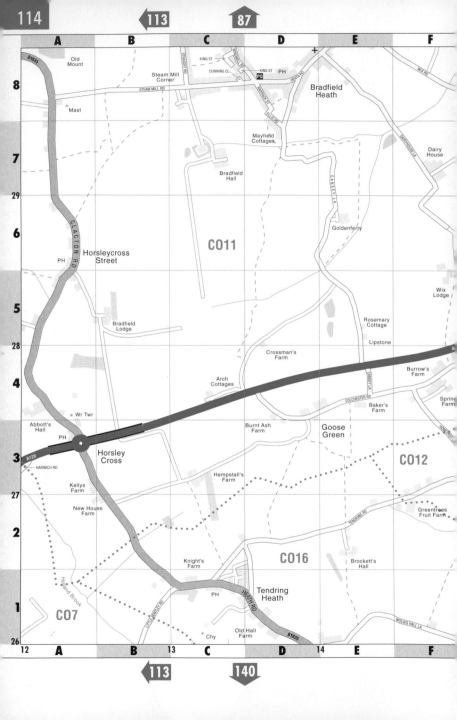

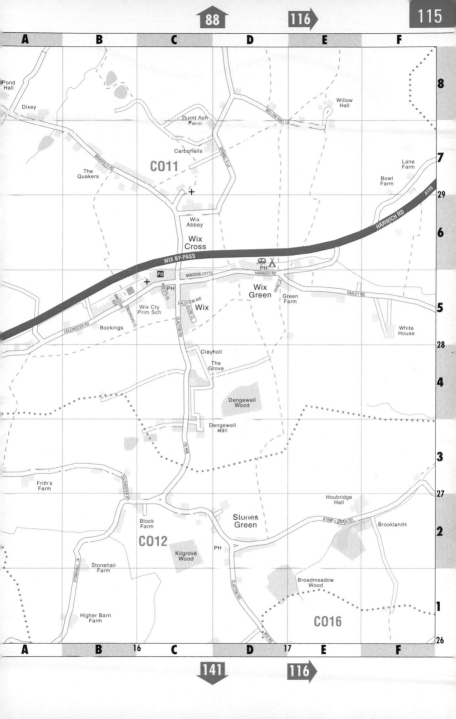

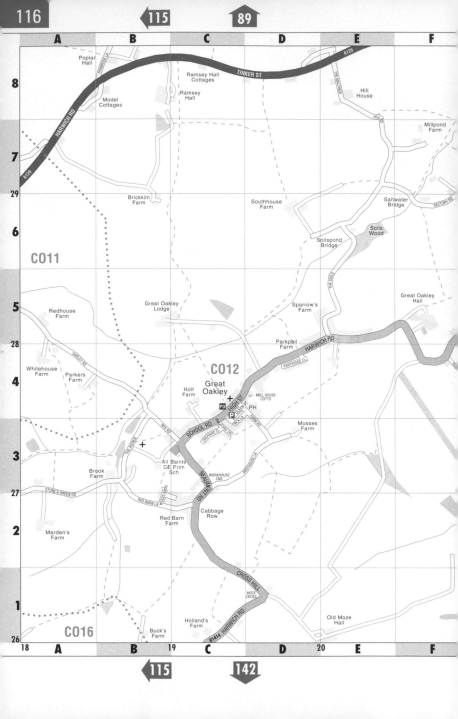

A    B    C    D    E    F

8

Poplar
Hall

TINKER ST

A120

Model
Cottages

Ramsey Hall
Cottages

Ramsey
Hall

THE MALTINGS

Hill
House

Millpond
Farm

HARWICH RD

A120

7

29

Brickkiln
Farm

Southhouse
Farm

Saltwater
Bridge

RECTORY RD

6

CO11

Soilspond
Bridge

Soils
Wood

5

Redhouse
Farm

Great Oakley
Lodge

Sparrow's
Farm

THE SIDE RD

Great Oakley
Hall

28

OAKLEY RD

Parkpail
Farm

HARWICH RD

4

Whitehouse
Farm

Parkers
Farm

CO12

Great
Oakley

Holt
Farm

PO

PH

MILL HOUSE
COTTS

PARTRIDGE CL

THE AVENUE

MILL LA

Mosses
Farm

3

WIX RD

SCHOOL RD

ORCHARD CL

HIGH ST

BEACH LA

QUAY RD

RESTHOUSE LA

All Saints
CE Prim
Sch

Brook
Farm

WORKHOUSE
CNR

BEAUMONT RD

27

STONE'S GREEN RD

RED BARN LA

POND FIELDS

Red Barn
Farm

Cabbage
Row

2

Marden's
Farm

CROSS HILL

1

MOZE
CROSS

Buck's
Farm

CO16

Holland's
Farm

HARWICH RD

B1414

Old Moze
Hall

26

18    A    19    B    C    D    20    E    F

A B C D E F

8

7

29

6

5

28

4

3

27

2

1

26

Little
Oakley

Triangle
Point

Jubilee
Houses

White
House

Little Oakley
CF Inf Sch

PH

Newhouse
Farm

CO12

Little Oakley
Hall

Burnthouse
Farm

Foulton
Hall

Essex Way

South Hall Creek

Long Bank

Sewage
Works

Boat Creek

Dugmore Creek

Great Oakley
Dock (dis)

Oakley Creek

Great Oakley
Works

Bramble Island

Pewit Island

New Island

CO14

Landing
Stage

Old
Moze
Dock

Bramble Creek

Rectory La

RECTORY RD

CLACTON RD

HARWICH RD

OAKLEY RD

B1414

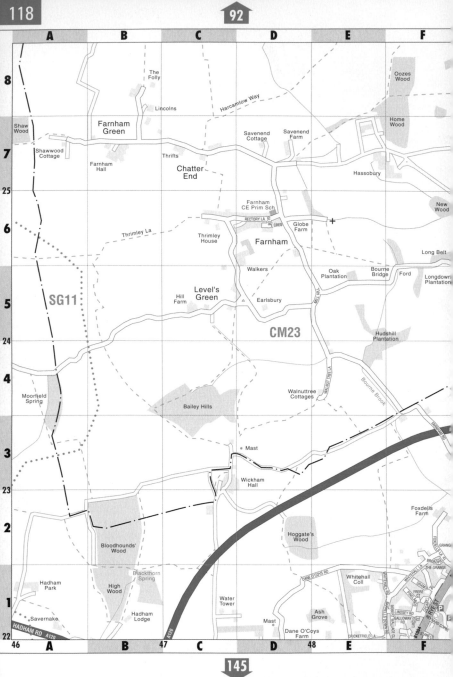

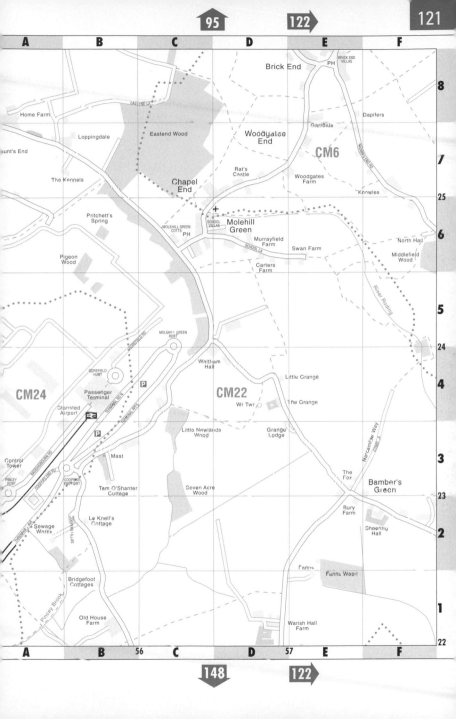

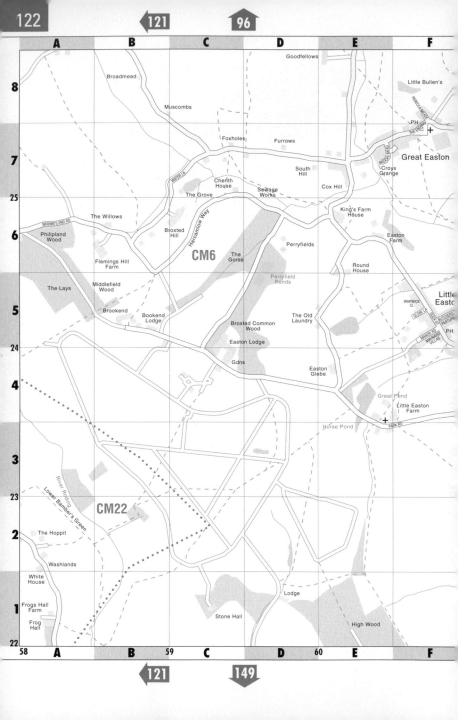

121
96

A   B   C   D   E   F

8   Broadmead

Muscombs

Goodfellows

Little Bullen's

PH
Great Easton

7   Foxholes   Furrows

South Hill

Cox Hill

Croys Grange

25   Cherith House   Sewage Works

The Grove

King's Farm House

The Willows   BROWN'S END RD

WATER LA

Harcamlow Way

6   Philipland Wood   Broxted Hill

CM6   The Gorse   Perryfields

Easton Farm

Flemings Hill Farm   Perryfield Ponds

Round House

The Lays   Middlefield Wood   Little Easto

Brookend   WARWICK CL

5   Bookend Lodge   The Old Laundry   BUTCHERS PASTURE

Broxted Common Wood   MANOR RD   MAYNARD VILLAS

PH

24   Easton Lodge

Gdns   Easton Glebe

4   Great Pond

Little Easton Farm

Horse Pond   PARK RD

3   River Roding

23   Lower Bamber's Green

CM22

2   The Hoppit

Washlands

White House

Lodge

1   Frogs Hall Farm

Frog Hall   Stone Hall

High Wood

22
58   A   B   59   C   D   60   E   F

121
149

**A** **B** **C** **D** **E** **F**

8

7

25

6

5

24

4

3

23

2

1

22

Great Easton CE Prim Sch

PH

Morris Trim La

Little Rakefairs

Rogers' Piece

Andrews Farm

Great Easton

Bigods Wood

The Spinney

Hill Farm

Ridley Wood

Battailes

New Farm

Bigods Hall Farm

ck dge

Bush Wood

Maysland

Bigods Hall

The Grove

CM6

DUCK ST

IVY COTTS

Marks Farm

B1057

Mill End

Elmbridge Farm

Bowyer's Bridge

Green La

Lower Hall

FAR RD

Brookfield Farm

River Chelmer

Elms Farm

THE BROADWAY

Walthams

Parsonage Farm

Markshill Wood

L Ctr

The Parsonage

Crouches

Crouches Farm

Helena Romanec Sch

ens m

Newton Hall

PH

BEAUMONT HILL

THE OAKS

CHURCH END VILLAS

CHURCH GDNS

Church End

Merks Hill Wood

Broomhills

B1057

CHURCH ST

PH

Hoglands Wood

Buildings Farm

BRADLEY

WAY

NORTH ST

THE CAUSEWAY

COUNTING HOUSE LA

KING'S RD

EDMUNDS

Brick Kiln Farm

Windmill

ST EDMUNDS CROFT

WDBRIDGE WY

LAUREL DR

WOODLANDS WLK

WOODLANDS

THE

Dunmow Inf Sch

B184

KNIGHT'S WAY

MILLERS CROSS

WINDMILLS

LARCH WAY

CYPRESS CT

JUNIPER

WALD GROOMS

ROSEMARY CL

Liby

TENTERFIELD

CRAYFIELDS

MAYBIRD CL

BOYES CROFT

THE DELL

Ford Farm

WOODLANDS PARK DR

NEWTON GR

JUBILEE CL

STORTFORD RD

WHITE ST

MILL LA

RIVERS

A120

Braintree Rd

BRAINTREE RD

**A** **B** 62 **C** **D** 63 **E** **F** 22

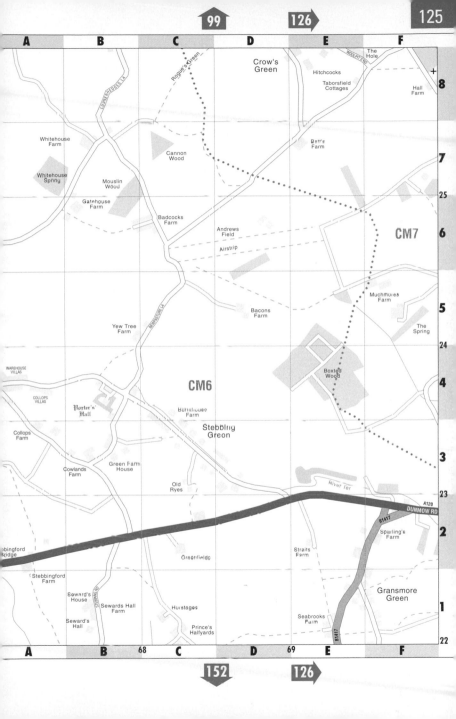

A B C D E F

The Hole
WOOLPIT END

Crow's Green

Hitchcocks

Taborsfield Cottages

Hall Farm

8

Whitehouse Farm

Cannon Wood

Bett's Farm

7

Whitehouse Spnny

Mouslin Wood

25

Gatehouse Farm

Badcocks Farm

Andrews Field

CM7

6

Airstrip

Muchmores Farm

The Spring

Yew Tree Farm

Bacons Farm

5

WAREHOUSE VILLAS

Boxted Wood

24

4

COLLOPS VILLAS

CM6

Porter's Hall

Burnthouse Farm

Collops Farm

Stebbing Green

Cowlands Farm

Green Farm House

Old Ryes

River Ter

3

23

A120
DUNMOW RD

Stebbingford Bridge

B1417

Sparling's Farm

2

Stebbingford Farm

Greenfields

Straits Farm

Seward's House

Sewards Hall Farm

Horstages

Gransmore Green

Seward's Hall

Prince's Halfyards

Seabrooks Farm

B1417

1

22

A B 68 C D 69 E F

Oxney Wood
Cow Wood
Great Priory Farm
Little Priory Farm
B1053
Bocking Churchstreet
Schs
ST NICHOLAS GDNS 1
CANTERBURY GRANGE 2
HANOVER CT 3
KINGSBRIDGE CL 4
BOVINGDON RD
SPENCER SQ
PH
PO
8
Choats Farm Stables
River Pant
Panfield
ST MARYS CT
CHURCH END
PO
PH
HALL RD
Panfield Hall
Panfield Farm
Towerlands L Ctr
CHARTWELL
The Old Deanery
King's Bridge
COUNCIL BLDGS
DEANERY HILL
Cemy
7
Towerlands Equestrian Ctr
Matthew's Farm
Park Farm
ST DEAN
ROGERS PL GDNS
BLENHEIM
BLANTFORD
WORDSWORTH RD
GAUDEN RD
DOVER CT
WINSTON
CHURCHILL
CLAVERIN
HYTHE
CAMB
MILLING RD
CHURCHILL
Polly's Hill
25
6

CM7
Panfield Wood
BRAINTREE
MAYSENT AVE
FAGGOT
EAGLE LA
B1053
EXETER CL
Bocking
5

Mast
Flanders Cl
DUKES RD
HAWKES WAY
SIX BELLS
WOOLPACK LA
24
Braintree Tabor High Sch (Upper Sch) L Ctr
FINCH END
COOPER DR
CRITTALL DR
WARNER DR
ARNHEM DR
MEADOWS
PILGRIM
ST JAMES
CT
FRIARS CL
PO
DANA
CL
1 VALENTINE CT
2 DALE HO
LANCASTER WAY
John Bunyan Cty Jun & Inf Sch
Sch
B1053
4
Air Strip
Sewage Wrks
Rayne Lodge
SPRINGWOOD IND EST
SPRINGWOOD DR
BRADBURY DR
St Michael's
Playing Field
ELM GLWS
ERN ENGL DR
CHURCH ST
PRIGT
Tabor High (Mid) Sch
BUNYAN RD
WEAVERS WK
ST PETER'S WK
THE FIELDS
Sch
I lby
CUGGESHALL RD
B1256
3
Rayne Hall
Rayne Hall Farm
Clap Bridge
BIRCH CL
GILDA TERR
SWINBORNE DR
CHILFORD
CT
SPRINGWOOD CT
H
CONSTABLE
HO
GODRIC PL
COLLEGE
RD
PO
MANOR ST
Mus
Liby
Victoria
Ct
23
RAYNE RD
FRANCIS RD
STATION RD
CLARE RD
ST MICHAELS
STATION AVE
SOUTH ST
B1255
Mus
P
2
Nursery
River Drain
Flitch Way
SWALLOW
BROOK LA
MAPLE
Sch
MARLING
FREEPORT
MALYON DR
William Julien Courtauld
NEW
H
THE
KENTS
GAINSBORO
Hoppit Bridge
THE STREET
GORE TERR
Hall
Cemy
HASTEL
HAZEL
MARSHALLS RD
EOWEN RD
RIVER
ST JOHNS
MARSH FARM
RIFLE HILL
RIFLE HILL
WORKS
Marsh Farm
1
Naylinghurst
B1256
A120
A131
A120
Bridge Farm
Marshalls Park
P
FORTUNES
COMMA SQ
WINDSOR
SANDOWN
P
1 COPPER CL
2 GRAYLING CL
3 MEADOW BROWN CT
RUCKWOODS
RD
CHALLIS L
22
Wenas Farm
OVERBROUGH LA

F1
1 HILLSIDE TERR
2 HILLSIDE HO
3 EDISON CL
4 NEWTON CL
5 DARWIN CL
6 WALL CL
7 FLEMING CL
8 GATEKEEPER CL

F2
1 ST MICHAEL'S LA
2 RUE DE JEUNES
3 THE BRAINTREE FOYER
4 ST MICHAEL'S CT
5 MAZERS CT
6 CHELSEA MEWS
7 COLLINS CL
8 TOM DAVIES HO
9 JAYMAN CT

10 STRUDWICK CL
11 CLAIRMONT CL

F3
1 CHERRY BGLWS
2 WRIGHT CT
3 ST LAWRENCE CT
4 DRURY LA
5 LEATHER LA
6 LITTLE SQ
7 GEORGE YD

8 SANDPIT LA
9 GREAT SQ
10 MARKET ST
11 MARKET PL
12 TOFTS WLK

A B C D E F

8 Kerami
Henham's Farm
Tumbler's Green
Warley Farm
MADGEMENTS RD
Baines Farm
Gower's Farm
BRAIN'S LA

7 Coven Plantation
Peckstone's Farm
Woodhouse Farm

25 RECTORY RD
BACK LA
Stisted Prim Sch
Liby
Slisted
Grassy Piece

6 KING'S LA
PH PO
CH
Stisted Hall
Hall Farm
Stistedhall Park
Sewage Works
Harvey's Farm
CL END
COMMERCE RD

5 Sisted Mill
China Bridge
CM7
Pattiswick Hall Farm
Pattiswick
CHURCH RD

24 Boathouse Plantation
Pattiswick Hall
STISTED RD
Shelborn Bridge

4 Milles Farm
Prior's Wood
New Plant
STOCKSTREET RD

3 PH
Baytree Farm
Runton Farm
COGGESHALL RD
Blackwater Bridge
MILL VIEW
Orange Wood
CO6
A120

23 GREY'S LA
FORGE CN
CHAPEL RISE
HILLARY CL
Bradwell
Mill View

2 Withies Farm
Stisted Cottage Farm
Rectory Farm
FOSTER'S COTTS
Highelms Farm
The Pits
Park Farm House
CHURCH RD

1 Fells Farm
Glazenwood
Perry Green Farm
Perry Green
Park House
Hoppits
PERRY LA
Bradwell Hall

22

A B 80 C D 81 E F

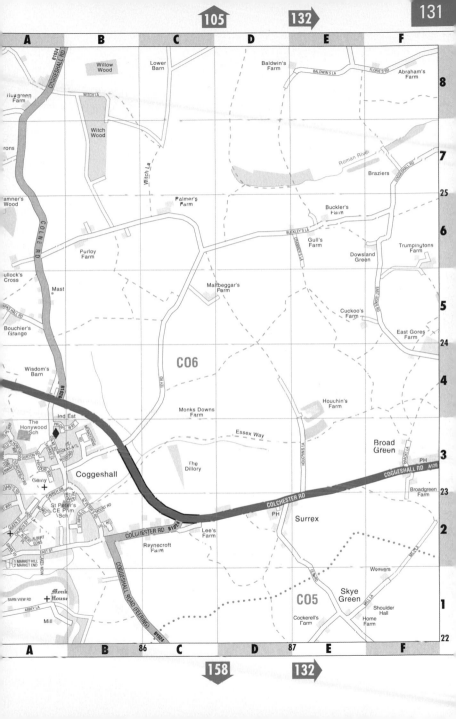

A　　B　　C　　D　　E　　F

8

7

25

6

24

5

4

23

3

2

1

22

Hoxgreen
Farm

Willow
Wood

Lower
Barn

WITCH LA

Baldwin's
Farm

BALDWIN'S LA

FLORIE'S RD

Abraham's
Farm

rons

Witch
Wood

Witch La

Roman River

Braziers

COGGESHALL RD

amner's
Wood

Palmer's
Farm

Buckler's
Farm

BUCKLEY'S LA

COLNE RD

B1024

Purloy
Farm

STANWELL'S LA

Gull's
Farm

Dowsland
Green

Trumpington's
Farm

ullock's
Cross

Mast

Maltbeggar's
Farm

EAST GORES RD

Bouchier's
Grange

MAX HALL RD

Cuckoo's
Farm

East Gores
Farm

Wisdom's
Barn

A1018

CO6

FEN RD

Monks Downs
Farm

Houchin's
Farm

The
Honywood
Sch

Ind Est

Essex Way

Broad
Green

PH

COGGESHALL RD　A120

Coggeshall

The
Dillory

HOUCHIN'S LA

SHACK LA

Broadgreen
Farm

Gerry

St Peter's
CE Prim
Sch

COLCHESTER RD

PH

Surrex

Lee's
Farm

Raynecroft
Farm

COLCHESTER RD　B1024

23

Weavers

MILL LA

1 MARKET HILL
2 MARKET END

CO5

Skye
Green

Shoulder
Hall

BARN VIEW RD

Monk
House

Cockerell's
Farm

Home
Farm

ABBEY LA

LONG RD

COGGESHALL ROAD (FEERING)

Mill

B1024

A　　B　　C　　D　　E　　F

86

87

Brookhouse

Great
Tey

Moor
Farm

Hoe
Farm

Church House
Farm

Walcott's
Farm

Walcott's
Hall

Brick Kiln
Cottage

Warren's
Farm

NEW
COTTS

Tey Brook
Piggeries

LC

Chase
Cottage

Teybrook
Farm

Little Tey
House

Little Tey House
Farm

Stonefield
Grove

Sparrow
Grove

CO6

Knave's
Farm

East
Gores

Upp Hall
Farm

Little
Tey

Church
Farm

Mott's
Farm

Marks Tey

Godbolt's
Farm

PH

Salmon's
Corner

COGGESHALL RD

Elm
Farm

Honeylands
Farm

Norman Cl 1
Roxborough Cl 2

St Andrew's
Prim Sch

LC

Wk

CO5

Hornigals

LONDON RD

A12

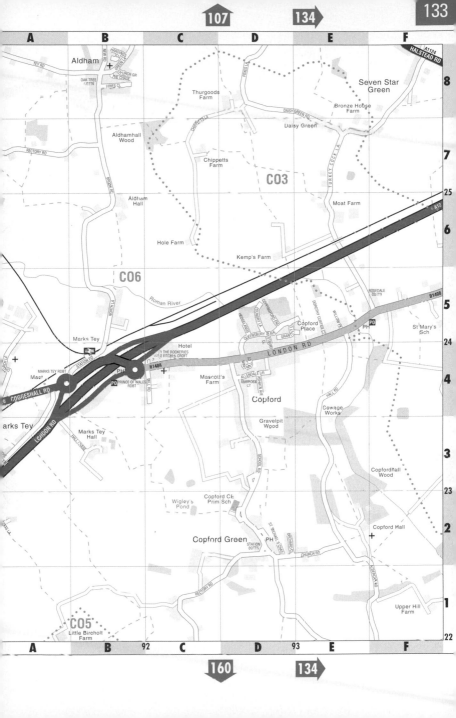

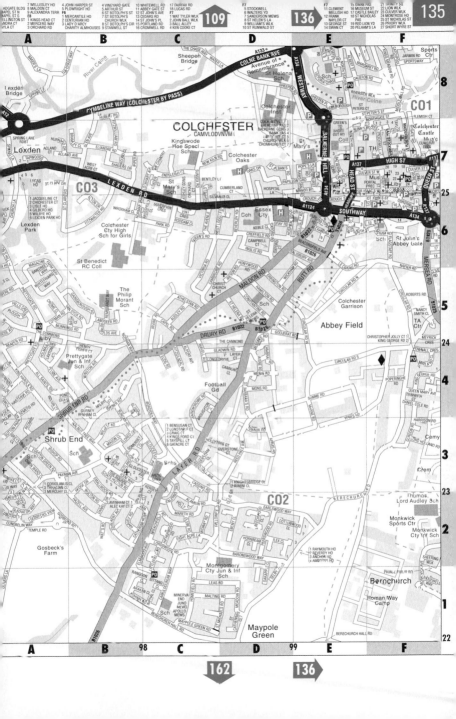

141
116

| | A | B | C | D | E | F |

**8**

Oldhouse Farm

Glebe Farm

Potland

B1414

HARWICH RD

The Horseshoes

New Moze Hall

CO12

Maze Creek

**7**

**25**

Northfield Farm

B1414

**6**

CHURCH LA

HARWICH RD

Lower Barn Farm

Landermere Creek

**5**

Quay Farm

Quay (dis)

Beaumont Cut

**24**

QUAY LA

Beaumont Bridge

Beaumont Quay

White House

**4**

CO16

GULL COTTS

GOLDEN LA

Landermere Hall

Landermere

**3**

Thorpe Lodge

New Hall

Kentshill Farm

**23**

LANDERMERE RD

WALTON RD

**2**

NEW TOWN

NEW RD

NEWNOTH DR

PALMERSTON RD

ARGYLE RD

THORPE DR

LONSDALE RD

1 HILLSIDE COTTS
2 LANDERMERE VIEW

2

RIDOLPH CT

DAMANT'S FARM LA

CO13

Dale Hill Farm

**1**

THE STREET

OAK CL

Tendring Tech Coll

ABBEY ST

Elm Farm

BYNG HO

Thorpe-le-Soken

Folly Farm

Damont's Farm

Sneating Hall

B1414

ABBEY ST

B1033

FRINTON RD

B1033

B1034

SNEATING HALL LA

**22**

| 18 | A | | B | 19 | C | | D | 20 | E | | F |

141
169

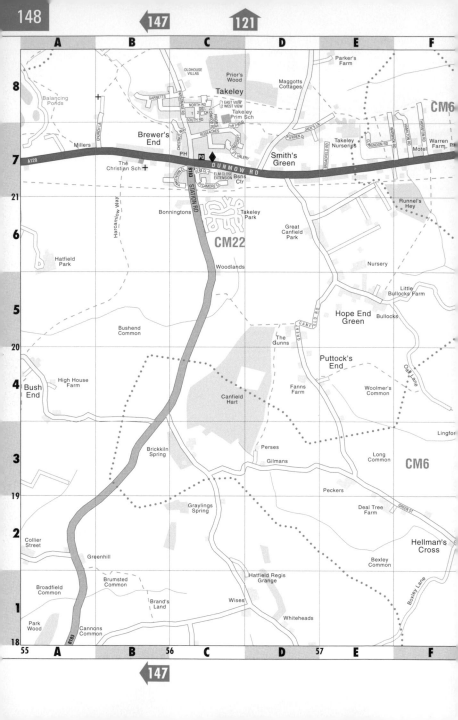

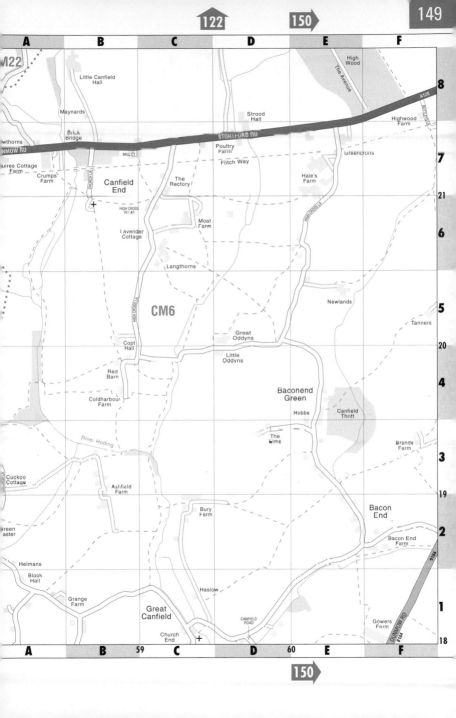

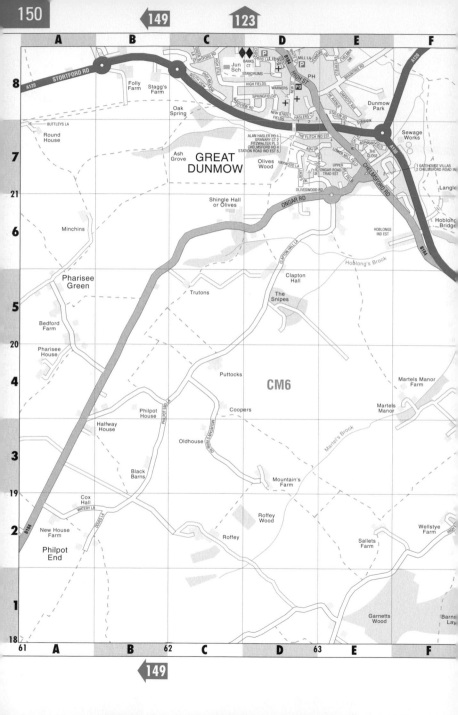

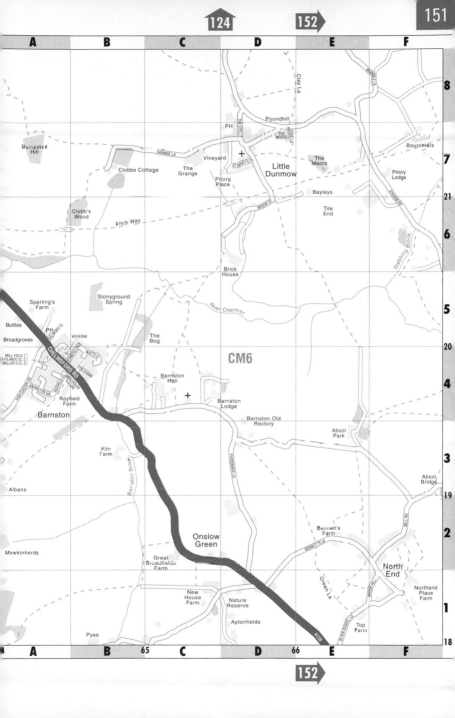

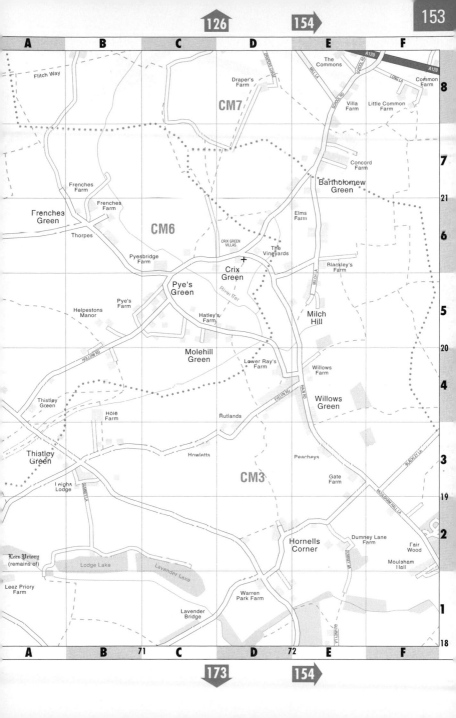

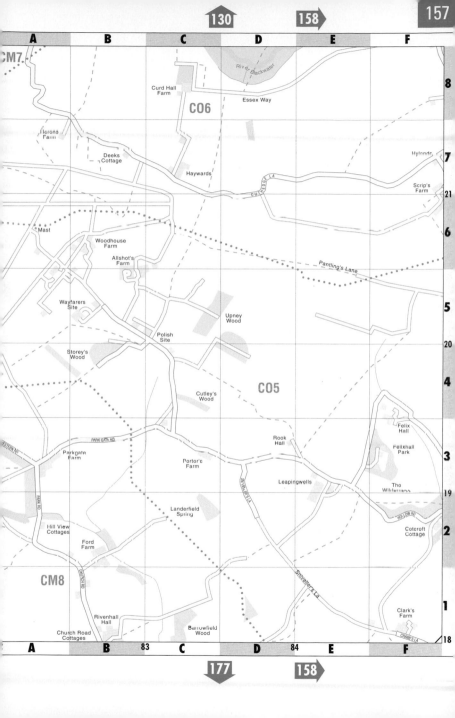

130
158
177
158

A    B    C    D    E    F

8

River Blackwater

Curd Hall
Farm

Essex Way

CO6

Herons
Farm

Deeks
Cottage

7

Hylands

Haywards

CULVERGE LA

Scrip's
Farm

21

Mast

6

Woodhouse
Farm

Allshot's
Farm

Pantling's Lane

Wayfarers
Site

Upney
Wood

5

Polish
Site

Storey's
Wood

20

Cutley's
Wood

CO5

4

Felix
Hall

PARK GATE RD.

Parkgate
Farm

Rook
Hall

Felixhall
Park

FESTEN RD.

Portor's
Farm

Leapingwells

The
Wilderness

3

RIVENHALL LA.

19

PARK RD.

Landerfield
Spring

Cotcroft
Cottage

2

Hill View
Cottages

HOLLOW RD.

Ford
Farm

CM8

SHRIVELLERS LA.

Clark's
Farm

1

CHURCH RD.

Rivenhall
Hall

Barrowfield
Wood

Church Road
Cottages

CRAB'S LA.

18

A    B    83    C    D    84    E    F

A B C D E F

8

CO6

Easthorpegreen Farm

Great Domsey

Popps

Great Domsey Farm

EULLA

DOMSEY CHASE

Domsey Brook

7

Little Domsey

EASTHORPE RD

Badcock's Farm

LONDON RD

B1024

Hill House Farm

21

6

Scottie's Farm

Long Grove

Prested Hall Farm

CO5

5

Fan Wood

ested Hall

Domsey Brook

EASTHORPE RD

20

4

Messing Grove

Messing Lodge

LARGO RD

3

Messing

PH

19

Yewtree Farm

THE STREET

HARBOROUGH HALL RD

2

Bouchier's Hall

KELVEDON RD

Messing-cum-Inworth Cty Prim Sch

Harborough Hall Farm

SCHOOL RD

Parsonage Farm

B1022

Messing Park

Haynes Green Cottages

1

Conyfield Wood

B1022

18

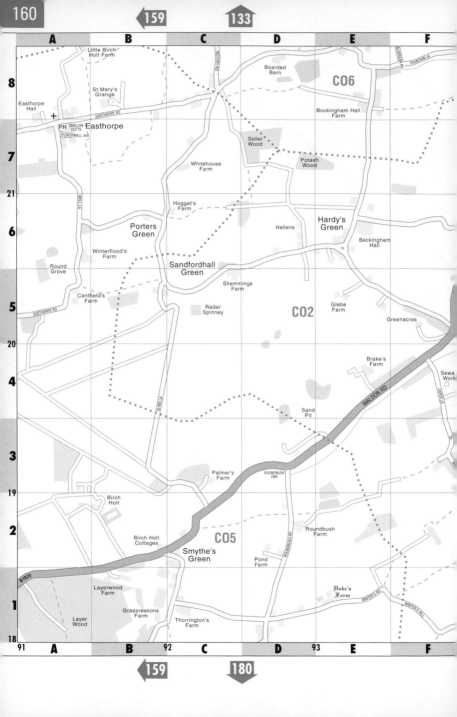

159
133

A B C D E F

8

CO6

Little Birch
Holt Farm

St Mary's
Grange

Boarded
Barn

Easthorpe
Hall

PH ONSLOW
COTTS Easthorpe

Bockingham Hall
Farm

EASTHORPE RD

CHURCHWELL AVE

7

Seller
Wood

Potash
Wood

Whitehouse
Farm

21

Hogget's
Farm

6

Porters
Green

Hellens

Hardy's
Green

Beckingham
Hall

Winterflood's
Farm

Round
Grove

Sandfordhall
Green

Shemmings
Farm

5

EASTHORPE RD

Cantfield's
Farm

Radar
Spinney

CO2

Glebe
Farm

Greenacres

20

Brake's
Farm

Sewa
Work

4

BLIND LA

MALDON RD

CAPEL LA

Sand
Pit

3

Palmer's
Farm

ROUNDBUSH
CNR

19

Birch
Holt

2

Birch Holt
Cottages

CO5

ROUNDBUSH RD

Roundbush
Farm

Smythe's
Green

Pond
Farm

Duke's
Farm

WINTERS RD

WINTERS HILL

B1022

Layerwood
Farm

1

Layer
Wood

Grassreasons
Farm

Thorrington's
Farm

18

91 A B 92 C D 93 E F

WELL LA

A B C D E F

8

7

21

6

5

20

4

3

19

2

1

18

03 A B 04 C D 05 E F

DE VERE LA
CHAPEL RD 1
BLITHE CT 2
BLYTHE LA 3
FALCON YD 4
ALMA ST 5
BLACK BOUY HILL 6
DENTON'S TERR 7
COLNE TERR 8
ALMSHOUSES 9

Wivenhoe
PH

Liby

Ballast Quay
Farm

BLACK BOUY HILL 6

STEPHEN CRANFIELD CL

Works

Sewage
Works

Sewage
Works

Marsh
Farm

WIVENHOE RD

Ballast Quay
Farm

High Park
Corner

CO7

Alresford
Grange

Mill

CHURCH RD

Holmwood
Farm

Lower Brickhouse
Farm

River Colne

Faringhoe
Hall

Tower

CO5

Sand Pit

Alresford
Lodge

Jaggers

Fingringhoe Wick
Nature Reserve

South
Green

WICK LA

Visitor Ctr

Aldboro
Point

DANGER AREA

North Geedon Creek

DANGER AREA

Fingringhoe Ranges

Fingringhoe
Marsh

Geedon
Saltings

A    B    C    D    E    F

Eden Farm

Risby's Farm

WEELEY RD

SWALLOW'S KNW

Weeley

WILLOW WLK

SECOND AVE

B1441 WEELEY BYPASS RD

THE STRD

CLACTON RD B1441

8

Weeley CE Prim Sch

Reedlands

Tye Farm

Weeley Brook

Gutteridge Hall

OUTTERIDGE GATE LA

St Mary's Farm

TOWER'S LA

Gutteridge Wood

7

21

Jubilee Cottage

CO7

Tye Homestead

Cole's Farm

SILTA

SOURCE RD

6

Coppice Farm

CO16

Oakhurst

BENTLEY RD

WESLOCK RD

Moynes Farm

WICK RD

AINGER'S DAZEN RD

The Cottage

Norwood Lodge

A133

5

College Farm

Simplebirch Wood

Landing Strip

20

Stockets Grove

4

Row Heath

St Osyth Wick Farm

STRAIGHT RD

Bowshots Wood

Maldon Wood

WICK LA

High Birch

Woodlands Farm

OLD HOStreigh RD

3

Ampers Wick Farm

Milton Wood

19

FANNY'S LA

Jaggards

OLD HOStreigh RD

2

Martin's Grove

TEGWICK LA

Welches

Little Ampers Wick Farm

PH

owick Hall Farm

Crosslands Farm

St Osyth Heath

B1027

HEATH RD

Huntleywood Farm

Newhouse Farm

Heath Farm

Lower Heath Farm

Riddles Wood

The Leys

1

18

A    B    13    C    D    14    E    F

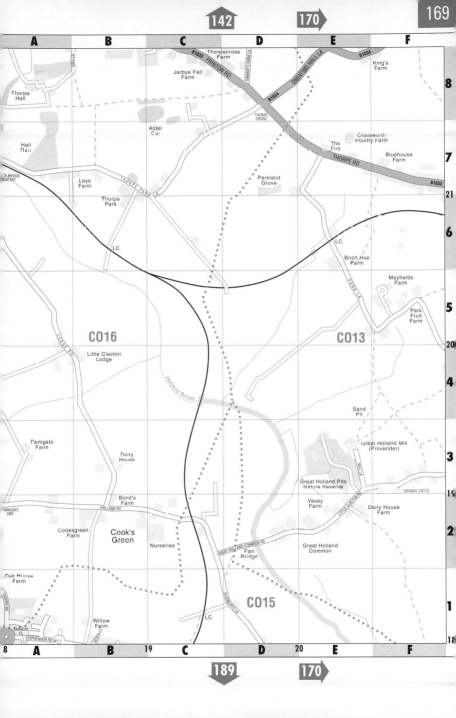

144

C8
1 MARINA MEWS
2 VICARAGE LA
3 HAVENCROFT CT
4 STRATFORD PL
5 NEWGATE ST
6 PATERNOSTER ROW
7 NEW PIER ST
8 MARTELLO RD
9 AGAR RD
10 AGAR ROAD APP
11 ST BOTOLPH'S TERR

**WALTON-ON-THE-NAZE**

Albion Breakwater

New Walton Pier

Winchester Breakwater

Lifeboat Station

CO14

CO13

Walton-on-Naze

Pedlars Wood

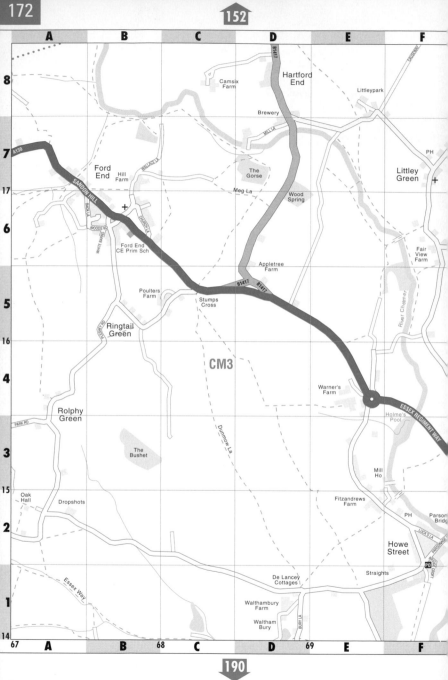

152

A B C D E F

8

Camsix
Farm

Hartford
End

Littleypark

B1417

7

A130

Ford
End

Hill
Farm

WALLACE LA

The
Gorse

Littley
Green

PH

17

Meg La

SANDON HILL

Wood
Spring

BACK LA

CHURCH LA

6

+

Ford End
CE Prim Sch

WHITE BARNS

B0005 RD

Appletree
Farm

Fair
View
Farm

Poulters
Farm

B1417

B1417

5

Stumps
Cross

River Chelmer

GREEN LA

Ringtail
Green

16

CM3

4

Warner's
Farm

ESSEX REGIMENT WAY

PARK RD

Rolphy
Green

Holme's
Pool

3

The
Bushet

Dunmow La

Mill
Ho

15

Oak
Hall

Dropshots

Fitzandrews
Farm

PH

Parson
Bridg

LUCK'S LA

2

Howe
Street

PO

BURY LA

LAWN LA

BESSONBRIDGE

1

Essex Way

De Lancey
Cottages

Straights

Walthambury
Farm

Waltham
Bury

14

67 A B 68 C D 69 E F

190

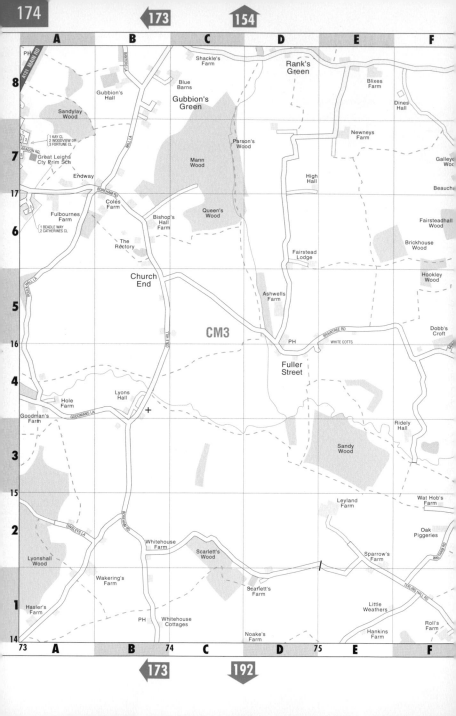

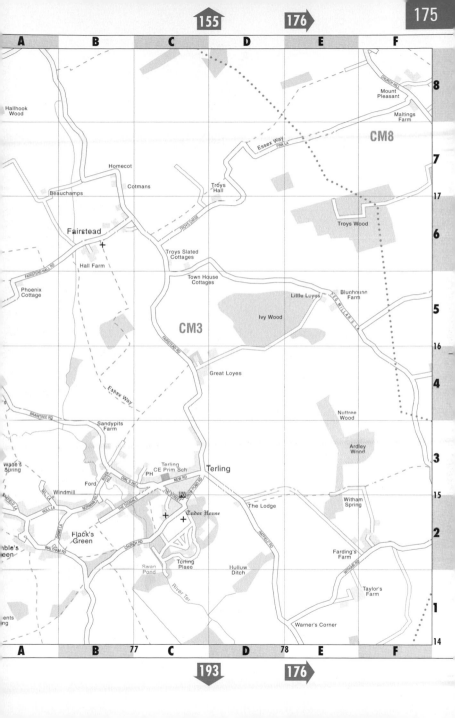

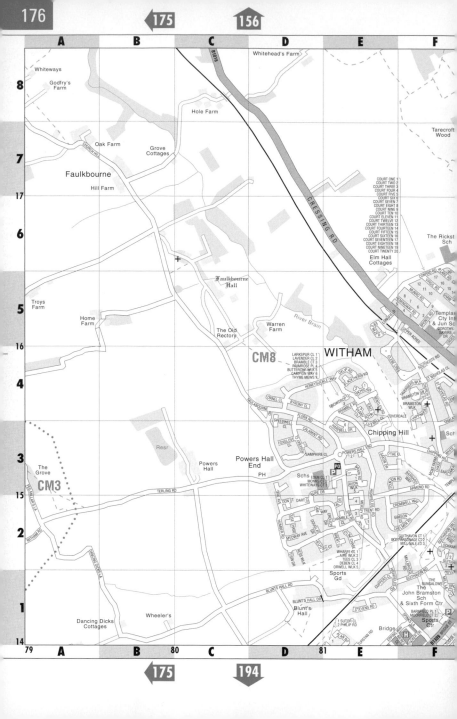

A B C D E F

8 Whiteways
Godfry's Farm
Whitehead's Farm
Tarecroft Wood

Hole Farm

7 Oak Farm
Grove Cottages
Faulkbourne
Hill Farm
CRESSING RD

17 COURT ONE 1
COURT TWO 2
COURT THREE 3
COURT FOUR 4
COURT FIVE 5
COURT SIX 6
COURT SEVEN 7
COURT EIGHT 8
COURT NINE 9
COURT TEN 10
COURT ELEVEN 11
COURT TWELVE 12
COURT THIRTEEN 13
COURT FOURTEEN 14
COURT FIFTEEN 15
COURT SIXTEEN 16
COURT SEVENTEEN 17
COURT EIGHTEEN 18
COURT NINETEEN 19
COURT TWENTY 20

6 The Rickst Sch
Elm Hall Cottages

5 Troys Farm
Home Farm
Faulkbourne Hall
River Brain
Templa Cty Inf & Jun Sc
DOROTHY DR

16 The Old Rectory
Warren Farm
CM8
LARKSPUR CL 1
LAVENDER CL 2
BRAMBLE CT 3
PRIMROSE PL 4
BUTTERCUP WLK 5
CAMPION WAY 6
THYME MEWS 7
WITHAM
ST NICHOLAS LA

4 HONEYSUCKLE WAY
SNOWDROP
BRAMSTON WLK
COVERDALE
BRAMSTON WLK
Sch

3 The Grove
CM3
Resr
Powers Hall
Powers Hall End
PH
SAMPHIRE CL
FOXGLOVE
P PO
THE CL
Chipping Hill

15 THE MALTINGS LA
WITHAM RD
TERLING RD
Schs
EDEN CL 1
MONKS CO 2
WHITEWAYS CT 3
ARMOND RD

2 WITHAM RD
FRANCIS DRACKLEY
MEDWAY AVE
TRENT RD
CROMWELL WAY
GIBSON
CHELMER RD
GUITHAVON CT 1
PARSONAGE CT 2
MILL VALE LO 3

1 SUTOR CL 1
PHILIP RD 2
WHARFE CT 1
AIRE WLK 2
TEES CL 3
DEBEN CL 4
ORWELL WLK 5
Sports Gd
BLUNTS HALL RD
BLUNT'S HALL DR
Blunt's Hall
S STEVENS RD
CLIPPERS CL
The Bungalows
The John Bramston Sch & Sixth Form Ctr
BARFIELD PL 1
MOORRELLE CT 2
Sports Ctr

14 Dancing Dicks Cottages
Wheeler's
Bridge
TURSTAN RD
H
B1389

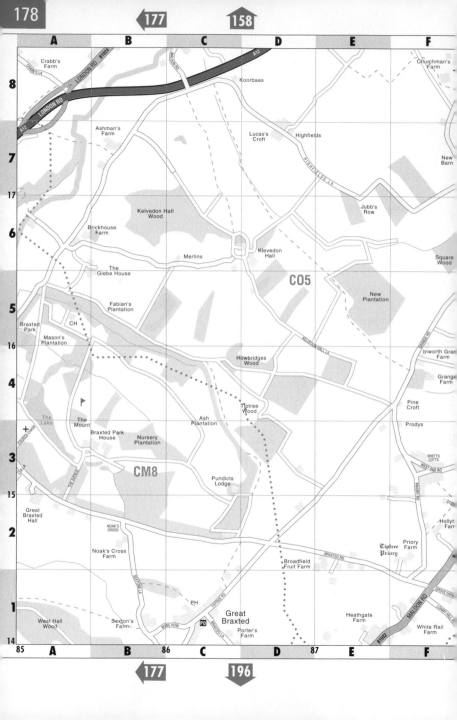

A B C D E F

8

Crabb's Farm

LONDON RD B1024

MALDON RD

A12

Koorbaes

Churchman's Farm

LONDON RD

A12

7

Ashman's Farm

Lucas's Croft

Highfields

HIGHFIELDS LA

New Barn

17

Kelvedon Hall Wood

Jubb's Row

6

Brickhouse Farm

Merlins

Klevedon Hall

Square Wood

The Glebe House

CO5

5

Fabian's Plantation

New Plantation

Braxted Park

CH

KELVEDON HALL LA

GRANGE RD

16

Mason's Plantation

Howbridges Wood

Inworth Gran Farm

4

The Lake

The Mount

Ash Plantation

Tiptree Wood

Grange Farm

Pine Croft

Prodys

CHURCH CHASE

Braxted Park House

Nursery Plantation

BRETTS COTTS

WEST END RD

3

THE AVENUE

CM8

Pundicts Lodge

PRIORY RD

15

Great Braxted Hall

NOAK'S CROSS

STON

2

SEXTON'S LA

Noak's Cross Farm

BRAXTED RD

Tiptree Priory

Priory Farm

Hollyt Farr

Broadfield Fruit Farm

GROVE FARM

1

West Hall Wood

CHURCH RD

TIPTREE RD

BUNG ROW

PH

Sexton's Farm

PO

BRAXTED LA

Great Braxted

Porter's Farm

Heathgate Farm

MALDON RD

B1022

LOMMY HILL RD

White Rail Farm

14

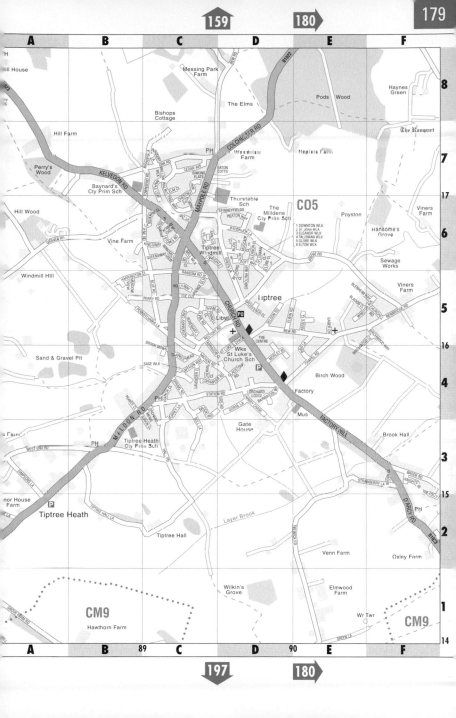

A B C D E F

8

White Lodge

Layer Woodlands Farm

WOODVIEW COTTS

Layer Marney

CO2

Layer Marney Tower
+

Wick Farm

STOCKHOUSE RD

Parkhouse Farm

Parkgate Farm

7

Oak Farm

Hall Farm

17

Layer Brook

6

Stockridge Farm

CO5

Silverthorn

Rockingham's Farm

5

Cadgers Wood

16

Long Wood

4

Park Farm

Beatbush Wood

CM9

3

Paternoster Heath

PARK LA

15

BROOK RD

HAWTHORN

ST THORN WAY

STOCKHOUSE CL

Gobolt's Farm

Barn Hall Farm

2

Tolleshunt Knights

ELIZABETH VILLAS

D'ARCY RD

TOP RD

Palmers Farm

BARNHALL RD

1

The Plough Inn (PH)

B1026

OXLEY HILL

Oxley Green

BE LA

HONEYPOT LA

RECTORY RD

Krissimon Farm

Wigborough Springs

Manifold Wick Farm

Lovedowns Farm

14

91 A B 92 C D 93 E F

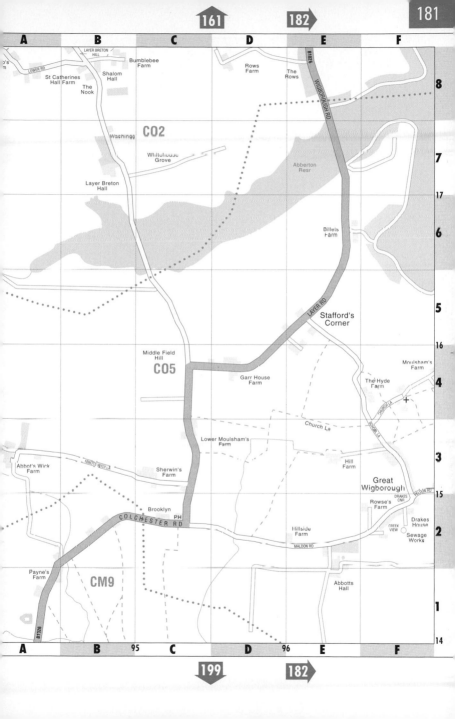

CO2

Abberton Resr

Haxells
Farm

Pete
Farm

Peldon
Lodge

Rolls
Farm

Malting
Farm

Peldon

Peldon
Hall

St Ives
Farm

BUTCHER'S
VIEW

PO

PH

Harvey's
Farm

Council
Hos

Peldon
Cres

Kemps
Farm

CO5

Moulsham's
Farm

Seaborough

Little
Wigborough

Copthall
Grove

Newpots

Samps
Farm

Kestons
Farm

Grove
Farm

New
Hall

Chestnuts
Farm

Coopers
Farm

The Old
Rectory

Copt
Hall

Lower
Barn

P

Decoy
Pond

Sampse
Cree

Nature
Trail

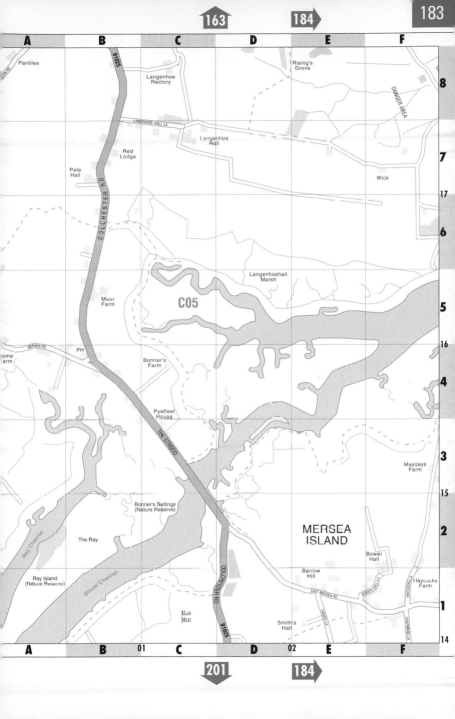

A   B   C   D   E   F

Pantiles

Langenhoe
Rectory

8

DANGER AREA

LANGENHOE HALL LA

Langenhoe
Hall

Red
Lodge

7

Pete
Hall

Wick

17

COLCHESTER RD

6

Langenhoehall
Marsh

Moor
Farm

C05

5

MERSEA RD

PH

16

Bonner's
Farm

ome
arm

4

THE STROOD

Pyefleet
House

Mausays
Farm

3

15

Bonner's Saltings
(Nature Reserve)

MERSEA
ISLAND

2

Ray Channel

The Ray

Bower
Hall

Barrow
Hill

BOWER HALL LA

Haycocks
Farm

Ray Island
(Nature Reserve)

Stroud Channel

COLCHESTER RD

EAST MERSEA RD

SHARPE LA

CHAMPAR LA

1

Red
Hill

Smith's
Hall

B1025

14

A   B   01   C   D   02   E   F

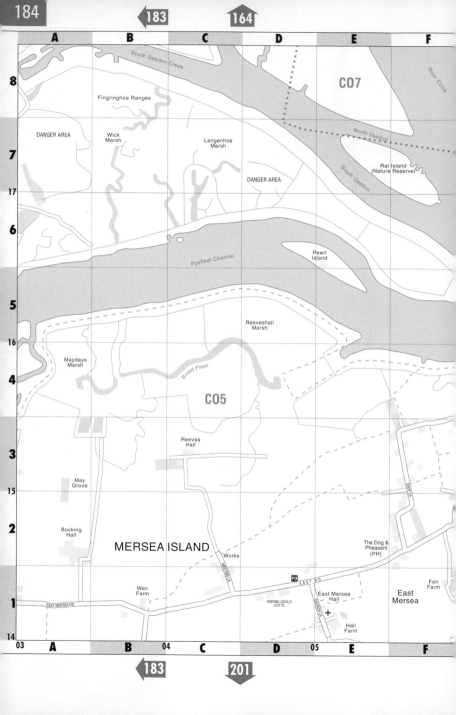

183
164

A B C D E F

8

South Geedon Creek

CO7

River Colne

Fingringhoe Ranges

DANGER AREA

Wick Marsh

Langenhoe Marsh

7

North Geedon

17

DANGER AREA

South Geedon

Rat Island (Nature Reserve)

6

Pyefleet Channel

Pewit Island

5

Reeveshall Marsh

16

Maydays Marsh

Broad Fleet

4

CO5

Reeves Hall

3

May Grove

15

Bocking Hall

2

MERSEA ISLAND

The Dog & Pheasant (PH)

Works

PO

EAST RD

Fen Farm

East Mersea

1

EAST MERSEA RD

Weir Farm

BARING-GOULD COTTS

East Mersea Hall

Hall Farm

14

**BRIGHTLINGSFA**

CO7

CO5

CO16

Point Clear
Bay

Wapping
La

Sewage
Works

Queech

Lodge
Farm

Wick's
Wood

The Great Divide

Furze
Hill

Boating
Lake
OYSTER TANK

Bateman's Tower

Westmarsh
Point

St Osyth Stone
Point

Cindery
Island

Mersea
Stone

River Colne

Ivy
House

North
Barn

Mersea Point
Nature Reserve

East Essex
Aviation Mus

Martello Tower

Brightlingsea Creek

Brightlingsea Reach

ads Green
Farm

Broman's
Farm

Visitor
Ctr

Cudmore Grove
Country Park

Stranger's
Corner

Sports
Ctr

Sch

MORSES
LA

Schs

Schs

SHIPYARD
EST

St JAMES CT 1
WELLINGTON ST 2
OSBOURNES CT 3
JOHN KING CT 4
JACOBS CT 5
FLORENCE COTTS 6

CHURCH

STATION RD

NEW ST

LADYSMITH AVE

PROMENADE WAY

WESTERN PROM

Lib

PO

Mus

07    08

A    B    C    D    E    F

8
17
7
6
5
16
4
15
3
2
1
14

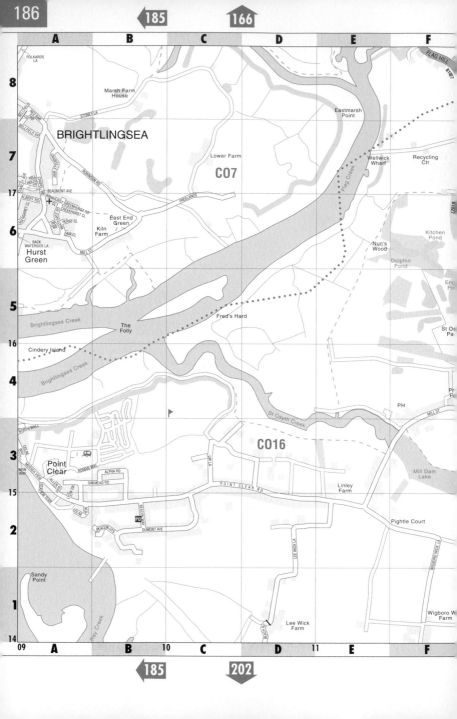

185
166

FLAG HILL

FOLKARDS LA

Marsh Farm House

STONEY LA

BRIGHTLINGSEA

Lower Farm

CO7

Eastmarsh Point

Wellwick Wharf

Recycling Ctr

ROBINSON RD

GREENHILL WAY

Beaumont Ave

GREENHURST RD

GREENHURST CL

FREELANDS

Flag Creek

B1027

East End Green

Kiln Farm

Hurst Green

HURST CL

FAIR CL

MILL ST

Kitchen Pond

Nun's Wood

Dolphin Pond

End Po

BACK WATERSIDE LA

Brightlingsea Creek

The Folly

Fred's Hard

St Os Pa

Cindery Island

Brightlingsea Creek

St Osyth Creek

PH

MILL ST

Pr Fe

NORTH WALL

Point Clear

ROMAN WAY

ALPHA RD

OAKMEAD RD

POINT CLEAR RD

CO16

Linley Farm

Milt Dam Lake

Pr

NEW WAY

BEACON HTE

DUMONT AVE

LEE WICK LA

Pightle Court

WIGBORO WICK LA

Sandy Point

Ray Creek

BLACKS RD

Lee Wick Farm

Wigboro W Farm

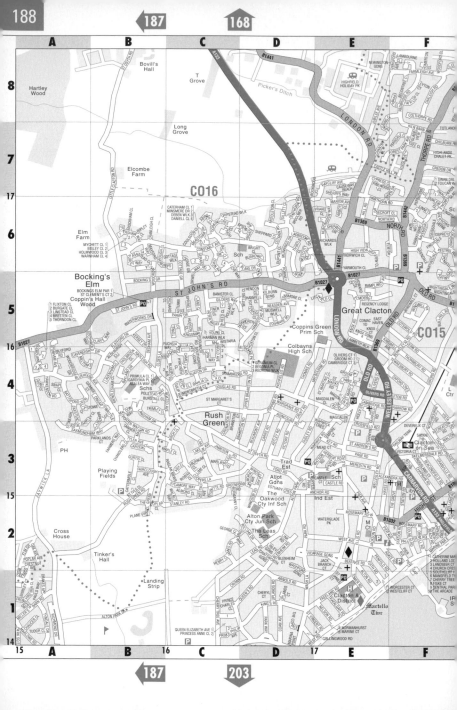

CO13

8

Sladbury's Old House

Sladburies

Treasure Holt Farm

Pond House

7

Burrsville Park
Cemy

17

Smythie's Farm

Pickers Ditch

CO15

6

AKERS WAY

FLEETWOOD AVE

BARKERS WAY
FLEETWOOD AVE

BRIARWOOD AVE

AYLESBURY DR

FRINTON RD

Liby

Sch

1 CUMBERLAND CT
2 SILVERDALE CT
3 MERRYMOUNT GDNS
4 ST BRELADES CT

Mast

SHRUBLAND

VALLEY RD
B1027

Bonham St

Ramsden
Clayhall Rd

Clarendon Pk

Holland Park Prim Sch

ST PETERS CT

Holland Pk

Collindale Gdns

Barrington Gdns
Deanhill Ave

Seafields Gdns

THE CHASE

CANTERBURY RD

HEREFORD CT

CLIFF RD

MEDINA CT

1 HOVE CT
2 BOSCOMBE CT
3 THE LODGE
4 SUNDALE CL
5 SOUTHVIEW DR

Holland-on-Sea

5

16

Playing Field

Sports Gd

Clacton ty High Sch

Windsor Sch

CLACTON-ON-SEA

1 AVONDALE HO
2 HOLLAND HO
3 COTSWOLD CT

1 CONNAUGHT CT
2 CONNAUGHT CL
3 HEYBRIDGE CT
4 WESTMINSTER CT
5 KNIGHTSBRIDGE CT

4 AMBLESIDE CT
5 WINDERMERE CT
6 HADLEIGH CT

Colchester Inst

7 SURREY CT
8 HAROLD RD
9 HARROLD CT
10 ROSEBANK CT

170

4

G                H

CO13

8

Holland Haven Country Park

Nature Reserve

CO15

B1032

CLACTON RD

7

Holland Bridge

Holland Haven

17

Mast

6

HAVEN AVE

THE ESPLANADE

21    G              H    22

3

15

2

1

A       B    19    C       D    20    E       F

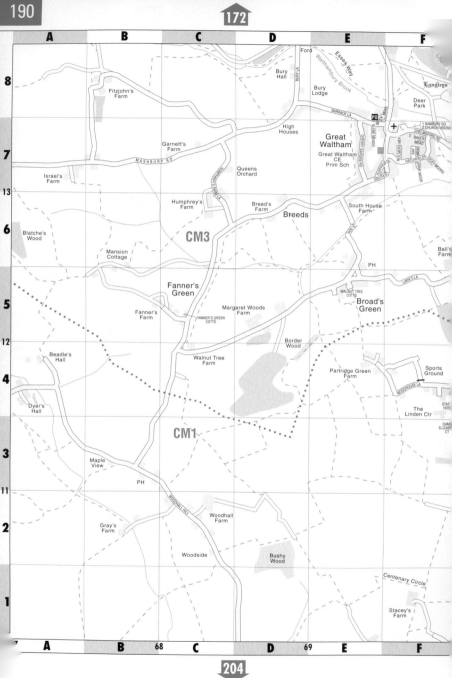

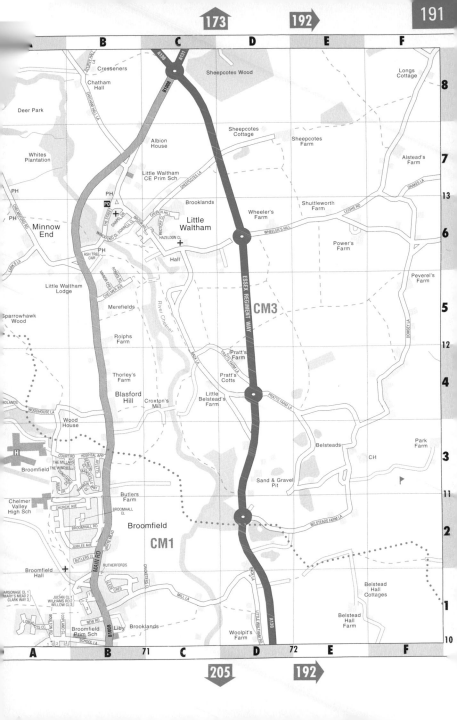

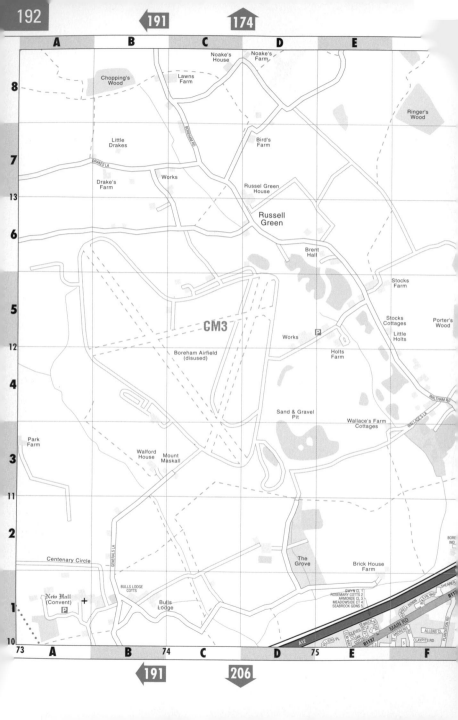

191
174
191
206

Noake's House
Noake's Farm
Chopping's Wood
Lawns Farm
Ringer's Wood
Little Drakes
Bird's Farm
DRAKE'S LA
Works
Russel Green House
Drake's Farm
Russell Green
Brent Hall
Stocks Farm
CM3
Stocks Cottages
Porter's Wood
Works
P
Little Holts
Boreham Airfield (disused)
Holts Farm
WALTHAM RD
Sand & Gravel Pit
Wallace's Farm Cottages
WALLACE'S LA
Park Farm
Walford House
Mount Maskall
BORE IND
Centenary Circle
The Grove
Brick House Farm
SHEARER

GWYN CL 1
ROSEMARY COTTS 2
ARMONDE CL 3
MEADOWSIDE CT 4
SEABROOK GDNS 5

New Hall (Convent)
P
BULLS LODGE COTTS
Bulls Lodge
B11ST
ALLENS CL
CLAYPITS RD
MAIN RD
A12

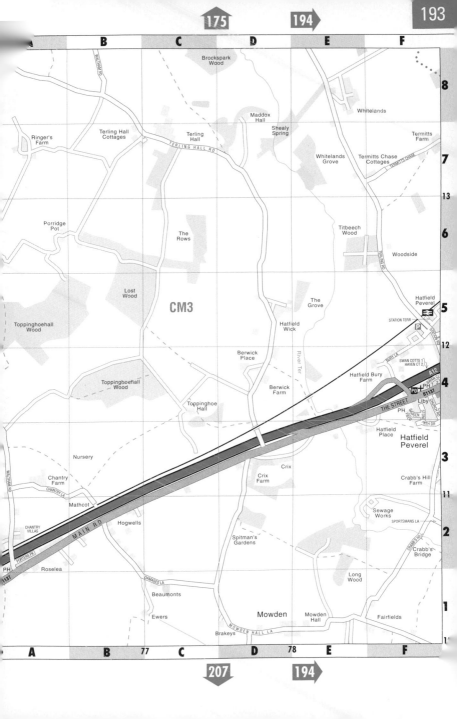

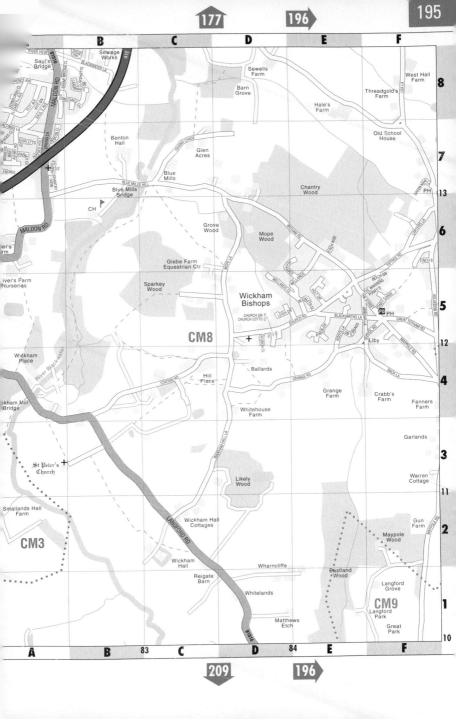

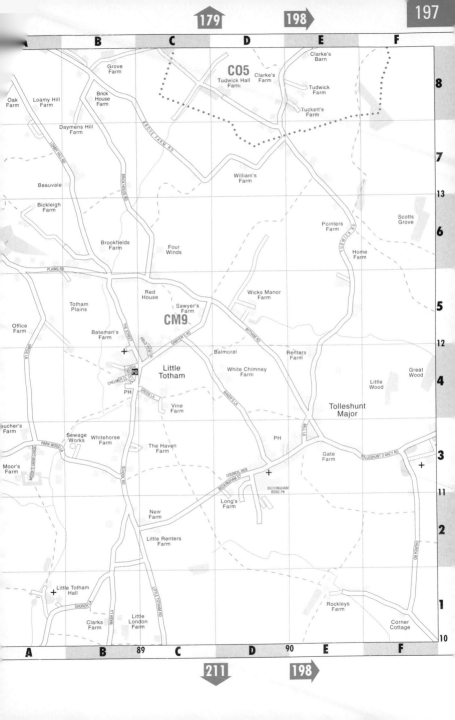

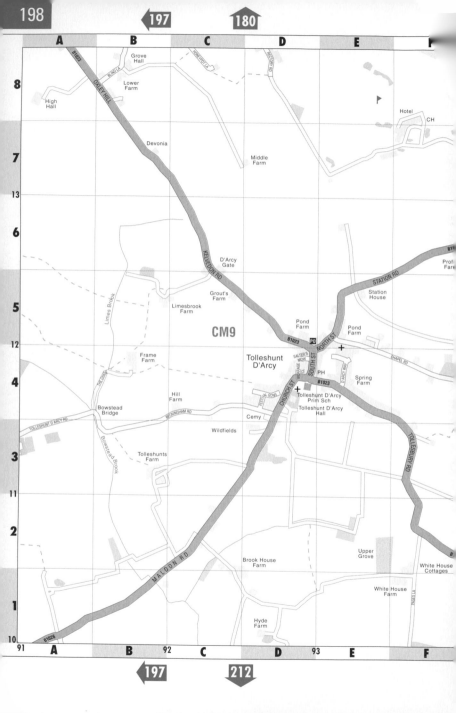

197
180

**A** **B** **C** **D** **E** **F**

8

B1023
OAKLEY HILL
BLUNTS LA
HONEYPOT LA
RECTORY RD

Grove
Hall

Lower
Farm

High
Hall

Hotel
CH

7

Devonia

Middle
Farm

13

6

KELVEDON RD

STATION RD
B10

Prof
Fare

D'Arcy
Gate

Station
House

5

Limes Brook

Limesbrook
Farm

Grout's
Farm

Pond
Farm

Pond
Farm

**CM9**

B1023
PO
NORTH ST
CHAPEL RD

12

Frame
Farm

Tolleshunt
D'Arcy

SALTER'S
MDW
THE CHASE CL
SOUTH ST
PH

Spring
Farm

4

THE CHASE

Hill
Farm

BECKINGHAM RD

CHURCH ST
D'ARCY WAY
B1023

Tolleshunt D'Arcy
Prim Sch

Tolleshunt D'Arcy
Hall

Bowstead
Bridge

TOLLESHUNT D'ARCY RD

Cemy

TOLLESBURY RD

3

Bowstead Brook

Tolleshunts
Farm

Wildfields

11

2

MALDON RD

Brook House
Farm

Upper
Grove

White House
Cottages

B

1

White House
Farm

PERRY LA

Hyde
Farm

10

B1026

**A** 92 **B** **C** 93 **D** **E** **F**

91

CO5

8

7

13

6

Salcott Creek

Virley
Hall

MILL LA

Horn
Farm

RISE LA

SALCOTT ST

Marsh
Farm

Salcott-cum-Virley

Green
Farm

THE STREET

SHARLANDS
ROW

B1026
RD

COLCHESTER RD

WHITEHOUSE HILL

STATION RD

urways
Farm

Bridge
Farm

tal
rm

CM9

Old Hall
Marsh Farm

Old Hall
Farm

5

12

COLCHESTER RD

Bourchier's
Farm

CHAPEL RD

Bourchier's
Hall

The
Rookery

BACK RD

OLD HALL LA

Old Hall Creek

4

Red
Hill

The
rove

snes
ourt

Gorwell
Hall

3

11

Carrington
Farm

Tollesbury

MALLARD

GANNET CL

CHAMBERS CL

SHELDRAKE CL

THURSTABLE CL

REDSHANK CL

SEAVIEW CL

KENTS GRASS

HUSTABLE WAY

2

P

Works

WOODROLFE RD

MOSSLEIGH

Garland's
Farm

NORTH RD

THE SLIPPERS

NEW RD

THE CHASE

SCOTTS CL

WEST ST

HIGH ST
PH

B1023  EAST ST

ORCHARD CL

KINGS CL

Marina

Woodrolfe
Farm

TOLLESBURY RD

Garlands
Farm

Cemy

ST JOHN'S
CT

ELYSIAN GDNS

MEAD CT

KINGS RD

MALL RD

THE MOUNT

MILL RD

VINEYARD LA

WHARF RD

Tollesbury
Cty Prim Sch

WOODROLFE FARM LA

Prentice Hall
Farm

PRENTICE HALL LA

Bohun's
Hall

WYCKE
LA

1

10

A  B  95  C  D  96  E  F

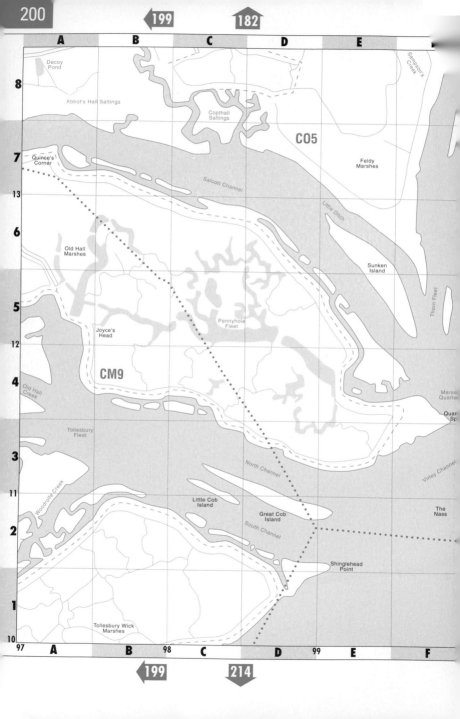

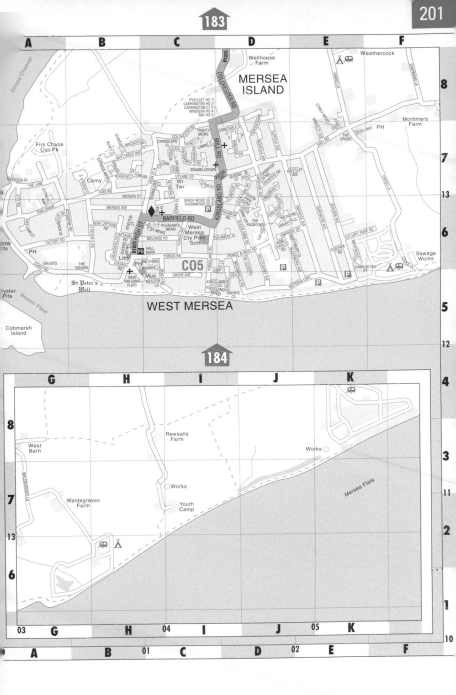

MERSEA ISLAND

Weathercock

Wellhouse Farm

Mortimers Farm

Firs Chase Cvn Pk

Strod Channel

The Cross

THE CROSS

BRAMBLEDOWN

Cemy

Wr Twr

West Mersea Cty Prim Sch

BARFIELD RD

Sewage Works

CO5

St Peter's Well

WEST MERSEA

Besom Fleet

Oyster Pits

Cobmarsh Island

Rewsalls Farm

Works

West Barn

Waldegraves Farm

Youth Camp

Works

Mersea Flats

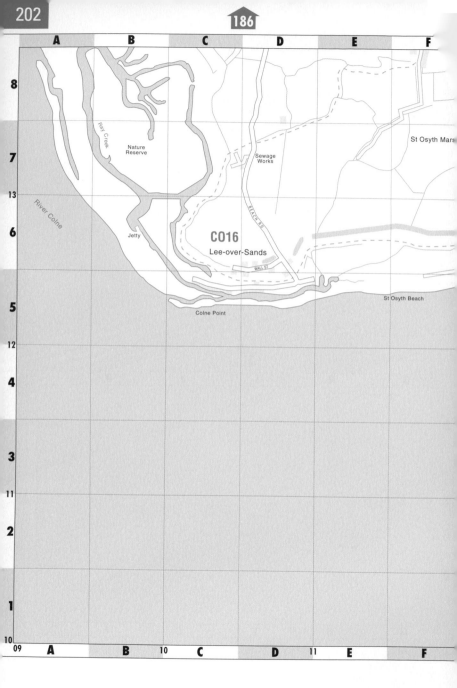

186

St Osyth Mars

River Colne

Ray Creek

Nature
Reserve

Sewage
Works

BEACH RD

Jetty

**CO16**
Lee-over-Sands

WALL ST

St Osyth Beach

Colne Point

09    10    11

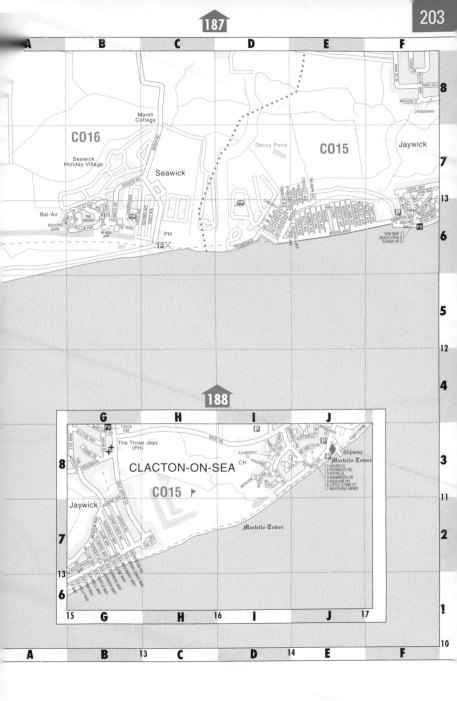

CO16

Marsh Cottage

Seawick
Holiday Village

Seawick

CO15

Jaywick

Decoy Pond

Bel-Air

BISHOPS
GDNS

THE GREEN

CLUB PAR

BEACH
APP

PH

PROMENADE

BROOKLANDS

YEW WAY 1
BEACH CRES 2
ELVINA HO 3

GORSE WAY
FERN WAY

BROADWAY

CROSSWAYS

ARAGON CL

PARK SQ E

The Three Jays
(PH)

TUDOR PAR

WEST RD

CLACTON-ON-SEA

CO15 ▶

Jaywick

LULWORTH
CL

PENZANCE

CH

BRIXHAM

Martello Tower

Slipway

𝕸artello 𝕿ower

1 DOVER CL
2 PLYMOUTH RD
3 HYTHE CL
4 SHAMROCK HO
5 AQUILINE HO
6 LITTLE STONE CT
7 WORTHING MEWS

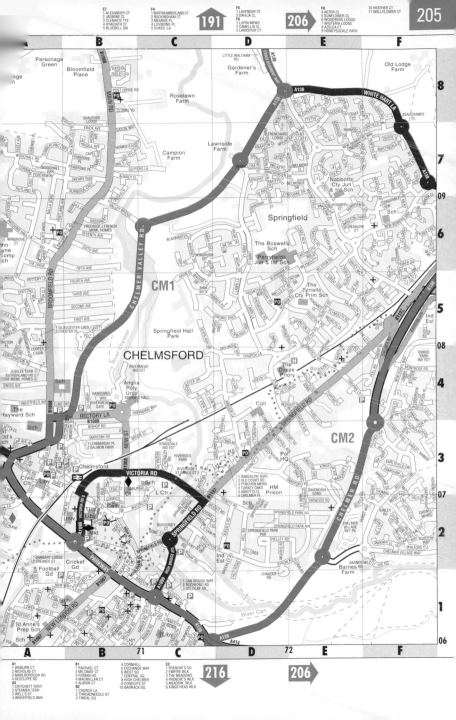

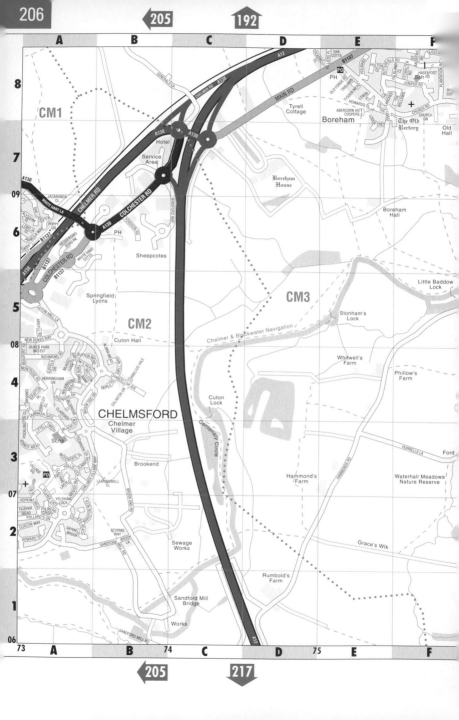

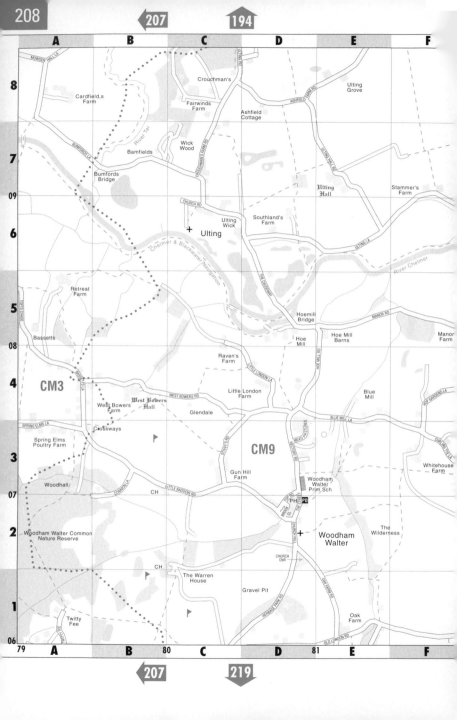

**A** **B** **C** **D** **E** **F**

MOWDEN HALL LA

8

Cardfield,s
Farm

Crouchman's

Fairwinds
Farm

Ashfield
Cottage

Ulting
Grove

ASHFIELD FARM RD

River Ter

BUMFORDS LA

7

Bamfields

Wick
Wood

ULTING HALL RD

Bumfords
Bridge

09

CHOUCHMAN'S FARM RD

CHURCH RD

Ulting
Hall

Stammer's
Farm

6

Ulting
Wick

+  Ulting

Southland's
Farm

ULTING LA

Chelmer & Blackwater Navigation

River Chelmer

Retreat
Farm

MANOR RD

5

Hoemill
Bridge

08

Bassetts

Hoe
Mill

Hoe Mill
Barns

Manor
Farm

THE CAUSEWAY

4

CM3

BASSETTS LA

WEST BOWERS RD

Raven's
Farm

LITTLE LONDON LA

Little London
Farm

Blue
Mill

HOE MILL RD

HOP GARDENS LA

West Bowers
Farm

West Bowers
Hall

Glendale

BLUE MILL LA

SPRING ELMS LA

Crossways

CM9

CURL HILL TYE LA

3

Spring Elms
Poultry Farm

MEAD PATH

BECHCROFT RD

Whitehouse
Farm

07

Woodhall

CORNER LA

CH

LITTLE BADDOW RD

Gun Hill
Farm

Woodham
Walter
Prim Sch

BRICK CL

PH  PO

2

Woodham Walter Common
Nature Reserve

+  Woodham
Walter

CHURCH HILL

The
Wilderness

CHURCH
CNR

CH

The Warren
House

Gravel Pit

HEYBRIDGE PARK RD

TOP RD

CURLING TYE LA

1

Twitty
Fee

CORR LA FARM RD

Oak
Farm

OLD LONDON RD

06

79    **A**    **B**    80    **C**    **D**    81    **E**    **F**

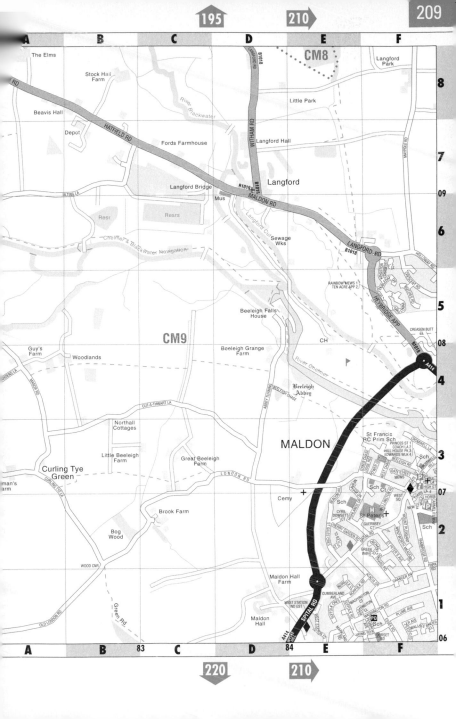

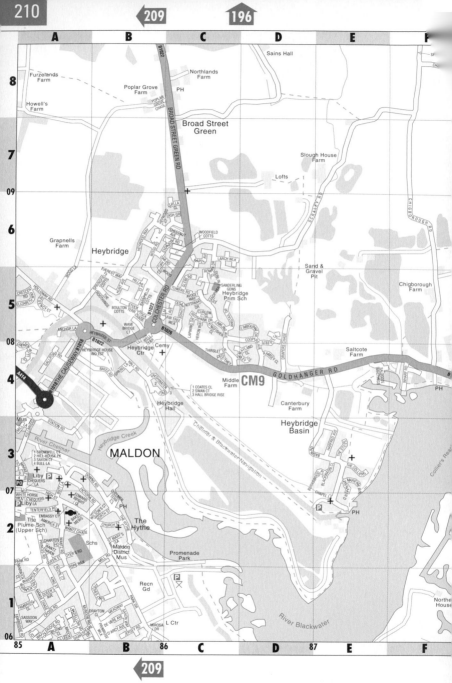

A    B    C    D    E    F

8

Furzelands
Farm

Howell's
Farm

Northlands
Farm

Sains Hall

SF

CH

Poplar Grove
Farm

PH

Broad Street
Green

POPLAR GROVE CHASE

7

09

BROAD STREET GREEN RD

B1022

Slough House
Farm

Lofts

LEZGALE'S RD

CHIGBOROUGH RD

6

Grapnells
Farm

Heybridge

Woodfield
Cotts

HONEYSUCKLE
GR

LARCH WLK

MAPLE

Sand &
Gravel
Pit

Chigborough
Farm

5

08

Elizabeth
CT

WOOD LA

POLLWAY RD

CHESER WAY

EVEREST WAY

BOULTON
COTTS

STEER
TERR

B1022

COLCHESTER RD

SANDERLING
GDNS

Heybridge
Prim Sch

AVOCET

CURLEW

KITTIWAKE

LIMBOURNE
DR

COOPER

STEE'S

DRAPERS CHASE

Saltcote
Farm

ANCHOR LA

WAVE
BRIDGE

B1026

Heybridge
House
Ind Est

Heybridge
Ctr

Cemy

FISH TREE
WLK

THISRLE

HERON WAY

THIRSLET DR

Middle
Farm

CM9

GOLDHANGER RD

PH

A414

100 THE CAUSEWAY B1018

GALLOWAY RD

BATTS RD

SPITAL LA

HALL RD

COLCHESTER RD

1 COATES CL
2 SWAN CT
3 HALL BRIDGE RISE

Canterbury
Farm

Heybridge
Basin

THE COLLIERY

4

Mus

STATION RD

River Chelmer

Heybridge
Hall

Chelmer & Blackwater Navigation

3

07

MALDON

Heybridge Creek

1 BROMWELL
2 HILL HOUSE PK
3 SAXON CT
4 BULL LA

PO

Liby

CHEQUERS LA

WHITE HORSE

CHEQUERS LA

P

Liby

TENTERFIELD RD

EDWARD
BRIGHT

PH

The
Hythe

P

CHAPEL

PH

2

The
Plume Sch
(Upper Sch)

EMBASSY CT

AMERICA ST

WANTZ CHASE

CHARTER

Schs

ST MARY'S RD

CHURCH ST

Maldon
District
Mus

Promenade
Park

PARK RD

STEER'S RD

ROPE WLK

MILL RD

1

SASSOON
WAY

DRAYTON
CL

MEADOW

MIROSA
DR

Recn
Gd

L Ctr

P

River Blackwater

Northe
House

06

85    A    B    86    C    D    87    E    F

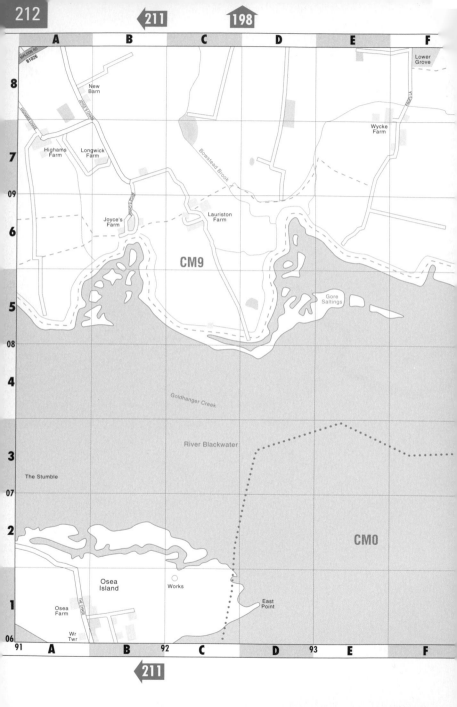

New Barn

MALDON RD
B1026

JOYCE'S CHASE

HIGHAMS CHASE

Highams Farm

Longwick Farm

Joyce's Farm

JOYCE'S CHASE

Lauriston Farm

Bowstead Brook

Wycke Farm

Lower Grove

JAMES LA

CM9

Gore Saltings

Goldhanger Creek

River Blackwater

CM0

The Stumble

Osea Island

Works

THE CHASE

Osea Farm

East Point

Wr Twr

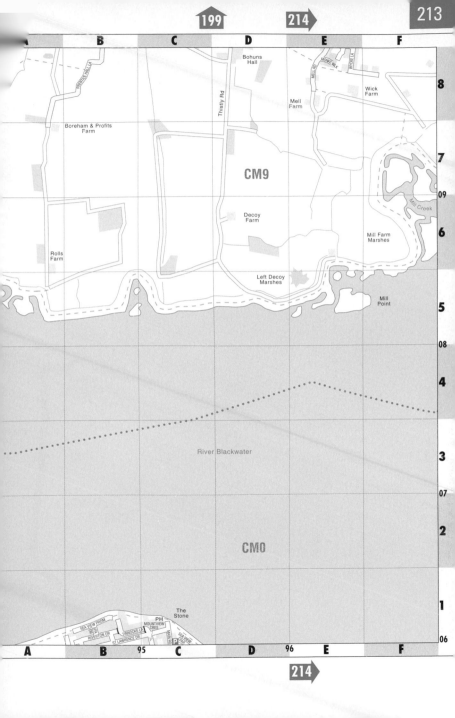

199
214

**A** **B** **C** **D** **E** **F**

Bohuns
Hall

Thistly Rd

Wick
Farm

**8**

Mell
Farm

Boreham & Profits
Farm

**CM9**

**7**

09

Decoy
Farm

Mill Creek

Mill Farm
Marshes

**6**

Rolls
Farm

Left Decoy
Marshes

Mill
Point

**5**

08

**4**

River Blackwater

**3**

07

**CM0**

**2**

**1**

The
Stone

PH
SEA VIEW PROM
MOUNTVIEW
CRES
RIVERTON DR
TINNOCKS LA
ST LAWRENCE DR
SEA VIEW

06

**A** **B** 95 **C** **D** 96 **E** **F**

8

CM9

7

09

6

Jetty

5

09

Pewet
Island

08

P0

PARKER
CT

Bradwe
Watersi

4

B1021

OLD
COASTGUARD
COTTS

PH

River Blackwater

Bradwell Creek

TRUSSES RD

3

Westwick
Farm

WATERSIDE RD

WOODYARDS

07

Down
Westwick

2

CM0

ORPLANDS
COTTS

Orplands

1

Kennel
Barn

MALDON RD

MALDON RD

06

B1021

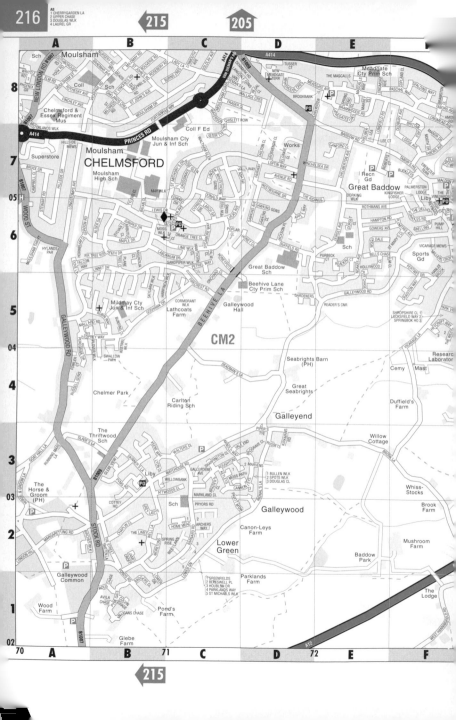

217
207

Gravel Pit

Lingwood Common

St Clere's Hall

WOODSIDE

Elm Green

Bellhill Wood

Danbury

MAIN RD

St John's Danbury CE Prim Sch

The Main Lodge

BELL HILL

Danbury Park Cty Prim Sch

MAIN RD

Liby

CM2

A414

Ind Est

Danbury

Ind Est

Danbury Country Park

Heathcote Sch

MALDON RD

Danbury Palace

PH

Danbury

CM3

Woodhill House

PH

Horne Row

Danbury Common

Danecourt

Woodhill

Paternoster Farm

Ludgores Farm

Gay Bowers Farm

Chamberlains Farm

Backwarden Nature Reserve

Poplar Farm

Springate Farm

Sporhams Farm

Thorn Farm

Overshot Bridge

Peartree Farm

Thorn Wood

Little Gibcracks

Overshot Farm

SUNNYWAY COTTS

PEARTREE LA

Butt's Green Farm

The Priory Cty Prim Sch

CM2

GREAT GIBCRACKS CHASE

St Giles

Bicknacre

PH

Mill Hill House

Mead's Grove

Priory Farm

PO

Great Gibcracks

Broadoaks Farm

South Gibcracks

MAIN RD

PH

BICKNACRE RD

Great Claydons Farm

Salesfrith Farm

Mill Farm

PH

B4118

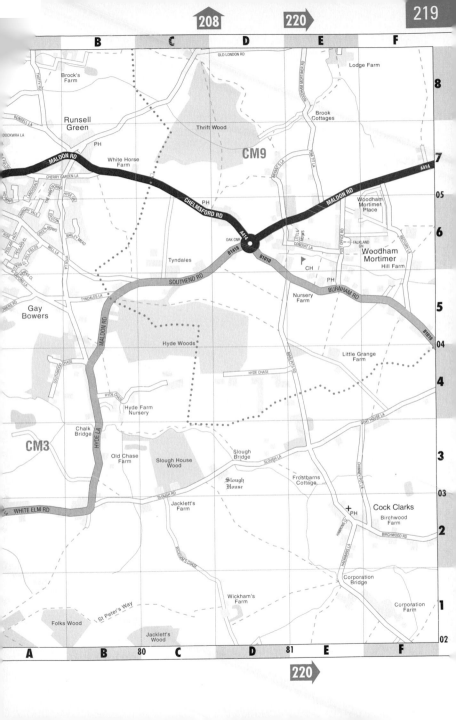

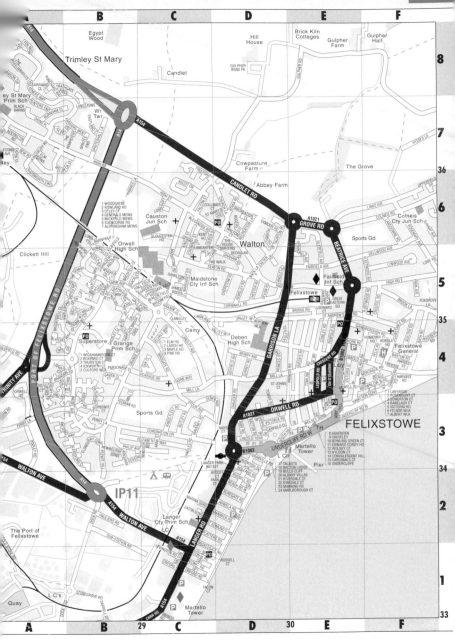

Street names are listed alphabetically and show the locality, the Postcode District, the page number and a reference to the square in which the name falls on the map page

**Gatekeeper Cl** 🎱 Braintree CM7..............**127** F1

---

**Full street name**
This may have been abbreviated on the map

**Location number**
If present, this indicates the street's position in a congested area of the map instead of the name

**Town, village or locality** in which the street falls.

**Postcode District**
for the street name

**Page number** of the map on which the street name appears

**Grid square** in which the centre of the street falls

---

## Abbreviations used in the index

| | | | | | | | |
|---|---|---|---|---|---|---|---|
| App | Approach | Cl | Close | Espl | Esplanade | Mans | Mansions | Rdbt | Roundabout |

App **Approach**
Arc **Arcade**
Ave **Avenue**
Bvd **Boulevard**
Bldgs **Buildings**
Bsns Pk **Business Park**
Bsns Ctr **Business Centre**
Bglws **Bungalows**
Cswy **Causeway**
Ctr **Centre**
Circ **Circle**
Cir **Circus**

Cl **Close**
Comm **Common**
Cnr **Corner**
Cotts **Cottages**
Ct **Court**
Ctyd **Courtyard**
Cres **Crescent**
Dr **Drive**
Dro **Drove**
E **East**
Emb **Embankment**
Ent **Enterprise**

Espl **Esplanade**
Est **Estate**
Gdns **Gardens**
Gn **Green**
Gr **Grove**
Hts **Heights**
Ho **House**
Ind Est **Industrial Estate**
Intc **Interchange**
Junc **Junction**
La **Lane**

Mans **Mansions**
Mdw **Meadows**
N **North**
Orch **Orchard**
Par **Parade**
Pk **Park**
Pas **Passage**
Pl **Place**
Prec **Precinct**
Prom **Promenade**
Ret Pk **Retail Park**
Rd **Road**

Rdbt **Roundabout**
S **South**
Sq **Square**
Strs **Stairs**
St **Street, Saint**
Stps **Steps**
Terr **Terrace**
Tk **Track**
Trad **Trading Est**
Wlk **Walk**
W **West**
Yd **Yard**

## Town and village index

Abberton ..............162 B3
Aldham ...............133 B8
Alphamstone .........54 F3
Alresford ............165 B8
Ardleigh .............111 E7
Arkesden ..............41 E2
Ashdon .................6 B1
Ashen ................11 D1
Bardfield Saling ......99 C2
Barnston .............151 A4
Bartlow ................6 B7
Beaumont ............141 F7
Beazley End .........101 C6
Belchamp St Paul .....13 A2
Belchamp Walter ......31 F5
Belstead ..............36 C7
Bentley ...............60 E7
Berden ................92 C8
Bicknacre ............218 F2
Birch ................161 A3
Birchanger ...........119 D2
Birdbrook .............28 B7
Bishop's Stortford ...145 E6
Black Notley .........155 B5
Blackheath ...........163 A8
Boreham ..............206 E8
Borley ................14 F3
Boxted ................82 F7
Bradfield .............87 F2
Bradwell .............129 D2
Bradwell Waterside ..214 F4
Braintree ............128 B5
Brantham ..............60 E1
Brightlingsea ........185 F6
Broomfield ...........191 B2
Bulmer ................32 F5
Bures .................79 E8
Canfield End .........149 B2
Capel St Mary .........35 B2
Castle Camps ...........7 E3
Castle Hedingham .....51 E4
Cavendish ..............1 C1
Chappel ..............106 C5
Chelmondiston ........63 E8
Chelmsford ...........205 B2
Chrishall .............19 D3
Clacton-on-Sea .......189 B5
Clare .................12 C6
Clavering .............65 C5
Coggeshall ...........131 A3

Colchester ...........135 F7
Colne Engaine .........77 F2
Copford ..............133 D4
Cressing .............156 A6
Danbury ..............218 F7
Debden ................68 B7
Dedham ................84 F7
Duddenhoe End .........41 A6
Earls Colne ..........105 B6
East Bergholt .........59 C2
East Mersea ..........184 E1
Easthorpe ............160 A7
Eight Ash Green ......134 A8
Elder Street ..........44 E1
Elmdon ................20 B4
Elmstead .............138 A6
Elsenham ..............94 C1
Farnham ..............118 D6
Feering ..............158 E5
Felixstowe ...........221 E4
Felsted ..............152 B5
Finchingfield .........72 C5
Fingringhoe .........163 F5
Ford End .............172 B6
Fordham ..............107 D5
Fordham Heath .......107 F1
Foxearth ..............14 C6
Frating ..............139 A3
Frinton-on-Sea .......170 F6
Galleywood ...........216 C3
Gestingthorpe ........31 E1
Glemsford ..............2 C4
Goldhanger ..........211 E7
Gosfield .............102 E8
Great Baddow ........216 F6
Great Bardfield .......72 C1
Great Bentley .......166 E8
Great Braxted .......178 C1
Great Bromley .......112 E1
Great Chesterford ......3 D2
Great Cornard ........34 B5
Great Dunmow ........150 D8
Great Easton .........122 F7
Great Hallingbury ...146 E4
Great Henny ..........54 C8
Great Holland .......170 A3
Great Horkesley ......82 B1
Great Leighs ........173 F7
Great Maplestead .....52 D2
Great Notley .........154 C6

Great Oakley ........116 C4
Great Sampford .......47 B3
Great Tey ...........132 C8
Great Totham ........196 B4
Great Waltham .......190 F7
Great Wigborough ...181 F2
Great Yeldham ........30 A1
Greenstead Green ....104 A5
Hadstock ...............5 C6
Halstead ..............76 D2
Harkstead ............63 B2
Harwich ...............91 E5
Hatfield Peverel ....194 A4
Haverhill ..............9 C7
Hazeleigh ............220 A4
Helions Bumpstead ...26 C8
Hempstead ............25 F1
Henham ................94 F6
Heybridge ...........210 C5
Heybridge Basin .....210 E3
Highwoods ...........110 B4
Hinxton ...............3 B7
Holbrook ..............62 C5
Holland-on-Sea ......189 B6
Howe Green ..........217 D3
Howe Street .........172 F2
Ickleton ...............3 A4
Ipswich ...............17 C7
Jaywick ..............188 A1
Kelvedon .............158 C2
Kirby Cross .........170 B6
Kirby-le-Soken ......170 C6
Lamarsh ...............55 B4
Langham ..............83 F4
Langley ...............40 C2
Lawford ...............86 B3
Layer-de-la-Haye ....161 F5
Lindsell ..............98 A3
Little Baddow .......207 E3
Little Bentley ......139 F8
Little Bromley .......113 B6
Little Clacton ......168 C3
Little Dunmow .......151 D7
Little Easton .......122 F5
Little Horkesley .....81 E4
Little Leighs .......173 E6
Little Maplestead ....53 B1
Little Oakley .......117 B7
Little Totham .......197 B4
Little Waltham ......191 B6

Little Yeldham ........30 E4
Littlebury ............21 E4
Long Melford .........15 D7
Maldon ..............210 A3
Manningtree ..........86 E4
Manuden ..............92 F2
Margaretting ........215 D1
Marks Tey ...........132 E3
Messing .............159 D2
Mistley ..............86 F8
Nayland ...............56 B1
New Mistley ..........87 B4
Newport ...............43 A1
North End ...........151 F2
Nuthampstead ........39 A2
Panfield ............127 A7
Pattiswick ..........129 F5
Peldon ..............182 E6
Pentlow ..............13 F6
Point Clear Bay .....186 A3
Purleigh ............220 D1
Quendon ..............66 F2
Radwinter ............45 F8
Rayne ...............126 F2
Rickling Green .......93 D8
Ridgewell ............29 B7
Rivenhall ...........177 B7
Rowhedge ............163 F8
Rushmere St Andrew ..18 E8
Saffron Walden .......22 D2
Salcott-cum-virley ..199 B8
Sandon ..............217 C6
Sewards End ..........23 E1
Shalford ............100 D3
Shotley Gate .........91 A8
Shudy Camps ...........7 B6
Sible Hedingham .....51 E1
Silver End ..........156 D4
Sproughton ...........16 B6
St Lawrence .........213 B1
St Osyth ............187 A4
Stambourne ...........28 D3
Stanstead .............2 F7
Stansted Mountfitchet 119 C8
Stebbing ............124 E5
Steeple Bumpstead ...27 B8
Stisted .............129 C6
Stoke by Clare .......11 C4
Stoke by Nayland .....56 E5

Stratford St Mary ....58 C2
Sturmer ...............9 F4
Stutton ...............61 F2
Sudbury ..............33 D8
Takeley .............148 C7
Tattingstone .........61 C7
Tendring ............140 F5
Terling .............175 C3
Thaxted ..............70 A3
Thorington Street ....57 C4
Thorpe-le-Soken .....142 A1
Thorrington .........166 A5
Tiptree .............179 D5
Tollesbury ..........199 D2
Tolleshunt D'arcy ...198 D4
Tolleshunt Knights ..180 A2
Tolleshunt Major ....197 E3
Toppesfield ..........50 C7
Trimley St Mary .....221 A7
Ugley ................93 E6
Ulting ..............206 D6
Wakes Colne .........106 B6
Walton-on-the-Naze ..171 C8
Washbrook ............35 B3
Weeley ..............140 F1
Weeley Heath ........168 A6
Wendens Ambo .........42 E5
West Bergholt .......108 E4
West Mersea .........201 C6
Wethersfield .........73 C3
Wherstead ............37 B6
White Colne .........105 E6
White Notley ........155 F1
Wickham Bishops ....195 E5
Wickham St Paul ......53 C5
Widdington ...........67 E4
Wimbish ..............45 C6
Witham ..............176 F2
Wivenhoe ............137 C1
Wix .................115 C5
Woodham Mortimer ...219 E6
Woodham Walter .....208 D2
Woolverstone .........38 B1
Wormingford .........80 E4
Wrabness ............88 E4
Writtle .............204 B1

...163 D3
...162 C5
esr Nature
.02 ...........161 F2
Wildfowl Ctr
...........161 E1
Cl CM1 ......204 E2
Cres CO16 ....142 A1
y Gate St CM2 ...135 F6
ey La Coggeshall CO6 .131 A1
ifton Walden CB10 ....92 D2
obey Rd CO10 .......51 D2
obey Rd CO10 .......15 E1
obey St Ickleton CB10 ...3 A4
Thorpe-le-S CO16 ....142 A1
bbey Turning CM9 ....209 D4
bbey View CM6 .....96 E2
bbot's Rd CO12 ....136 B3
bbots Cl
Clacton-on-S CO15 ...188 E6
Manningtree CO11 ....115 C5
bbots Gdns CO16 ...187 C4
bbots La CO4 ......134 A7
bbots Wick La CO5 ...181 B3
bbotsbury Cl IP2 ....17 A1
bbott Rd CO12 .....90 F2
bbotts Cl CM7 ......203 A6
bbotts Ct CB9 .......9 E5
bbey Ave CM23 ....145 E3
bdy Ave CO12 ......90 E2
bell Way CM2 .....206 B4
bels Rd CO9 .......103 D8
bercorn St CB9 .....8 F7
bercorn Ho CM3 ...206 E8
bercorn Way CM8 ...177 A2
bingdon Cl IP2 ....17 A1
binger Cl CO16 ....188 C6
bington IP2 .......9 A8
braham Dr CM6 ...156 E4
bram's La SG8 ....19 C4
cacia Ave CO6 ....136 E8
cacia Cl IP3 ......18 E1
cacia Ct CO11 .....60 D1
cacia Dr CM9 .....209 F1
cacia Gdns CO8 ....77 A5
ccommodation Rd CO4 .109 D7
cer Gr IP8 ........16 C1
chilles Way CM7 ...128 B5
chnacone Dr CO4 ..109 C3
cland Ave CO3 ....135 B7
cland Ct CO3 .....135 A7
corn Ave Braintree CM7 .127 E2
  Halstead CO9 .....76 D1
corn Ct Colchester CO4 .110 D4
  Harwich CO12 .....90 F1
  Ipswich IP2 ......16 C2
corn Wlk CO7 .....166 A5
corns The CM24 ...119 E7
cors End CM1 .....204 E4
cton Cl CO10 .....33 F8
cton Gn CO10 .....33 E7
cton La CO10 .....33 F8
cton Sq 4 CO10 ..33 E7
cland Rd CO8 .....a8
dams Cl IP2 ......17 C3
dams Ct Halstead CO9 ..76 D2
  Saffron Walden CB11 ..43 C8
dderley Rd CM23 ..145 F7
ddington Rd IP11 ..221 A7
ddison Rd CO13 ..170 B5
delaide Dr CO2 ...136 A1
delaide Rd IP4 ....18 D6
delaide St CO12 ...90 F5
dmiral Rd IP8 ....36 E8
dmirals Wlk CM1 ...204 F3
dethric Rd CM7 ...127 E3
fleck Rd CO4 .....136 E7
gar Rd 9 CO14 ..171 C8
gar Road App 10 CO14 .171 C8
gate Rd CO15 ....188 F2
gincourt Rd CO4 ..188 D4
Agricultural/Domestic
  Mus CM9 ......211 E7
inger Rd CO12 ....90 E2
ingers Green Rd CO7 .167 A5
inslie Rd IP1 .....17 A6
ire Wlk CM4 .....176 E2
isne Rd CO2 .....135 D4
jax Cl CM7 ......128 B5
Alamein Rd
  Chelmsford CM1 ...204 F6
  Colchester CO2 ...135 C2
Alan Dr CO16 .....168 D1
Alan Hasler Ho CM6 .150 D7
Alan Rd Ipswich IP3 ..17 F4
  Witham CM8 .....163 A4
Alan Way CO3 ....134 F4
Alanbrooke Rd CO2 .136 D2
Albany Chase CO15 .189 B4
Albany Cl Chelmsford CM1 .204 E5
  West Bergholt CO6 .108 E4
Albany Gdns 6 CO15 .189 B3
Albany Gdns W CO15 .189 B3
Albany Rd CO6 ....108 E4
Albany The IP4 ...17 E8
Albany Villas IP11 .221 D3
Albemarle Gdns CM7 .128 C5
Albemarle St CO12 ..91 D5
Albert Gdns
  Clacton-on-S CO15 .189 B3
  Coggeshall CO6 ...131 A2
Albert Pl IP4 .....17 B4
Albert Pl CO6 ....131 A2
Albert Rd Braintree CM7 .128 A3

Albert Rd continued
  Brightlingsea CO7 ...186 A6
  Witham CM8 ......177 A3
Albert St Colchester CO1 .135 E8
  Harwich CO12 ....91 D5
Albert Wlk IP11 ....221 E4
Albertine Cl CO3 ..134 C6
Albion Cl 5 CM2 ..205 B1
Albion Gr CO2 ....136 A1
Albion Hill IP4 ....17 F7
Albion St CO5 ....164 A8
Albra Mead CM3 ..206 B4
Albrighton Croft CO4 .110 C4
Alconbury CM23 ...119 B1
Alde Rd CO9 ......9 A8
Aldeburgh Cl
  Clacton-on-S CO16 .188 B4
  Haverhill CB9 .....8 E7
Aldeburgh Gdns CO4 .110 B3
Aldeburgh Way CM1 .205 D5
Alder Cl CM23 ....145 D4
Alder Dr CM7 .....216 B6
Alder Wlk CM8 ....177 A4
Alderbury Lea CM3 .218 F1
Alderbury Rd CM24 .119 E8
Aldercar Rd CO6 ..133 F1
Alderford St CO9 ..75 E8
Alderlee IP2 ......36 F8
Alderman Blaxhill Sch
  CO2 ...........135 B3
Alderman Howe Lodge
  CO4 ...........110 B4
Alderman Rd IP1 ..17 B5
Alderton Cl CM6 ..152 C6
Alderton Rd CO4 ..136 C8
Aldham Ct 8 CO8 ..56 F6
Aldon Cl CO12 ....90 C1
Aldous Cl CO7 ....59 C3
Aldridge Cl CO4 ..206 A4
Aldringham Mews IP11 .221 B5
Alec Hunter High Sch
  The CM7 ......128 C1
Alec Kay Ct CO2 ..135 C2
Aletha Farm Pl CO9 .29 D6
Alexander Ct 1 CM1 .205 E7
Alexander Mews CM2 .217 D2
Alexander Rd CM7 .127 E4
Alexandra Ave CO5 .201 E6
Alexandra Dr CO7 .137 C3
Alexandra Rd
  Clacton-on-S CO15 .188 F3
  Colchester CO3 ...135 E6
  Felixstowe IP11 ..221 C6
  Harwich CO12 ....91 D5
  Ipswich IP4 .....17 E6
  Sible Hedingham CO9 .51 D1
  Sudbury CO10 ....34 A7
  Weeley CO16 .....140 F1
Alexandra St CO12 ..91 D5
Alexandra Terr 9 CO13 .135 E6
Alf Eounder Cl CO4 .136 E6
Alfells Rd CO7 ....171 C8
Alfred Terr CO14 ..171 C8
Alfreg Rd CM8 ....194 D8
Alienor Ave CM7 ..72 B1
All Hallows Rd CO4 .18 A1
All Saints Ave CO3 .135 A4
All Saints CE Prim Sch
  Great Oakley CO12 .116 C3
  Harwich CO12 ....90 F3
  Maldon CM9 .....209 E2
  Maldon CM9 .....209 F3
All Saints CE Sch CM23 .146 B8
All Saints Cl
  Bishop's Stortford CM23 .146 A8
  Chelmsford CM1 ..205 B4
All Saints' Rd IP1 ..17 A8
Allectus Way CM8 ..194 D8
Allen Cotts CO6 ...106 E5
Allen Way CO16 ...186 A3
Allenby Rd IP2 ....16 F6
Allendale Dr CO6 ..133 D4
Allens Cl CM23 ...192 F1
Alleyne Way CO15 .203 G8
Allfields CO12 ....91 A2
Allington Cl IP4 ..17 F7
Allington Wlk CB9 .8 E8
Alma Dr CM1 .....205 A2
Alma Sq 4 CO11 .86 D4
Alma St CO7 .....164 B8
Almond Cl
  Clacton-on-S CO15 .188 C3
  Tiptree CO5 .....179 C6
  Wivenhoe CO7 ...137 C2
Almond Way CO4 ..136 E8
Almondhayes IP2 ..16 F3
Almshouses CO7 ..164 B8
Alpe St IP1 ......17 B7
Alpha Cl CM7 ....128 A2
Alpha Pl
  4 Bishop's Stortford CM23 .145 F8
  2 Saffron Walden CB11 ..22 E1
Alpha Rd CO3 ....186 B3
Alphamstone Rd CO8 .55 E8
Alport Ave CO3 ..135 C4
Alresford Cty Prim
  Sch CO7 .......138 A6
Alresford Rd CO7 ..164 E8
Alresford Sta CO7 ..165 A8
Alsa Bsns Pk CM24 .93 F1
Alsa Gdns CM22 ..94 C2
Alsa Leys CM22 ..94 C2
Alsa St CM24 ....93 F1
Alston Rd IP3 ....18 D1
Alstone Ct IP3 ...18 D1
Altbarn Cl CO4 ..110 D5
Altbarn Rd CO4 ..136 D5
Alton Dr CO3 ....135 B6

Alton Hall La IP9 ..61 F3
Alton Park Cty Jun Sch
  CO15 ..........188 D2
Alton Park La CO15 .188 B1
Alton Park Rd CO15 .188 D3
Alton Rd CO15 ...188 E1
Alton Water (Nature
  Reserve) IP9 .....62 A4
Aluf Cl CM8 ......194 E8
Alverton Cl CM7 ..154 B6
Alverton Way CO4 .110 B3
Alvis Ave CO15 ...203 E6
Alyssum Cl CM1 ..206 A6
Alyssum Wlk CO4 ..136 D6
Amberley Cl CO7 ..137 D1
Ambridge Rd CO6 .130 E3
Ambrose Ave CO3 .134 F4
Ambrose Ct CO6 ...133 D4
Ambross Ho CO2 ..126 A7
Amerells Rd CO7 ..168 C4
America Rd CO6 ...105 C2
America St CM9 ...210 A2
Amos Hill CO10 ...54 B8
Amoss Rd CM2 ...216 F8
Ancaster Rd IP2 ..37 B4
Anchor End CO11 ..87 A4
Anchor Hill CO7 ..164 B7
Anchor Ho CO2 ...135 E2
Anchor La Heybridge CM9 .210 A5
  New Mistley CO11 ..87 A4
Anchor Rd
  Clacton-on-S CO15 .188 E3
  Tiptree CO5 .....179 C4
Anchor St
  Bishop's Stortford CM23 .146 A6
  Chelmsford CM2 ..205 B1
Anderson Ave CM1 .204 F5
Anderson Cl CM23 .92 F2
Andover CO15 ....189 A6
Andrew Cl CM7 ...127 F5
Andrews Farm La CM3 .218 C3
Andrews Pl CM1 ..204 F3
Andros Cl IP3 ....38 A8
Anemone Cl CO4 ..109 C2
Angel La Glemsford CO10 .2 B4
  Great Dunmow CM6 .150 D8
  8 Ipswich IP4 ...17 C6
Angelgate CO12 ...91 E6
Angelgate Cotts CO12 .91 E6
Angle Side CM7 ...128 B2
Anglefield CO15 ..189 A7
Anglesea Rd Ipswich IP1 .17 B7
  Wivenhoe CO7 ...164 C8
Anglesey Ct CM23 .145 C7
Anglia Cl CO2 ....135 B3
Anglia Poly Univ CM1 .205 B2
Anglia Univ CM1 ..205 B2
Anglia Way CM7 ..128 B2
Anita Cl E IP2 ...16 E5
Anita Cl W IP2 ...16 E5
Ann Coles Cl CB9 .27 C6
Ann St IP1 ......17 C7
Annbrook Rd IP2 ..16 E1
Annex Cl CO4 ....185 F6
Anne St IP11 ....221 C3
Ansgar Rd CB11 ..43 E7
Anson Cl CO12 ...91 A2
Anson Ct CO4 ....128 D4
Anthony Cl CO4 ..110 D2
Antonia Cl CB9 ..9 E7
Antonio Wlk CO4 ..136 F7
Antonius Way CO4 .110 B6
Anvil Way CM1 ...205 E8
Anzani Arr IP11 ..221 A4
Anzio Cres CO2 ...135 C1
Apollo Ho IP2 ....16 E1
Apollo Mews CO2 ..135 C1
Apple Cl CM1 ....204 F2
Apple Way CO2 ..216 D6
Appleby Cl IP2 ...16 F1
Appleton Fields CM23 .145 E4
Appletree Cl CM7 ..155 F5
Appletree Wlk CM7 .128 A1
Approach The CO15 .203 G8
Apsley Cl CM23 ..146 A8
Apsley Ct 3 IP1 ..17 A7
Apton Ct CM23 ...146 A7
Apton Fields 7 CM23 .145 F7
Apton Rd CM23 ..145 F7
Aquiline Ho CO15 ..203 J8
Aragon Cl CO15 ..203 F8
Aragon Rd CM7 ..154 B6
Arakan Cl CO15 ..135 B1
Arbour La Chelmsford CM1 .205 D4
  Wickham Bishops CM8 .195 F5
Arbour Way CO4 ..110 C4
Arbutus Cl CM2 ..216 B6
Arcade St 15 IP1 ..17 C6
Arcade The CO15 ..188 F2
Archangel Gdns IP2 .16 E4
Archers Way CM2 .216 C2
Archery Fields CO15 .189 A5
Arden Cl CO4 ....110 C3
Arderne Cl CO12 ..90 F2
Ardleigh Ct CO7 ..111 E8
Ardleigh Rd Dedham CO7 .84 D2
  Great Bromley CO7 .112 B4
  Little Bromley CO11 .112 E5
Argents La CO10 ..108 C2
Argyle Ct CO3 ...158 C2
Argyle Rd
  Thorpe-le-S CO16 .141 F2
  Thorpe-le-S CO16 .142 A2
Argyle St CM7 ...127 E4
Argyll Ct 10 CB9 ..27 B7
Ariel Cl CO4 .....136 F7
Arkwright Rd IP2 ..16 E7

Armadale Wlk CO2 .136 A2
Armiger Way CM8 .177 B2
Armond Rd CM8 ...176 F3
Armonde Cl CM3 ..192 E1
Armourers Cl CM23 .145 B4
Armoury Rd CO6 ..108 F4
Armstrong Cl CM3 .218 F8
Armstrong Way CO9 .30 A2
Arnhem Gr CM7 ...127 E5
Arnhem Rd CM1 ..204 E6
Arnold Cres CM8 ..176 E5
Arnold Dr CO4 ...136 E6
Arnold Rd CO15 ..188 D1
Arnold Villas CO5 .179 C6
Arnold Way CM2 ..216 C3
Arnstones Cl CM3 .136 C8
Arras Rd CO2 ....135 D3
Arras Sq 12 IP1 ..17 C6
Arrow Rd CO4 ....136 F7
Arthur Cl CM7 ...204 F5
Arthur St 8 CO2 ..135 F6
Arthur's Terr IP4 ..17 C5
Arthy Cl CM3 ....194 A4
Artillery St CO1 ..136 B6
Arun Cl CM1 ....205 C5
Arundel Way CM1 ..18 E3
Arundel Wlk 1 CB9 .8 E8
Arwela Rd IP11 ...221 D2
Asbury Cl CO4 ...136 D8
Asbury Dr CO6 ...132 E3
Ascot Cl CM23 ...146 C8
Ascot Dr Felixstowe IP11 .221 C6
  Ipswich IP3 .....18 B4
Ascot Gdns CO3 ..134 E7
Ash Bglws CM7 ...127 E3
Ash Cl Brightlingsea CO7 .185 E7
  Colchester CO3 ..188 C3
  Hatfield Peverel CM3 .194 A4
Ash Ct CO12 .....90 E2
Ash Fall CM6 ....177 A5
Ash Gn CB10 .....11 D1
Ash Gr Blackheath CO2 .163 A8
  Capel St M IP9 ...35 A2
  Chelmsford CM2 ..216 D7
  Great Bromley CO7 .139 A6
  Great Cornard CO10 .34 C5
  Great Dunmow CM6 .150 D7
  Heybridge CM9 ...210 C6
  Wivenhoe CO7 ...137 C3
Ash Ground Cl CO11 .86 D8
Ash Ho IP2 ......16 E1
Ash Rd CO7 .....165 B8
Ash Rise CO9 ....103 F8
Ash Tree Cl CM1 ..204 F2
Ash Tree Cnr CM3 .191 B6
Ash Way CO3 ....134 F3
Ashby Rise CM23 ..119 B1
Ashdale CO4 .....145 D4
Ashdon Cty Prim Sch CO .6 B1
Ashdon Rd CB10 ..23 C3
Ashdown Rd CB10 ..24 C4
Ashdown Way
  Colchester CO4 ..136 D2
  Ipswich IP3 .....18 A4
Ashen Cl CO10 ...11 D1
Ashen Hill CO10 ..11 C3
Ashen La CO10 ...11 C3
Ashen Rd Ashen CO10 .12 A1
  Clare CO10 .....12 B5
  Ridgewell CO9 ...29 B8
Ashenden IP11 ...221 E4
Ashes Cl CM7 ....170 F8
Ashes Rd CM7 ...155 B6
Ashfield Ct IP4 ...17 C4
Ashfield Farm Rd
  Hatfield Peverel CM3 .194 E1
  Ulting CM9 ......208 D8
Ashford Rd CM1 ..204 A3
Ashlea Cl CB9 ....9 B6
Ashlea Rd CB9 ...9 B6
Ashley Ct CO12 ..91 B3
Ashley Gdns CO3 .135 C6
Ashley Rd CO12 ..91 B3
Ashley St IP2 ....17 C4
Ashlong Gr CB9 ..9 C7
Ashlyn's Rd CO13 .170 E4
Ashmere Gr IP4 ..17 F6
Ashmere Rise CO10 .34 A8
Ashmole Dr CO13 .170 F6
Ashpole Rd CM7 ..202 B1
Ashstead Cl CO16 .188 B6
Ashton Cl IP2 ....16 C2
Ashton Pl CM2 ...206 A3
Ashurst Cl CM1 ..163 F8
Ashurst Dr CM1 ..205 B8
Ashwells Mdw CO6 .105 B6
Ashwin Ave CO6 ..133 D4
Askins Rd CO7 ...59 C3
Aspall Sq CO10 ..34 B8
Aspen Way
  3 Colchester CO4 ..136 D8
  Little Oakley CO12 .117 B8
Aspens The CM23 ..119 B3
Aspin Mews CO10 ..22 D2
Asquith Dr CO4 ..110 C5
Aster Cl CO3 ....170 F4
Aster Cl
  Bishop's Stortford CM23 .145 D4
  4 Chelmsford CM1 ..205 F6
  Clacton-on-S CO16 .188 C4
Aster Rd IP2 .....16 E4
Astley Rd CO15 ..188 D3
Ataka Rd IP11 ...221 A3
Athelstan Rd CO3 .135 A6
Atherton Rd IP2 ..16 D2
Atholl Rd CM2 ...205 F5
Atlantic Sq CM8 ..177 A3
Atlas Bglws CO6 ..105 A6

Atlas Ct CO6 .....105 A7
Atlas Ho 3 IP4 ...17 E6
Atlas Rd CO6 ....104 F4
Attlee Gdns 7 CO1 .136 A4
Attwood Cl CO4 ..110 B5
Attwoods Cl CM2 ..216 C3
Aubrey Cl CM1 ...205 B7
Auckland Cl CM4 ..204 E5
Audley End Miniature
  Rly CB11 ......43 A8
Audley End Rd CB11 .43 C8
Audley End Sta CB11 .42 F5
Audley Rd Colchester CO3 .135 C5
  Great Leighs CM3 ..173 F7
  Saffron Walden CB11 ..22 E1
Audley Way CO12 ..171 B6
Audrey Gdns CM23 .145 F4
Audries Est CO14 .171 A8
Augustine Way CM3 .218 F2
Augustus Cl
  Colchester CO4 ..110 B6
  Haverhill CB9 ....9 D7
Augustus Way CM8 .194 E8
Austen Cl CM7 ...155 A8
Austin Ave CO15 ..203 E6
Austin St IP2 ....17 C4
Auston Croft CB11 .43 D7
Autoway CO4 ....110 C5
Autumn Cl CO16 ..188 C5
Aveley Way CM9 ..220 F8
Aveline Rd CO7 ..111 E7
Avenue Rd
  Bishop's Stortford CM23 .146 B6
  Chelmsford CM2 ..216 D7
  Clacton-on-S CO15 .188 F1
  Colchester CO3 ..135 C6
  Danbury CM3 ....218 F7
  Great Baxted CM3 .178 A3
  Great Dunmow CM6 .150 B8
  Great Oakley CO12 .116 B3
  Ipswich IP1 ......17 C8
  Trimley St M IP11 .221 A7
  West Bergholt CO6 .108 D3
  Witham CM8 .....177 A2
  Wivenhoe CO7 ...137 B1
Avignon Cl CO2 ..136 B4
Avila Chase CM2 ..216 B1
Avocet Cl
  Frinton-on-S CO13 .170 E6
  Kelvedon CO5 ...158 D2
  West Mersea CO5 ..201 D7
Avocet Ct IP11 ...221 D2
Avocet Way CO15 ..210 C5
Avon Rd CM1 ....204 C5
Avon Way CO4 ...134 F6
Avon Way Ho CO4 .136 F6
Avon Wlk CM8 ...176 E3
Avondale Ho CO15 .189 A3
Avondale Rd
  Clacton-on-S CO15 .189 A3
  Ipswich IP3 .....18 A2
Aylesbury Dr CO15 .189 F6
Ayletts CM1 .....191 B3
Ayloffe Rd CO4 ...110 C1
Aynsworth Ave CM23 .146 D8
Azalea Ct CO4 ...136 D8
Azalea Way CO16 .188 C4
Azalea Ct 9 CM1 ..205 F6

## B

Back Hamlet IP3 ..17 E5
Back Hill CM1 ....5 B6
Back La Broomfield CM1 .191 D2
  Colchester CO3 ..134 E8
  Felixstowe IP11 ..221 D5
  Ford End CM3 ....172 B6
  Great Oakley CO12 .116 C4
  Ickleton CB10 ....3 A3
  Little Waltham CM3 .191 F4
  Stisted CM7 .....129 C7
  Tattingstone IP9 ..61 C6
  Thaxted CM6 .....69 F3
  Washbrook IP8 ...35 E8
  Wickham Bishops CM8 .195 F4
Back La W CO7 ...138 F7
Back Rd Ardleigh CO7 .112 B5
  Tollesbury CM9 ...199 C4
  Writtle CM1 .....204 A1
Back Waterside La CO7 .185 F5
Backwarden Nature
  Reserve CM3 .....218 E5
Bacon's La CO6 ...106 C3
Bacon Lodge IP11 .221 D3
Bacton Rd CM1 ...217 A6
Bacton St La 4 CO7 .138 C7
Baddow Hall Ave CM2 .217 A6
Baddow Hall Cres CM2 .217 B6
Baddow Hall Cty Jun &
  Inf Sch CM2 .....217 A6
Baddow Place Ave CM2 .217 A6
Baddow Rd
  Chelmsford CM2 ..205 C1
  Great Baddow CM2 .216 E7
Baden Powell Dr CO3 .135 A4
Bader Cl CM7 ....128 B3
Badger Gr CM7 ...128 B3
Badgers CM23 ...145 E5
Badgers Bank IP2 ..16 E1
Badgers Cl CM23 ..216 B1

Badgers Gn C06 .......132 E3
Badgers Gr C06 .......82 B1
Badley Hall Rd C07 .......112 F2
Badminton Rd C015 .......203 G7
Badshah Ave IP3 .......18 B3
Bagshaw Rd C012 .......91 D4
Bailey Bridge Rd CM7 .......127 E5
Bailey Cl Haverhill CB9 .......9 D7
  Ipswich IP2 .......16 F2
Bailey Dale C03 .......134 C4
Bailey La C010 .......12 C7
Bainbridge Dr C05 .......179 D4
Baines Cl C03 .......135 A5
Baird Cl IP2 .......16 F7
Baker Ave CM3 .......194 A3
Baker Mews CM9 .......210 A2
Baker Rd IP9 .......91 A8
Baker St CM2 .......205 A1
Baker's La Colchester C04 .......109 A2
  Great Notley CM7 .......154 D6
  Tolleshunt Major CM9 .......197 D4
Baker's Rd C010 .......12 F2
Bakers Cl 6 CM23 .......146 A7
Bakers La Danbury CM3 .......218 E7
  Felsted CM6 .......152 C4
Bakers Mead CM7 .......190 F7
Bakers Terr C07 .......85 A5
Bakery Ct CM24 .......119 D6
Baldry Cl IP8 .......16 C1
Baldwin's La C06 .......131 E8
Bale Cl C03 .......134 C4
Balfe Cl C04 .......136 E6
Balkerne Gdns C01 .......135 E7
Balkerne Hill C03 .......135 E7
Balkerne Pas C01 .......135 E7
Ball Alley 8 C01 .......135 E7
Ball La Abberton C02 .......162 F5
  Blackheath C02 .......163 B5
Ballast Quay Rd
  Fingringhoe C05 .......164 B6
  Wivenhoe C07 .......137 D1
Ballingdon Hill C010 .......33 C5
Ballingdon Hill Ind Est
  C010 .......33 C6
Ballingdon St C010 .......33 D6
Ballingdon Trad Est C010 .......33 C6
Balmoral Ave C015 .......188 D3
Balmoral Cl IP2 .......16 F1
Balmoral Ct CM2 .......205 C2
Balmoral Dr CM9 .......210 A1
Balton Way C012 .......90 F2
Banham Dr C010 .......33 F8
Banister Cl C016 .......188 C5
Bank Pas C01 .......135 E7
Bank Rd IP4 .......17 E6
Bank St CM7 .......127 F3
Bankart La CM2 .......205 F4
Banks Ct CM6 .......150 D8
Bannister Green
  Villas CM6 .......152 E6
Bantams La CM3 .......158 A1
Bantoft Terr IP3 .......18 C2
Barbary Lodge CM2 .......205 A2
Barbel Rd C04 .......110 F1
Barbour Gdns C02 .......134 F2
Barbrook La C05 .......179 B6
Barbrook Way CM3 .......218 E1
Barclay Cl CM7 .......217 A6
Bardell Cl CM1 .......204 F6
Bardfield Cottage Mus
  CM7 .......72 A1
Bardfield Rd
  Bardfield Saling CM7 .......99 A1
  Colchester C02 .......136 A1
  Thaxted CM6 .......70 D2
Bardfield Way C013 .......170 F6
Bardfield Gdns C02 .......201 C6
Bargate La C07 .......85 C3
Baring-gould Cotts C05 .......184 D1
Barker Cl Ipswich IP2 .......16 D5
  Stanway C03 .......86 B4
  Steeple Bumpstead CB9 .......27 B6
Barker Rd C010 .......13 E2
Barkers Mead CM7 .......146 B1
Barkis Cl CM1 .......204 D7
Barkstead Rd C04 .......110 C1
Barlee Cl CB11 .......65 C3
Barley Ct CB11 .......22 D1
Barley Fields CM8 .......177 A1
Barley Hills CM23 .......145 E4
Barley Mead CM3 .......219 B6
Barley Way C03 .......134 E5
Barlow Rd CM2 .......205 C3
Barlow Road Cotts CB10 .......6 B2
Barlow's Reach CM2 .......206 A4
Barn Gn CM1 .......205 E8
Barn Hall Ave C02 .......136 C4
Barn La C011 .......112 F7
Barn Mead CM7 .......228 D2
Barn View Rd C06 .......131 A1
Barnaby Rudge CM4 .......204 F7
Barnard Cl CB11 .......66 F8
Barnard Rd C016 .......216 C2
Barnardiston Rd C04 .......110 C1
Barnardiston Way CM8 .......176 F3
Barnards Field CM6 .......70 B2
Barncroft Cl C04 .......110 B3
Barnes Farm Cty Jun &
  Inf Sch CM2 .......206 A3
Barnes Mill Rd CM2 .......205 F2
Barnfield Capel St M IP9 .......35 B1
  Feering C05 .......158 D3
  Felixstowe IP11 .......221 B6

Barnfield continued
  Manningtree C011 .......86 D4
Barnfield Cotts CM9 .......210 B5
Barnfield Mews CM1 .......205 A6
Barnfield Pl CM8 .......176 F1
Barnfield Rd C06 .......109 C6
Barnhall Rd CM9 .......180 D2
Barnham Pl IP5 .......18 F6
Barnston Gn CM6 .......151 A4
Baron's Ct 5 CB9 .......8 E7
Baron's La CM3 .......220 E1
Baronia Croft C04 .......110 C3
Barons The CM23 .......145 F6
Baronswood Way C02 .......135 D2
Barr Cl C07 .......137 C1
Barrack Cnr 5 IP1 .......17 B6
Barrack La
  Great Waltham CM3 .......190 E8
  Harwich C012 .......91 E4
  Ipswich IP1 .......17 B6
Barrack Sq 10 CM2 .......205 B2
Barrack St Bradfield C011 .......114 D8
Barrack Cl C016 .......136 B6
Barrel Cl C07 .......139 A3
Barrells Down Rd CM23 .......118 E1
Barrett La 5 CM23 .......145 F7
Barrington Cl
  Great Baddow CM2 .......217 A6
  Little Clacton C016 .......168 C2
Barrington Gdns C015 .......189 C5
Barrington Rd C02 .......136 A5
Barrow Marsh CM9 .......211 A4
Barryfields CM7 .......100 E7
Bartholomew Cl CB10 .......3 E2
Bartholomew Rd 8
  CM23 .......145 F6
Bartholomew St IP4 .......17 F6
Bartletts CB10 .......22 C1
Bartlow Rd Castle Camps CB1 .......7 D4
  Hadstock CB1 .......5 D7
Barton Cl IP2 .......16 E2
Barton Rd IP11 .......221 F4
Bartram Ave CM7 .......128 C3
Barwell Way CM8 .......177 B2
Basbow La 2 CM23 .......145 F7
Basin Rd CM9 .......210 D3
Bassetts La CM3 .......208 A4
Bassingbourn Rd CM24 .......121 A3
Bateman Rd C02 .......185 E8
Bateman's Rd C016 .......168 B4
Bates Rd CM9 .......219 B6
Bath Ct CB9 .......8 F6
Bath Rd IP11 .......221 F4
Bath St Ipswich IP2 .......17 D3
  Wivenhoe C07 .......164 B8
Bathurst Cl 1 C02 .......136 A1
Battery La IP9 .......91 B8
Battisford Dr C016 .......188 A4
Battlesbrook Rd C02 .......136 D2
Bawdsey Cl C016 .......188 B3
Bawtree Way C03 .......135 A5
Baxters CM3 .......128 A4
Bay Rd C012 .......91 D4
Bay View Cres
  Harwich C012 .......90 C1
Bayard Ave C07 .......185 F7
Bayley St C09 .......51 F4
Baynard's Cty Prim Sch
  C05 .......179 B7
Baynards Cres C013 .......170 E6
Bayning Ho C07 .......139 F8
Baytree Ct CM7 .......126 F2
Beach App C016 .......203 B6
Beach Cres C015 .......203 F6
Beach Rd
  Clacton-on-S C015 .......188 F2
  Harwich C012 .......91 C2
  Point Clear B C016 .......202 D6
  St Osyth C016 .......187 B2
  West Mersea C05 .......201 B7
Beach Rd W IP11 .......221 D2
Beach Station Rd IP11 .......221 C1
Beach's Dr CM1 .......204 D3
Beachcroft Ave C013 .......170 D6
Beacon Cl C07 .......185 G6
Beacon Field IP11 .......221 C5
Beacon Hill Maldon CM9 .......209 E2
  Wickham Bishops CM8 .......196 A6
Beacon Hill Ave C012 .......91 E4
Beacon Hill Sch IP7 .......16 F3
Beacon Hts C016 .......186 B2
Beacon Way
  Colchester C03 .......134 C6
  Point Clear B C016 .......186 B2
Beaconsfield Ave C03 .......135 E6
Beaconsfield Cl C010 .......33 E8
Beaconsfield Ct 7 CB9 .......8 F7
Beaconsfield Rd
  Clacton-on-S C015 .......188 F3
  Ipswich IP4 .......16 F7
  Maldon CM9 .......209 F2
  Thaxted CM6 .......70 A3
Beadel Cl CM6 .......194 E8
Beadle Way CM3 .......174 A6
Beadon Dr CM7 .......128 A1
Bear St C06 .......56 A1
Beard's La CB11 .......41 A4
Beardsley Dr CM7 .......205 D7
Beardwin Bsns Pk CB11 .......42 F5
Beatrice Ave IP11 .......221 E5
Beatrice Cl IP3 .......18 A3
Beatrice Rd
  Clacton-on-S C015 .......188 E2
  Walton-on-t-N C014 .......144 D2
Beatty Gdns CM7 .......128 C4
Beatty Rd IP3 .......18 B2

Beauchamps Cl CM1 .......205 F8
Beaufort Ct 5 CB9 .......8 F7
Beaufort Gdns CM7 .......128 A4
Beaufort Rd CM2 .......206 A4
Beaufort St IP1 .......17 A7
Beaumont Ave
  Brightlingsea C07 .......186 A7
  Clacton-on-S C015 .......188 D3
Beaumont Cl
  Colchester C04 .......109 F4
  Walton-on-t-N C014 .......170 F7
Beaumont Ct CB9 .......9 B6
Beaumont Hill CM6 .......123 D2
Beaumont Pk C03 .......218 C6
Beaumont Pl CM7 .......128 B3
Beaumont Rd C012 .......116 C2
Beaumont Vale CB9 .......9 B6
Beaumont Way CM7 .......210 B1
Beaumont Wlk CM1 .......204 D5
Beaver Cl C03 .......134 E7
Beche Rd C02 .......136 B5
Beck Rd CB11 .......22 D1
Becker Rd C03 .......134 E4
Beckers Green Cty Prim
  Sch CM7 .......128 D2
Beckers Green Rd CM7 .......128 D2
Becketts La IP7 .......57 D8
Beckford Rd C011 .......87 A4
Beckingham Bsns Pk
  CM7 .......197 D3
Beckingham Rd
  Great Totham CM9 .......196 D5
  Tolleshunt D'arcy CM9 .......198 C4
  Beckingham St CM9 .......197 D3
Beckmere Ct C015 .......188 F8
Bedells Ave CM7 .......155 B5
Bedford Cl Braintree CM7 .......128 B4
  Tiptree C05 .......179 D5
Bedford Ct 9 CB9 .......8 F7
Bedford St IP1 .......17 B6
Bedwell Rd CM22 .......94 B3
Beech Ave Braintree CM7 .......127 F5
  Halstead C09 .......77 A2
  Wivenhoe C07 .......137 B7
Beech Cl Sproughton IP8 .......16 A6
  Takeley CM22 .......148 C8
Beech Gn CM8 .......195 F5
Beech Gr
  Bourham Heath C03 .......107 F1
  Haverhill CB9 .......9 A8
  Ipswich IP3 .......17 F3
  Little Oakley C012 .......117 B7
  Sible Hedingham C09 .......51 D1
Beech Ho IP2 .......16 D2
Beech Rd
  Great Cornard C010 .......34 B6
  Rivenhall CM8 .......177 B7
Beech Rise CM3 .......194 A3
Beeches Cl
  Chelmsford CM1 .......204 E2
  Saffron Walden CB11 .......43 C7
Beeches Rd
  Chelmsford CM1 .......204 E2
  Heybridge CM9 .......209 F5
Beeches The Ipswich IP3 .......17 F4
  Wendens Ambo CB11 .......42 F5
Beechholm 2 IP4 .......17 E6
Beechlands C06 .......145 F5
Beechwood Ct C02 .......136 C2
Beehive La CM2 .......216 C5
Beehive Lane Cty Prim
  Sch CM2 .......216 D5
Beeleigh Chase CM9 .......209 D4
Beeleigh Cl C02 .......136 A1
Beeleigh Link CM2 .......205 B8
Beeleigh Rd CM9 .......209 F3
Begonia Cl CM1 .......205 F6
Begonia Pl C016 .......188 C4
Bekeswell La CM2 .......215 F2
Bekeswell Pl CM2 .......216 C2
Belcham's La CB11 .......93 E8
Belcham St Paul CE
  Prim Sch C010 .......13 A1
Beldams Cl C010 .......142 A1
Beldams La CM23 .......146 B5
Belgrave Cl
  Chelmsford CM2 .......216 D7
  Ipswich IP4 .......17 E8
Belgrave Ho 6 CM23 .......146 B8
Bell Cl Colchester CM2 .......136 C2
  Ipswich IP7 .......17 C4
Bell College C011 .......43 E8
Bell Farm Ind Est SG8 .......39 B2
Bell Hill Danbury CM3 .......218 C7
  Lamarsh C08 .......55 C3
Bell La Great Bardfield CM7 .......72 A2
  Ipswich IP2 .......17 C6
  Nuthampstead SG8 .......39 B2
  Panfield CM7 .......127 A7
  Thaxted CM6 .......70 A3
Bellamy Cl C013 .......170 D6
Bellcroft CM8 .......177 A3
Belle Vue C04 .......205 A1
Belle Vue Rd
  Colchester C01 .......109 E1
  Ipswich IP4 .......17 C4
  Sudbury C010 .......33 F7
  Wivenhoe C07 .......137 C1
Bellevue Terr C09 .......76 E2
Bellfield Ave C07 .......186 A7
Bellfield Cl C07 .......186 A8
Bellmead CM1 .......205 B2
Bells Chase CM2 .......216 E6
Bells Cl CB11 .......43 D6

Bells Hill
  Bishop's Stortford CM23 .......145 E7
  Bures C08 .......80 A4
Bells La C010 .......2 C5
Bells Rd C010 .......31 F6
Belmans Ct C012 .......91 A2
Belmer Rd CM24 .......120 D4
Belmonde Dr CM1 .......205 E7
Belmont Cl CM1 .......205 E7
Belmont Cres C04 .......110 C3
Belmont Ct 6 CB9 .......8 F7
Belmont Hill CB11 .......43 A1
Belmont Pl C01 .......136 C5
Belmont Rd IP2 .......16 C1
Belsay Ct CB9 .......8 D8
Belsize Ave C015 .......203 D6
Belstead Ave IP2 .......17 B3
Belstead Rd IP2 .......17 A3
Belstead Sch IP8 .......16 C2
Belsteads Farm La CM3 .......191 E2
Belvawney Cl CM1 .......204 E6
Belvedere Cl CM3 .......218 F7
Belvedere Ct CM7 .......215 F8
Belvedere Pl CM9 .......220 F8
Belvedere Rd
  Danbury CM3 .......218 F7
  Ipswich IP4 .......17 F7
Belvoir Ct 4 CB9 .......8 E7
Bembridge Cl C015 .......188 F8
Bemerton Ct C013 .......170 B6
Bemerton Gdns C013 .......170 C6
Benacre Rd IP3 .......18 A2
Bendalls Ct 12 C011 .......86 D4
Bendlowes Rd CM7 .......72 C1
Benedict Dr CM1 .......204 E2
Benezet St IP1 .......17 B6
Benfield Way CM7 .......128 B2
Benhooks Ave CM23 .......145 E5
Benhooks Pl 1 CM23 .......145 E5
Bennet Ct C04 .......136 E6
Bennett Cl Braintree CM7 .......155 A8
  Walton-on-t-N C014 .......171 A8
Bennett Rd IP1 .......16 D8
Bennett Way CM3 .......194 A4
Bennett's La CM6 .......151 E2
Benskins Cl CM23 .......92 A8
Bensusan Ct C02 .......135 B3
Bentall Cl CM1 .......205 C3
Bentfield Cty Prim Sch
  CM24 .......119 D8
Bentfield End Cswy
  CM24 .......119 D7
Bentfield Gdns CM24 .......119 D8
Bentfield Green CM24 .......119 D8
Bentfield Rd CM24 .......119 D7
Bentleigh Ct 8 C01 .......136 D7
Bentley Ave C015 .......203 E6
Bentley CE Prim Sch IP9 .......60 F7
Bentley Cl CM23 .......145 F5
Bentley Ct C013 .......135 C7
Bentley La Belstead IP8 .......36 C6
  Stutton IP9 .......61 A3
Bentley Rd
  Little Bromley C011 .......113 D3
  Weeley Heath C07, C016 .......167 E6
  Witham CM8 .......176 E4
Benton Cl Cressing CM7 .......155 E6
  Witham CM8 .......195 A7
Berberis Wlk 5 C04 .......110 C4
Bercolta Ct C06 .......108 E4
Berechurch Hall Rd C02 .......162 D8
Berechurch Rd C02 .......135 E2
Berecroft CM3 .......194 A3
Berent Cl C016 .......188 C5
Bergen Ct CM9 .......220 E8
Bergholt Rd Brantham C011 .......86 B7
  Colchester C04 .......109 D8
Beridge Rd C09 .......76 D2
Beriffe Pl C07 .......185 F7
Berkeley Cl IP4 .......17 E8
Berkeley Rd C015 .......188 F5
Berkely Dr CM2 .......205 F2
Berkley Cl C04 .......110 C4
Bermuda Rd IP3 .......38 E7
Bernard Cl C013 .......170 E6
Bernard Cres IP3 .......18 A2
Berners End CM6 .......151 B4
Berners St IP1 .......17 B6
Bernside CM7 .......127 F2
Berrimans Cl C04 .......136 D6
Berry Cl IP3 .......18 F1
Berryfield Cotts C09 .......136 B7
Bertram Ave C016 .......168 D1
Berwick Ave CM1 .......204 E4
Beryl Rd C012 .......90 D1
Beslyns Rd CM7 .......72 A3
Bethany St C07 .......164 B7
Betjeman Cl CM7 .......155 A8
Betony Vlle C09 .......205 A1
Betts Green Rd C016 .......168 D5
Betty Dent's Cnr C016 .......141 C5
Beverley Ave C07 .......201 E7
Beverley Ct 5 IP4 .......17 D6
Beverley Dr C013 .......170 E7
Beverley Rd
  Colchester C03 .......135 D6
  Ipswich IP4 .......17 F8
Bevington Mews CM7 .......177 B2
Bevan Cl C013 .......170 C6
Bewick Ct 7 CM1 .......205 F6
Bexfield Cl C015 .......203 B8
Bexley Ave C012 .......90 F1
Bibb Way IP1 .......17 A5
Bicknacre Rd CM3 .......218 D1
Bignalls Croft C04 .......110 C4
Bignells Croft C04 .......110 C4
Bigods La CM6 .......123 D4
Bijou Cl C05 .......179 D6

Bilberry End CB1
Billy's La C07
Bilsdale Cl C04
Bilton Rd CM1
Binley Rd CM2
Birch Ave
  Great Bentley C07
  Harwich C012
Birch CE Prim Sch C02
Birch Cl Braintree CM7
  Brightlingsea C07
  Clacton-on-S C015 .......18?
Birch Dr Brantham C011 .......60?
  Halstead C09
Birch Dr C07
Birch Rd C02 .......161 E?
Birch Rise CM8 .......161 A?
Birch St Birch C02 .......161 A?
  Nayland C06 .......56 A?
Birch Wood Cl C05 .......201 D?
Birchalls CM24 .......119 D?
Birchanger CE Prim Sch
  CM23 .......119 D?
Birchanger Ind Est CM23 .......119 D?
Birchanger La CM23 .......119 D?
Birches The C013 .......170 E?
Birches Wlk CM2 .......216 A?
Birchway C02 .......161 A?
Birchwood CM23 .......119 D?
Birchwood Cl C015 .......179 F?
Birchwood High Sch
  CM23 .......146 C?
Birchwood Rd
  Dedham C07 .......84 B?
  Hazeleigh CM3 .......219 F?
  Langham C04 .......84 A?
  Purleigh CM3 .......220 B?
Birchwood Way C05 .......179 E?
Bird La C05 .......179 E?
Birdbrook Rd C09 .......28 A?
Birdbush Ave C011 .......43 D?
Birds Cl C010 .......34 C?
Birk Beck CM1 .......205 C?
Birkdale Rise CM3 .......194 B?
Birkfield Cl IP2 .......17 A?
Birkfield Dr IP2 .......16 F?
Birkin Cl C015 .......179 C?
Biscay Cl CB9 .......9 C?
Bishop Mews IP8 .......16 B?
Bishop Rd Chelmsford CM1 .......205 A?
  Colchester C02 .......135 A?
Bishop William Ward
  Sch C06 .......109 B?
Bishop's Ave CM23 .......145 F?
Bishop's CE & RC Aided
  Prim Sch The CM1 .......205 F?
Bishop's Cl 3 CB9 .......8 E?
Bishop's Ct 7 CB9 .......8 E?
Bishop's Hall La CM1 .......205 B?
Bishop's Hill IP3 .......17 F?
Bishop's La C09 .......54 B?
Bishop's Stortford Bsns
  Ctr CM23 .......146 A?
Bishop's Stortford Coll
  CM23 .......145 E?
Bishop's Stortford High
  Sch The CM23 .......145 F?
Bishop's Stortford Sta
  CM23 .......146 A?
Bishops Ave CM7 .......128 B?
Bishops Dr C016 .......203 B?
Bishops Gdns C03 .......203 A?
Bishops La C05 .......179 C?
Bishops Park Way CM23 .......145 E?
Bishopscourt Gdns CM2 .......205 E?
Bishopsgarth IP3 .......17 F?
Bisley Cl C016 .......188 B?
Bittern Cl Ipswich IP2 .......16 E?
  Kelvedon C05 .......158 D?
Bixley Dr IP4 .......18 E?
Bixley La IP4 .......18 E?
Bixley Rd IP3 .......18 E?
Black Barns IP11 .......221 A?
Black Bouy Hill C07 .......164 B?
Black Boy La C011 .......89 A?
Black Chapel La CM6 .......151 E?
Black Horse La IP1 .......17 C?
Black La CM7 .......71 F?
Blackberry Rd C03 .......134 C?
Blackbrook Rd C06 .......109 C?
Blackbushe CM23 .......119 C?
Blackdown Ave IP5 .......18 F?
Blackfriars C010 .......33 D?
Blackfriars Ct 8 IP4 .......17 D?
Blackheath C02 .......163 A?
Blackhouse La C010 .......34 C?
Blacklands Cl CB11 .......43 C?
Blackley La Braintree CM3 .......153 F?
  Great Notley CM7 .......154 A?
Blacklock CM2 .......206 A?
Blackman Way CM8 .......177 A?
Blacksmith Cl CM1 .......205 E?
Blacksmith's Corner C04 .......53 E?
Blacksmith's La C012 .......90 F?
Blacksmiths Cl CM23 .......145 B?
Blacksmiths Hill C010 .......11 B?
Blacksmiths La
  Bulmer C010 .......32 F?
  Shudy Camps CB1 .......7 C?
  Wickham Bishops CM8 .......195 E?
Blacksmiths La C07 .......164 B?
Blackthorn Cl Ipswich IP3 .......18 E?
  Writtle CM1 .......204 A?
Blackthorn Rd
  Harwich C012 .......90 ?
  Witham CM8 .......176 E?
Blackthorn Way CM9 .......180 A?
Blackwater Ave C04 .......110 E?

| | |
|---|---|
| ...W1 | .....205 C6 |
| ....asin CM9 | .....210 E3 |
| ..ar Dr CO5 | .....201 A6 |
| ...er La CM5 | .....195 B8 |
| ...er Way CM7 | .....128 A4 |
| ...dl Dr CM7 | .....127 C4 |
| ....er Dr IP4 | .......18 F5 |
| ...n Cl Braintree CM7 | .....127 E7 |
| ....er CO5 | .....179 E5 |
| ...e Dr CO13 | .....170 F7 |
| ...r Cl | |
| ...ishop's Stortford CM23 | .....145 C7 |
| ...ushmere St A IP4 | .......18 E5 |
| ...lair Par C8 | .......8 E8 |
| Blake Cl CO11 | .......86 B4 |
| Blake Dr Braintree CM7 | .....128 C4 |
| Clacton-on-S CO16 | .....188 D6 |
| Blake Rd CM8 | .....176 F5 |
| Blamsters Cres CO9 | .....103 D8 |
| Blanchard Cl CO13 | .....170 A7 |
| Blanche St IP4 | .......17 C6 |
| Blandford Rd IP3 | .......18 D3 |
| Blaxhall Cl **17** C89 | .......8 E7 |
| Blenheim Cl | |
| Braintree CM7 | .....127 E7 |
| Brantham CO11 | .......60 D1 |
| Danbury CM3 | .....218 F2 |
| Blenheim Ct | |
| Bishop's Stortford CM23 | .....145 C7 |
| Clacton-on-S CO15 | .....188 D2 |
| **4** Ipswich IP1 | .......17 A7 |
| Blenheim Dr CO2 | .....163 A8 |
| Blenheim Rd | |
| Clacton-on-S CO15 | .....188 D2 |
| Ipswich IP1 | .......17 A7 |
| Blenheim Way CO5 | .....179 F5 |
| Blickling Cl IP2 | .......17 B2 |
| Blind La Easthorpe CO2 | .....160 B4 |
| Eight Ash G CO6 | .....134 A8 |
| Goldhanger CM9 | .....211 C7 |
| Howe Green CM2 | .....217 F4 |
| Tolleshunt Knights CM9 | .....180 B1 |
| Blithe Ct CO7 | .....164 B8 |
| Blofield Rd IP11 | .....221 A4 |
| Blois Mdws CB9 | .......27 C7 |
| Blois Rd | |
| Steeple Bumpstead CB9 | .......27 D8 |
| Sturmer CB9 | .......9 F1 |
| Bloom Cl CO13 | .....170 F6 |
| Bloomfield Ave CO13 | .....170 E7 |
| Bloomfield St IP4 | .......18 B6 |
| Blooms Hall La CO10 | .......2 F8 |
| Blott Rise CM8 | .....194 F8 |
| Blue Mill La CM9 | .....208 E4 |
| Blue Mills Hill CM8 | .....195 B7 |
| Blue Rd CO5 | .....179 C5 |
| Bluebell Ave CO16 | .....188 C4 |
| Bluebell Cl Ipswich IP2 | .......16 A7 |
| Witham CM8 | .....176 E3 |
| Bluebell Gn **5** CM1 | .....205 E7 |
| Bluebell Way CO4 | .....109 C2 |
| Bluebridge Cotts CO9 | .......77 A1 |
| Bluebridge Ind Est CO9 | .......77 A2 |
| Bluegate La IP9 | .......60 B7 |
| Bluehouse Ave CO16 | .....188 A4 |
| Bluestem Rd IP3 | .......38 E8 |
| Blundens The CO6 | .......56 C6 |
| Blunt's Hall Dr CM8 | .....176 D1 |
| Blunts Hall Rd CM8 | .....176 D1 |
| Blyford Rd CO16 | .....188 A4 |
| Blyford Way IP11 | .....221 A4 |
| Blyth Cl IP2 | .......17 A1 |
| Blyth's Mdw CM7 | .....127 F3 |
| Blyth's Way CM7 | .....126 F2 |
| Blythe La CO7 | .....164 B8 |
| Blythwood Gdns CM4 | .....119 D6 |
| Boadicea Cotts CO6 | .......79 F6 |
| Boadicea Way CO2 | .....135 C4 |
| Boars Tye Rd CM8 | .....156 D6 |
| Bobbits La IP9 | .......36 F8 |
| Bobbits Way CO7 | .....164 C8 |
| Bober Ct CO2 | .....163 B7 |
| Bocking Church Street | |
| Cty Prim Sch CM7 | .....127 F3 |
| Bocking End CM7 | .....127 F3 |
| Bocking's Gr CO16 | .....188 B5 |
| Bockings Elm Par CO16 | .....188 B5 |
| Bodiam Cl IP3 | .......18 A4 |
| Bodiam Rd IP3 | .......18 D4 |
| Bodiam Wlk **8** CB9 | .......8 E8 |
| Bodmin Rd CM1 | .....205 D5 |
| Bogmoor Rd SG8 | .......39 A8 |
| Bohun Cl CM3 | .....173 F7 |
| Bois Field Terr CO9 | .......76 E2 |
| Bois Hall Gdns CO9 | .......76 F3 |
| Boley Dr CO5 | .....189 A4 |
| Boley Rd CO6 | .....106 A8 |
| Boleyn Way Boreham CM3 | .....192 F1 |
| Clacton-on-S CO15 | .....203 F8 |
| Boleyns Ave CM7 | .....127 F6 |
| Bolford St CM6 | .....123 F3 |
| Bolingbroke Cl CM3 | .....173 F7 |
| Bolton La IP4 | .......17 D5 |
| Bonham Cl CO15 | .....189 C6 |
| Bonington Chase CM1 | .....205 E6 |
| Bonneting La CM23 | .......92 B8 |
| Bonnington Rd IP3 | .......17 F1 |
| Boone Pl CM8 | .....177 A2 |
| Booth Ave CO4 | .....136 C8 |
| Borda Cl CM1 | .....205 A5 |
| Boreham Cty Prim Sch | |
| CM3 | .....206 F8 |
| Boreham Ind Est CM3 | .....192 F2 |
| Boreham Rd | |
| Great Leighs CM3 | .....174 B7 |

| Boreham Rd *continued* | |
|---|---|
| Little Waltham CM3 | .....174 B2 |
| Borehamgate CO10 | .......33 F7 |
| Borley Rd CO8 | .......15 B4 |
| Borough La CB11 | .......43 D8 |
| Borradale Ct CB9 | .......27 B6 |
| Borrowdale Ave IP4 | .......17 E8 |
| Boscawen Gdns CM7 | .....128 C4 |
| Boscombe Ct CO15 | .....189 F6 |
| Boss Hall Bsns Pk IP1 | .......16 E7 |
| Boss Hall Rd IP1 | .......16 E7 |
| Bostock Rd IP1 | .......17 C1 |
| Boston Rd IP4 | .......17 F7 |
| Boswells Dr CM2 | .....205 C2 |
| Boswells Sch The CM1 | .....205 D6 |
| Botanical Way CO16 | .....187 A5 |
| Botany La CO16 | .....168 B5 |
| Bouchers Mead CM1 | .....205 F7 |
| Bouchiers Barn Visitors | |
| Ctr CO6 | .....130 D7 |
| Boudicca Wlk CO7 | .....137 C3 |
| Boulton Cotts CM9 | .....210 E5 |
| Boundary Rd | |
| Bishop's Stortford CM23 | .....146 A5 |
| Colchester CO4 | .....136 F4 |
| Sturmer CB9 | .......9 D1 |
| Wivenhoe CO7 | .....137 A4 |
| Bounderby Gr CM1 | .....204 E7 |
| Bounstead Hill CO2 | .....162 C5 |
| Bounstead Rd CO2 | .....162 D7 |
| Bourchier Ave CO9 | .....103 D8 |
| Bourchier Way CO9 | .....103 D8 |
| Bourne Ct CO9 | .....103 D8 |
| Bourne Ct CO2 | .....136 A4 |
| Bourne Hill IP2 | .......37 B7 |
| Bourne Mill CO2 | .....136 B4 |
| Bourne Rd Colchester CO2 | .....136 B4 |
| Haverhill CB9 | .......9 A8 |
| West Bergholt CO6 | .....108 E2 |
| Bourne The CM23 | .....146 A8 |
| Bournebridge Hill CO9 | .....103 B6 |
| Bournemouth Rd CO15 | .....189 F6 |
| Bouverie Rd CM2 | .....216 C7 |
| Bovills Way CO16 | .....168 C1 |
| Bovingdon Rd CM7 | .....101 D2 |
| Bowdens La CO6 | .......80 F7 |
| Bower Gdns CM9 | .....209 F3 |
| Bower Hall Dr CB9 | .......27 B6 |
| Bower Hall La CO5 | .....183 F1 |
| Bowers Cl CM8 | .....156 E3 |
| Bowes Rd CO7 | .....137 D1 |
| Bowland Dr IP8 | .......16 C1 |
| Bowling Cl **4** CM23 | .....145 F6 |
| Bowling Green Ct IP11 | .....221 E4 |
| Bowmans Pk CO9 | .......51 E4 |
| Bowsers La CB10 | .......5 C3 |
| Bowthorpe Cl IP1 | .......17 B7 |
| Box Mill La CO9 | .......76 E3 |
| Boxford Ct | |
| Felixstowe IP11 | .....221 A4 |
| Haverhill CB9 | .......9 B8 |
| Boxhouse La Dedham CO7 | .......84 C5 |
| Langham CO7 | .......84 B6 |
| Boxted Ave CO16 | .....188 C4 |
| Boxted CE Prim Sch CO4 | .......82 F7 |
| Boxted Church Rd CO6 | .......82 C7 |
| Boxted Rd Colchester CO4 | .......83 A5 |
| Great Horkesley CO6 | .......82 C3 |
| Boxted Straight Rd CO4 | .......83 A5 |
| Boyd Cl **8** CM23 | .....146 B8 |
| Boydell's Dairy Farm | |
| CM7 | .....100 E8 |
| Boydin Cl CM8 | .....194 E8 |
| Boydlands IP9 | .......35 A1 |
| Boyes Croft CM6 | .....123 D1 |
| Boyles Ct CO2 | .....163 B7 |
| Boyne Dr CM1 | .....205 D6 |
| Boyton Rd IP3 | .......18 B1 |
| Boyton's La CB10 | .......26 A1 |
| Bracken Way CO5 | .....163 B2 |
| Brackenbury Cl IP11 | .......17 B8 |
| Brackenden Dr CM1 | .....205 D7 |
| Brackenhayes Cl IP2 | .......16 E2 |
| Brackens The CO4 | .....110 B3 |
| Brackley Cl IP11 | .....221 C5 |
| Bracks La CO6 | .....131 F3 |
| Bradbrook Cotts CO6 | .....108 F4 |
| Bradbury Dr CM7 | .....127 D3 |
| Braddy Ct CO5 | .....184 A4 |
| Bradfield Cty Prim Sch | |
| CO11 | .......87 E1 |
| Bradfield Rd CO11 | .......61 A5 |
| Bradford St Braintree CM7 | .....128 A4 |
| Chelmsford CM2 | .....205 A1 |
| Bradfords Ct CM7 | .....128 A4 |
| Brading Ave CO15 | .....189 A7 |
| Bradley Cl CM6 | .....123 C2 |
| Bradley Comm CM23 | .....119 C3 |
| Bradley Mews **2** CB10 | .......22 F2 |
| Bradley St **17** IP7 | .......17 C4 |
| Bradwell Cr CM7 | .....155 C8 |
| Braemar Ave CM2 | .....216 B8 |
| Braemore Cl CO4 | .....110 D3 |
| Braggon's Hill IP29 | .......2 B4 |
| Brain Rd CM8 | .....176 E3 |
| Brain Valley Ave CM7 | .....155 B6 |
| Braintree Coll CM7 | .......75 F6 |
| Braintree Coll CM7 | .....128 A5 |
| Braintree Ent Ctr CM7 | .....127 D5 |
| Braintree Foyer The **3** | |
| CM7 | .....127 F2 |
| Braintree Rd | |
| Cressing CM7 | .....155 E7 |
| Felsted CM6 | .....152 C6 |
| Gosfield CO9 | .....102 E5 |
| Great Bardfield CM7 | .....72 B7 |
| Great Dunmow CM6 | .....124 A1 |
| Great Dunmow CM6 | .....123 F1 |

| Braintree Rd *continued* | |
|---|---|
| Shalford CM7 | .....100 E6 |
| Terling CM3 | .....174 E5 |
| Wethersfield CM7 | .......73 D2 |
| Cogeshall La CM6 | .....130 F1 |
| Finchingfield CM7 | .......72 C6 |
| Great Bardfield CM7 | .......72 B2 |
| Great Yeldham CO9 | .......30 A1 |
| Halstead CO9 | .......76 A2 |
| Ipswich IP1 | .......17 C4 |
| Saffron Walden CB10 | .......22 D2 |
| Witham CM8 | .....176 F1 |
| Wickham St Paul CO10 | .......31 C5 |
| Bramble Ave IP3 | .......18 E1 |
| Bramble La | |
| Great Dunlow CM6 | .....124 E1 |
| Little Dunmow CM6 | .....151 F8 |
| Bramble Rd CM8 | .....176 E4 |
| Brambledown CO5 | .....201 C7 |
| Brambles CO14 | .....171 B7 |
| Brambles The | |
| Bishop's Stortford CM23 | .....145 C6 |
| Colchester CO3 | .....134 F3 |
| Bramblewood **1** IP8 | .....116 C2 |
| Bramford La IP1 | .......16 F8 |
| Bramford Rd IP1 | .......16 E8 |
| Bramhall Cl IP2 | .......16 D1 |
| Bramley Chase IP4 | .......18 B7 |
| Bramley Cl Alresford CO7 | .....165 B8 |
| Braintree CM7 | .....128 A1 |
| Colchester CO3 | .....135 B7 |
| Bramleys The CO6 | .....131 A3 |
| Bramston Cl CM2 | .....216 F8 |
| Bramston Gn CM8 | .....176 F4 |
| Bramston Sports Ctr | |
| CM8 | .....176 F1 |
| Bramston Wlk CM8 | .....176 F4 |
| Bramwoods Rd CM2 | .....216 E8 |
| Bran End Fields CM6 | .....124 F7 |
| Brand Ct CM7 | .....127 F7 |
| Brand Dr CO5 | .....163 B3 |
| Brandon Rd | |
| Braintree CM7 | .....127 D2 |
| Felixstowe IP11 | .....221 A4 |
| Brands Cl CO10 | .......34 C5 |
| Bransby Gdns IP4 | .......17 E7 |
| Branscombe Cl CO13 | .....170 E5 |
| Branston Ct CO16 | .....188 C4 |
| Branston Rd CO15 | .....188 D3 |
| Brantham Hill CO11 | .......86 C8 |
| Brantham Mill Ind Est | |
| CO11 | .......86 B7 |
| Braxted La | |
| Great Braxted CM8 | .....178 C1 |
| Great Totham CM9 | .....196 D8 |
| Braxted Rd Tiptree CO5 | .....178 E2 |
| Wickham Bishops CM8 | .....196 A6 |
| Brazier's Wood Rd IP3 | .......38 B8 |
| Braziers Cl CM2 | .....216 C3 |
| Braziers Quay CM23 | .....146 A6 |
| Breach La CM6 | .......97 B2 |
| Breachfield Rd CO2 | .....135 C2 |
| Brecon Cl IP2 | .......17 B2 |
| Bredfield Cl IP11 | .....221 B5 |
| Bree Ave CO4 | .....132 E3 |
| Brendon Dr IP5 | .......18 F6 |
| Brendon Pl CM1 | .....204 E1 |
| Brent Cl Frinton-on-S CO13 | .....170 F7 |
| Witham CM8 | .....176 E2 |
| Brent Hall Rd CM7 | .......72 B6 |
| Brentwood Rd CO15 | .....189 C6 |
| Bretten Cl CO16 | .....188 A4 |
| Brettenham Cres CM7 | .....17 D8 |
| Bretts Cotts CM8 | .....178 F3 |
| Brewers Cl CM23 | .....145 C5 |
| Brewery Chapel Mus CO9 | .......76 D2 |
| Brewery Cres CM7 | .....217 A5 |
| Brewery La CM23 | .....119 C2 |
| Brewery Yd CM23 | .....119 F7 |
| Brian Bishop Cl CO14 | .....171 B8 |
| Brian Cl CM2 | .....216 B6 |
| Briar Rd CO7 | .....112 B4 |
| Briardale Ave CO12 | .......90 F3 |
| Briarfields CO13 | .....170 C8 |
| Briarhayes Cl IP2 | .......17 B3 |
| Briarsford Ind Est CM8 | .....177 B1 |
| Briarswood CM5 | .....205 D7 |
| Briarwood End CO4 | .....110 B3 |
| Brices Way CO10 | .......2 B5 |
| Brick Cotts IP9 | .......62 F4 |
| Brick End Villas CM6 | .....121 E8 |
| Brick House La CM3 | .....192 E1 |
| Brick House Rd CM7 | .....197 B7 |
| Brick Kiln Cl CO6 | .....131 A3 |
| Brick Kiln La | |
| Rickling Green CB11 | .......66 D1 |
| Stebbing CM6 | .....124 D7 |
| Thorrington CO7 | .....165 E5 |
| Brick Kiln Rd | |
| Colchester CO1 | .....109 E1 |
| Great Horkesley CO6 | .....109 C7 |
| Harkstead IP9 | .......63 C5 |
| Sandon CM2 | .....217 B3 |
| Brick Kiln Way CM7 | .....128 D2 |
| Brick Row SG8 | .......19 D3 |
| Brick St CO3 | .....108 B1 |
| Brickburn Cl CM6 | .....152 C4 |
| Brickfield Cl IP2 | .......17 D3 |
| Brickhouse Cl CO5 | .....158 E4 |
| Brickhouse Rd CO6 | .......78 A3 |
| Brickmakers La CO4 | .....109 F2 |
| Brickmarsh's Hill CO11 | .......87 D3 |
| Brickspring La CM9 | .....196 D7 |
| Brickway Ct CO6 | .....105 B6 |
| Bridewell St CO10 | .......12 C8 |
| Bridge Cotts CO10 | .......1 D2 |
| Bridge Croft CM7 | .....172 F2 |
| Bridge Foot CO10 | .......33 D6 |
| Bridge Hall Rd CM7 | .....129 C3 |
| Bridge Hill CO6 | .....107 C7 |
| Bridge Hospl CM1 | .....176 F1 |

| Bridge Rd IP11 | .....221 E5 |
|---|---|
| Bridge St | |
| Bishop's Stortford CM23 | .....145 F7 |
| Bures CO8 | .......55 F1 |
| Coggeshall CO6 | .....130 F1 |
| Finchingfield CM7 | .......72 C6 |
| Great Bardfield CM7 | .......72 B2 |
| Great Yeldham CO9 | .......30 A1 |
| Halstead CO9 | .......76 A2 |
| Ipswich IP1 | .......17 C4 |
| Saffron Walden CB10 | .......22 D2 |
| Witham CM8 | .....176 F1 |
| Wickham St Paul CO10 | .......31 C5 |
| Bridge Terr CO10 | .......33 F8 |
| Bridgebrook Cl CO4 | .....110 D1 |
| Bridgefield Cl CO4 | .....136 C7 |
| Bridgeford Ho **13** CM23 | .....145 F6 |
| Bridgwater Rd IP2 | .......16 D2 |
| Bridewalk CO3 | .....134 D6 |
| Bridport Ave IP3 | .......18 D3 |
| Bridport Rd CM1 | .....205 D5 |
| Bridport Way CM7 | .....128 D4 |
| Brierley Ave CO5 | .....201 E7 |
| Bright Cl CO16 | .....188 D6 |
| Brightlingsea Cty Inf | |
| Sch CO7 | .....136 F4 |
| Brightlingsea Cty Inf | |
| Sch CO7 | .....185 E6 |
| Brightlingsea Cty Jun | |
| Sch CO7 | .....185 E6 |
| Brightlingsea Rd | |
| Thorrington CO7 | .....165 E3 |
| Wivenhoe CO7 | .....137 C4 |
| Brighton Rd CO15 | .....189 F6 |
| Brightside CO13 | .....170 E7 |
| Brightwell Cl IP11 | .....221 A5 |
| Brimstone Ct CM7 | .....154 E8 |
| Brimstone Rd IP8 | .......36 E8 |
| Brindley Rd CO15 | .....189 B8 |
| Bringey The CM2 | .....217 A6 |
| Brinkley Cres CO4 | .....110 D2 |
| Brinkley Grove Prim Sch | |
| CO4 | .....110 B5 |
| Brinkley Grove Rd CO4 | .....110 A5 |
| Brinkley La CO4 | .....110 B5 |
| Brinkley Pl CO4 | .....109 F3 |
| Brisbane Rd IP4 | .......18 D6 |
| Brisbane Way CO2 | .....136 A1 |
| Brise Cl CM7 | .....128 A1 |
| Bristol Cl CM8 | .....156 E3 |
| Bristol Hill IP9 | .......91 B8 |
| Bristol Rd Colchester CO1 | .....136 A8 |
| Ipswich IP4 | .......18 A7 |
| Bristowe Ave CM7 | .....217 A6 |
| Britannia Cres CO7 | .....137 B1 |
| Britannia Ct CO7 | .....137 B1 |
| Britannia Pl **3** CM23 | .....145 E5 |
| Britannia Rd IP4 | .......18 B6 |
| Britannia Cty Prim Sch | |
| IP4 | .......18 B5 |
| Brittany Way CO2 | .....136 B4 |
| Britten Cl CO4 | .....136 E6 |
| Britten Cres CM7 | .....216 F8 |
| Brixham Cl CM1 | .....205 A5 |
| Brixton La CB11 | .......93 B6 |
| Broad La CO6 | .......82 C2 |
| Broad Meadow **3** IP8 | .......16 C2 |
| Broad Oaks Cl CO10 | .......44 E2 |
| Broad Oaks Pk CO14 | .....110 E3 |
| Broad Oak CM6 | .......17 B6 |
| Broad Rd Braintree CM7 | .....128 B7 |
| Wickham St P CO9 | .......53 B8 |
| Broad St CB9 | .......8 E8 |
| Broad Street Green Rd | |
| Great Totham CM9 | .....196 B1 |
| Heybridge CM9 | .....210 C7 |
| Broadcroft Cres CB9 | .......9 F8 |
| Broadfield CM23 | .....118 F2 |
| Broadfield Rd CM2 | .....148 C7 |
| Broadfields CO7 | .....137 C3 |
| Broadlands CO13 | .....170 E3 |
| Broadlands Way | |
| Colchester CO4 | .....110 B1 |
| Rushmere St A IP4 | .......18 F5 |
| Broadleaf Ave CM23 | .....145 D4 |
| Broadmead Rd CO4 | .....110 E1 |
| Broadmere Cl CO15 | .....189 E7 |
| Broadmere Rd IP1 | .......16 E8 |
| Broadoaks Cres CM7 | .....128 D4 |
| Broadstrood CO16 | .....187 B5 |
| Broadwater Gdns IP9 | .......91 A8 |
| Broadway | |
| Clacton-on-S CO15 | .....203 G7 |
| Glemsford CO10 | .......2 B5 |
| Silver End CM8 | .....156 D4 |
| Broadway Cl CM8 | .....156 D5 |
| Broadway The CM6 | .....123 F3 |
| Brock Cl CM8 | .....194 E8 |
| Brockenhurst Way CM3 | .....218 F1 |
| Brockham Cl CO16 | .....188 B6 |
| Brockley Cres IP1 | .......16 D8 |
| Brockley Rd CM2 | .....205 D2 |
| Brocks Mead CM6 | .....122 E7 |
| Brockwell La CO5 | .....158 C1 |
| Brograve Cl CM2 | .....216 D3 |
| Broke Hall Gdns IP3 | .......18 E4 |
| Broke Hall Prim Sch IP3 | .......18 E5 |
| Broman's La CO5 | .....185 A2 |
| Bromfield CB11 | .......43 E8 |
| Bromley Cl IP2 | .......17 C3 |
| Bromley Cnr CO11 | .......86 A2 |
| Bromley La CB11 | .......43 B1 |
| Bromley Rd | |
| Colchester CO7, CO4 | .....111 C2 |
| Elmstead CO7 | .....138 B5 |
| Frating CO7 | .....139 A4 |
| Lawford CO11 | .......86 B2 |
| Brompton Gdns CM9 | .....220 E8 |
| Bronte Cl CM7 | .....155 A8 |

| | |
|---|---|
| Bla–Bro | **225** |
| Bronte Rd CM8 | .....176 F5 |
| Brook Cl Braintree CM7 | .....127 C2 |
| Great Totham CM9 | .....196 A3 |
| Tiptree CO5 | .....179 F3 |
| Woodham Walter CM9 | .....208 D2 |
| Brook Cotts Boxted CO4 | .......82 E5 |
| Stansted | |
| Mountfitchet CM24 | .....119 E5 |
| Brook End Rd | |
| Chelmsford CM2 | .....206 A4 |
| Chelmsford CM2 | .....206 B2 |
| Brook Farm Cl CM7 | .....127 F4 |
| Brook Farm La IP9 | .......62 D6 |
| Brook Hall Rd CO5 | .....164 B5 |
| Brook Hill | |
| Little Waltham CM3 | .....191 B6 |
| North End CM6 | .....151 F1 |
| Brook La Chelmsford CM2 | .....206 B2 |
| Felixstowe IP11 | .....221 F5 |
| Galleywood CM2 | .....216 E3 |
| Brook Mdw CO9 | .......51 D1 |
| Brook Mead CM3 | .....190 E8 |
| Brook Meadows CO5 | .....179 C4 |
| Brook Rd Aldham CO6 | .....133 B7 |
| Great Tey CO6 | .....132 C7 |
| Stansted | |
| Mountfitchet CM24 | .....119 E6 |
| Tiptree CO5 | .....179 F3 |
| Tolleshunt Knights CO5 | .....180 A2 |
| Brook Service Rd CB9 | .......9 A7 |
| Brook St Chelmsford CM1 | .....205 B3 |
| Colchester CO1 | .....136 B7 |
| Colne Engaine CO6 | .......77 F1 |
| Glemsford CO10 | .......84 F7 |
| Glemsford CO10 | .......2 B6 |
| Great Bardfield CM7 | .......72 B2 |
| Great Bromley CO7 | .....112 C1 |
| Little Dunmow CM6 | .......86 D4 |
| Manningtree CO11 | .......86 D4 |
| Wivenhoe CO7 | .....164 C8 |
| Brook Terr CO9 | .......51 E1 |
| Brook Vale CO16 | .....187 B3 |
| Brook View Sandon CM2 | .....217 C6 |
| Thaxted CM6 | .......70 A3 |
| Brook Wlk CM8 | .....194 F8 |
| Brookbank CO4 | .....216 E8 |
| Brooke Ave CO10 | .......22 E2 |
| Brooke Gdns CM23 | .....146 C7 |
| Brooke Sq CM9 | .....210 A1 |
| Brookes Nature | |
| Reserve CM7 | .....103 E2 |
| Brookfield Rd IP1 | .......16 F8 |
| Brookfields CM6 | .....124 D7 |
| Brookhampton St CO10 | .......3 A5 |
| Brookhill Way IP4 | .......18 F4 |
| Brookhouse Bsns Pk IP2 | .......16 F1 |
| Brookhouse Pl **3** CM23 | .....145 F8 |
| Brookhouse Rd CO6 | .....132 B8 |
| Brookhurst Cl CM2 | .....205 D3 |
| Brookland CO5 | .....179 C4 |
| Brooklands | |
| Clacton-on-S CO15 | .....203 E6 |
| Colchester CO1 | .....136 B7 |
| Brooklands Cty Prim Sch | |
| CM7 | .......86 D8 |
| Brooklands Gdns CO15 | .....203 E6 |
| Brooklands Rd CO11 | .......86 D8 |
| Brooklands Rise CO11 | .......86 D8 |
| Brooklands Wlk CM2 | .....216 A7 |
| Brooklyn Ct CO15 | .......91 C3 |
| Brooklyn Mews CO12 | .......91 C3 |
| Brooklyn Rd CO12 | .......91 C3 |
| Brooks Hall Rd IP1 | .......17 A7 |
| Brooks Maltings **3** CO11 | .......86 D4 |
| Brooksdale CO6 | .....136 B4 |
| Brooksies CO12 | .......36 E8 |
| Brookview IP2 | .......36 E8 |
| Broom Cres IP3 | .......17 F1 |
| Broom Farm Rd CM2 | .....204 C2 |
| Broom Field IP11 | .....221 C5 |
| Broom Hill Rd IP1 | .......17 A8 |
| Broom Knoll CO7 | .......60 C2 |
| Broom St CO10 | .......34 B5 |
| Broom Way Abberton CO5 | .....163 B2 |
| Capel St M IP9 | .......35 B2 |
| Broomedown Villas CM7 | .....100 E5 |
| Broome Gr CO7 | .....137 B2 |
| Broome Way CO15 | .....203 F6 |
| Broomfield CM8 | .....156 C5 |
| Broomfield Comm IP8 | .......16 C2 |
| Broomfield Cres CO7 | .....137 B2 |
| Broomfield Hospl CM1 | .....191 A3 |
| Broomfield Prim Sch | |
| CM1 | .....191 B1 |
| Broomfield Rd CM1 | .....205 A5 |
| Broomhall Cl CM1 | .....191 B2 |
| Broomhall Rd CM1 | .....191 B2 |
| Broomhayes IP2 | .......17 A2 |
| Broomhills Ind Est CM7 | .....127 D2 |
| Broomhills Rd CO15 | .....203 D5 |
| Brotherton Ave CO11 | .......21 A5 |
| Broton Dr CO9 | .......76 E2 |
| Brougham Glades CO3 | .....134 D5 |
| Broughton Cl CO2 | .....135 C4 |
| Broughton Rd IP1 | .......17 B7 |
| Brown's End Rd CM7 | .....121 F7 |
| Browning Cl CO3 | .....134 F6 |
| Browning Rd | |
| Braintree CM7 | .....155 A8 |
| Brantham CO11 | .......86 C7 |
| Brownings Ave CM1 | .....205 A5 |
| Brownlow Rd IP11 | .....221 F4 |
| Brownsea Way CO3 | .....135 A4 |

Bruce Gr CM7 ....216 A7
Bruce Rd CM1 ....204 B1
Bruff Cl CO4 ....109 E2
Bruff Dr CO14 ....171 A7
Brundells Rd CO7 ....139 A5
Brundon La CO10 ....33 C7
Brunel Cl CO4 ....110 C6
Brunel Rd Braintree CM7 ....128 A1
  Clacton-on-S CO15 ....189 B8
  Ipswich IP2 ....16 F6
Brunel Way CO4 ....110 C6
Brunswick House Cut
  CO11 ....87 A3
Brunswick Rd IP4 ....17 F8
Brunwin Rd CM7 ....126 F2
Brussels Cl CO12 ....91 B1
Bryan Rd CM3 ....145 F8
Bryanstone Mews CO3 ....134 E5
Bryant's La CM9 ....219 D7
Bryon Ave IP11 ....221 A2
Buchan Cl CM7 ....155 A8
Buck Hill CM7 ....154 F6
Buck's Horns La IP8 ....36 B6
Buckenhoe Rd CO10 ....22 E3
Buckfast Ave CO13 ....170 D6
Buckfast Cl 5 IP2 ....17 A2
Buckingham Ct 2 CM2 ....205 F4
Buckingham Dr CO4 ....136 E7
Buckingham Rd CB9 ....8 E6
Bucklesham Rd IP3 ....18 E2
Buckley's La CO6 ....131 E6
Bucks Cl CM7 ....155 A7
Buckleys Cl CM8 ....195 E5
Bucks La CO10 ....12 B7
Buckwoods Rd CM7 ....128 A1
Buddleia Cl IP2 ....16 E4
Buddleia Cl CO2 ....137 A2
Buffett Way CO4 ....136 E8
Buglers Rise CM1 ....215 B8
Buick Ave CO15 ....203 D6
Building End Rd
  Chrishall SG8 ....19 C1
  Duddenhoe End SG8 ....40 B7
  Duddenhoe End SG8 ....40 B8
Bulford La CM7 ....155 C5
Bulford Mill La CM7 ....155 D5
Bull Hill Rd CO15 ....188 F5
Bull La Langley CB11 ....42 D8
  Long Melford CO10 ....15 E8
  Long Melford CO10 ....15 F8
  Maldon CM9 ....210 A3
  Tiptree CO5 ....179 C3
Bull's Hill CO9 ....51 E4
Bullace Cl CO14 ....110 D3
Bullen Wlk CM2 ....216 C3
Bullfields CB11 ....67 A8
Bullfinch Cl CO4 ....136 F8
Bullock Wood Cl CO4 ....110 D4
Bullocks La CO10 ....33 E6
Bulls Cliff IP11 ....221 D3
Bulls Lodge Cotts CM3 ....192 B1
Bulmer Rd CO10 ....33 C6
Bulmer Road Ind Est CO10 ....33 C6
Bulmer St CO10 ....32 D4
Bulstrode Rd IP2 ....17 D4
Bulwer Rd IP1 ....17 A6
Bumfords La CM3 CM9 ....208 A7
Bumpstead Rd CM9 ....
Bundick's Hill CM1 ....204 F3
Bung Row CM8 ....178 C1
Bungalows The CM6 ....176 F1
Bunting Cl CM2 ....216 B5
Bunting Rd IP2 ....16 D3
Buntingford Ct 2 CO2 ....136 A1
Bunyan Rd CM7 ....127 E5
Burdun Cl CM8 ....194 D8
Bure Dr CM8 ....176 D3
Buregate Rd IP11 ....221 D2
Bures CE Prim Sch CO6 ....79 F8
Bures Hl 11 CB9 ....9 E7
Bures Ho CO6 ....79 F8
Bures Rd
  Great Cornard CO10 ....34 B3
  Nayland CO6 ....81 B8
Bures Sta CO6 ....79 F8
Burgate Cl CO16 ....188 A4
Burgess Field CM2 ....205 F4
Burghley Ave CM23 ....145 C7
Burghley Cl
  Great Notley CM7 ....154 B6
  4 Ipswich IP2 ....17 A2
Burgundy Ct CM2 ....205 C2
Burkitts Ct 8 CO10 ....33 E7
Burkitts La CO10 ....33 E7
Burley Rd CM23 ....146 A4
Burlington Ho IP2 ....17 B4
Burlington Rd
  Colchester CO3 ....135 E6
  Ipswich IP1 ....17 B4
Burmanny Cl CO15 ....188 C3
Burnells Way CM24 ....119 E7
Burnham Cl Ipswich IP4 ....17 F7
  Trimley St M IP11 ....221 A7
  Walton-on-N CO14 ....171 B8
Burnham Rd
  Chelmsford CM1 ....205 D5
  Woodham Mortimer
  CM9, CM3 ....219 E5
Burns Ave CO3 ....134 F6
Burns Cl CM9 ....210 A1
Burns Cres CM2 ....216 C8
Burnsall Cl CB11 ....43 F8
Burnside Cres CM1 ....205 B2
Burnstie Rd CM6 ....152 F6
Burnt Dick Hill CO4 ....82 D7

Burnt Oak Cnr CO7 ....59 D1
Burnthouse Rd CO6 ....105 E2
Burrell Rd IP2 ....17 C4
Burrell Rd IP2 ....
Burroughs Piece Rd CO10 ....33 F7
Burrows Cl
  Clacton-on-S CO16 ....188 D6
  Lawford CO11 ....86 B4
Burrows Rd CO6 ....105 B7
Burrs Rd CO15 ....189 A7
Burrsville Cty Jun & Inf
  Schs CO15 ....188 F6
Burrswood Pl CM9 ....210 E3
Burstall Cl CO16 ....188 B4
Burstall La IP8 ....16 A6
Burton End CB9 ....8 E7
Burton End CB9 ....8 E7
Burton End Cty Prim Sch
  CB9 ....8 D7
Burton Pl CM2 ....205 F4
Burton's Green Rd CO9 ....104 B4
Burwood Ct CM2 ....205 C1
Bury Cl Colchester CO1 ....136 A8
  Marks Tey CO6 ....132 F4
Bury Fields CM6 ....152 A5
Bury La Chrishall SG8 ....19 D1
  Great Waltham CM3 ....190 D8
  Hatfield Peverel CM3 ....193 F4
  Howe Street CM3 ....172 D1
Bury Lodge La
  Great Hallingbury CM22 ....147 C7
  Stansted
  Mountfitchet CM24 ....120 A2
Bury The CO16 ....187 A4
Bury Water La CB11 ....42 E1
Burywater Cotts CB11 ....42 F1
Burywoods CO4 ....109 B3
Bush Gr CO10 ....33 C6
Bush La CB10 ....46 A8
Bush Rd CB10 ....46 E2
Bushell Way CO13 ....170 E6
Bushey Cl IP9 ....35 A1
Butcher Row CB10 ....22 D1
Butcher's View CO5 ....182 E6
Butchers La Capel St M IP9 ....35 E1
  Walton-on-N CO14 ....171 B7
Butchers Pasture CM6 ....122 F5
Butchers Row CO2 ....22 D1
Bute Ct CB9 ....8 F6
Butler Cl CB11 ....42 E7
Butler Rd CO9 ....76 D2
Butler's La CO11 ....88 E1
Butlers Cl CM1 ....191 B2
Butlers La CB10 ....23 C5
Butlers Way CO9 ....30 A1
Butley Cl IP2 ....36 F8
Butley Rd IP11 ....221 C3
Butley Rd IP11 ....
Butt La Maldon CM9 ....210 A3
  Manuden CM23 ....92 E2
Butt Rd Colchester CO2 ....135 E5
  Great Cornard CO10 ....34 B6
  Stoke-by-N CO6 ....56 C5
Butt's Green Rd CM2 ....217 F3
Butter Market IP1 ....17 C6
Buttercup Cl IP8 ....16 C2
Buttercup Wlk CM8 ....176 E4
Butterfield Rd CM3 ....206 E8
Butterfly Gdns IP4 ....18 E5
Buttermarket Sh Ctr 3
  IP1 ....17 C5
Buttermere CM7 ....154 C7
Buttleys La CM6 ....149 F8
Butts La CM3 ....218 F7
Butts Way CM2 ....205 C1
Buxey Cl CO5 ....201 B7
Buxton Rd Coggeshall CO6 ....130 F3
  Colchester CO2 ....136 A3
Bylam La IP9 ....63 C6
Byland Cl IP2 ....17 A2
Bylands Cl CM23 ....145 D6
Byng Cres CO16 ....142 B1
Byng Cl CO2 ....136 A1
Byng Gdns CM7 ....128 C4
Byng Ho CO16 ....142 B1
Bypass Rd CO16 ....187 B5
Byrd's Farm La CB10 ....22 E3
Byron Ave CO3 ....134 F7
Byron Cl CM7 ....155 A8
Byron Dr CM8 ....195 E5
Byron Rd CM2 ....205 D2
Byrony Cl CM8 ....176 D4

**C**

Cadenhouse Mews CO3 ....134 C7
Caernarvon Wlk CB9 ....8 E8
Cage La Boxted CO4 ....83 E4
  Felixstowe IP11 ....221 D5
Cairns Rd CO2 ....136 B2
Caithness Cl IP4 ....18 B8
Calamint Rd CM8 ....176 D3
Caldbeck Way CM7 ....154 C6
Caledonia Rd IP9 ....91 B8
California Cl CO4 ....110 B4
California Rd CO11 ....87 A4
Callis Ct CO10 ....12 C8
Callis St CO10 ....12 B8
Callowood Croft CM3 ....202 D1
Calverley Cl CM23 ....145 E4
Calves La CO8 ....56 B8
Cam Way CM8 ....176 D2
Camberley Rd IP4 ....18 D7
Camberton Rd CM7 ....127 F2
Camborne Cl CM1 ....205 E5
Cambrai Rd CO2 ....135 D4

Cambria Cl CO11 ....87 B3
Cambridge Ave CO9 ....75 E8
Cambridge Ct
  Clacton-on-S CO15 ....188 E4
  Frinton-on-S CO13 ....171 A5
Cambridge Dr IP2 ....16 F1
Cambridge Rd
  Clacton-on-S CO15 ....188 E4
  Colchester CO3 ....135 C8
  Felixstowe IP11 ....221 F4
  Frinton-on-S CO13 ....171 A5
  Littlebury CB11 ....21 F4
  Newport CB11 ....43 A2
  Stansted
  Mountfitchet CM24 ....119 E8
Cambridge Way CO8 ....79 F8
Camden Rd IP3 ....18 B4
Camellia Ave CO16 ....188 C4
Camellia Cl CM1 ....205 F6
Camellia Ct CO16 ....188 C5
Camellia Ct 2 CM1 ....136 D8
Camelot Cl CM1 ....204 F5
Cameron Cl CO10 ....15 C6
Camoise Cl CO9 ....50 B7
Camomile Way CO4 ....109 C2
Camp Rd CO7 ....139 A7
Campbell Cl CM2 ....216 A7
Campbell Ct CO3 ....135 D6
Campbell Dr CO4 ....110 E2
Campbell Rd Ipswich IP3 ....18 C1
  Witham CM8 ....176 F5
Campernell Cl CO7 ....185 F8
Campion Rd
  Colchester CO3 ....136 A5
  Ipswich IP2 ....16 F4
Campion Way CM8 ....176 E3
Campions Hill CO6 ....81 D8
Campions The CM24 ....119 E8
Camps Rd Bartlow CB1 ....6 B7
  Haverhill CB9 ....8 F7
  Helions Bumpstead CB9 ....8 A1
Camulodunum Way CO2 ....135 C1
Camulus Cl CO2 ....135 A2
Camwood Gdns CO1 ....18 B4
Can Bridge Way CM2 ....205 C1
Canberra Cl
  Chelmsford CM1 ....204 E5
  9 Colchester CO2 ....136 A1
  Ipswich IP4 ....18 D6
Candlet Gr IP11 ....221 D5
Candlet Rd IP11 ....221 D6
Candytuft Rd CM1 ....205 F6
Canes Mill Ct CM7 ....128 A5
Canfield CM23 ....145 E8
Canfield Rd CM6 ....149 D1
Canford Cl CM2 ....216 E7
Canham Cl CM7 ....17 B6
Canhams Rd CO10 ....34 C5
Cann Hall Cty Prim Sch
  CO16 ....188 D6
Canning St CO12 ....91 D5
Cannock Mill Ct CO2 ....136 C4
Cannon Circ CM7 ....73 D6
Cannon Leys CM3 ....216 D3
Cannon Rd CO1 ....136 B6
Cannon St CO1 ....136 B6
Cannons Cl
  Bishop's Stortford CM23 ....119 A1
  Colchester CO2 ....135 D4
Cannons Mead CM24 ....119 D7
Cannons The CO10 ....135 D4
Canons Cl CM3 ....219 E1
Cansey La CO11 ....114 E6
Cant Way CM7 ....128 C1
Canterbury Cl IP2 ....36 F8
Canterbury Grange CM7 ....127 F8
Canterbury Rd
  Colchester CO2 ....136 A5
  Holland-on-S CO15 ....189 E5
  Sudbury CO10 ....15 C2
Canterbury Way CM1 ....204 E4
Canuden Rd CM1 ....204 E2
Canvey Wlk CM1 ....205 F6
Canwick Gr CO2 ....136 C4
Cap Pillar Cl CO7 ....137 B2
Capel Cl CO3 ....134 F5
Capel Cl Chelmsford CM1 ....205 B7
  Rayne CM7 ....126 F2
Capel Dr IP11 ....221 A4
Capel Pk CO13 ....170 E7
Capel St Mary CE Prim
  Sch IP9 ....35 A1
Caper La CO2 ....160 F4
Capons La CM3 ....219 A5
Captains Rd CO5 ....201 B6
Captains Wood Rd CM9 ....196 A3
Card's Rd CM2 ....217 D6
Cardiff Ave IP2 ....17 B2
Cardigan St IP1 ....17 B7
Cardinal Cl CO4 ....137 A7
Cardinal St IP1 ....17 C5
Cardinals Ct IP11 ....221 E3
Carisbrooke Ave CO15 ....189 A7
Carlisle Cl CO1 ....136 A8
Carlton Cl CO4 ....30 A2
Carlton Rd CO15 ....189 B5
Carlton Way IP11 ....17 E8
Carmarthen Cl IP2 ....17 A2
Carmel St CB10 ....3 D2
Carmelite Way CM9 ....209 F2
Carmen St CB10 ....3 D3
Carnarvon Rd CO15 ....188 F3
Carnation Cl CM1 ....205 F5
Carnation Dr CB10 ....22 E2
Carolbrook Rd IP2 ....16 E1

Carolina Way CO5 ....179 D5
Caroline Cl CO7 ....137 C3
Carpenters The CM23 ....145 B5
Carr St IP4 ....17 D6
Carraways CM6 ....195 B8
Carriage Cl IP11 ....221 A8
Carriage Dr CM1 ....205 E7
Carriers Cl CO6 ....201 A7
Carrigans CM23 ....145 E8
Carrington Ct CO5 ....201 D7
Carrington Ho CO5 ....201 D7
Carrington Way CM7 ....127 F8
Carringtons Rd CO7 ....112 D4
Carrs Rd CO15 ....188 D3
Carsey Hill CM1 ....7 B6
Carshalton End CO10 ....134 F4
Carsons Dr CO10 ....34 D5
Carstone Pl CM1 ....204 F2
Cartbridge Cl CO14 ....171 B8
Carters Cl CO16 ....188 B3
Carters Croft CO15 ....6 B1
Carters Hill Boxted CO4 ....83 A6
  Manuden CM23 ....93 A1
Carters La Henham CM22 ....94 F5
  Wickham Bishops CM8 ....195 F6
Carters Leys CM23 ....145 D8
Cartwright Wlk CM7 ....205 F2
Case La IP9 ....60 D7
Cassino Rd
  Chelmsford CM1 ....204 E6
  Colchester CO2 ....135 C3
Castle Ave CB9 ....
Castle Bailey 6 CO1 ....135 F7
Castle Camps Prim Sch
  CB1 ....7 E3
Castle Cl
  Castle Hedingham CO9 ....51 E4
  Great Leighs CM3 ....173 F6
Castle Cross CB10 ....22 E2
Castle Ct CO15 ....188 E3
Castle Hill Dedham CO7 ....84 F4
  Saffron Walden CB10 ....22 D2
Castle Hill Mid Sch CB9 ....8 D8
Castle Hill Pk CO16 ....188 E7
Castle House CO7 ....85 A5
Castle La
  Castle Hedingham CO9 ....51 F4
  Haverhill CB9 ....
Castle Manor Upper Sch
  CB9 ....8 E8
Castle Mdw CO9 ....51 D2
Castle Rd
Castle Wlk CM23 ....146 A7
Castle Way CO16 ....187 A4
Castle Wlk Haverhill CB9 ....8 E7
  Stansted
  Mountfitchet CM24 ....119 E6
Castlegate St CO12 ....91 D4
Castleward Cl CO7 ....164 C8
Caswell Mews CM2 ....205 F2
Cat's La CO10 ....34 A7
Catchpole Cl 12 CO10 ....33 E7
Catchpole La CM9 ....196 A4
Catchpool Rd CO1 ....135 F8
Caterham Cl CO16 ....188 C6
Cates Cnr CB10 ....22 E1
Cathedral Sch The CM1 ....205 C3
Cathedral Wlk CM1 ....205 B3
Catherine Cl CO15 ....189 A5
Catherine Hunt Way CO2 ....135 C2
Catherine May Ct CO15 ....188 F3
Catherines Cl CM3 ....174 A6
Catons La CB10 ....22 D2
Cattawade St CO11 ....86 C7
Cattermole Cl CO16 ....188 B3
Catts Cl IP9 ....61 F2
Cattsfield IP9 ....61 F2
Cauldwell Ave IP4 ....17 F7
Cauldwell Hall Rd IP4 ....18 A6
Causeway CM23 ....152 F1
Causeway Cl CO10 ....15 D2
Causeway End CO11 ....86 B5
Causeway End Rd CM6 ....152 C3
Causeway Reach CO15 ....188 D7
Causeway The
  1 Bishop's Stortford CM23 ....146 A7
  Braintree CM7 ....127 F4
  Colchester CO4 ....110 C1
  Finchingfield CM7 ....72 D6
  Great Baddow CM2 ....216 F7
  Great Leighs CM3 ....123 D2
  Great Horkesley CO6 ....82 B2
  Halstead CO9 ....76 E1
  Harkstead SG9 ....64 B1
  Haverhill CB9 ....8 E7
Cavendish Dr
  Clacton-on-S CO16 ....188 A4
  Lawford CO11 ....86 B3
Cavendish Gdns
  Braintree CM7 ....128 C5

Cavendish Gdns cor...
  Chelmsford CM2 ....
Cavendish La CO10 ....
Cavendish Prim Sch C...
Cavendish Rd Clare CO10 ...
  Felixstowe IP11 ....
Cavendish St IP3 ....
Cavendish Way CO10 ....
Cawkell Cl CM24 ....
Cawkell Cl CM2 ....
Caxton Cl CO4 ....
Cecil Cl CM23 ....14(
Cecil Rd IP1 ....17 (
Cecilia St IP1 ....17 (
Cedar Ave
  Brightlingsea CO7 ....185 E7
  Chelmsford CM1 ....205 A3
  Tiptree CO5 ....179 C7
Cedar Ave W CM1 ....205 A3
Cedar Chase CM9 ....210 C5
Cedar Cl Brantham CO11 ....60 E8
  Great Dunmow CM6 ....123 A1
  Walton-on-t-N CO14 ....171 A7
Cedar Cres CO11 ....86 C3
Cedar Ct
  Bishop's Stortford CM23 ....118 F1
  West Bergholt CO6 ....108 D5
Cedar Dr CM8 ....177 A5
Cedar Pk CM23 ....145 C4
Cedar Way CO7 ....166 E8
Cedar Rd CO2 ....135 F6
Cedars The CO9 ....102 E7
Celandine Ct CO4 ....109 C2
Cemetery La
  East Bergholt CO7 ....59 B2
  Ipswich IP4 ....17 E8
Cemetery Rd
  Bishop's Stortford CM23 ....145 F6
  Ipswich IP4 ....17 E6
Centaury Cl CO3 ....134 C7
Centenary
  Way CO15, CO16 ....168 E1
Central Arc CB10 ....22 D1
Central Ave
  Frinton-on-S CO13 ....171 A6
  Ipswich IP3 ....38 E8
Central Ho CO12 ....91 D4
Central Par CO15 ....188 F2
Central Sq 7 CM1 ....205 B2
Centre The
  2 Colchester CO1 ....136 E7
  Halstead CO9 ....76 E2
  Ipswich IP2 ....17 A1
  Tiptree CO5 ....179 D5
Centurion Ho 2 CO2 ....136 C5
Centurion Way CO2 ....135 A3
Chadburn Rd CO10 ....15 D8
Chaffinch Gdns CO4 ....136 F8
Chaffix CM4 ....152 C6
Chaffix Cl CM6 ....152 C6
Chainey Pieces 12 CB9 ....8 E7
Chalfont Rd CO4 ....110 C3
Chalfont Sq 18 IP4 ....17 D6
Chalklands
  Saffron Walden CB10 ....22 E3
  Sandon CM2 ....217 D3
Chalkners Cl 2 IP9 ....35 A1
Chalks Rd CM8 ....176 F4
Chalkstone Mid Sch CB9 ....9 A8
Chalkstone Way CB9 ....9 A7
Chalky La SG8 ....19 C1
Challenge Way CO1 ....136 B6
Challis La CM7 ....155 A8
Chalon St IP1 ....17 B5
Chamberlain Ave CO14 ....171 B7
Chamberlain Way IP8 ....16 C2
Chamley Ct CO15 ....189 D5
Chancellor Ave CM2 ....206 B4
Chancery Gr CO2 ....163 A8
Chancery Pl CM1 ....204 B1
Chancery Rd IP1 ....17 C6
Chandlers Cl
  Bishop's Stortford CM23 ....145 C4
  Clacton-on-S CO16 ....188 B3
  West Mersea CO5 ....201 C7
Chandlers Ct CO5 ....201 C7
Chandlers Row CO1 ....136 C5
Chaney Rd CO7 ....137 A2
Chant Ct CO4 ....110 D3
Chanterelle CO4 ....110 B3
Chantry Cl
  Bishop's Stortford CM23 ....145 F7
  Clacton-on-S CO16 ....188 E7
Chantry Gn IP2 ....16 F3
Chantry High Sch IP2 ....16 F3
Chantry Jun & Inf Sch IP2 ....16 E3
Chantry La CM3 ....172 B3
Chantry Mount CM23 ....145 E8
Chantry Rd CM2 ....205 D3
Chantry The
  18 Bishop's Stortford CM23 ....145 F8
  Colchester CO3 ....135 C7
Chantry View CM8 ....195 A7
Chantry Villas CM3 ....193 A2
Chanute Ave CM7 ....73 D7
Chapel Cl IP9 ....35 A1
Chapel Ct CO7 ....111 C7
Chapel Cut CO11 ....87 A4
Chapel Dr CM3 ....191 B6
Chapel End Way CO9 ....28 B2
Chapel Hill
  Belchamp Walter CO10 ....31 D4
  Braintree CM7 ....128 B2
  Halstead CO9 ....76 D2
  Stansted
  Mountfitchet CM24 ....119 C6
Chapel Hill Bsns & Ret
  Pk CM7 ....128 C1

**...hill Cty Prim Sch** ...................128 B2
..La Belstead IP8 .......36 C7
..s CO4 .............................83 A3
..lester CO7 ......................111 B1
..stead CO7 .....................138 A6
..at Bromley CO7 ............139 A5
Chelmond CO10 ............34 C2
..eybridge Basin CM9 ....210 E2
..orty Cross CO13 ..........170 A6
..ittle Baddow CM3 .......207 B3
Newport CB11 ..................67 A8
St Osyth CO16 .................187 A4
Tendring CO16 ................140 E8
Thorington Street CO6 ....32 B7
Thorrington CO7 ...........166 B5
Washbrook IP8 .................16 A1
West Bergholt CO6 .........108 E3

**Chapel Rd** Beaumont CO16 ...141 E7
Boxted CO4 .......................83 A3
Brightlingsea CO7 ...........186 A7
Colchester CO3 ...............134 C6
Fingringhoe CO5 .............163 F5
Great Totham CM9 ..........196 D6
Langham CO4 .....................83 D4
Ridgewell CO9 ...................29 B7
Tiptree CO5 .....................179 E4
Tolleshunt D'arcy CM9 ...198 F4
West Bergholt CO6 ..........108 E4
Wivenhoe CO7 .................164 B8

**Chapel Rise** CM7 .............129 D2
**Chapel Row 3** CM23 ........145 F6
**Chapel St** Halstead CO9 ....76 E2
Rowheage CO5 ................164 A8
Steeple Bumpstead CB9 ....27 C2
Stoke by CO10 ....................11 A3
**Chapel St N 2** CO2 .........135 E6
**Chapel St S 3** CO2 ..........135 E6
Chapelfields CO13 ...........170 E6
**Chaplin CI** CM7 ..............216 B2
**Chaplin Dr** CO4 ..............110 D1
**Chaplin Rd** CO7 ..............59 D3
**Chaplin Wlk** CO10 ..........34 D5
Chaplins CO7 ...................170 F7
**Chapman Rd** CO15 ..........188 F3
**Chappel Cres** CO5 ..........201 F8
**Chappel CE Prim Sch**
CO6 ................................106 D5
**Chappel Cnr** CO6 ...........106 D6
**Chappel Hill** CO6 ...........106 D6
**Chappel Rd** Bures CO6, CO8 ....79 E3
Fordham CO6 ...................107 D7
Great Tey CO6 .................106 D7
**Chappel & Wakes Colne**
**Sta** CO6 ........................106 D6
**Charlecote Rd** CM7 .........154 C7
**Charles Ct** Colchester CO3 ..134 D6
Wivenhoe CO7 .................137 C3
**Charles Pell Rd** CO4 .......136 E7
**Charles Rd**
Brightlingsea CO7 ...........185 F6
Ipswich IP1 ......................221 C3
**Charles St** Colchester CO1 ..136 A6
Ipswich IP1 .......................17 C6
**Charles Wheeler Ho** CO3 ..134 E6
**Charleston St** CO5 ..........201 E6
**Charlotte Dr** CO13 ..........170 E6
**Charlotte Way** CM8 .........177 B2
**Charnock CI** CO13 ..........170 E6
**Charnwood Ave** CM1 .......204 E1
**Charnwood CI** IP2 ............17 B4
**Charrington CI** CB9 ..........9 C6
**Charter Ct** CO4 ..............110 C6
**Charter Ho** CM9 ..............210 A2
**Charter Way** CM7 ...........128 C1
**Charters The** CM6 ...........123 D2
**Chartfield Dr** CO13 .........170 D8
**Chartwell CI**
Braintree CM7 .................127 E7
Ipswich IP4 .......................18 A5
**Chase Ct** CO4 .................136 D7
**Chase La** CO12 .................90 E2
**Chase Lane Prim Sch**
CO12 ...............................90 E2
**Chase Rd E** CO7 ..............139 C8
**Chase Rd W** CO7 ............139 A6
**Chase The** Aldham CO6 ......133 B8
Barnston CM6 ...................151 A4
Bishop's Stortford CM23 ..145 F6
Boreham CM3 ..................206 E8
Braintree CM7 .................128 A7
Brantham CO11 ................60 F1
**6** Colchester CO1 ...........136 D7
Dedham CO7 .....................85 A4
Elmstead CO7 ..................138 B6
Foxearth CO10 ..................14 C6
Goldhanger CM9 ..............212 A1
Great Baddow CM2 ..........216 F6
Great Notley CM7 ............154 C5
Great Tey CO6 .................132 C8
Henham CM22 ...................94 F6
Holland-on-S CO15 ..........189 E5
Kelvedon CO5 ..................158 C2
Mistley CO11 ....................86 D3
Steeple Bumpstead CB9 ...199 D2
Tollesbury CM9 ................199 D2
Tolleshunt D'arcy CM9 .....198 B4
West Mersea CO5 .............201 C6

**Chase Way The**
Colchester CO3 ...............109 B1
Colchester CO3 ...............109 C1
**Chaseway The** CM7 .........128 C2
**Chaters Hill** CB10 .............22 E2
**Chatham Hall La** CM3 .......173 A1
**Chatley Rd** CM3 .............173 F7
**Chatsworth CI** CM23 .......145 C7
**Chatsworth Cres**
Ipswich IP2 .......................17 B2

**Chatsworth Cres** continued
Trimley St M IP11 ..............221 A6
**Chatsworth Dr** IP4 ..........18 E5
**Chatsworth Gdns** CO15 ...188 D2
**Chatsworth Rd** CO5 .........201 C7
**Chattisham Rd** IP8 ...........35 C8
**Chaucer CI** CO15 .............188 A1
**Chaucer Cres** CM7 ..........155 A8
**Chaucer Rd**
Chelmsford CM2 ..............205 D1
Felixstowe IP11 ...............221 D3
Sudbury CO10 ...................15 D2
**Chaucer Way** CO3 ...........134 F6
**Chauntry Rd** CO9 ..............8 F7
**Chauntry The 2** CB9 .........9 A7
**Chedburgh PI 3** CB9 .........9 A8
**Chelmer Ave** CM3 ...........191 B5
**Chelmer CI**
Kirby Cross CO13 .............170 E7
Little Totham CM9 ............197 B4
**Chelmer Dr** CM6 .............150 E8
**Chelmer Lea** CM2 ...........216 E7
**Chelmer PI** CM2 .............205 D3
**Chelmer Rd**
Braintree CM7 .................128 D1
Chelmsford CM2 ..............205 E2
Haverhill CB9 .....................9 B8
Witham CM8 ....................176 F2
**Chelmer Terr** CM9 ...........210 B2
**Chelmer Valley High Sch**
CM1 ................................205 B5
**Chelmer Valley Rd** CM1 ...205 B5
CM2 ................................205 E2
**Chelmer Village Way**
CM2 ................................206 A3
**Chelmerton Ave** CM2 ......216 E7
**Chelmondiston CE Prim**
**Sch** IP9 ...........................63 E7
**Chelmsford Coll F Ed**
Chelmsford CM2 ..............216 C7
Chelmsford CM2 ..............216 C7
**Chelmsford Cty High**
**Sch** CM1 ........................205 A4
**Chelmsford & Essex**
**Regiment Mus** CM2 .......216 A8
**Chelmsford Ho** CM6 ........150 E7
**Chelmsford Rd**
Barnston CM6 ..................151 A4
Felsted CM6 ....................152 B4
Great Dunmow CM6 .........150 E7
Great Waltham CM3 .........191 A7
Holland-on-S CO15 ..........189 D6
Purleigh CM3 ...................220 C3
Woodham Mortimer CM9 ..216 D2
Writtle CM1 .....................204 C1
**Chelmsford Road Ind**
**Est** CM6 ..........................150 E7
**Chelmsford Sta** CM1 .......205 B3
**Chelsea CI** CO10 ..............33 F7
**Chelsea Mews 6** CM7 ......127 F2
**Chelsea Rd** CO10 ..............33 F7
**Chelsworth Ave** CO10 .......34 B7
**Chelsworth Rd** IP11 .........221 B3
**Chelwater** CM2 ................216 D8
**Chenies Gn** CM23 ...........145 D6
**Chepstow Rd** IP11 ..........221 D5
**Chequers** CM23 ..............145 C8
**Chequers Ct** CM8 ...........177 B2
**Chequers La** Glemsford CO10 ..2 C6
Great Dunmow CM6 .........150 D8
Maldon CM9 ....................210 A2
**Chequers Rd** CO10 .........113 C6
**Chequers The** CO7 ..........165 A7
**Cheriton Rd** CM7 ...........128 C1
**Cherry Bglws 1** CM7 ......127 F3
**Cherry Blossom CI** IP8 .....16 B2
**Cherry Chase** CO5 ...........179 D4
**Cherry Garden La**
Danbury CM3 ..................219 B7
Newport CB11 ...................66 F8
**Cherry Garden Rd**
Great Waltham CM3 .........190 E7
Maldon CM9 ....................209 E2
**Cherry Gdns** CM23 ..........146 A8
**Cherry La** CO9 ..................51 A8
**Cherry La Gdns** CM4 .........18 B7
**Cherry Row** CO3 .............134 F5
**Cherry Tree Ave** CO15 ....188 C1
**Cherry Tree CI**
Halstead CO9 .....................77 A2
Little Oakley CO12 .............17 C7
**Cherry Tree Cty Prim Sch**
CO2 ................................163 A8
**Cherry Tree Ho** CO5 .......158 C3
**Cherry Tree La**
Abberton CO2 ..................162 F6
Blackheath CO2 ...............163 A7
**Cherry Trees** CO15 ..........188 F2
**Cherrygarden La 1** CM2 ..216 A8
**Cherrytree CI** CO3 ..........134 F5
**Cherrytree Rd** CO10 .........34 B7
**Cherrytree Rise** CM8 .......177 A5
**Cherrywood Dr** CO3 .......134 F5
**Cherrywoods** CO7 ...........166 D8
**Chervil CI** CO5 ................158 C4
**Cherwell Dr** CM1 ............204 C5
**Cheryl CI** CO15 ..............188 D1
**Chesapeake CI** IP9 ............63 F7
**Chesapeake Rd** IP3 ...........38 A8
**Chesfield CI** CM23 ...........145 F5
**Chesham Rd** IP2 ..............17 B4
**Chess La** CM8 .................177 A2
**Chessington Gdns** IP1 .....16 F8
**Chester PI** CM1 ...............205 A5
**Chester Rd** IP11 ..............221 D5
**Chesterton CI** IP2 .............16 F1

**Chestnut Ave**
Blackheath CO2 ...............163 A8
Clacton-on-S CO15 ..........188 C3
Clare CO10 .......................12 B8
Hatfield Peverel CM3 .......194 A3
Heybridge CM9 ................210 C6
Jaywick CO16 ..................188 A2
Kirby Cross CO13 .............170 C6
Littlebury CB11 .................21 C1
**Chestnut CI**
Bishop's Stortford CM23 ..145 E6
Haverhill CB9 ......................8 F8
**Chestnut Gr** CM11 ............67 A8
**Chestnut Gr** CM7 .............127 E2
**Chestnut Rd**
Alresford CO7 ..................165 B8
Glemsford CO10 .................2 B5
**Chestnut Terr** CO10 .........15 C8
**Chestnut Way**
Brightlingsea CO7 ...........185 E2
Takeley CM22 ..................148 C7
Tiptree CO5 .....................179 C7
**Chestnut Wlk**
Chelmsford CM1 ..............205 A5
Felsted CM6 ....................152 C6
Little Baddow CM3 ..........207 E1
Witham CM8 ....................177 B4
**Chestnuts The** IP2 ............16 C2
**Chevalier Rd** IP11 ...........221 F4
**Chevallier St** IP1 ...............17 A7
**Cheveley** IP11 .................221 E4
**Cheveling Rd** CO2 ...........136 D2
**Cheviot Dr** CM1 ..............204 D6
**Chevy Ct** CO12 ................90 C2
**Cheyne Ct** CO10 ...............33 E7
**Chichester Ct** CO3 ..........135 A7
**Chichester Dr** CM1 ..........205 C4
**Chichester Rd** CB11 .........43 E8
**Chickney Rd** CM22 ...........95 C7
**Chigborough Rd** CM9 ......210 F6
**Chignall Rd** CM1 .............204 D5
**Chilburn Rd** CO15 ...........189 F7
**Childers Field** IP11 .........221 B5
**Childwell Alley** CO1 ........136 A6
**Chilford Ct** CM7 ..............127 D3
**Chiltern CI** CO1 ...............109 E1
**Chilton CI** Chelmsford CM2 ..216 D7
Great Horkesley CO6 ........109 B7
**Chilton Cotts** CO6 .............80 E4
**Chilton Ct** Ipswich IP2 ......17 B3
Sudbury CO10 ..................34 A6
**Chilton Ind Est**
Sudbury CO10 ..................34 A8
Sudbury CO10 ..................34 B8
**Chilton Lodge Rd** CO10 ...34 A7
**Chilton Rd** IP3 .................18 C4
**Chimney Pot La** CM3 .......219 E3
**Chimswell Way** CB9 ..........8 C8
**Chingford Ave** CO15 ........188 F8
**Chinnel La** CB11 ..............42 D5
**Chinnery Hill** CM23 .........145 F5
**Chinook** CO4 ..................110 B4
**Chippetts La** CO13 ..........133 C7
**Chipping Hill**
**2** Halstead CO9 ...............76 F2
Witham CM8 ....................176 F3
**Chipping Hill Cty Inf Sch**
CM8 ................................176 F3
**Chippingdell** CM8 ...........176 F4
**Chipstead Wlk** CO16 .......188 C6
**Chishill Rd** SG8 .................19 A4
**Chislett Row** CM2 ...........216 C8
**Chitts Hill** CO3 ...............108 D1
**Chivers Rd** CO9 .................8 D7
**Choat's Cotts** CO6 ...........107 E1
**Choats Wood** CO3 ..........107 F1
**Chrishall CE Prim Sch**
SG8 ..................................19 C3
**Chrismund Way** CM6 .......106 C1
**Christ Church Ct** CO3 ......135 D5
**Christchurch CI 4** IP4 .......17 D6
**Christchurch Mansion**
**(Mus)** IP4 .......................17 D6
**Christchurch Park Hospl**
**(private)** IP4 ...................17 C7
**Christchurch St** IP4 .........17 D6
**Christian Sch The** CM22 ..148 B7
**Christies Warehouse 15**
IP4 ..................................17 D5
**Christina Rd** CM8 ............194 E8
**Christine Chase** CO3 .......134 F5
**Christmas Field** CO9 ..........51 D2
**Christopher Ct 9** CO10 .....33 E7
**Christopher Dr** CO16 .......168 D1
**Christopher Jolly Ct** CO2 ..135 F4
**Christopher La** CO10 .........33 E7
**Christy Ave** CM1 .............204 F4
**Church Ave** CM1 .............191 A2
**Church Chase** CM6 .........178 A3
**Church CI** Cavendish CO10 ..1 D2
West Bergholt CO6 ..........108 E4
Wickham Bishops CM8 .....195 D5
**Church Cnr** CM9 ..............208 D2
**Church Cotts** CM8 ..........195 D5
**Church Cres**
Clacton-on-S CO15 ..........188 F2
Sproughton IP8 .................16 A6
**Church Dr** CM23 ...............92 B8
**Church End**
Great Dunmow CM6 .........123 E2
Panfield CM7 ...................127 B7
**Church End Villas** CM6 ....123 E3
**Church Farm Way** CO4 ....109 E4
**Church Field** CM3 .............43 E7
**Church Field Rd** CO10 .......34 C8
**Church Fields** CM23 .........146 B7
**Church Gdns** CM6 ...........123 D2
**Church Gn** Boreham CM3 ..206 F8

**Church Gn** continued
Coggeshall CO6 ...............131 A3
Himston CB10 .....................3 B7
Little Yeldham CO9 ............30 D4
Wickham Bishops CM8 .....195 D5
**Church Gr** CO6 ................133 B8
**Church Hill** Ashdon CB10 ...24 A8
Earls Colne CO6 ...............105 C6
Finchingfield CM7 ............72 C6
Harwich CO12 ...................90 B1
Helions Bumpstead CB9 ....26 C8
Lawford CO11 ...................85 F3
Little Waltham CM3 ..........191 C6
Purleigh CM3 ...................220 C3
Rowhedge CO5 ................163 F8
White Notley CM8 .............175 F8
Woodham Walter CM9 ......208 D2
**Church Housen** CM3 .......190 F7
**Church La** Beaumont CO16 ..142 A6
Bishop's Stortford CM23 ..145 F6
Braintree CM7 .................127 F6
Brantham CO11 .................60 E1
Canfield End CM6 ............149 B7
Castle Camps CB1 ...............7 E3
Castle Hedingham CO9 .....51 E4
**1** Chelmsford,
Moulsham CM9 ................205 B2
Chelmsford,
Springfield CM1 ...............205 D4
Clare CO10 .......................12 B7
Colchester, Lexden CO3 ...135 A6
Colchester, Stanway CO3 ..134 A4
Debden CB11 .....................68 A7
East Mersea CO5 .............183 E1
Elsenham CM22 ...............120 E8
Felixstowe IP11 ...............221 D6
Ford End CM3 ..................172 B6
Great Henny CO10 ............54 D8
Great Holland CO13 .........170 B3
Great Leighs CM3 .............173 D7
Great Tey CO6 .................132 C4
Great Wigborough CO5 ....181 F4
Harkstead IP9 ....................63 B3
Harwich CO12 ...................91 E6
Heybridge CM9 ................211 A8
Little Totham CM9 ............197 B1
Marks Tey CO6 .................133 A4
Mistley CO11 .....................86 E4
Nayland CO6 .....................56 B1
Ridgewell CO9 ...................29 B6
Sproughton IP8 .................16 B6
Takeley CM22 ..................148 B7
Toppesfield CO9 ................50 C8
Washbrook IP8 ..................35 D8
Weeley Heath CO16 .........168 A7
Widdington CB11 ...............67 D4
Wrabness CO11 .................88 C1
**Church Manor** CM23 .......146 B8
**Church Mead** CM8 ..........155 F1
**Church Path** CB1 ...............5 B6
**Church Pk** CO10 ...............11 C3
**Church Rd**
Alphamstone CO10 ............54 C6
Alresford CO7 ..................165 B7
Bentley IP9 .......................60 F7
Black Notley CM7 .............154 B6
Boxted CO4 .......................82 E6
Bradwell CM7 ..................129 E1
Brightlingsea CO7 ...........185 E8
Bulmer CO10 .....................32 F4
Capel St M IP9 ..................35 F1
Chrishall SG8 .....................19 C3
Clacton-on-S CO15 ..........189 A3
Copford CO6 ....................133 E2
Cressing CM7 ...................156 A5
Elmstead CO7 ..................138 A7
Fingringhoe CO5 .............164 A5
Fordham CO6 ...................107 D5
Frating CO7 .....................138 D2
Gosfield CO9 ...................102 E8
Great Cornard CO10 ..........34 A5
Great Hallingbury CM22 ...146 D3
Great Holland CO13 .........170 F6
Great Totham CM9 ..........196 E3
Great Yeldham CO9 ...........29 F2
Greenstead Green CO9 ....104 A5
Hatfield Peverel CM3 .......194 A3
Hempstead CB10 ..............46 F8
Holbrook IP9 ....................62 D5
Kelvedon CO5 ..................158 C2
Layer-de-l-H CO2 .............161 F4
Little Baddow CM3 ..........207 A6
Little Bentley CO7 ............140 A5
Little Bromley CO11 ........113 B4
Pattiswick CM7 ................129 F5
Peldon CO5 .....................182 D6
Rivenhall CM8 ..................157 B1
Shudy Camps CB1 ..............7 C5
Stisted CM7 ......................28 D2
Stutton IP9 ........................62 A2
Tattingstone IP9 ...............37 D3
Terling CM3 .....................175 B2
Thorrington CO7 ..............166 A6
Tiptree CO5 .....................179 D5
Tolleshunt Major CM9 ......197 F2
Ulting CM9 ......................208 C6
Walton-on-t-N CO14 ........171 C8
Wendens Ambo CB11 .........42 E5
Wickham Bishops CM8 .....195 D6
Wickham St P CO9 .............53 B6
Wormingford CO6 .............80 E5
Wrabness CO11 .................88 F4
Writtle CM1 .....................204 C8
St Osyth CO16 .................187 A4
**Church St**
Belcham St P CO10 ...........13 B3

**Church St** continued
Bishop's Stortford CM23 ..145 F7
Boxted CO4 .......................82 F7
Braintree CM7 .................102 B1
Chelmondiston IP9 ............63 E7
Chelmsford CM1 ..............205 B2
Clare CO10 .......................12 B7
Coggeshall CO6 ...............131 A2
Colchester CO1 ...............135 E7
Colne Engaine CO6 ............78 E1
Gestingthorpe CO9 ...........31 E1
Goldhanger CM9 ..............211 E7
Great Baddow CM2 ..........217 A6
Great Chesterford CB10 ......3 D2
Great Dunmow CM6 .........123 D2
Great Maplestead CO9 ......52 D1
Harwich CO12 ...................91 E6
Henham CM22 ...................94 F6
Ickleton CB10 .....................3 B4
Kelvedon CO5 ..................158 E2
Maldon CM9 ....................209 F2
Newport CB11 ...................43 A1
Rowhedge CO5 ................164 A8
Saffron Walden CB10 ........22 D2
Sible Hedingham CO9 .......51 D1
Steeple Bumpstead CB9 .....27 B7
Stoke-by-N CO6 ................56 D5
Sudbury CO10 ...................33 D6
Tollesbury CM9 ................199 D1
Tolleshunt D'arcy CM9 .....198 D4
Wendens Ambo CB11 .........42 E5
Witham CM8 ....................176 F4
**Church Terr** CO10 .............10 D2
**Church View** Ardleigh CO7 ..111 E7
Stoke by CO10 ..................10 D3
**Church Wlk**
Colchester CO1 ...............135 E7
Littlebury CB11 .................21 F4
Sturmer CB9 ......................9 E4
**5** Sudbury CO10 ..............33 E7
**Churchfield Rd**
Coggeshall CO6 ...............131 A3
Walton-on-t-N CO14 ........171 C8
**Churchfields** Stansted
Mountfitchet CM24 ..........119 F6
Steeple Bumpstead CB9 ....27 B6
West Mersea CO5 .............201 B6
**Churchfields Dr** CB9 .........27 B6
**Churchgate** CO10 ...............2 C5
**Churchill Ave** Halstead CO9 ..77 A3
Ipswich IP4 .......................18 B5
**Churchill CI** CO7 ..............185 F8
**Churchill Ct** CO12 .............91 A4
**Churchill Dr** CO10 .............15 E2
**Churchill Rd**
Braintree CM7 .................127 E7
Tiptree CO5 .....................179 F5
**Churchill Rise** CM1 ..........205 D7
**Churchill Terr** CM7 ..........127 E6
**Churchill Way** CO2 ..........136 B4
**Churchponds** CO9 .............51 E4
**Churchwell Ave** CO5 ........160 A7
**Churnwood CI** CO4 ..........110 D1
**Churnwood Rd** CO4 .........110 D1
**Chuzzlewit Dr** CM1 .........204 E2
**Cinque Port Rd** CO7 ........185 F7
**Circular Rd E** CO2 ...........135 F5
**Circular Rd N** CO2 ...........135 E5
**Circular Rd S** CO2 ...........135 E5
**Circular Rd W** CO2 ..........135 E5
**City Rd** CO5 ...................201 A6
**Civic Dr** IP1 .....................17 B6
**Civic Ind Est** CB9 ..............8 F5
**Clachar CI** CM2 ..............206 A3
**Clacton Cty High Sch**
CO15 ...............................189 A4
**Clacton & District Hospl**
CO15 ...............................188 E1
**Clacton- on-Sea Sta**
CO15 ...............................188 F3
**Clacton Rd** Bradfield CO11 ..114 A6
Elmstead CO7 ..................137 C5
Elmstead CO7 ..................138 C5
Great Holland CO13 .........170 A2
Holland-on-S CO15 ..........189 F7
Little Oakley CO12 ...........117 B5
Mistley CO11 .....................86 E2
St Osyth CO16 .................187 B4
Thorrington CO7 ..............166 C4
Weeley Heath CO16 .........166 B8
Wix CO11 ........................115 C5
Wix CO11 ........................115 D1
**Claire Rd** CO13 ...............170 B6
**Clairmont CI 11** CM7 .......127 F2
**Clairmont Rd** CO3 ...........134 E5
**Claredon Ho** CO13 ..........170 F4
**Clapgate Dr** CO16 ...........168 C2
**Clapgate La** IP3 ...............18 A2
**Clapton Hall La** CM6 ........150 D6
**Clara Reeve CI** CO3 .........134 C4
**Clare Castle Cty Pk** CO10 ..12 C7
**Clare CI** CO9 ...................103 D7
**Clare Ct** CO6 .....................69 F3
**Clare Cty Prim Sch** CO10 ..12 C8
**Clare Mid Sch** CO10 .........12 C8
**Clare Priory (remains**
**of)** CO10 .........................12 C6
**Clare Rd** Braintree CM7 ....127 E2
Ipswich IP4 .......................17 F8
**Clare Way** CO16 ..............188 B5
**Claremont Hts** CO1 ..........109 E1
**Claremont Rd** CO7 ...........164 C8
**Clarence CI** CM2 .............206 A4
**Clarence Rd** Clare CO10 ....12 B8
Ipswich IP3 .......................18 B1

**Clarence Rd** *continued*
 Stansted
 Mountfitchet CM24 ..........119 E7
 Sudbury CO10 ...............15 E1
**Clarendon Pk** CO15 .........189 B5
**Clarendon Rd** Haverhill CB9 ..8 F6
 Takeley CM6 ................148 E7
**Clarendon Way** CO1 .........109 E1
**Clark Way** CM1 .............191 A1
**Clark's Rd** CO12 ...........90 F3
**Clarkesmead** CO5 ...........179 C4
**Clarkia Wlk** CO4 ...........136 D7
**Clarks Farm Rd** CM8 ........218 F8
**Clarks Wood Dr** CM7 ........128 D3
**Clarkson St** IP1 ...........17 B6
**Clatterbury La**
 Arkesden CB11 ..............41 E1
 Clavering CB11 .............65 D5
**Claude Ince Ave** CM7 .......155 E6
**Claude Oliver Cl** CO11 .....86 A2
**Claude St** IP1 .............17 C6
**Claudian Cl** CB9 ...........9 D7
**Claudius Rd** CO2 ...........136 A5
**Claudius Way** CM8 ..........194 E8
**Clavering Cty Prim Sch**
 CB11 ......................65 C4
**Clavering Rd** CM7 ..........127 F6
**Claverton Way** IP4 .........18 E4
**Clay Hill** CO10 ............54 C8
**Clay La** St Osyth CO16 .....187 C7
 Stebbing CM6 ...............124 D7
**Clay Lane Gr** CO4 ..........110 C4
**Clay Pit Piece** CB11 .......43 E6
**Clay Pits Way** CM7 .........128 D3
**Claydon Cl** CB1 ............7 E4
**Clayhall Rd** CO15 ..........189 A5
**Clayhive Dr** CB9 ...........8 F7
**Claypit Hall** CM22 .........120 E8
**Claypits Ave** CO8 ..........80 A8
**Claypits La** CO10 ..........14 D5
**Claypits Rd** CM3 ...........192 F1
**Claypits Villas** CM6 .......70 B2
**Clayponds** CM23 ............146 B7
**Clays Rd** CO14 ............171 B7
**Clayshotts Dr** CM8 .........195 B8
**Clayton Rd** CO12 ...........90 C2
**Claywall Bridge** CB9 .......27 C7
**Claywall Cotts** CB9 ........27 C7
**Clear Springs Chalet**
 Site CO12 .................91 A1
**Clearwater** CO2 ............136 B3
**Clematis Tye** 🔲 CM1 .......205 E7
**Clematis Way** CO4 ..........136 E7
**Clement Mellish Ho** 🔲
 CO1 .......................135 F7
**Clement's La** CB9 ..........8 F7
**Clements Cty Prim Sch** CB9 ..8 F7
**Clements Dr** CB9 ...........8 F7
**Clench Cl** 🔲 IP4 ..........17 D6
**Clench Rd** IP9 .............62 D7
**Clenent Ave** CO10 ..........15 E2
**Clevedon Cl** CM7 ...........154 C7
**Cleveland Cl** CO4 ..........110 C4
**Cleves Ct** CM3 .............192 E1
**Cricket Hill** CO8 ..........88 B8
**Cliff Cres** CM7 ............100 E7
**Cliff Ct** CO13 .............171 B6
**Cliff La** IP3 ..............17 E3
**Cliff Lane Prim Sch** IP3 ...17 E3
**Cliff Par** CO14 ............144 E2
**Cliff Rd** Harwich CO12 .....91 D3
 Holland-on-S CO15 .........189 E5
 Ipswich IP3 ...............17 E3
**Cliff Way** CO13 ............171 B5
**Cliffield** CM7 .............100 E7
**Clifford Ct** 🔟 CM23 .......146 A7
**Clifford Rd** IP4 ...........17 F5
**Clifford Road Prim Sch**
 IP4 .......................17 F5
**Clifton Terr** CO7 ..........164 B8
**Clifton Way** IP2 ...........16 D2
**Clifton Wood** IP9 ..........62 D6
**Clive Rd** CO1, CO2 .........136 A6
**Cliveden Cl** CM1 ...........204 E3
**Clobbs Yd** CM1 .............205 B8
**Clockhouse Way** CM7 ........128 E7
**Cloes La** CO15 .............188 B4
**Cloisters The**
 Braintree CM7 .............128 A5
 Kelvedon CO5 ..............158 B1
**Cloncurry Gdns** IP11 .......221 B3
**Clopton Dr** CO10 ...........15 C6
**Close The**
 Clacton-on-S CO15 .........203 H7
 Colchester CO3 ............134 D6
 Cressing CM7 ..............155 E6
 Debden CB11 ...............68 B7
 Frinton-on-S CO13 .........170 E5
 Great Dunmow CM6 .........150 E7
 Great Holland CO13 ........170 A3
 Harwich CO12 ..............91 A3
 Sudbury CO10 ..............33 F8
 Tattingstone IP9 ..........61 D7
**Clouded Yellow Cl** CM7 .....154 E8
**Clough Rd** CO4 .............110 D6
**Clovelly Cl** IP4 ...........18 E4
**Clover Ave** CM23 ...........145 B6
**Clover Cl** IP2 .............16 F4
**Clover Ct** Colchester CO13 .134 D5
 Great Holland CO13 ........34 C6
**Clover Dr** CO7 .............166 A5
**Clover Way** CO7 ............111 B5
**Cloverlands** CO4 ...........110 C2
**Clovers** 🔲 CM6 ...........76 D1

**Cluanie Orch** CO10 .........1 E1
**Club Par** CO16 .............203 B6
**Clump Field** IP2 ...........16 F2
**Clyde Cres** CM1 ............204 D4
**Clydesdale Rd** CM7 .........127 E2
**Coach House Way** 🔟
 CM8 .......................177 A2
**Coach La** CM9 ..............209 F3
**Coach Rd** Alresford CO7 ....165 B8
 Great Horkesley CO6 .......109 A7
 Hempstead CB10 ............25 F2
**Coachman's Paddock** IP9 ....62 D6
**Coachmans Ct** 🔲 IP4 .......17 C5
**Coast Ave** CO15 ............188 D1
**Coast Rd** CO5 ..............201 A6
**Coastguard Cotts** CO14 .....144 D1
**Coates Cl** CM9 .............210 B4
**Coats Hutton Rd** CO2 .......135 B3
**Coats Quay** CM7 ............205 C2
**Cobbold Mews** 🔟 CM9 ......17 D6
**Cobbold Rd** IP11 ...........221 E4
**Cobbold St** IP4 ............17 D6
**Cobbs La** CM22 .............121 F3
**Cobden Pl** IP4 .............17 D6
**Cobden St** IP4 .............18 C2
**Cock & Bell La** CO10 .......15 C8
**Cock La** CB11 ..............64 F3
**Cock & Pye Ct** CO1 .........135 E7
**Cock Rd** CO9 ...............53 B1
**Cockaynes La** CO7 ..........138 A1
**Cockett Wick La** CO16 ......187 C1
**Cockrell's Rd** CO6 .........81 B4
**Codham Little Park Dr**
 CM7 .......................101 C6
**Cody Rd** IP3 ...............18 C1
**Coeur De Lion** CO4 .........109 F2
**Coggeshall Pieces** CO9 .....77 A2
**Coggeshall Rd**
 Ardleigh CO7 ..............84 F2
 Braintree CM7 .............128 C3
 Coggeshall CO6 ............131 F3
 Coggeshall CO6 ............131 F7
 Earls Colne CO6 ...........165 B3
 Great Tey CO6 .............132 B7
 Kelvedon CO5 ..............158 B5
 Marks Tey CO6 .............132 C3
**Coggeshall Rd**
 (Feering) CO5 .............158 D7
**Coggeshall Road**
 (Feering) CO5 .............131 B1
**Coggeshall Way** CO9 ........77 A2
**Cogmore** CB11 ..............41 B8
**Cohort Cr** CO2 .............135 A2
**Coke St** CO12 ..............91 D5
**Cokers Cl** CM7 .............155 C5
**Colam La** CM3 ..............207 C3
**Colbayns High Sch** CO15 ....188 D4
**Colchester Boys High**
 Sch CO3 ...................135 E6
**Colchester Bsns Pk** CO4 ....110 C6
**Colchester Castle** CO1 .....135 F7
**Colchester Castle**
 Mus CO1 ...................135 F7
**Colchester Cty High Sch**
 Girls CO3 .................135 B6
**Colchester General**
 Hospl CO4 .................109 E3
**Colchester Inst** CO15 ......189 A3
**Colchester Institute** CO13 .135 D8
**Colchester Oaks Hospl**
 CO3 .......................135 D7
**Colchester Rd**
 Abberton CO5 ..............163 B1
 Ardleigh CO7 ..............111 C6
 Bures CO8 .................79 F8
 Chappel CO6 ...............106 E5
 Chelmsford CM2 ............206 A6
 Coggeshall CO6 ............131 D2
 Dedham CO7 ................84 E6
 Elmstead CO7 ..............137 F6
 Frating CO7 ...............139 E3
 Great Bentley CO7, CO16 ...186 F8
 Great Bromley CO7 .........112 A3
 Great Totham CM9 ..........196 D7
 Great Wigborough
  CO5, CM9 .................181 C2
 Halstead CO9 ..............77 A1
 Heybridge CM9 .............210 B5
 Holland-on-S CO15 .........189 D6
 Ipswich IP4 ...............18 B8
 Lawford CO11 ..............86 C5
 Little Horkesley CO6 ......81 B1
 Peldon CO5 ................183 B6
 Salcott-cum-virley CM9 ....199 A5
 St Osyth CO16 .............187 A4
 St Osyth CO16 .............187 A7
 Thorpe-le-S CO16 ..........194 B5
 Tiptree CO5 ...............179 D7
 Weeley CO16 ...............140 C2
 West Bergholt CO6 .........108 D6
 West Mersea CO5 ...........201 C7
 White Colne CO6 ...........105 E6
 Witham CM8 ................177 B3
 Wivenhoe CO7 ..............137 B4
 Wix CO11 ..................114 E4
 Wix CO11 ..................115 B3
 Wormingford CO8 ...........80 A6
**Colchester Royal Gram**
 Sch CO3 ...................135 D6
**Colchester Sta** CO1 ........109 E1
**Colchester Zoo** CO3 ........134 C1
**Cold Hall Chase** CO7 .......138 E6
**Cold Store Rd** IP11 ........221 A1
**Coldhanger Cl** CM7 .........155 D8
**Coldnailhurst Ave** CM7 .....127 F5
**Cole End La** CB10 ..........44 E6
**Cole Hill** CM3 .............174 B5

**Cole Ness Rd** IP3 ..........38 A8
**Colehills Cl** CB11 .........65 C4
**Coleman's La** CM3 ..........218 D7
**Coleman's La** CM3 ..........218 D7
**Coleridge Rd** CM9 ..........210 A1
**Coles La** CO14 .............144 A1
**Coles Oak La** CO7 ..........84 C6
**College Cl** CM23 ...........141 F4
**College Ct** CO11 ...........86 C4
**College Ho** CM7 ............127 E2
**College Rd** Braintree CM7 ..127 E2
 Clacton-on-S CO15 .........189 A3
**College St** IP4 ............17 C5
**Coller Rd** CO12 ............90 F5
**Colles Brook Rd** CO7 .......166 F4
**Colletts Chase** CO6 ........80 F4
**Colley Rd** CM2 .............217 A6
**Colliers The** CM9 ..........210 E8
**Collimer Cl** IP9 ...........63 E7
**Collimer Ct** IP11 ..........221 C6
**Collindale Gdns** CO15 ......189 C5
**Collingwood Ave** IP3 .......18 B3
**Collingwood Cl** CM7 ........128 C5
**Collingwood Fields** CO7 ....59 B4
**Collingwood Rd**
 Clacton-on-S CO15 .........188 D1
 Colchester CO3 ............134 E6
 Witham CM8 ................177 A2
**Collins Cl** 🔲 CM7 .........127 E2
**Collins Cross** CM23 ........119 B1
**Collins Rd** CO7 ............53 D1
**Collinson's** IP2 ...........16 D5
**Collops Villas** CM6 ........125 A4
**Colne Bank Avenu** CO3 ......135 D8
**Colne Chase** CM6 ...........176 C2
**Colne Com Sch & Colne**
 Coll The CO7 ..............185 E8
**Colne Cswy** CO2 ............136 D5
**Colne Ct** CM7 ..............128 C1
**Colne Engaine Prim CE**
 Sch CO4 ...................78 A2
**Colne Park Rd** CO6 .........105 D7
**Colne Rd**
 Brightlingsea CO7 .........185 E6
 Bures CO8 .................79 E8
 Clacton-on-S CO15 .........188 F2
 Coggeshall CO6 ............131 A6
 Halstead CO9 ..............77 A2
 Sible Hedingham CO9 .......75 E8
**Colne Rise** CO5 ............163 B8
**Colne Springs** CO9 .........29 B6
**Colne Terr** CO7 ............164 B8
**Colne Valley Cl** CO9 .......76 D2
**Colne Valley Railway** CO9 ..51 C5
**Colne Valley Rd** CB9 .......9 A7
**Colne View**
 Colchester CO2 ............136 D2
 Point Clear B CO16 ........186 A2
**Colne View Ret Pk** CO1 .....110 A1
**Colne Way** CO16 ............185 F4
**Colneford Hill** CO6 ........105 D7
**Colneis Cty Jun Sch** IP11 ..221 F6
**Colneis Rd** IP11 ...........221 F6
**Colneys Cl** CO10 ...........15 D1
**Colthorpe Rd** CO15 .........188 F8
**Coln The** CM23 .............145 C4
**Coltsfield** CM24 ...........119 E8
**Coltsfoot Cl** CO4 ..........109 C2
**Coltsfoot Rd** IP2 ..........16 E4
**Columbine Gdns**
 Ipswich IP2 ...............16 E5
 Walton-on-t-N CO14 ........171 B7
**Columbine Mews** CO3 ........134 C7
**Columbines The** CO10 .......1 E2
**Colvin Chase** CM2 ..........216 B1
**Colvin Cl** CO3 .............134 F7
**Colyers Reach** CM2 .........216 A6
**Colyn Pl** CB10 .............22 E3
**Comac Yd** CO15 ............188 E5
**Comma Cl** CM7 .............127 E1
**Commerce Pk** CO2 ..........136 D4
**Commerce Way**
 Colchester CO2 ............136 D4
 Lawford CO11 ..............86 C5
**Commercial Rd** IP1 .........17 B4
**Common Hill** CB10 ..........22 D2
**Common La**
 Duddenhoe End SG8 .........40 B7
 Little Baddow CM3 .........207 E2
 Woodham Walter CM9 .......208 B3
**Common St** CO10 ...........12 B8
**Commons The** CM6 ..........218 C4
**Commons The** CO3 ..........135 A5
**Compasses Rd** CM7 .........129 F5
**Compton Mews** 🔲 CO4 ......136 C8
**Compton Rd** CO4 ...........136 C8
**Comyns Pl** IP11 ............204 B1
**Conan Doyle Cl** CM7 ........155 A8
**Concil Houses** CM7 .........156 A4
**Conder Way** CO2 ...........136 D4
**Conduit La** CM9 ............219 E6
**Conduite St** 🔲 CM1 .......205 B2
**Conies Rd** CO9 ............103 D7
**Conifer Cl** Alresford CO7 ..164 F7
 Colchester CO4 ............136 E8
**Conifer St** 🔲 CM23 .......145 F8
**Coniston Cl** CM7 ...........154 D6
**Coniston Rd** IP3 ...........18 B2
**Coniston Sq** IP3 ...........18 B2
**Connaught Ave** CO13 ........170 F4
**Connaught Cl** CO15 .........189 B3
**Connaught Ct** CO15 .........189 B3
**Connaught Gdns** CM7 .......128 A4
**Connaught Gdns E** CO15 ....189 B3
**Connaught Gdns W** CO15 ....189 B3
**Connaught Ho**
 Clacton-on-S CO15 .........189 A4
 Frinton-on-S CO13 .........170 F5

**Connaught Rd** Haverhill CB9 ..8 E7
 Weeley Heath CO16 .........168 C5
**Connaught Sq** CM3 ..........194 B3
**Conrad Rd** CM6 ............176 F5
**Constable Ave** CO16 ........188 C6
**Constable Cl**
 Colchester CO4 ............109 E4
 Lawford CO11 ..............86 B4
 West Mersea CO5 ...........201 D7
**Constable Ct** CO2 ..........135 B3
**Constable Ho** CM7 ..........127 E3
**Constable Rd**
 Felixstowe IP11 ...........221 F4
 Ipswich IP4 ...............17 D8
 Sudbury CO10 ..............33 E8
**Constable View** CM1 ........205 F6
**Constance Cl**
 Broomfield CM1 ............191 A3
 Witham CM8 ................195 B8
**Constantine Rd**
 Colchester CO3 ............135 D5
 Ipswich IP1 ...............17 B5
 Witham CM8 ................194 E8
**Constitution Hill**
 Ipswich IP1 ...............17 B8
 Sudbury CO10 ..............33 D8
**Convalescent Hill** IP11 ....221 E3
**Convent Hill** CM7 ..........128 A5
**Convent La** CM7 ............128 A5
**Conway Cl** Halstead CO9 ....103 D8
 Haverhill CB9 .............8 E6
 Ipswich IP2 ...............17 B2
 Wivenhoe CO7 ..............164 C8
**Conyer Cl** CM9 .............220 F8
**Cook Cl** CO12 ..............90 F1
**Cook Cres** CO4 .............136 E7
**Cook Pl** CM2 ...............205 F3
**Cook's Corner** CO11 ........88 E2
**Cook's Hall Rd** CO6 ........148 C8
**Cook's La** Colchester CO3 ..134 E8
 Colchester CO3 ............134 F7
 Great Bardfield CM7 .......71 E4
**Cooks Cl** CO9 ..............103 F8
**Cooks Hill** CO4 ............83 B6
**Coolyne Way** CO15 .........189 B7
**Coombe Lodge** CO6 .........105 B6
**Coombe Rise** CM1 ..........205 B7
**Cooper Dr** CM7 ............127 D4
**Cooper's La** CO7 ...........84 F5
**Cooper's Row** CM1 .........205 A5
**Coopers** CM3 ..............206 E8
**Coopers Ave** CM9 ..........210 D5
**Coopers Cl** CM23 ..........145 B4
**Coopers Cres** CO3 .........108 F4
**Coopers End Rd** CM24 ......121 A3
**Coopers End Rdbt** CM24 ....121 B3
**Coopers La**
 Clacton-on-S CO15 .........188 C3
 Great Leighs CM3 ..........173 F7
**Coopers Villas** CM22 ......121 B2
**Copdock Cty Prim Sch**
 IP8 .......................35 F8
**Copford CE Prim Sch**
 CO6 .......................133 D2
**Copland Cl**
 Broomfield CM1 ............191 A1
 Great Baddow CM2 .........216 F8
**Copleston High Sch** IP4 ....18 C5
**Copleston Rd** IP4 ..........18 B5
**Coploe Rd** CB10 ...........3 A2
**Copper Beeches** CO3 ........134 D5
**Copper Ct** CM7 ............127 E1
**Copperas Rd** CO7 ..........185 F5
**Copperfield Rd**
 Chelmsford CM1 ............204 E7
 Ipswich IP2 ...............16 D4
**Copperfields** CB11 .........43 C8
**Coppice Cl** CM6 ...........123 D1
**Coppice End** CO4 ..........110 B3
**Coppice Rd** CO7 ...........165 B8
**Coppice The** CO15 .........188 D1
**Coppingford End** CO6 ......133 D5
**Coppins Cl** CM2 ...........216 D4
**Coppins Green Prim Sch**
 CO15 ......................188 D4
**Coppins Rd** CO15 ..........188 D4
**Coprolite St** IP3 ..........17 F5
**Copse The**
 Bishop's Stortford CM23 ...146 C8
 Colchester CO3 ............109 F3
 Felsted CM6 ...............152 F6
**Copt Hall La** CO5 .........182 C3
**Copt Hill** CM3 ............218 E6
**Copthall Ct** CM23 .........146 F4
**Copthall La** CM6 ..........70 B3
**Copy Hill** CB9 ............8 F3
**Coral Dr** IP1 .............16 D8
**Coralin Wlk** CO3 ..........134 C6
**Cordell Pl** CO10 ..........15 D8
**Cordell Rd** CO10 ..........15 D8
**Corder Rd** IP4 ............17 D8
**Cordwinders** CO7 ..........59 F1
**Coriander Rd** CO5 .........179 C4
**Corinda Ho** CO13 ..........170 F4
**Coriolanus Cl** CO2 ........135 A3
**Cormorant Wlk** CO16 .......216 C5
**Corn Mill Ct** CO11 ........43 E8
**Cornard Rd** CO10 ..........33 F7
**Cornel Cl** CM8 ............177 D3
**Cornelius Vale** CM2 .......206 B4
**Cornells La** CB11 .........67 E3
**Corner Pk** CB10 ...........22 E3
**Cornerth Cres** CO10 .......34 B6
**Cornflower Cl**
 Colchester CO3 ............134 C7
 Ipswich IP2 ...............16 E4
**Cornflower Dr** CM1 ........205 F6
**Cornflower Rd** CM1 ........203 G7

**Cornford Way** CO11 ........2 ...
**Cornhill**
 🔲 Chelmsford CM1 ........2 ...
 🔟 Ipswich IP1 ...........2 ...
**Cornish Hall End Rd**
 Stambourne CO9 ............2 ...
 Steeple Bumpstead CO9 ....4 ...
**Cornwall Cl** CO15 .........186 ...
**Cornwall Cres** CM1 ........205 ...
**Cornwall Gdns** CM7 ........128 ...
**Cornwall Ho** CM23 .........145 E...
**Cornwall Rd** IP11 .........221 D5
**Cornwallis Pl** CB10 .......22 E3
**Cornwallis Rd** CB9 ........8 F3
**Cornwalls Dr** CO6 .........132 F3
**Coronation Ave**
 Braintree CM7 .............127 F2
 Colchester CO2 ............136 A2
**Coronation Dr** IP11 .......221 C3
**Coronation Rd**
 Bishop's Stortford CM23 ...145 E5
 Clacton-on-S CO15 .........188 C3
 Ipswich IP4 ...............18 ...
**Coronation Villas** CO16 ...141 F7
**Coronation Way** CM7 .......155 D5
**Corporation Ave** IP2 ......37 A8
**Corporation Rd** CM1 .......205 A4
**Corriander Dr** CM2 ........94 D2
**Corry Cl** 🔲 CO4 ..........136 D8
**Corton Rd** IP3 ............18 B1
**Cortoncroft Cl** CO13 ......170 F7
**Cotman Ave** CO11 ..........86 B4
**Cotman Rd**
 Clacton-on-S CO16 .........188 D6
 Colchester CO3 ............135 A5
 Ipswich IP3 ...............18 A1
**Cotswold Cres** CM1 ........204 D6
**Cotswold Cl**
 Clacton-on-S CO15 .........189 A3
 Highwoods CO4 ............110 C4
**Cotswold Dr** CO10 .........15 C6
**Cotswold Rd** CO15 .........188 F5
**Cottage Dr** CO2 ...........136 D3
**Cottage Gn** CO6 ...........188 C6
**Cottage Gr** CO16 ..........188 C6
**Cottage Pl**
 Chelmsford CM1 ............205 B3
 🔲 Ipswich IP1 ...........17 B6
**Cottage Wlk** CO4 ..........188 C6
**Cottey Ho** CM2 ............216 B2
**Cottingham Rd** IP8 ........16 B1
**Cottonwood Cl** CO2 ........135 D2
**Coulsdon Cl** CO16 .........188 C6
**Council Bglws**
 Braintree CM7 .............127 F2
 Hazeleigh CM3 .............220 A4
**Council Cotts**
 Great Holland CO13 ........169 F3
 Helions Bumpstead CB9 ....8 E1
**Council Hos**
 Bicknacre CM3 .............218 F1
 Chelmondiston IP9 ........63 E7
 Great Bromley CO7 .........139 A6
 Hadstock CB1 ..............5 B6
 Holbrook IP9 ..............62 D7
 Peldon CO5 ................182 E5
 Thorrington Street CO6 ....57 B3
 Thorpe-le-S CO16 ..........141 E2
 Tolleshunt Major CM9 .....197 D3
 Wakes Colne CO8 ...........79 C1
**Council Rd** CM23 ..........146 B7
**Counting House La** CM6 ....123 D1
**County Pl** CM2 ............205 B1
**Coupals Cl** CB9 ...........9 E6
**Coupals Cty Prim Sch** CB9 ..9 D7
**Coupals Rd** CB9 ...........9 E6
**Court Cl** CM23 ............145 E5
**Court Eight** CM8 ..........176 F5
**Court Eighteen** CM8 .......176 F5
**Court Eleven** CM8 .........176 F5
**Court Farm** CO11 ..........61 A1
**Court Fifteen** CM8 ........176 F5
**Court Five** CM8 ...........176 F5
**Court Four** CM8 ...........176 F5
**Court Fourteen** CM8 .......176 F5
**Court Nine** CM8 ...........176 F5
**Court Nineteen** CM8 .......176 F5
**Court One** CM8 ............176 F5
**Court Rd** CM1 .............191 A3
**Court Seven** CM8 ..........176 F5
**Court Seventeen** CM8 ......176 F5
**Court Six** CM8 ............176 F5
**Court Sixteen** CM8 ........176 F5
**Court St** CO6 .............56 A1
**Court Ten** CM8 ............176 F5
**Court Thirteen** CM8 .......176 F5
**Court Three** CM8 ..........176 F5
**Court Twelve** CM8 .........176 F5
**Court Two** CM8 ............176 F5
**Courtauld Cl** CO9 .........76 F1
**Courtauld Homes of**
 Rest CO9 ..................76 E3
**Courtauld Rd** CM7 .........127 D4
**Courtenay Cl** CO10 ........15 D2
**Courtland Mews** CM9 .......220 F8
**Courtland Pl** CM9 .........220 F8
**Courtlands**
 Chelmsford CM1 ............205 A6
 Halstead CO9 ..............103 D8
**Coval Ave** CM1 ............205 A3
**Coval La** CM1 .............205 A2
**Covehithe Cl** 🔲 CB9 .....8 E4
**Coventry Cl** CO1 ..........136 A8
**Coverdale** CM8 ............176 E4
**Coverts The**
 West Mersea CO5 ...........201 D6
 Writtle CM1 ...............204 B1

...CB10 ..... 4 A5
....... .186 C3
ox's Hill C011 .... 204 A3
...nall Rd IP7 .... 109 F1
....to C01 .... 135 F7
....The C01 .... 110 A1
....P2 .... 204 E5
....G2 .... 17 C3
....arm La CM6 .... 97 E5
....xd IP11 .... 221 E4
....Mews CM7 .... 155 A8
....St IP4 .... 18 A6
....ip Cl IP2 .... 16 E4
....slip Ct C03 .... 134 C7
....La IP4 .... 17 D5
....x Rd C07 .... 165 B8
....x's Hill C011 .... 36 E1
...xhall Rd IP7 .... 36 E1
oytes Gdns **2** IP1 .... 17 C5
rabb's Hill CM3 .... 193 F2
rabb's La C05 .... 178 A8
rabbe St IP4 .... 18 A6
rabs Croft CM7 .... 128 D3
rabtree C013 .... 170 C8
rabtree Hill CB11 .... 67 C3
raiston Way CM2 .... 216 F5
ramphorn Wlk CM1 .... 204 D2
ranbrook La C010 .... 2 F1
rane Hill IP2 .... 16 E4
ranford Cl C07 .... 170 E5
ranham Rd CM6 .... 95 F3
ranleigh Cl C016 .... 188 B6
ranmer Ho CM2 .... 215 F7
ranmer's La C06 .... 131 E6
ranmere Ct C01 .... 136 A7
ranmore Cl CM22 .... 94 C2
ranmoregreen La C010 .... 2 E3
ranmore St IP3 .... 18 C1
ranwell Gdns CM23 .... 119 C1
raven Dr C04 .... 110 C3
rawley End SG8 .... 19 D4
rayfields CM6 .... 123 E1
rayford Cl CM7 .... 220 E8
rayford Rd C010 .... 15 D2
reance Ct CM2 .... 205 A2
reasen Butt Cl CM9 .... 210 A4
redon Cl C015 .... 188 F7
redon Dr C015 .... 188 F7
reek Cotts C014 .... 144 E4
reek View C05 .... 181 F2
reekhurst Cl C07 .... 186 A6
reffield Rd C03 .... 135 D6
repping Hall Dr IP9 .... 61 F1

Crescent Rd
Bishop's Stortford CM23 .... 146 A6
Felixstowe IP11 .... 221 E4
Great Baddow CM2 .... 217 A7
Heybridge CM9 .... 209 F6
Ipswich IP1 .... 17 B6
Tollesbury CM9 .... 199 E1
Walton-on-t-N C014 .... 171 C8

Crescent The
Clacton-on-S C015 .... 189 B7
Colchester C04 .... 110 C7
Frinton-on-S C013 .... 170 F4
Great Holland C013 .... 170 A4
Great Horkesley C06 .... 82 B1
Great Leighs CM3 .... 173 E5
Marks Tey C06 .... 133 A3
Steeple Bumpstead CB9 .... 27 B7
Thorpe-le-S C016 .... 141 F2
West Bergholt C06 .... 108 D5
Crest Croft CM7 .... 128 D1
Cressages Cl CM6 .... 152 F6

Cressing Cty Prim Sch
CM7 .... 155 C6

Cressing Rd
Braintree CM7 .... 128 C2
Witham CM8 .... 176 D6
Cressing Sta CM7 .... 155 D5

Cressing Temple Barns
CM7 .... 156 B2
Crestlands C07 .... 165 B7
Cricket Hill Rd IP11 .... 221 B5

Cricketers Cl
Broomfield CM1 .... 191 C1
Sudbury C010 .... 33 E6
Cricketfield La CM23 .... 145 E8
Crispin Cl CB9 .... 8 D7
Critchett Terr **1** CM1 .... 205 A3
Crittall Cl CM8 .... 156 E4
Crittall Dr CM7 .... 127 D4
Crittall Rd CM8 .... 177 B3
Crix Green Villas CM6 .... 153 D6
Croasdaile Rd CM24 .... 119 E8
Croasdale Cl CM24 .... 119 E8
Crocklands C09 .... 104 A5
Crocus Cl IP2 .... 16 F4
Crocus Fields CB10 .... 22 E3
Crocus Way CM1 .... 205 E7
Croft Cl CM7 .... 128 D1
Croft Ct C04 .... 205 E8
Croft Ho **3** C08 .... 76 F2
Croft La CB9 .... 9 B6

Croft Rd
Clacton-on-S C015 .... 188 D4
Kelvedon C05 .... 158 B2
Sudbury C010 .... 33 E8
Croft St IP2 .... 17 C3
Croft The Bures C08 .... 55 F1

Croft The continued
Earls Colne C06 .... 105 A6
Elsenham CM22 .... 94 C1
Glemsford C010 .... 2 C4
Great Yeldham C09 .... 30 A2
Croft Way CM8 .... 177 A3
Crofton Cl IP4 .... 18 B7
Crofton Rd IP4 .... 18 B7
Cromarty Rd IP4 .... 18 B8
Crome Cl C03 .... 135 A5
Crome Rd C016 .... 188 D5
Cromer Rd IP1 .... 16 F8
Cromhurst Ct C03 .... 135 E7
Crompton Rd IP2 .... 16 F7
Crompton St CM1 .... 204 F1

Cromwell Cl
Bishop's Stortford CM23 .... 145 B7
Boreham CM3 .... 206 D8

Cromwell Ct
**11** Ipswich IP1 .... 17 C5
Maldon CM9 .... 210 A3
Cromwell Ctr CM8 .... 177 B2
Cromwell Hill CM7 .... 209 F3
Cromwell La CM9 .... 209 F3
Cromwell Pk CM6 .... 152 B5

Cromwell Rd
**16** Colchester C02 .... 135 F6
Saffron Walden CB11 .... 43 E7
Cromwell Sq **8** IP1 .... 17 C5
Cromwell Way CM8 .... 176 F2
Croquet Gdns C07 .... 137 C1
Cross Cotts C04 .... 83 B6
Cross Field Way C04 .... 83 B5
Cross Hill C012 .... 116 D1
Cross La C05 .... 201 F7
Cross Rd Maldon CM9 .... 210 A1
Witham CM8 .... 176 F5
Cross St Felixstowe IP11 .... 221 C6
Saffron Walden CB10 .... 22 D1
Sudbury C010 .... 33 D7
Cross The C05 .... 201 E7
Cross Way C05 .... 201 E7
Crossfield Rd C015 .... 188 E3
Crossfield Way C013 .... 170 B6
Crossfields C06 .... 58 C5
Crossgate Field IP11 .... 221 C5
Crossley Ave C015 .... 203 E7
Crosstree Wlk C02 .... 136 A3

Crossways
Chelmsford CM2 .... 216 C2
Clacton-on-S C015 .... 203 G8
Colne Engaine C06 .... 77 F1
Crotchets Cl IP9 .... 35 A1
Crouch CM7 .... 128 D1
Crouch Dr CM8 .... 176 E2
Crouch St C03 .... 135 E6

Crouchman's Farm Rd
CM9 .... 208 C2

D'arcy Ave CM9 .... 210 B1
D'Arcy Cl C014 .... 170 F6
D'Arcy Ho C014 .... 144 D2
D'Arcy Hts CM2 .... 136 C3
D'Arcy Rd Colchester C02 .... 136 C3
St Osyth C016 .... 187 B4
Tiptree C05 .... 179 F2

D'arcy Way
Brightlingsea C07 .... 185 E7
Tolleshunt D'arcy CM9 .... 198 E4
Daen Ingas CM3 .... 217 A3
Daffodil Cl IP2 .... 16 E3
Daffodil Way CM1 .... 205 E7
Dagnets La CM7 .... 154 D3

Dahlia Cl
**4** Chelmsford CM1 .... 205 F5
Clacton-on-S C016 .... 188 C4
Dahlia Wlk C04 .... 136 D7
Daimler Ave C015 .... 203 D6
Dains Pl IP11 .... 221 A7
Dairy Rd CM2 .... 216 C7
Dairyhouse La C011 .... 114 F7
Daisleys La CM3 .... 174 A2
Daisy Ct CM1 .... 206 A6
Daisy Green Rd C03 .... 133 E8
Daisyley Rd CM6 .... 98 B4
Dale Cl C03 .... 134 B7
Dale Hall La IP1 .... 17 C8
Dale Ho CM7 .... 127 E4
Dale The C07 .... 164 C8
Dales The C012 .... 90 F1
Dales View IP8 .... 35 E8
Dales View Rd **11** IP1 .... 17 A8
Daleview Ave C011 .... 115 C5
Dalham Pl **4** CB9 .... 9 A8
Dallwood Way CM7 .... 128 B3
Dalrymple Cl CM1 .... 205 D3
Daltes La C016 .... 187 C3
Dalton Gdns CM23 .... 145 E4
Dalton Rd IP1 .... 16 C8
Damant's Farm La C016 .... 142 D1
Damases La CM3 .... 193 C1
Damask Rd C03 .... 134 C7
Dame Elizabeth Ct CM1 .... 190 F3

Dame Johane Bradbury's
Sch CB10 .... 22 F2
Dammant Ct **8** C04 .... 136 D8
Dampier Rd C04 .... 130 F3
Danbury Cl C06 .... 132 F3
Danbury Ctry Pk C05 .... 218 B7

Danbury Park Cty Prim
Sch CM3 .... 218 C7
Danbury Vale CM3 .... 218 A7
Dancing Dicks La CM8 .... 176 A2
Dandalan Cl IP1 .... 16 E8
Dane Acres C03 .... 145 D8
Dane House CM3 .... 145 D8
Dane O'Coys Rd CM23 .... 145 F7
Dane Pk CM23 .... 145 D8
Dane Rd CM1 .... 204 E2
Dane St CM23 .... 146 A7
Danes Ct C010 .... 34 B4
Daneum Holt C010 .... 12 A6
Daniel Cole Rd C02 .... 135 F4
Daniel Way CM8 .... 156 E4
Daniell Cl C016 .... 188 C6
Daniell Dr C02 .... 135 D2
Dansie Ct CM8 .... 176 E1

Curds Rd C06 .... 105 A4

Curlew Cl
Clacton-on-S C015 .... 188 F6
Heybridge CM9 .... 210 C5
Kelvedon C05 .... 158 D2
Curlew Croft C04 .... 136 F8
Curlew Rd IP2 .... 16 D4

Curling Tye La
Maldon CM9 .... 209 A3
Woodham Walter CM9 .... 208 F3
Currants Farm Rd CM7 .... 127 E5
Currents La C012 .... 91 E6
Curriers' La IP1 .... 17 C5

Curtis Cl
Clacton-on-S C016 .... 188 B3
Ipswich IP8 .... 16 C1
Curzon Rd C010 .... 34 B8
Curzon Way CM2 .... 206 A6
Cusak Rd CM1 .... 205 F3
Custerson Ct CB11 .... 22 D1
Custom House La C012 .... 91 D6
Cut Hedge CM7 .... 154 C6
Cut The C05 .... 179 C5
Cut Throat La CM8 .... 177 A4
Cut-A-Thwart La CM9 .... 209 C4
Cuthedge La C06 .... 157 D7
Cutler St IP1 .... 17 C5
Cutlers La C07 .... 75 E4
Cutmaple C09 .... 75 F6
Cutmore Pl CM2 .... 215 F8
Cuton Hall La CM2 .... 206 A5
Cutting Dr C09 .... 76 E1

Cygnet Ct
Bishop's Stortford CM23 .... 145 F6
Sible Hedingham C09 .... 51 E1

Cymbeline Way
(Colchester By Pass)
C03 .... 135 B8
Cypress Cl C015 .... 188 D7
Cypress Ct CM6 .... 123 B1
Cypress Dr CM2 .... 216 C6
Cypress Gr **5** C04 .... 136 F8
Cypress Mews C05 .... 201 B7
Cypress Rd CM8 .... 177 A4
Cyril Child Cl C04 .... 136 E7
Cyril Dowsett Ct CM7 .... 209 E2

# D

D'Arcy Ave CM9 .... 210 B1
D'Arcy Cl C014 .... 170 F6
D'Arcy Ho C014 .... 144 D2
D'Arcy Hts CM2 .... 136 C3
D'Arcy Rd Colchester C02 .... 136 C3
St Osyth C016 .... 187 B4
Tiptree C05 .... 179 F2

Daphne Cl CM7 .... 154 C7
Daphne Ct **8** C04 .... 136 D8
Dapier Dr CM7 .... 128 D3
D'Arcy Rise CM1 .... 207 E1
Darkhouse La C05 .... 164 A8
Darnay Rise CM1 .... 204 D6
Darnel Way C03 .... 134 B7
Darnet Rd CM9 .... 199 E1
Darrell Cl CM1 .... 205 B6
Darrell Rd IP11 .... 221 B1
Darsham Cl IP11 .... 221 B4
Dart Cl CM8 .... 176 D2
Dartmouth Rd CM1 .... 205 E6

Darwin Cl
**5** Braintree CM7 .... 127 C1
Colchester C02 .... 136 B1
Darwin Rd IP4 .... 17 F5
Dashwood Cl IP8 .... 16 C1
Datchet Ho C03 .... 134 E7
Daundy Cl IP2 .... 16 D5
Davall Cl C02 .... 90 C1
Davey Cl Colchester C01 .... 136 D6
Ipswich IP3 .... 17 F1
Davidson Cl C010 .... 34 D4
Davy Rd C015 .... 189 C8
Daw St Birdbrook C09 .... 28 B7
Finchingfield CM7 .... 72 E4

Daw's Hall (Wildfowl
Farm) C06 .... 55 B6
Dawes La C05 .... 201 E8
Dawlish Rd C015 .... 203 1B
Dawnbrook Cl **1** IP2 .... 16 E1
Dawnford Cl C03 .... 134 C7
Dawnford Ct C03 .... 134 C7
Dawson Cl C010 .... 22 F2
Dawson Dr IP11 .... 221 A8
Days Cl CM1 .... 205 B8
Dazeley's La C07 .... 85 F8

De Bohun Cl CB10 .... 22 E2
De Burgh Rd C03 .... 134 E6
De Greys Cl C010 .... 34 C5
De Mandeville Rd CM22 .... 94 C2
De Staunton Cl C07 .... 165 B7
De Vere Ave CM9 .... 210 B1

De Vere Cl
Hatfield Peverel CM3 .... 194 B3
Wivenhoe C07 .... 164 B8
De Vere Cty Prim Sch C09 .... 51 E4
De Vere Ct C07 .... 166 D8
De Vere La C07 .... 164 B8

De Vere Rd
Colchester C03 .... 135 A5
Earls Colne C06 .... 104 F7
De Vere Way C012 .... 90 F2
De Veres Rd **7** C09 .... 76 D1
De Vigier Ave C010 .... 23 A2
Dead La Ardleigh C07 .... 111 C8
Great Bentley C07 .... 166 F2
Lawford C011 .... 86 C2
Little Clacton C016 .... 168 B2
Wix C011 .... 115 D5
Deadman's La C07 .... 216 C4
Deal Cl Braintree CM7 .... 122 E6
Clacton-on-S C015 .... 203 J8
Deal Way C07 .... 185 E8
Dean Rd C01 .... 6 B8
Dean Rogers Pl CM7 .... 127 F7
Dean St C07 .... 185 F7
Dean Wlk CM1 .... 204 E1
Deane's Cl C012 .... 91 A2
Deanery Gdns CM7 .... 127 F7
Deanery Hill CM7 .... 127 F7
Deanes Ct C012 .... 91 A2
Deanhall Ave C015 .... 189 C5
Deans Wlk CM7 .... 122 F8

Debden CE Prim Sch
CB11 .... 68 B7
Debden Dr CB10 .... 44 E2
Debden Rd Newport CB11 .... 67 C8
Saffron Walden CB11 .... 43 D8
Saffron Walden CB11 .... 43 E8
Deben Dr CM8 .... 176 E2
Deben Dr C010 .... 34 A8
Deben High Sch CM1 .... 221 D4
Deben Rd Colchester C04 .... 110 D3
Haverhill CB9 .... 9 B8
Deben Way IP11 .... 221 C3
Deben Wlk C016 .... 188 C6
Dedham Ave C015 .... 188 B5
Dedham CE Prim Sch C07 .... 85 A6
Dedham Meade C07 .... 84 F3
Dedham Pl **7** IP4 .... 17 D5
Dedham Rd Ardleigh C07 .... 84 D1

Dellwood Ave IP11 .... 221 F5
Delvyn's La C09 .... 52 C6
Dene Ct CM1 .... 204 D5
Dengie Ct CM8 .... 194 E8
Denham Ct C07 .... 164 C8
Denholm Ct CM8 .... 194 E8
Denmark Gdns IP9 .... 62 D6
Denmark Ho CM2 .... 216 D8
Denny Ct CM23 .... 119 B2
Denton Cl IP2 .... 16 C4
Denton's Terr C07 .... 164 B8
Derby Cl IP4 .... 18 A5
Derby Rd IP3 .... 18 A4
Derby Road Sta IP3 .... 18 A4
Dereham Ave IP3 .... 17 F3
Dereham Cl C02 .... 135 C3
Derwent Gdns C015 .... 189 C6

Derwent Rd
Highwoods C04 .... 110 C4
Ipswich IP3 .... 17 F3

Derwent Way
Chelmsford CM1 .... 204 D4
Great Notley CM7 .... 154 C7
Devereaux Cl C014 .... 170 F8
Devereaux Pl C014 .... 109 C3
Devereux Ct C015 .... 188 F3
Devereux Pl C04 .... 109 C3
Devoils La **9** CM23 .... 145 F7
Devon Rd Colchester C02 .... 135 B3
Felixstowe IP11 .... 221 D5
Devon Way Harwich C012 .... 90 C2
Holland-on-S C015 .... 189 E7
Devonshire Gdns CM7 .... 128 B4
Devonshire Rd IP3 .... 17 F5
Dewberry Cl **8** C04 .... 136 D7

Dewes Green Rd
Berden CM23 .... 92 A8
Clavering CM23 .... 64 F1
Dewlands CM7 .... 155 D6
Deynes Rd CM11 .... 68 B7
Dial Cnr C07 .... 166 C3
Dial La IP1 .... 17 C6
Dial Rd C07 .... 166 E3
Diana Ho C013 .... 170 E5
Diana Way C015 .... 188 C2
Dickens Cl CM7 .... 155 A8
Dickens Pl CM1 .... 204 D7
Dickens Rd IP2 .... 16 F5
Dicksons Cnr IP1 .... 16 C7
Dicky Moors CM3 .... 173 F6
Didsbury Cl IP7 .... 16 D2
Digby Mews C05 .... 201 C6
Digby Rd IP4 .... 18 C7
Dilbridge Rd E C04 .... 136 C8
Dilbridge Rd W C04 .... 136 C8
Dillestone Ct CB9 .... 9 E5
Dillwyn St IP1 .... 17 A6
Dilwyn St W IP1 .... 17 A6
Dilston IP3 .... 219 A6
Dimsdale Cres CM23 .... 146 B6
Dinants Cres C06 .... 132 E3
Dinsdale Cl **1** C04 .... 136 C8
Dinsdale Ct IP11 .... 221 D3
Dismals The CM3 .... 175 B2
Distillery La C02 .... 136 C4
Ditchingham Gr IP11 .... 18 F6
Dixon Ave Chelmsford CM1 .... 204 F4
Clacton-on-S C016 .... 188 C6
Dixon Cl C011 .... 86 B4
Dixon Way C07 .... 137 A2
Dobbies La C06 .... 132 F3
Dock La C012 .... 117 A4
Dock Rd IP11 .... 221 B2
Dock St IP2 .... 17 C4
Docker Ct C04 .... 136 B4
Dockfield Ave C012 .... 90 F3
Dockwra La CM5 .... 218 F7
Doctor's La C010 .... 11 D2
Docwra Rd C05 .... 158 C2
Doddenhill Cl CB10 .... 22 E3
Dodmans **7** IP9 .... 35 A1
Doe's Cnr Halstead C09 .... 76 D5
Hatfield Peverel CM9 .... 194 F1
Dog Chase CM7 .... 73 C3
Doggetts La C06 .... 132 F2
Doghouse Rd CM7 .... 17 C5
Dogs Head St **8** IP4 .... 17 C5
Dogwood Cl IP3 .... 18 D2
Dolby Rise CM2 .... 205 F2
Dolphin Ct C013 .... 171 B6
Dolphin Way CM23 .... 146 A8
Dombey Cl CM1 .... 204 F7
Dombey Rd IP2 .... 16 F5
Doms La CM3 .... 175 B2
Domsey Bank CM3 .... 132 L3
Domsey Chase C05 .... 159 C8
Domsey La CM3 .... 191 F5
Don Ct CM8 .... 176 D2
Donald Way CM2 .... 216 C7
Donard Dr C06 .... 108 D4
Donne Dr C015 .... 203 G8
Donyland Way C05 .... 163 F7
Dooley Rd Felixstowe IP11 .... 221 A3
Halstead C07 .... 76 D1
Dorchester End C02 .... 136 B3
Dorchester Rd IP3 .... 18 D3
Dordell Ct C09 .... 50 B8
Dorewards Ave CM7 .... 128 C2
Dorking Cres C016 .... 188 C6
Dorking Wlk CM2 .... 216 E7
Dorothy Curtice Ct C06 .... 133 C5
Dorothy Sayers Dr CM8 .... 177 A5
Dorset Ave CM2 .... 216 E6

## Dorset Cl

Dorset Cl
Great Baddow CM2 . . . . . .216 E6
Halstead CO9 . . . . . . . . .76 E1
Holland-on-S CO15 . . . .189 E6
Dorset Ho **10** CM23 . . . .145 F7
Dorset Rd CM9 . . . . . .220 F8
Dorvis La CB10 . . . . . . .6 B1
Doubleday Cnr CO6 . . .130 F2
Doubleday Dr CM9 . . . .209 F5
Doubleday Gdns CM7 .128 B5
Doucecroft Sch CO5 . .158 C3
Douglas Cl CM2 . . . . . .216 D3
Douglas Gr CM8 . . . . . .176 D2
Douglas Rd
Clacton-on-S CO15 . . .188 C4
Harwich CO12 . . . . . . . . .91 B3
Douglas Wlk **3** CM2 . .216 A8
Dove Cl
Bishop's Stortford CM23 . .145 E3
Stansted
Mountfitchet CM24 . . . .119 E8
Dove Cres CO12 . . . . . . . .90 D2
Dove House Rd CB9 . . . .9 A8
Dove La CM2 . . . . . . . . .216 A6
Dove St IP4 . . . . . . . . . . .17 E5
Dove Tree Ct CO3 . . . .134 C5
Dovedale IP11 . . . . . . . .221 B3
Dovedale Gdns CO15 .189 C6
Dover Cl Braintree CM7 . .127 E6
Clacton-on-S CO15 . . . .203 J8
Dover Rd
Brightlingsea CO7 . . . .185 F8
Ipswich IP3 . . . . . . . . . . .18 B4
Dovercourt Sta CO12 . .91 D4
Doves La CM6 . . . . . . . .150 B2
Dowches Cotts CO5 . .158 C2
Dowches Dr CO5 . . . . .158 C3
Dowches Gdns CO5 . .158 C3
Dowding Cl CO2 . . . . .136 A4
Dowling Rd CO6 . . . . . .79 F3
Downing Prim Sch IP2 .16 F2
Downs Cres
Great Dunmow CM6 . .123 C1
Haverhill CB9 . . . . . . . . .8 F8
Downs Pl **5** CB9 . . . . . . .8 F8
Downs Rd CM9 . . . . . .210 B3
Downs The
Felixstowe IP11 . . . . . .221 B5
Great Dunmow CM6 . .123 D1
Downside Cl IP2 . . . . . . .36 F8
Downsway CM1 . . . . . .205 D6
Downton Dr CB9 . . . . . . .8 E8
Downton Wlk . . . . . . . .179 D6
Dragon's Gn CB10 . . . .23 D1
Drake Ave IP1 . . . . . . . . .18 B2
Drake Gdns CM7 . . . . . .18 B2
Drake Sq N IP3 . . . . . . .18 B2
Drake Sq S IP3 . . . . . . .18 B2
Drakes App CO15 . . . . .188 A1
Drakes Cnr CO5 . . . . . .181 F2
Drakes La Boreham CM3 . .192 B7
Little Waltham CM3 . .191 F7
Drapers Chase
Heybridge CM9 . . . . . .210 D4
Rayne CM7 . . . . . . . . . .153 D8
Drapers La **13** CB9 . . . . .8 B2
Drapery Comm CO10 . .2 A4
Dray Ct CO6 . . . . . . . . . .108 F4
Drayman's Cl CM23 . .145 B5
Drays The CO10 . . . . . . .15 B5
Drayton Cl CM9 . . . . . .210 A1
Drays The CB10 . . . . . .40 D8
Driberg Way CM7 . . . .128 A1
Driffield Cl CO5 . . . . .158 D4
Drift The
Great Cornard CO10 . .34 C5
Ipswich, Priory Heath IP3 .18 E2
Ipswich, Rose Hill IP4 .18 A6
Stutton IP9 . . . . . . . . . . .62 C2
Driftway The IP4 . . . . . .18 B6
Drive The Chelmsford CM1 .205 A6
Clacton-on-S CO15 . . .189 B7
Harwich CO12 . . . . . . . .91 B2
Rivenhall CM8 . . . . . . .177 E6
Thaxted CM6 . . . . . . . . . .69 F3
Drood Cl CM11 . . . . . . .204 F7
Drovers Way CM23 . . .145 C5
Druce The CB11 . . . . . . .65 D4
Drum Field CO7 . . . . . . .58 D1
Drury La **4** Braintree CM7 .127 F3
Ridgewell CO9 . . . . . . . .29 A6
Drury Rd CO2 . . . . . . . .135 C5
Du Cane Pl **6** CM8 . . .177 A2
Duchess Cl CM23 . . . .145 C7
Duck St Little Easton CM6 .122 F5
Wendens Ambo CB11 . .42 E5
Ducketts Wharf **10** CM23 .145 F6
Duddery Hill CB9 . . . . . .9 A7
Duddery Rd CB9 . . . . . .9 A7
Dudley Cl Boreham CM3 .192 E1
Colchester CO2 . . . . . .136 A4
Dudley Rd
Clacton-on-S CO15 . .188 D3
Earls Colne CO6 . . . . .104 F7
Fingringhoe CO5 . . . . .163 E3
Duffield Dr CO4 . . . . . .136 E7
Duffield Rd CM2 . . . . .216 D6
Duffries Cl CM3 . . . . . .190 E7
Duffs Hill CO10 . . . . . . .2 B6
Dugard Ave CO3 . . . . .134 E4
Duggers La CM7 . . . . .128 A1
Dugmore Ave CO13 . .170 C8
Duke St Brightlingsea CO7 .185 E6
Chelmsford CM1 . . . . .205 B2

Duke St continued
Ipswich IP3 . . . . . . . . . . .17 E4
Dukes La **8** CM2 . . . . .205 F4
Dukes Orch CM1 . . . . .204 B1
Dukes Park Ind Est CM2 .206 A4
Dukes Priory Hospl The
CM1 . . . . . . . . . . . . . . .205 D4
Dukes Rd CM7 . . . . . . .127 F5
Dukes Ride CM23 . . . .145 C7
Dulverton Cotts CO3 .134 C4
Dulwich Ct CO15 . . . . .189 D4
Dulwich Rd CO15 . . . .189 D5
Dumbarton Rd IP4 . . . .18 C8
Dumfries Rd IP4 . . . . .18 C8
Dumney La Braintree,
Hornells Corner CM3 . .153 E2
Braintree, Thistley
Green CM6 . . . . . . . . . .153 B3
Great Leighs CM3 . . . .173 E8
Dumont Ave CO16 . . .186 B2
Duncan Rd CO2 . . . . . .135 B4
Duncan Rise CO9 . . . . .29 F2
Dunlin Cl CM9 . . . . . . .210 C5
Dunlin Ct CO5 . . . . . . .158 C2
Dunlin Rd IP2 . . . . . . . .16 E2
Dunlop Rd IP2 . . . . . . . .16 F6
Dunmore Rd CM2 . . . .206 A3
Dunmow Inf Sch CM6 .123 D1
Dunmow Rd
Bishop's Stortford CM23 .146 C7
Felsted CM6 . . . . . . . . . .125 F2
Great Bardfield CM7 . .98 F8
Great Hallingbury CM22 .147 C7
Great Easton CM6 . . . .69 B2
Takeley CM22 . . . . . . . .148 C7
Thaxted CM6 . . . . . . . . . .97 A7
Dunning Cl CO11 . . . .114 C8
Dunnock Way CO4 . .137 A7
Dunnon Cl CM7 . . . . .128 D4
Dunster Dr CB9 . . . . . . .8 F8
Dunthorne Rd CO4 . .110 E2
Dunthorpe Rd CO16 .188 D6
Duntons Almshouses CO7 .84 F6
Dunwich Ct
Colchester CO2 . . . . . .135 F4
Ipswich IP1 . . . . . . . . . .16 E8
Dupont Cl CO16 . . . . .188 D6
Durham Cl CM7 . . . . . .72 A1
Durham Sq CO1 . . . . .136 A7
Durfold Rd CB10 . . . . .3 A7
Dyer's Rd Colchester CO3 .134 C3
Maldon CM9 . . . . . . . . .210 A2
Dyers Rd CO9 . . . . . . . . .28 E1
Dyke St IP1 . . . . . . . . . . .17 C7
Dykes Chase CM9 . . .209 F3
Dyne's Hall Rd CO9 . .76 C8

## E

Eagle Ave CO14 . . . . . .144 D1
Eagle La CM7 . . . . . . . .127 F6
Eagle St **3** IP4 . . . . . . .17 D5
Eaglegate CO1 . . . . . . .136 A7
Eagles Cl IP11 . . . . . . .221 D4
Earlhams Cl CO12 . . . .90 F1
Earls Cl CM23 . . . . . . . .145 D6
Earls Colne Prim Sch
CO6 . . . . . . . . . . . . . . .105 C6
Earls Colne Rd CO6 . .106 A1
Earls Hall Dr CO16 . .187 E5
Earlsfield Dr CM2 . . .205 F3
Earlsmead CM4 . . . . . .176 F3
Earlswood Way CO2 .135 D2
East Anglian Rly Mus
CO6 . . . . . . . . . . . . . . .106 D6
East Area IP1 . . . . . . . .16 C7
East Bay CO1 . . . . . . . .136 B7
East Bergholt CE Prim
Sch CO7 . . . . . . . . . . .59 B3
East Bergholt High Sch
CO7 . . . . . . . . . . . . . . .59 D3
East Bergholt Place Gdns
CO7 . . . . . . . . . . . . . . .59 F1
East Dock Rd CO12 . . .90 F6
East Donyland CE Prim
Sch CO2 . . . . . . . . . . .163 F8
East End Rd CO7 . . . . . .60 A3
East Essex Aviation Mus
CO16 . . . . . . . . . . . . . .185 E4
East Gores Rd CO6 . .131 F5
East Hanningfield Rd
CM2 . . . . . . . . . . . . . . .217 E2
East Haven CO15 . . . .188 E5
East Hill CO1 . . . . . . . .136 A7
East La CO7 . . . . . . . . . .85 B5
East Lawn IP4 . . . . . . . .18 C8
East Mersea Rd CO5 .183 E1
East Mill CO9 . . . . . . . . .76 F2
East Rd
Bishop's Stortford CM23 .146 B7
East Mersea CO5 . . . .184 D1
West Mersea CO5 . . .201 E7
East Row IP9 . . . . . . . . .62 D6
East Side CO4 . . . . . . . .83 A4
East St Braintree CM7 .128 A3
Coggeshall CO6 . . . . .131 A2
Colchester CO1 . . . . . .136 B8
Harwich CO12 . . . . . . . .91 D4
Saffron Walden CB10 .22 E1
Sudbury CO10 . . . . . . . .33 F8
Tollesbury CM9 . . . . . .199 D1
Wivenhoe CO7 . . . . . .137 C3
East Stockwell St CO1 .135 F7
East Terr CO14 . . . . . .144 D1
East View CM22 . . . . .148 C8
East View IP4 . . . . . . . . .45 F8

Eastacre CB10 . . . . . . .22 E2
Eastby Cl CB11 . . . . . .43 F8
Eastcliff Ave CO15 . .189 B4
Eastcliff Rd CM1 . . . .121 C8
Easterford Rd CO5 . .158 C2
Easterling Cl CO2 . . . .91 A4
Eastern App CM2 . . .205 F5
Eastern Ave CB9 . . . . .8 F8
Eastern Cl IP4 . . . . . . .18 E4
Eastern Cres CO4 . . .204 F5
Eastern Prom CO16 .185 F3
Eastern Rd CO7 . . . . .185 E6
Eastgate
Great Chesterford CB10 . .3 D2
**15** Ipswich IP4 . . . . . .17 D6
Eastgate St CO12 . . . .91 D6
Easthorpe Rd
Easthorpe CO5 . . . . . .159 D7
Messing CO5 . . . . . . . .159 F5
Eastland Ct IP11 . . . . .221 B7
Easton Rd CM8 . . . . . .177 A3
Easton Way CO13 . . .171 B6
Eastway Ent Ctr IP1 . .16 D8
Eastways CM8 . . . . . . .177 B4
Eastwood Dr CO4 . . .110 B3
Eaton Cl IP11 . . . . . . . .221 A7
Eaton Cotts CO5 . . . .179 D7
Eaton Gdns IP11 . . . .221 C2
Eaton Ho **12** CM23 . . .146 A8
Eaton Mews CO3 . . .136 B3
Eaton Way CM9 . . . . .196 F7
Ebenezer Cl CM8 . . .176 E5
Ebenezer Terr CM2 . .216 F7
Ebony Cl CO2 . . . . . . .159 D2
Eccles Rd IP2 . . . . . . . .16 D1
Eckersley Rd CM1 . .205 C3
Eden Cl CM8 . . . . . . . .176 E3
Eden Rd Haverhill CB9 . .9 A7
Ipswich IP4 . . . . . . . . . .18 B5
Eden Way CM1 . . . . .204 B5
Edens Cl CM23 . . . . . .146 B7
Edenside CO7 . . . . . . .170 E7
Edgefield Ave CO11 . .86 B3
Edgeworth Rd IP2 . . .16 E2
Edgeworth Rd CO6 .188 D5
Edgworth Rd CO10 . . .33 E7
Edinburgh Cl CM8 . .195 A8
Edinburgh Gdns
Bishop's Stortford CM23 .145 E6
Braintree CM7 . . . . . .128 C4
Edison Cl **3** CM7 . . . .127 F2
Edison Gdns CO4 . . .110 C1
Edison Rd CO4 . . . . . .110 C1
Edith Borthwick Sch The
CM7 . . . . . . . . . . . . . . .127 F8
Edith Cavell Way CB9 . .27 C6
Edith Rd
Clacton-on-S CO15 . .188 E2
Kirby-le-S CO13 . . . . .170 D8
Edmund Cl CB9 . . . . . . .8 F8
Edmund Gn CO10 . . .128 C8
Edmund Rd CM8 . . . .194 E8
Edward Ave CO7 . . . .185 F8
Edward Bright Cl CM9 .210 A2
Edward Cl Ipswich IP1 .16 E8
Little Clacton CO16 . .168 E5
Edward Cordy Ho IP11 .221 E3
Edward Dr CM2 . . . . .216 C7
Edward Marke Dr CO5 .163 B3
Edward Rd CO16 . . .168 E7
Edward St CO12 . . . . . .90 E5
Edward Terr CO10 . . .168 E5
Edwards Wlk CM9 . .209 F3
Egerton Green Rd CO2 .135 A3
Egglestone Cl IP2 . . . .16 F1
Eggshell La CM7 . . . . .27 E2
Egremont Dr CM2 . .206 B4
Egremont St CO10 . . .137 C4
Egret Cres CO4 . . . . .137 A8
Ehringshausen Way CB9 . .9 B7
Eight Acre La CO2 . .135 C2
Eight Ash Green CE
Prim Sch CO3 . . . . . .107 F1
Eld La CO1 . . . . . . . . . .135 F7
Elder Field CM7 . . . . .154 B5
Elderberry Gdns CM8 .177 B4
Elden Cl CO4 . . . . . . . .110 C1
Eldred Ave CO2 . . . . .135 B3
Eldred Dr CO10 . . . . . .34 C4
Eleanor Cl CO15 . . . .179 D6
Eleanor Wlk CO5 . . .179 D6
Eleventh Ave CM24 .120 B2
Elgin Ave CM1 . . . . . .205 A2
Elianore Rd CO3 . . . .135 B7
Eliot Way CM9 . . . . . .210 A1
Elisabeth Ct CO4 . . .144 E3
Elizabeth Ave CM8 .195 A8
Elizabeth Cl
Highwoods CO4 . . . . .110 C4
Saffron Walden CB10 .22 F2
Elizabeth Rd
Bishop's Stortford CM23 .145 E5
Ipswich IP2 . . . . . . . . . .91 A3
Elizabeth Villas CM9 .180 A2
Elizabeth Way
Brightlingsea CO7 . .185 F6
Felixstowe IP11 . . . .221 C3
Halstead CO9 . . . . . . . .76 E2
Hatfield Peverel CM3 .194 A4
Heybridge CM9 . . . . .210 A5
Saffron Walden CB10 .22 F2
Sudbury CO10 . . . . . . .33 C5
Wivenhoe CO7 . . . . .137 C3
Ellen Friend Ho CM23 .145 D5
Ellen Way CM7 . . . . . .154 D7
Ellenborough Cl IP2 . .16 D1
Ellenbrook Gn IP2 . .16 D1

Ellenbrook Rd IP2 . . . .16 D1
Elliots Dr CO14 . . . . . .171 B8
Elliot St IP1 . . . . . . . . . .17 A6
Ellis Rd Boxted CO4 . .82 F3
Bradfield CO11 . . . . . .114 D8
Clacton-on-S CO15 . .188 E2
Elm Ave CM9 . . . . . . . .210 C5
Elm Bglws CM7 . . . . .127 D4
Elm Cl Alresford CO7 .165 B8
Brantham CO11 . . . . . .60 D1
Chelmsford CM1 . . . .205 A8
Elsenham CM22 . . . . . .94 C2
Great Baddow CM2 .216 F6
Great Bentley CO7 . .166 E8
Haverhill CB9 . . . . . . . . .8 F8
Sible Hedingham CO9 . .51 D2
Takeley CM22 . . . . . . .148 C7
Tiptree CO5 . . . . . . . . .179 C7
Elm Close Extension
CM22 . . . . . . . . . . . . . .148 C7
Elm Cres CO4 . . . . . . .136 D7
Elm Ct Elmdon CB11 . .20 B4
Sturmer CB9 . . . . . . . . .9 E5
Elm Dr Brightlingsea CO7 .185 D7
Halstead CO9 . . . . . . . . .76 F1
Harwich CO12 . . . . . . . .91 B3
Elm Est CO7 . . . . . . . . .59 C3
Elm Gdns IP11 . . . . . .221 A7
Elm Gr
Bishop's Stortford CM23 .146 B7
Clacton-on-S CO15 . .188 F6
Jaywick CO16 . . . . . . .188 A2
Kirby Cross CO13 . . .170 D6
Saffron Walden CB10 .22 D1
Wivenhoe CO7 . . . . . .137 B1
Elm Green La
Danbury CM3 . . . . . . .218 C6
Sandon CM3 . . . . . . . .207 D3
Elm Ho IP11 . . . . . . . .221 C4
Elm La Capel St M IP9 . .35 A1
Marks Tey CO5 . . . . .132 B2
Washbrook IP8 . . . . . . .35 E8
Elm Rd
Bishop's Stortford CM23 .145 F8
Chelmsford CM2 . . . .216 A8
East Bergholt CO7 . . .59 C3
Little Clacton CO16 . .168 C3
Rushmere St A IP5 . .181 F7
Sudbury CO10 . . . . . . . .34 A7
Elm Rise CM8 . . . . . . .177 A5
Elm St IP1 . . . . . . . . . . .17 C6
Elm Tree Ave CO13 . .170 F7
Elm Tree Cl CO13 . . .170 F7
Elm Way CM3 . . . . . . .192 E1
Elm Wlk CM7 . . . . . . .126 F2
Elmbrook Dr CM23 . .145 E3
Elmcroft CO2 . . . . . . . .136 A4
Elmdale Dr CO11 . . . .86 D3
Elmden Ct CO15 . . . .188 E5
Elmdon Pl **1** CB9 . . . .9 B8
Elmfield Cl CO15 . . .189 E7
Elmhurst Cl CB9 . . . . .9 B7
Elmhurst Dr IP3 . . . . .17 F3
Elmhurst Rd CO12 . .91 C3
Elms Dr CM2 . . . . . . . .205 A4
Elms Hall Rd CO6 . . .104 E8
Elms The East Bergholt CO7 . .60 C3
Elmstead Prim Sch CO7 .137 F6
Elmstead Rd
Colchester CO4 . . . . .136 E5
Wivenhoe CO7 . . . . .137 D4
Elmwood Ave CO2 . .135 B2
Elmwood Dr CO5 . . .201 D7
Elsenham CE Prim Sch
CM22 . . . . . . . . . . . . . .94 D1
Elsenham Sta CM22 . .94 D2
Elsham Dr CM7 . . . . .154 B6
Elsmere Rd IP1 . . . . . .17 C8
Elthorne Pk CO16 . . .188 D6
Elton Park Bsns Ctr IP2 .16 E6
Elton Pk IP2 . . . . . . . . .16 D6
Elton Wlk CO5 . . . . . .179 D6
Elvina Ho CO15 . . . . .203 F6
Elwes Cl CO4 . . . . . . . .110 D1
Elwin Rd CO5 . . . . . . .179 D5
Elysian Gdns CM9 . .199 C1
Embassy Ct CM9 . . .210 A2
Emberson Ct CM2 . .205 F4
Emblems CM6 . . . . . .123 C1
Embra Ct CO2 . . . . . . .136 B5
Emily May Ct CO12 . .91 A3
Emlen St IP1 . . . . . . . . .17 A6
Emmanuel Cl IP2 . . .16 F1
Empire Ct CO15 . . . .188 E3
Empire Rd CO12 . . . . .91 D3
Empire Wlk **2** CM2 . .205 C2
Empress Ave CO5 . .201 E6
Empress Dr CO5 . . . .201 D6
Emson Cl CB10 . . . . . .22 D2
Endean Ct CO7 . . . . .137 A2
Endeavour Cl CM9 . .199 D2
Endsleigh Ct CO3 . . .135 C7
Endway The
Great Easton CM6 . .122 F8
Steeple Bumpstead CB9 . .27 C8
Englefic SG8 . . . . . . . .39 F8
Enid Way CO4 . . . . . .109 D2
Ennerdale Ave CM7 .154 C6
Enterprise Ct
Braintree CM7 . . . . . .128 B2
Witham CM8 . . . . . . . .177 A3
Enville Way CO4 . . . .110 B4
Epping Cl Chelmsford CM1 .204 E1
Clacton-on-S CO15 . .188 F8
Epping Way CM8 . . .176 E1
Epsom Cl CO16 . . . . .188 D6
Erbury Pl CO12 . . . . . .12 B8

Erica Wlk CO4 . . . . . . .
Erick Ave CM1 . . . . . . .
Eridge Cl CM1 . . . . . . .
Erle Havard Rd **4** CB9 . .
Erle Havard Rd CO6
Ernest Rd CO7 . . . . . . .
Ernleigh Rd IP4 . . . . . .
Errington Rd CO3 . . .
Erskine Rd CO11 . . . .
Esplanade
Frinton-on-S CO13 . .
Harwich CO12 . . . . . . .
Esplanade Ct
Frinton-on-S CO13 . .1 ,
Clacton-on-S CO15 . .203 E
Esplanade The CO15 .189
Essex Ave Chelmsford CM1 .
Clacton-on-S CO15 . .203 E
Sudbury CO10 . . . . . .15 F
Essex Cty Hospl CO3 .135 D
Essex Hall Rd CO1 . .109 E
Essex Hill CB11 . . . . .20 D
Essex Knowle CO6 . . .55 F
Essex Rd Braintree CM7 .128 B
Maldon CM9 . . . . . . . .209 F
Essex Regiment Way
Howe Street CM3 . . . .173 A
Little Waltham CM3 . .191 D
Essex Show Ground CM3 .154 A
Essex Way IP3 . . . . . . .18 E
Essex Yeomanry Way
CO3 . . . . . . . . . . . . . . .134 B
Estella Mead CM1 . .204 E
Estuary Cl CO4 . . . . .109 E
Estuary Cres
Clacton-on-S CO15 . .188 D
Shotley Gate IP9 . . . . .91 B
Estuary Mews CM9 .199 D
Estuary Park Rd CO5 .201 E
Estuary Rd IP9 . . . . . .91 B
Eton Ct CO13 . . . . . . .171 A
Eton Rd Clacton-on-S CO15 .188 F
Frinton-on-S CO13 . .171 A
Eudo Rd CO3 . . . . . . .135 C
Euro Ret Pk IP3 . . . . .18 D
Europa Way Harwich CO12 .90 F
Ipswich IP1 . . . . . . . . . .16 E
Eustace Rd IP1 . . . . . .16 E
Euston Ave IP4 . . . . .18 F
Euston Ct IP11 . . . . . .221 A
Evabrook Cl IP2 . . . . .16 E
Evelyn Rd CM3 . . . . .153 D
Evelyn Wood Rd CM7 .155 E
Everest Way CM9 . . .210 B
Everett Ho CO1 . . . . .136 B
Evergreen Dr CO4 . .110 D
Everitt Rd CB10 . . . .22 E
Everitt Way CO9 . . . .51 C
Eves Cnr CM3 . . . . . .218 E
Eves Cres CM1 . . . . .205 A
Eves Ct CO12 . . . . . . . .90 D
Eves Orch CO8 . . . . . .55 F
Evesham Cl IP2 . . . . . .16 F
Ewan Cl CO3 . . . . . . . .134 C
Ewan Way CO3 . . . . .134 C
Ewell Hall Chase CO5 .158 C
Exchange Way **5** CM1 .205 B
Exeter Cl Braintree CM7 .128 B
Great Horkesley CO6 . .109 C
Exeter Ct **6** CB9 . . . . . .8 A
Exeter Dr CO1 . . . . . .136 A
Exeter Rd Chelmsford CM1 .205 E
Felixstowe IP11 . . . .221 D
Ipswich IP3 . . . . . . . . . .18 B
Exmoor Cl CM1 . . . .204 D
Exmoor Rd IP11 . . . .221 D

## F

Faber Rd CM8 . . . . . .194 E8
Fabians Cl CO6 . . . . .131 A3
Factory Hill CO5 . . .179 E3
Factory La CO11 . . . . .86 E4
Factory La E CO9 . . . .76 E1
Factory Terr CO9 . . . .76 E2
Faggot Yd CM7 . . . . .127 F5
Fair Cl CO7 . . . . . . . . .186 A6
Fair Leas CB10 . . . . . .22 E5
Fairbrother Ct **1** CO4 .136 D2
Fairclough Ave CO16 .188 B3
Fairfax Mead CM2 . .206 A2
Fairfax Rd **8** CO2 . . .135 F4
Fairfield Ave IP11 . .221 E5
Fairfield Cl CO7 . . . .221 E5
Fairfield Gdns **2** CO4 .136 A1
Fairfield Inf Sch IP11 .221 E5
Fairfield Rd Braintree CM7 .127 F2
Chelmsford CM1 . . . .205 A3
Clacton-on-S CO15 . .188 E4
Ipswich IP3 . . . . . . . . . .18 A2
Fairfield Way CO9 . .76 F1
Fairfields CM3 . . . . . .220 D3
Fairhead Rd N CO4 .110 B6
Fairhead Rd S **6** CO4 .136 B8
Fairleads CO3 . . . . . . .218 F8
Fairlop Cl CO15 . . . . .188 E5
Fairstead Hall Rd CM3 .175 A5
Fairstead Rd CM3 . .175 C5
Fairway
Bishop's Stortford CM23 .146 C6
Great Notley CM77 . .154 E6
Hockley CM3 . . . . . .216 D2
Fairways CO4 . . . . . . .109 B3
Fairways The CM . . .127 A1
Fairy Hall La CM7 . .127 A1
Fairycroft Rd CB10 . .22 D1

Fal Dr CM8 .................176 E2
Falcon Cl CB9 ...................9 C8
Falcon Cres C01 .............136 B5
Falcon Fields CM9 ..........220 F8
Falcon Mews CM9 ...........220 F8
Falcon Rd C09 ................51 F4
Falcon St Felixstowe IP11 .221 C6
  Ipswich IP1 ..................17 C5
Falcon Way
  Chelmsford CM2 ...........216 A6
  Clacton-on-S C015 .........188 F6
Falcon Yd C07 ................164 B8
Falconer Rd CB9 .................9 C5
Falconer St CM23 ............145 C5
Falkland Cl CM3 ..............206 E8
Falkland Cl CM7 ..............128 B4
Falkland Gn CM6 .............219 E6
Falklands Wy **7** CO11 .....86 D4
Fallowden La CB10 ...........23 F8
Fallowfield Cl C012 ..........90 F3
Fallowfield Ct **11** CB9 .....9 B7
Fallowfield Rd C02 ..........135 C2
Falmouth Rd CM1 ............205 E5
Fambridge Chase CM6 ......155 F2
Fambridge Cl CM9 ...........210 A1
Fambridge Rd
  Maldon CM9 .................209 F2
  Maldon CM9 .................220 F6
Fanner's Green Cotts
  CM3 ...........................190 C5
Fanny's La C016 .............167 D2
Faraday Cl Braintree CM7 ..127 F1
  Felixstowe IP11 .............221 A4
Faraday Rd IP4 ................17 E5
Farford Field C010 ...........34 C6
Farm Rd C012 ................116 D3
Farm Wlk C07 ................185 E8
Farmadine Cl CB11 ...........22 E1
Farmadine Ct CB11 ...........22 E1
Farmadine Gr CB11 ..........22 E1
Farmadine Ho **5** CB11 ....22 E1
Farmers Way C016 ..........188 B3
Farmfield Rd C04 ............106 E8
Farmleigh Ave C05 ..........188 F1
Farnham CE Prim Sch
  CM23 .........................118 D6
Farnham Rd CM23 ...........118 F3
Farriers End C03 .............136 C6
Farriers Went IP11 ...........221 B7
Farrington Cl **3** C01 .......136 C6
Farrow Rd CM1 ...............215 E7
Farthing Cl CM7 .............128 D4
Farthing Rd IP1 ................16 C3
Farthing Road Ind Est IP1 ..16 C2
Farthings Went IP9 ..........35 B2
Fastnet Cl IP9 ..................9 D8
Faulds Wlk C02 ..............136 A3
Faulkbourne Rd CM8 ........176 D4
Faulkners Way IP11 ..........221 A8
Fawkner Cl CM2 ..............216 B7
Fawley Cl IP4 ...................18 C7
Feathers Field IP11 ..........221 B5
Feedhams Cl C07 ............137 C3
Feering CE Prim Sch
  C05 ...........................158 E4
Feering Hill C05 ..............158 D3
Feering Mus C05 .............158 B1
Felaw St IP2 ....................17 D4
Felix Rd Felixstowe IP11 ...221 F4
  Ipswich IP2 ...................18 C2
Felixstowe Cl C016 ..........188 A4
Felixstowe General
  Hospl IP11 ...................221 A4
Felixstowe Rd IP3 ............18 B3
Felixstowe Sta IP11 .........221 C5
Fell Christys CM1 .............205 B5
Fell Rd C09 ......................28 B8
Fellbrigg Ave IP5 .............18 F6
Felnor Wlk IP11 ..............221 E4
F[...]land Cl C010 .............163 A8
Felsted Almshouses _ CM6_ .152 D2
Felsted Cty Prim Sch
  CM6 ...........................152 D7
Felsted Sch CM6 .............152 C6
Feltwell Pl **2** CB9 ...........9 B8
Fen La C07 .....................60 C3
Fen Mdw IP11 .................221 A8
Fen St C06 ......................56 D1
Fen View IP8 ...................35 E8
Fenbridge La C07 .............59 B1
Fenman Ct CM22 ..............94 C2
Fenn Cl C07 ...................139 A3
Fenn Rd C09 ....................77 A1
Fennell Cl C05 ................179 C5
Fennells Cl CB9 ..................9 A7
Fennes Rd CM7 ..............124 A7
Fennings Chase C01 ........136 A7
Fenno Cl C03 ..................134 F4
Fenton Rd CB9 ..................9 B8
Ferdinand Wlk C04 ..........136 F7
Ferguson Cl CB11 .............23 A2
Fern Gr CB9 ......................9 A8
Fern Hill C010 ..................2 B7
Fern Way C015 ...............203 F7
Ferndale Cl C015 .............188 F7
Ferndale Rd C012 .............91 D5
Ferndown Rd C013 ..........170 E5
Ferndown Way CM3 .........194 B4
Fernhayes Cl IP2 ..............17 A2
Fernie CM7 .....................127 D2
Fernlea C04 ....................109 C2
Fernlea Rd C012 ..............91 D5
Fernwood Ave C015 ........189 F5
Ferny La Felixstowe IP11 ...221 A3
Ferry La IP11 ..................221 B3
Ferry Rd C016 ................164 B6
Festival Gdns CM9 ..........198 D4
Feverills Rd C016 ............168 D4

Fiat Ave C015 .................203 D6
Fiddlers Folly C03 ...........107 E1
Fiddlers Hill C03 .............107 E2
Fiddlers La C07 ................59 C3
Field Ct C04 ...................136 E8
Field Gate La CM22 ...........94 A3
Field View Dr C07 ...........197 C4
Field Way C07 ................137 C2
Fieldgate Dock C07 .........185 E5
Fields Cl C016 ................167 F6
Fields Farm Rd C02 .........205 D1
Fieldside CB11 .................43 E7
Fifth Ave Chelmsford CM1 .205 B6
  Frinton-on-S C013 .........170 E5
  Halstead C09 .................77 B1
Filbins Wlk IP4 ................17 F5
Finborough Cl IP4 .............18 F8
Finch Dr Braintree CM7 ....127 D4
  Great Bentley C07 .........139 D1
Finch Hill CO10 ...............33 A7
Finchingfield CE Prim
  Sch C07 .......................72 D6
Finchingfield Guildhall
  Mus C07 ......................72 D6
Finchingfield Rd
  Stambourne C09 ............49 C7
  Steeple Bumpstead CB9 ...27 C6
Finchingfield Way C02 .....162 A5
Finchley Ave CM2 ...........216 A8
Finchley Rd IP4 ................17 E6
Findley Cl IP7 .................61 F2
Finer Cl C010 .................188 C5
Fingringhoe CE Prim
  Sch C05 ......................163 F5
Fingringhoe Rd
  Abberton C05 ...............163 B3
  Colchester C02 ..............136 D1
Fingringhoe Wick
  Nature Reserve &
  Visitor Ctr C05 .............164 D3
Finham Cl C04 ................136 F7
Finsbury Pl C09 ...............76 F2
Fir Trec Cl C04 ...............110 B4
Fir Tree Hill IP9 ...............62 F4
Fir Tree La CM3 ..............207 E1
Fir Tree Rise
  Chelmsford CM2 ...........216 B6
  Ipswich IP8 ...................16 C2
Fir Tree Wlk CM9 ............210 C5
Fir Way C015 .................203 D6
Firebronds Rd IP9 .............62 D5
Firecrest Rd CM2 ...........216 C5
Firlands CM23 .................145 E6
Firlands Ho CM23 ...........145 E6
Firlie Wlk C02 ................136 E7
Firmins Cl C06 ...............108 D4
Firs Chase C05 ...............201 A6
Firs Dr CM1 ...................204 B1
Firs Hamlet C05 .............201 A6
Firs Jun & Mid Sch The
  CM3 ...........................145 F6
Firs Rd Tiptree C05 .........179 D4
  West Mersea C05 ..........201 B7
First Ave Chelmsford CM1 .205 B5
  Clacton-on-S C015 .........189 B4
  Frinton-on-S C013 .........170 E4
  Glemsford C010 ..............2 B5
  Halstead C09 ..................77 B1
  Harwich C012 ................91 C3
  St Osyth C016 ...............203 C6
Fishbane Cl IP3 ...............*7H H*9
Fisher Cl CB9 ....................9 D8
Fisher Way CM7 ..............128 C4
Fisher's La C07 .................60 C3
Fishmarket St CM6 ...........70 A2
Fishponds Hill C06 ...........81 F4
Fishponds La IP9 ..............62 E5
Fisin Wlk C03 .................134 E3
Fiske Ct C015 .................188 D7
Fitches Cres CM9 ............210 B1
Fitches Croft C06 ............133 C4
Fitzgerald Cl C011 ...........86 B4
Fitzgerald Cotts C012 .......90 F2
Fitzgilbert Rd C02 ...........135 B4
Fitzmaurice Rd IP3 ...........18 B3
Fitzpiers C010 .................22 E2
Fitzroy St **2** IP1 .............17 C6
Fitzwalter La CM3 ...........218 D6
Fitzwalter Pl
  Dunmow CM23 ..............204 E3
  Great Dunmow CM6 .......150 D8
Fitzwalter Rd
  Boreham CM3 ...............206 F8
  Colchester C03 .............135 B6
Fitzwilliam La IP2 .............16 F2
Fitzwilliam Rd C010 .........34 B5
Five Acres Danbury CM3 ...218 F3
  Holbrook IP9 ..................62 D5
Five Acres
  Mountfitchet CM24 ........119 E8
  Walton-on-t-N C014 ......171 B8
Five Ways C03 ...............134 D4
Fiveash La CM7 ..............129 E1
Flag Hill C07 ..................186 F8
Flagstaff Rd C02 .............135 F6
Flail Cl C07 ....................137 C6

Flanders Cl CM7 ..............127 E5
Flanders Field C02 ..........136 B3
Flatford Dr C016 .............188 B5
Flatford Mill C07 .............85 D7
Flatford Rd C07 ...............85 C8
Flavian Cl CB9 ....................9 D7
Flax La C010 .....................2 C3
Fleetwood Ave
  Felixstowe IP11 .............221 F5
  Holland-on-S C015 .........189 E7
Fleetwood Cl C015 ..........189 E7
Fleetwood Rd C011 ..........86 C4
Fleming Cl **7** CM7 .........127 F1
Flemish Ct C01 ...............135 F8
Fletcher Rd IP3 ................18 A1
Flint Cl IP7 ......................17 B2
Flintwich Manor CM1 .......204 E7
Flitch Ind Est The CM6 .....150 D7
Flitch La CM6 .................150 E7
Flixton Cl C016 ...............188 A4
Flora Ind CM7 .................176 D4
Florence Cl C07 ..............197 F8
Florence Rd C014 ...........144 E2
Florence Wlk **8** CM23 ...145 F8
Florie's Rd C06 ...............131 F8
Flowers Way C015 ..........203 G7
Flumsey Row CM1 ..........204 B1
Foley Cotts CM7 .............102 D3
Folkards La C07 ..............185 F8
Folly La IP8 .......................35 C4
Folly Mill La CM6 .............96 E6
Folly Thy Layer-de-l-H C02 ..162 A5
  Tiptree C05 ..................179 F2
  Wivenhoe C07 ..............164 C7
Fonnereau Rd IP1 ............17 C6
Ford End CE Prim Sch
  CM3 ...........................172 B6
Ford La Alresford C07 .......165 A5
  Colchester C04 ..............109 D5
Ford Rd C015 .................188 D3
Ford St C06 ....................107 C2
Fordham CE Prim Sch
  C06 ...........................107 D4
Fordham Pl IP4 ................18 F5
Fordham Rd Bures C06, C08 ..79 F2
  Wormingford C06 ...........80 E2
Fordson Rd IP3 ...............206 B6
Fordstreet Hill C06 ..........107 C2
Fordwater Cl C09 .............10 B3
Fordwich Rd C07 ............165 C1
Fore Field CM7 ...............128 D3
Fore Hamlet IP3 ...............17 E5
Fore St IP4 ......................17 D5
Forefield Gn CM1 ...........205 F7
Foresight Rd C04 ............136 D2
Forest Dr CM1 ...............204 E1
Forest Park Ave C015 ......188 F7
Forest Rd Colchester C04 ..136 D7
  Witham CM8 ................177 A5
Foresthall Rd CM24 .........119 E4
Forfar Cl IP4 ....................18 B8
Forfields Way CM7 ..........155 E6
Forge Cotts C010 ............22 D1
Forge Cres CM7 ..............129 D3
Forge St C07 ...................85 A6
Forties Cl CB9 ...................9 D8
Forsyth Dr CM7 ..............155 A8
Forsythia Cl CM1 ............205 E7
Forties C[...] Cl IP2 .........136 C3
Forthbras Way CM2 .........216 B8
Fortis Cl01 .....................194 E8
Fortune Cl C04 ...............174 A7
Fossatts La C04 ..............107 F4
Foster Ct **2** CM8 ..........177 A2
Foster La Braintree CM7 ...127 F4
  Maldon CM9 ...................90 E5
Foster's Cotts CM7 ..........129 D2
Foundation St **8** IP4 .....17 C5
Foundry La Copford CU6 ..133 D5
  Earls Colne C06 ............105 B6
  Ipswich IP2 ...................17 C5
Fountain Ct C012 .............91 E5
Fountain La Pesthall C06 ...134 A1
  Easthorpe C06 ..............108 F0
Fountains Rd IP2 ..............16 F1
Four Acres
  Great Chesterford CB10 ...3 E3
  Saffron Walden CB1 .......23 E1
Four Ash Hill C09 .............10 D4
Four Ashes CM7 ...............74 C1
Four Sisters C07 ..............59 B5
Fourth Ave
  Chelmsford CM1 ...........205 B6
  Clacton-on-S C015 .........189 C4
  Frinton-on-S C013 .........170 F4
  Harwich C012 ................91 C3
Fourways CM22 ................94 C1
Fowe's La C010 ...............31 B8
Fowler Ct CM7 ................204 E3
Fowlers Arc C013 ...........170 F4
Fowlmere Rd SG8 .............19 A6
Fox Burrows La CM1 ........204 B2
Fox Cres CM1 .................204 F4
Fox Yd C09 .......................53 C5
Fox's Rd C010 .................11 E1
Foxburrow Rd IP3 ............18 F1
Foxdells La CM23 .............43 A1
Foxden CM8 ...................177 D6
Foxendale Folly C03 ........134 C7
Foxes La C03 ..................133 D8
Foxglove Cl
  Bishop's Stortford CM23 ..145 C6
  Clacton-on-S C015 .........188 F7
  Witham CM8 ................176 D3
Foxglove Cres IP3 ............18 E1

Foxglove Way CM1 ..........205 F6
Foxglove Wlk **4** C04 .....136 E7
Foxgrove La IP11 .............221 F5
Foxhall Cl C07 .................59 C4
Foxhall Fields C07 ...........59 C3
Foxhall Rd IP3 .................18 D5
Foxholes Rd CM2 ............216 F6
Foxley Dr CM23 ..............146 B8
Foxmead CM8 .................177 D6
Foxtail Rd IP3 ..................38 E8
Foxwood Cl C011 .............85 C2
Foxwood Cres IP4 ...........18 F5
Frambury La C01 ..............66 F8
Framingham Ct **5** IP1 ....17 A8
Framlingham Cl CM7 ........154 C7
Frampton Rd IP3 ..............38 A8
Frances Cl C07 ...............137 B2
Francis Cl Haverhill CB9 .....8 F8
  Tiptree C05 ..................179 C4
Francis Ct CM8 ...............156 C5
Francis Rd Braintree CM7 ..127 D2
  Sudbury C010 ................33 E7
Francis St C07 ..................59 B2
Francis Way
  Colchester C04 ..............110 D1
  Silver End CM8 ..............156 C4
Franciscan Way IP1 ..........17 C5
Frank Clater Cl C04 .........136 C8
Frank Naylor Ct **12** C01 ..135 F7
Franklin Rd IP3 ................18 B2
Fraser Cl CM2 .................216 C8
Fraser Rd IP1 ...................16 F7
Frating Abbey Farm Rd
  C07 ...........................166 C6
Frating Cross C07 ............166 B7
Frating Hill C07 ..............128 D1
Frating Rd Ardleigh C07 ...111 F6
  Great Bromley C07 .........138 F6
  Thorrington C07 ............166 A7
Fredrick J French Meml
  Homes CM1 .................205 B6
Fredricks Cl C011 ............115 B5
Freebournes Ct **8** CM8 ..177 A2
Freebournes Rd CM8 ........177 B2
Freehold Rd IP4 ..............18 B6
Freeland Rd C015 ...........188 E1
Freelands C07 ................186 C6
Freewood La CM1 ............20 B3
Fremantle Rd C02 ...........136 B1
French's Way CM2 ..........205 C2
French's Wlk **4** CM2 .....205 C2
Frensham Ct C013 ...........134 D7
Freston Ct CM23 .............118 C1
Freston Hill IP9 ................37 E4
Freston St IP9 ..................37 E3
Friars **7** IP9 ..................60 B8
Friars Bridge Rd IP1 .........17 B5
Friars Cl
  Clacton-on-S C015 .........188 B6
  Colchester C02 ..............110 C2
  Sible Hedingham CO9 .......51 D2
  Wivenhoe C07 ..............164 C8
Friars Gr Jun & Inf
  Schs C04 ....................110 C2
Friars La Braintree CM7 ...127 F4
  Maldon CM9 ...................90 E5
  Saffron Walden IP1 .........17 C5
  Sudbury C010 ................33 E7
Friars Wlk CM7 ...............205 B1
Friars Wood CM23 ..........146 C8
Friday Wood Gn C02 ........162 A8
Friedberg Ave CM7 .........145 D4
Friends Field C08 ..............55 F1
Friends Sch CB11 .............43 D8
Friends Wk CB11 .............43 D7
Frinton Gn C04 ...............110 E3
Frinton Park Ct C014 ......171 A0
Frinton Rd
  Holland-on-S C015 .........189 E6
  Kirby Cross C013 ...........170 D6
  Thorpe-le-S C016 ..........142 B1
Frinton-on-Sea Cty
  Prim Sch C013 .............170 F5
Frinton-on-Sea Sta
  C013 ...........................170 F5
Fritillary Cl IP6 ................36 E0
Friton Cl IP2 ....................17 A1
Fritton Cl IP2 ...................17 A1
Fritton Ct **10** CB9 ...........8 E7
Frobisher Cty Prim Sch
  C015 ...........................187 F1
Frobisher Dr C015 ..........187 F1
Frobisher Rd Harwich C012 ..90 F1
  Ipswich IP3 ...................17 E1
Frobisher Way CM7 .........128 C4
Frog Hall Cl C05 .............164 B6
Frog Mdw C07 .................84 F7
Frogge St CB10 ...............11 A1
Frogs Cl CM22 ................91 C2
Fronk's Ave C012 .............91 B2
Fronk's Rd C012 ..............91 B2
Frowick La C016 ............167 B2
Fryatt Ave C012 ...............91 A4
Fuchsia Ct **2** C04 .........136 D8
Fuchsia La IP4 ..................18 A5
Fuchsia Way C016 ..........188 C5
Fulcher Ave CM2 ............205 F3
Fulfen Way CB11 ..............43 D7
Fullbridge CM9 ...............210 A3

Fuller Ct **3** CM23 ..........146 A7
Fuller's Cl C015 ..............158 B2
Fullers Rd C02 ................136 D2
Fulmar Cl C04 .................137 A8
Fulton Cres CM23 ...........146 C8
Furneaux La C05 .............163 F5
Furness Cl IP2 ..................36 F8
Furrow Ct CM23 .............145 C5
Furrow Cl C03 ................134 E5
Further Meadow CM1 .......215 A8
Furze Cres C07 ...............165 A7
Furze La C07 ..................139 A5

## G

Gablefields CM2 ..............217 D6
Gaces Acre CB11 ...............43 A1
Gadwall Reach C05 ..........158 D2
Gage's Rd
  Belchamp St P C010 ........13 A1
  Little Yeldham C09 .........30 F8
Gager Dr C05 .................179 E5
Gaiger Cl CM1 ................205 D7
Gainsborough Cl
  Clacton-on-S C016 .........188 B6
  West Mersea C05 ..........201 D6
Gainsborough Cres CM2 ...205 E3
Gainsborough Dr C012 .....86 C4
Gainsborough La IP3 .........37 F7
Gainsborough Rd
  Colchester C03 .............135 B5
  Felixstowe IP11 .............221 F4
  Ipswich IP4 ...................17 D8
  Sudbury C010 .................33 E8
Gainsborough's House
  Mus C010 .....................33 E7
Gainsford Ave C015 ........189 A4
Gainsford End Rd C09 .......50 B6
Gainsford Rd C02 ............201 A6
Gall End La CM24 ...........119 F7
Galleydene Ave CM2 ........216 C3
Galleywood Cty Inf Sch
  CM2 ...........................216 C2
Galleywood Rd
  Chelmsford CM2 ...........216 A5
  Great Baddow CM2 ........216 E5
Galliford Rd CM9 ............210 A4
Galloway Cl **3** CM2 .......145 F8
Galloway Dr C016 ...........168 D3
Galloway Rd CM23 ..........118 F1
Gallows Green Rd CM6 ......97 F2
Gallows Wlk CB11 ............43 C7
Galsworthy Cl CM7 .........155 A7
Gandish Cl C07 .................59 D1
Gandish Rd C07 ...............59 E2
Ganges Rd IP9 .................91 B8
Gannet Cl CB9 ...................9 C8
Gannet Rd IP2 ..................16 E3
Gaol La C010 ...................33 E7
Gap The Arlesden CB11 .....43 F1
Garden Cl
  Holland-on-S C015 .........189 G6
Garden Ct C013 ...............170 F3
Garden Farm C05 ............201 D7
Garden Field
  ..................................221 C5
  Hatfield Peverel CM3 ......193 I-4
Garden Field Cotts C06 .....81 E5
Garden Fields
  Great Tey C06 ...............132 C8
  Dunmow CM6 ................124 D6
Garden Pl C010 ................33 D7
Garden Rd
  Clacton-on-S C015 .........203 D7
  Walton-on-N C014 ........171 A7
Garden Terr C09 ..............76 F7
Gardeners Rd CM7 ..........216 D5
Gardeners Rd C07 .............76 F1
Gardenia Pl C016 ............188 B4
Gardenia Wlk C04 ...........136 E7
Garfield Cl IP11 ..............221 D3
Garfield Rd IP11 ..............221 D3
Garland Rd C010 ..............90 F5
Garnetts **1** CM6 ...........152 C5
Garnetts Bglws CM6 ........152 C5
Garnetts La CM6 .............152 C6
Garnetts Villas CM6 ........152 C5
Garnons Chase C06 ..........81 A5
Garrettlands C07 .............217 F6
Garrison La IP11 .............221 D4
Garrod Ct C02 .................163 B7
Garrods IP9 ......................35 B1
Garthwood Cl C06 ..........108 E4
Gascoigne Rd C04 ...........136 C8
Gasfield **5** CB11 .............86 D4
Gaston End C07 ...............59 C3
Gaston St C07 ..................59 C3
Gatacre Rd IP1 .................17 A7
Gate St CM9 ...................209 F3
Gate Street Mews CM9 .....209 F3
Gatefield Ct C014 ...........170 F7
Gatekeeper Cl
  **8** Braintree CM7 ........127 F1
  Ipswich IP8 ....................36 E8
Gatwick Cl CM23 .............119 B1
Gauden Rd CM7 ..............127 F7
Gavin Way C04 ...............110 B5
Gay Bowers La CM3 ........218 F6
Gay Bowers Rd CM3 ........218 F4
Gay Bowers Way CM8 ......195 A7
Gaye St **1** IP1 ................17 B6
Gazelle Ct C04 ................110 C4
Generals La CM3 .............192 B2

Generals Mews IP11 .....221 B5
Genesta Cl CM9 .....199 D2
Geneva Rd IP1 .....17 B7
Gentian Ct C04 .....109 C2
Geoff Seaden Cl 2 C01 ..136 C6
George Ave C07 .....185 F7
George Cl C015 .....188 C2
George Cut C07 .....185 F6
George Frost Cl IP4 .....17 D7
George Gent Cl CB9 .....27 B6
George Green CM22 .....146 B1
George La C010 .....2 B3
George Rd CM7 .....127 D2
George St Chelmsford CM2 205 B1
 ■ Colchester C01 .....135 F7
 Harwich C012 .....91 D6
 Saffron Walden CB10 .....43 E7
George Yd 7 CM7 .....127 F3
Georgian Ct IP11 .....221 D5
Geralds Ave .....18 A5
Geranium Cl C04 .....188 C4
Geranium Wlk C04 .....136 D7
Gerard Ave CM23 .....145 E4
Gerard Rd C016 .....188 C6
Gernon Cl CM1 .....191 B3
Gernon Rd C07 .....111 E7
Gestingthorpe Rd C010 ..31 F4
Gibbons Ct CM6 .....123 D1
Gibbons St 8 IP1 .....17 A6
Gibbs Field CM23 .....145 D5
Gibson Cl CB10 .....22 D1
Gibson Gdns CB10 .....22 D1
Gibson Rd C09 .....51 D1
Gibson Way CB10 .....22 D1
Giffins Cl CM7 .....127 F1
Gifford Cl IP9 .....62 D5
Giffords Pl IP4 .....18 F6
Gilberd Ct C04 .....110 C6
Gilberd Ho C03 .....135 A7
Gilberd Rd C02 .....136 B4
Gilberd Sch The C04 .....110 B5
Gilbert Rd C02 .....12 88
Gilbert Way CM7 .....128 C5
Gilbey Ave CM23 .....146 B6
Gilbey Cotts CM22 .....94 C1
Gilbey Cres CM24 .....119 E8
Gilbey Gn CB11 .....42 F1
Gilchrist Way CM7 .....127 E4
Gilda Terr CM7 .....127 E2
Gilderdale Cl C04 .....110 D3
Gilders Way C016 .....188 C5
Gili Cl CM9 .....209 F6
Gilmore Way CM7 .....217 B6
Gilpin Way CM7 .....154 C7
Gilson Cl CM2 .....205 F2
Gilwell Park Cl C03 .....135 A4
Gimson Cl CM8 .....176 F2
Gippeswyk Ave IP2 .....17 A4
Gippeswyk Rd IP2 .....17 B4
Gipping Cl CB9 .....8 E6
Gipping Way IP8 .....16 86
Gipsy La CM23 .....119 C4
Girling St C010 .....33 E8
Girton Rd CB9 .....9 87
Girton Way IP2 .....16 F1
Glade The C04 .....110 F2
Gladeview C015 .....188 F7
Gladiator Way CM2 .....135 A2
Gladstone Ct CM2 .....205 B1
Gladstone Rd
 Colchester C01 .....136 A5
 Ipswich IP3 .....17 F5
 Tiptree C05 .....179 D4
Gladwin Rd C04 .....135 D4
Glamis Cl CB9 .....8 D8
Glamorgan Rd IP2 .....17 B1
Glastonbury Cl IP2 .....16 F1
Glebe Ave CM7 .....127 F6
Glebe Cl Elmstead C07 ..138 A6
 Sproughton IP8 .....16 86
 Tattingstone IP9 .....61 C7
 Wix C011 .....115 C5
Glebe Cres
 Broomfield CM1 .....191 B1
 Witham CM8 .....176 E4
Glebe Ct CM23 .....146 B8
Glebe End Capel St M IP9 ..35 82
 Elsenham CM22 .....94 D1
Glebe Gdns C05 .....158 E5
Glebe La Chelmondiston IP9 ..63 A8
 Little Easton CM6 .....122 F5
 Woolverstone IP9 .....38 B1
Glebe Meadow CM3 .....190 E7
Glebe Rd Chelmsford CM1 205 B3
 Colchester C02 .....135 C2
 Heybridge CM9 .....210 C5
 Kelvedon C05 .....158 82
 Tiptree C05 .....179 C5
Glebe The Elsenham CM22 ..94 D1
 Peldon C05 .....182 E5
 Purleigh CM3 .....220 D1
 Saffron Walden CB11 .....43 E7
Glebe View CM2 .....216 B3
Glebe Way
 Clacton-on-S C015 .....203 G7
 Frinton-on-S C013 .....170 F5
Glebefield Rd CM3 .....194 B4
Glebelands C06 .....82 B1
Glemham Dr IP4 .....18 F3
Glemsford Cl IP11 .....221 B3
Glemsford Cty Prim Sch
 C010 .....2 85
Glemsford Pl 3 CB9 .....9 88
Glen Ave C010 .....135 B7
Glenavon Rd IP4 .....18 D7

Glencoe Rd IP4 .....18 C8
Glendale Gr C04 .....110 C3
Gleneagles Dr IP4 .....18 D5
Gleneagles Way CM3 ..194 84
Glenfield Ave IP11 .....221 E5
Glenhurst Ave IP4 .....18 88
Glenside C010 .....34 A6
Glenstevins Cl C04 .....110 D3
Glenway Ct C06 .....82 B1
Glisson Sq C02 .....135 B4
Globe Cl C05 .....179 C6
Globe Cres CM23 .....118 D6
Globe Wlk C05 .....179 D6
Globe Yd 4 C010 .....33 E8
Gloucester Ave
 Chelmsford CM2 .....216 C6
 Colchester C02 .....135 C3
 Maldon CM9 .....209 F1
Gloucester Cres CM1 ..205 A5
Gloucester Gdns CM7 ..128 B4
Gloucester Rd Haverhill CB9 ..8 F6
 Ipswich IP3 .....18 B2
Gloucester Way C010 ..15 D2
Goat Hall La
 Chelmsford CM2 .....215 F3
 Galleywood CM2 .....216 A3
Goat House La CM3 .....219 F4
Goat Lodge Rd CM9 ..196 A5
Goda Cl CM8 .....194 D8
Goddard Way
 Chelmsford CM2 .....205 F2
 Saffron Walden CB10 .....22 E3
Godfrey Way CM6 .....123 C1
Godfreys Mews CM7 ..205 B1
Godlings Way CM7 .....127 F2
Godmans La C06 .....132 E3
Godric Pl CM7 .....127 E3
Godric Rd CM8 .....194 E8
Godwin Cl C09 .....76 D1
Godwit Ct C05 .....158 D2
Goff's La C016 .....141 F8
Goings La C05 .....201 D6
Gold Cl CM22 .....94 83
Gold St CB10 .....22 D1
Goldcrest Cl C04 .....137 A8
Goldcrest Cl IP2 .....16 D3
Goldcrest Rd IP2 .....16 C3
Golden Dawn Way C04 ..109 E2
Golden La Radwinter CB10 ..25 A2
 Thorpe-le-S C016 .....141 F3
Golden Noble Hill C01 ..136 A6
Goldenacres CM1 .....205 F8
Goldenlond C06 .....56 C5
Goldfinch Cl C04 .....136 F7
Goldhanger Cl CM7 ..128 D1
Goldhanger Rd CM9 ..210 D4
Golding Thoroughfare
 Golding Way Glemsford C010 ..2 B4
 St Osyth C016 .....187 A5
Goldingham Dr CM7 .....155 A7
Goldings CM23 .....146 88
Goldings Ave CM2 .....216 C8
Goldlay Gdns CM2 .....205 C1
Goldlay Rd CM2 .....205 C1
Golds Nursery Bsns Pk
 C02 .....94 C3
Golf Green Rd C015* ..203 G8
Goodchild Way C09 .....30 A2
Goodey Cl C01 .....136 A6
Goodlake Cl C012 .....90 F2
Goodliffe Pk CM21 .....119 82
Goodmans La CM3 .....173 F4
Goodwin Stile CM23 ..145 D5
Goodwins Cl CB11 .....21 E3
Goojerat Rd C02 .....135 D5
Gordon Dr C04 .....110 C5
Gordon Rd
 Chelmsford CM2 .....216 A6
 Harwich C012 .....91 82
 Ipswich IP4 .....18 A7
Gordon Way C012 .....91 82
Gore La CM7 .....127 A2
Gore Rd CM7 .....127 A2
Gore Terr CM7 .....127 A2
Gorefield Rd CM22 .....121 B5
Gorefield Rdbt CM24 ..121 B4
Goring Rd Colchester C04 ..110 C1
 Ipswich IP4 .....18 C6
Gorse La
 Clacton-on-S C015 .....189 A8
 Tiptree C05 .....179 C4
Gorse Lane Ind Est C015 ..189 B8
Gorse Rd IP3 .....18 B2
Gorse Way
 Clacton-on-S C015 .....203 F7
 Colchester C03 .....134 D4
Gorse Wlk C06 .....136 D7
Gorsehayes IP2 .....17 B3
Gosbecks Cty Prim Sch
 C02 .....135 A3
Gosbecks Rd C02 .....135 A2
Gosbecks View C02 ..135 A2
Gosfield Cty Prim Sch
 C09 .....102 C8
Gosfield Hall C09 .....102 C8
Gosfield Rd
 Blackheath C02 .....163 A8
 Braintree CM7 .....102 D3
Gosfield Sch C09 .....75 F2
Gosford Cl C010 .....12 88
Goshawk Dr CM2 .....216 85
Goslings The CM6 .....156 C5
Goul La CB10 .....22 D1
Gouldings Ave C014 ..171 88
Goulds Rd C04 .....54 F2
Goulton Rd CM1 .....191 A1

Government Flats C012 ..91 E5
Gower St IP2 .....17 C4
Gowers Ave CM2 .....216 E6
Gowers End C010 .....2 C5
Goyfield Ave IP11 .....221 D4
Grace Gdns CM23 .....145 F4
Grace's Cross CM2 .....217 C7
Graces Cl CM8 .....195 A7
Graces La CM3 .....207 81
Graces Wlk C013 .....171 A6
Grafton Pl CM7 .....206 A4
Grafton Rd C012 .....91 D6
Grafton Way IP1 .....17 C5
Graham Ave IP1 .....17 88
Graham Rd
 Felixstowe IP11 .....221 D5
 Great Oak Ct C09 .....30 A1
 Ipswich IP1 .....17 B7
Grailands CM23 .....145 D8
Grammar School Pl 11
 C010 .....33 E7
Grampian Gr CM1 .....204 D6
Granary Barn Mus The
 .....85 D7
Granary Ct CM6 .....150 D7
Granary The C010 .....12 86
Grange Cl Felixstowe IP11 221 C5
 Halstead C09 .....102 E7
 Walton-on-t-N C014 .....171 A7
Grange Ct Chelmsford CM2 215 F7
 Clacton-on-S C016 .....188 A4
Grange Farm IP11 .....221 85
Grange Farm Rd C02 ..136 D4
Grange Hill C06 .....130 F1
Grange La CM6 .....151 C7
Grange Mill C06 .....130 F2
Grange Pk CM23 .....118 F1
Grange Prim Sch IP11 ..221 84
Grange Rd
 Bishop's Stortford CM23 ..146 A7
 Felixstowe IP11 .....221 84
 Great Horkesley C06 .....109 87
 Harwich C012 .....91 A3
 Ickleton CB10 .....22 A6
 Ipswich IP1 .....17 E6
 Lawford C011 .....85 F1
 Little Bromley C011 .....112 E7
 Tiptree C05 .....179 A6
 Wickham Bishops CM8 ..195 E4
Grange The CM23 .....118 F1
Grange Way C02 .....136 D3
Grange Wlk CM23 .....146 A7
Grange View CM9 .....209 F1
 Walton-on-t-N C014 .....144 D2
 Weeley Heath C016 .....168 A6
Granta Cl CB10 .....3 D1
Granta Cotts CB10 .....3 C2
Grantham Cres IP2 .....17 A4
Grantham Ct C01 .....136 A7
Grantham Rd C06 .....109 87
Grantley Cl C06 .....133 D5
Grants Ct C014 .....171 C8
Granville Cl C06 .....108 E3
Granville Rd
 Clacton-on-S C015 .....188 F3
 Colchester C01 .....136 85
 Felixstowe IP11 .....221 D3
Granville St 2 IP1 .....17 86
Granville Way C07 .....186 A7
Grasby Cl C07 .....137 82
Grasmere Cl
 Great Notley CM7 .....154 C6
 Ipswich IP3 .....18 81
Grasmere Gdns C013 ..170 F7
Grassfields C013 .....170 E6
Grassmere C04 .....110 B5
Gravel Hill C06 .....56 A2
Gravel Hill Way C012 ..90 F1
Gravel Pit La C011 .....60 E2
Gravel The C06 .....130 F2
Gray Rd C03 .....135 A6
Gray's Cotts C011 .....136 87
Gray's La CM7 .....73 E4
Grayling Cl CM7 .....127 E1
Grayling Dr C04 .....110 F1
Grayling Rd IP8 .....36 88
Grays Cl C05 .....201 C6
Grays Ct CM23 .....145 E8
Grays Mead C09 .....51 D2
Great Baddow Sch CM2 216 D6
Great Bardfield Cage CM7 ..72 82
Great Bardfield Cty Prim
 Sch CM7 .....72 82
Great Bentley Cty Prim
 Sch C07 .....166 E7
Great Bentley Rd C07 ..166 A8
Great Bentley Sta C07 ..166 C2
Great Bradfords Cty Jun
 & Inf Sch CM7 .....128 84
Great Canfield Rd CM22 ..148 D5
Great Chesterford CE
 Prim Sch C010 .....3 C1
Great Chesterford Ct
 CB10 .....3 C2
Great Chesterford Sta
 CB10 .....3 C1
Great Cob CM1 .....205 E5
Great Cornard Ctry Pk
 C010 .....34 C4
Great Cornard Mid Sch
 C010 .....34 C4
Great Cornard Upper Sch
 C010 .....34 84
Great Dunmow CE Jun
 Sch CM6 .....150 C8
Great Eastern Cl CM23 ..146 A6
Great Eastern Rd C010 ..33 E7
Great Eastern Sq IP11 ..221 E5

Great Easton CE Prim
 Sch CM6 .....123 A8
Great Field IP11 .....221 A8
Great Gibcracks Chase
 CM3 .....218 A2
Great Gipping St IP1 .....17 85
Great Hadham Rd CM23 ..145 C5
Great Harrods C014 .....171 A7
Great Holland Common
 Rd C013 .....169 D2
Great House Farm Rd
 C02 .....162 A5
Great Leighs Cty Prim Sch
 CM3 .....174 A7
Great Notley Ave CM7 ..154 C5
Great Oak Ct C09 .....30 A1
Great Sampford Cty Prim
 Sch CB10 .....47 A3
Great Tey CE Prim Sch
 C06 .....106 C1
Great Tey Rd C06 .....132 C4
Great Totham Prim
 Sch CM9 .....196 A5
Great Totham Rd CM8 ..195 F5
Great Tufts IP9 .....35 81
Great Waltham CE Prim
 Sch CM3 .....190 E7
Great Whip St IP2 .....17 C4
Great Yeldham Rd C09 ..50 D7
Grebe Cl IP2 .....16 E2
Green Acres Rd C02 ..162 A5
Green Cl Chelmsford CM1 ..205 D4
 Hatfield Peverel CM3 .....194 C3
 Writtle CM1 .....204 81
Green Cnr C07 .....139 E1
Green Ct C06 .....104 F7
Green End La C013 .....170 85
Green Farm Rd C06 .....78 82
Green La Aldham C06 ..107 C1
 Ardleigh C07 .....111 D6
 Black Notley CM8 .....155 A2
 Boxted C04 .....82 D5
 Colchester C04 .....110 E2
 Colchester, Crockleford
  Heath C07 .....111 C1
 Great Horkesley C06 .....109 C6
 Great Notley CM7 .....154 F2
 Little Totham CM9 .....197 C7
 Stratford St M C07 .....58 C4
 Tattingstone IP9 .....61 D7
 Tiptree C05 .....179 D6
Green Man La C07 .....179 E1
 Walton-on-t-N C014 .....144 D2
 Writtle CM1 .....204 81
Green Way C06 .....78 A2
Green's Yd C07 .....135 E7
Greenacres
 Clacton-on-S C015 .....189 A5
 Coggeshall C06 .....130 F1
 Colchester C04 .....109 E3
Greene View CM7 .....155 88
Greenfield C08 .....177 A1
Greenfield Cotts C04 .....82 E6
Greenfield Dr C06 .....106 81
Greenfields
 Galleywood CM2 .....216 C2
 Gosfield C09 .....102 F7
 Stansted
  Mountfitchet CM24 .....119 E7
Greenfields Way CB9 .....8 E6
Greenfinch Ave IP2 .....16 D3
Greenfinch End C04 .....136 F8
Greenford Rd C015 .....188 C3
Greengates Mobile
 Home Pk C016 .....168 C4
Greenhill Pk CM23 .....145 D5
Greenhurst Rd C07 .....186 A6
Greenhythe Cl C04 .....136 D6
Greens The IP4 .....18 C4
Greens Yd C013 .....170 F5
Greensmill C011 .....86 C5
Greenspire Gr IP8 .....16 82
Greenstead Cl C01 .....136 D6
Greenstead Ct C01 .....136 D6
Greenstead Rdbt C04 ..136 D6
Greenview Pk C015 .....189 A7
Greenway
 Bishop's Stortford CM23 ..146 C6
 Frinton-on-S C013 .....170 F5
 Green La C015 .....188 87
Greenway Gdns CM7 ..154 D7
Greenway The C015 .....189 87

Greenwood Sch C09 .....76 F2
Gregory St C010 .....13 86
Grendel Way C015 .....189 F6
Grenfell Ave C015 .....189 E6
Grenfell Cl C04 .....110 C1
Grenville Rd
 Braintree CM7 .....127 E2
 Sudbury C010 .....15 F2
Gresley Cl C04 .....109 F2
Gresley Gdns IP2 .....17 C3
Gretna Gdns IP4 .....18 89
Greville Cl C014 .....144 E2
Grey Friars Rd 10 IP1 ..17 C5
Grey Ladys CM7 .....216 82
Greyhound Hill C04 .....83 E5
Greyhound Rd C010 .....2 83
Greys Cl C010 .....1 C1
Greys Hollow CB11 .....93 D6
Greystones Cl C03 .....135 A3
Grieves Cl C03 .....134 C4
Grimston Rd C02 .....136 A4
Grimston Way C014 .....171 87
Grimwade Cl C011 .....86 D7
Grimwade St IP4 .....17 D5
Grindle The IP8 .....16 A7
Groom Ho C015 .....188 E4
Groom Pk C015 .....188 E4
Groome Ct 6 C04 .....136 D7
Grooms La CM8 .....156 E4
Groomside CM7 .....128 A2
Grosvenor Cl
 Bishop's Stortford CM23 ..145 D4
 Chelmsford CM2 .....216 D7
 Ipswich IP4 .....17 E8
 Tiptree C05 .....179 D5
Grosvenor Ct IP3 .....18 89
Grosvenor Ho 4 CM23 ..146 88
Grosvenor Rd C010 .....15 C2
Grove Ave
 Walton-on-t-N C014 .....171 88
 West Mersea C05 .....201 C5
Grove Cotts 1 CM8 .....177 A2
Grove Ctr The CM8 .....177 A1
Grove Farm Rd
 Tiptree CM9 .....179 A1
 Tolleshunt Major CM9 ..197 C7
Grove Field CM7 .....102 C1
Grove Hill Belstead IP8 ..36 C7
 Dedham C07 .....84 D4
 Ipswich IP8 .....16 E1
 Langham C04 .....83 F5
 Stansted
  Mountfitchet CM24 .....119 D5
Grove La Chelmondiston IP9 ..63 D5
 Ipswich IP4 .....17 E5
Grove Orch CM7 .....102 C1
Grove Pl 10 CM23 .....145 F7
Grove Rd Bentley IP9 .....60 86
 Brantham C011 .....86 D8
 Chelmsford CM1 .....205 D4
 Felixstowe IP11 .....221 E6
 Little Clacton C016 .....168 D5
 Tiptree C05 .....179 D5
Grove The Bicknacre CM3 ..218 F1
 Clacton-on-S C015 .....188 F2
 Earls Colne C06 .....105 86
 Great Hallingbury CM22 ..146 F2
 Witham CM8 .....177 A2
Grove Villas CM7 .....126 A8
Gryme's Dyke Ct C03 ..134 D6
Gryme's Dyke Way C03 ..134 E3
Guelph's La C06 .....70 A3
Guernsey Way CM7 .....127 D2
Guildford Rd C01 .....136 A8
Guildhall Way CB10 .....24 A7
Guinea Cl CM7 .....128 D4
Guithavon Ct CM8 .....176 F2
Guithavon Rise CM8 ..176 F2
Guithavon St CM8 .....176 F2
Guithavon Valley CM8 ..176 F2
Gull Cotts C016 .....142 D4
Gull Ct C010 .....141 F1
Gull's La C07 .....85 A3
Gulls Croft CM7 .....128 D3
Gulpher Bsns Pk IP11 ..221 D8
Gulpher Rd IP11 .....221 D7
Gun Hill C07 .....84 C7
Gunfleet Cl C05 .....201 87
Gunfleet Ct C015 .....189 C4
Gurdon Rd C02 .....135 F3
Gurney Benham Cl C02 ..135 84
Gurton Rd C06 .....131 A3
Gusford Prim Sch IP2 ..16 D1
Gutteridge Hall La C016 ..167 E7
Gutters La CM1 .....205 C7
Guy Cook Cl C010 .....34 C4
Guys Farm CM1 .....204 81
Gwendoline Rd IP4 .....18 F4
Gwyn Cl CM1 .....192 E1
Gwynne Rd C012 .....91 D4
Gymnasium St IP1 .....17 87
Gypsy La C05 .....159 C6

## H

Ha'penny Field IP9 .....62 D5
Hackmans La CM3 .....219 E2
Haddon Pk C01 .....136 C6
Hadfelda Sq C03 .....194 A4
Hadham Ct CM23 .....145 E8
Hadham Gr CM23 .....145 E8
Hadham Hall C010 .....145 D8
Hadham Rd CM23 .....145 D8
Hadleigh Cl
 Clacton-on-S C015 .....189 A3
 5 Saffron Walden CB10 ..22 F2

High St *continued*
Saffron Walden CB10 .........22 D1
Sproughton IP8 ...............16 A6
Stebbing CM6 ................124 E5
Thorpe-le-S CO16 ............141 F1
Tollesbury CM9 ...............199 D1
Walton-on-t-N CO14 .........171 C8
West Mersea CO5 ............201 B6
Wethersfield CM7 .............73 C3
Widdington CB11 .............67 D4
Wivenhoe CO7 ...............164 B8
High St N CO5 ...............201 C7
High Stile CM6 ...............150 C8
High Tree La CO14 ...........144 D2
High View CM23 ..............119 D3
High View Ave CO15 .........188 E6
High View Cl CO15 ...........188 E5
High View Rd IP1 .............16 D8
High Woods Ctry Pk CO4 ...110 A4
Higham Hill IP7 ...............58 A8
Higham Rd CO7 ...............58 B3
Highams Chase CM9 .........212 A8
Highbank CO10 ................2 B5
Highbirch Rd CO16 ..........167 D3
Highbury Terr **1** CO9 ......76 F2
Highbury Way CO10 ..........34 B5
Highclere Rd
Colchester CO4 ..............110 B4
Great Notley CM7 ............154 B6
Highfield CO10 ...............12 D7
Highfield Ave
Bishop's Stortford CM23 ....146 C6
Harwich CO12 .................91 B3
Highfield Cl
Braintree CM7 ...............128 A6
Danbury CM3 ................218 D6
Highfield Ct CO12 ............91 B3
Highfield Dr CO3 .............135 C7
Highfield Holiday Pk
CO16 .........................188 E8
Highfield Rd
Chelmsford CM1 .............204 E4
Felixstowe IP11 ..............221 E4
Sudbury CO10 .................34 A8
Highfield Stile Rd CM7 ......128 A6
Highfields Bentley IP9 .......60 E6
Debden CB11 ..................68 B7
Great Yeldham CO9 ..........30 A2
Halstead CO9 ................103 F8
Henham CM22 .................94 F6
Langley CB11 .................40 D2
Saffron Walden CB10 .........22 E2
Highfields Cty Prim Sch
CO11 .........................86 C4
Highfields La CO5 ............136 E7
Highfields Rd CM8 ...........176 E1
Highland Rd CM23 ...........145 F3
Highlands CO9 ................75 E1
Highlands Chalet Pk
CO15 .........................188 F7
Highlands Dr CM9 ...........209 E2
Highmead CM24 ..............119 E8
Highview Cl CO10 ............15 E2
Highwoods App CO4 .........110 C4
Highwoods Cty Prim Sch
CO4 ..........................110 B4
Highwoods Sq CO4 ..........110 B4
Hildabrook Cl **2** IP2 ........16 E1
Hill Cl CO16 ...................15 D8
Hill Cotts CO7 ...............166 E2
Hill Cres CM2 ...............205 D2
Hill Farm La IP9 ..............63 F7
Hill Fields CM3 ...............219 A6
Hill House Ct CO7 ...........186 A7
Hill House Pk CM9 ...........209 F3
Hill House Rd IP3 .............17 E5
Hill La CB9 .....................9 F5
Hill Rd Chelmsford CM2 ....205 D2
Clacton-on-S CO15 ..........188 E6
Coggeshall CO6 ..............131 B2
Harwich CO12 .................91 C4
Hempstead CB10 ..............46 D8
Ramsey CO12 .................116 E8
Hill Road S CM2 .............205 D2
Hill St CB10 ...................22 D1
Hill Top La CB11 ..............43 E7
Hill View CM3 ................218 F1
Hill View Cl CO5 .............163 F8
Hill View Rd CM1 ............205 C4
Hillary Cl Bradwell CM7 ....129 D2
Chelmsford CM1 .............205 D4
Thringstone CM9 .............210 B5
Ipswich IP4 ...................18 A5
Hillcrest
Clacton-on-S CO15 ..........189 A6
Kirby-le-S CO13 ..............170 D8
Hillcrest Cotts CO4 ..........83 E6
Hillcrest Cl CO12 .............91 C3
Hillcrest Rd CO10 .............15 E2
Hillhouse La CO16 ...........141 B3
Hilliards Rd CO7 .............113 C2
Hillie Bunnies CO6 ..........105 B7
Hillman Ave CO15 ...........203 E6
Hillman JMI Sch
CM23 .........................119 C1
Hillridge CO10 ...............110 B3
Hills Cl CM7 ..................127 F4
Hills Cres CM23 .............135 A5
Hills Rd CO9 ...................75 D8
Hillside CO13 .................170 E4
Hillside Ave CM23 ...........146 A7
Hillside Cotts
Birchanger CM23 ............119 C3
Sudbury CO10 .................34 A7
Thorpe-le-S CO16 ...........142 A2

Hillside Cres
Holland-on-S CO15 ..........189 C5
Ipswich IP3 ...................18 C3
Hillside End CM23 ...........119 C3
Hillside Gdns CM7 ..........127 F1
Hillside Gr CM2 ..............216 A7
Hillside Ho **2** CM7 ..........127 F1
Hillside Mews CM2 ..........216 A7
Hillside Prim Sch IP2 ........17 C3
Hillside Rd CO10 .............34 A7
Hillside Specl Sch CO13 ....15 F1
Hillside Terr **1** CM7 ........127 F1
Hillston CO12 .................136 B2
Hilltop Cl CO2 ...............136 D4
Hilltop Cres CO16 ...........140 F1
Hilltop Rise CO10 ...........140 E1
Hilton Cl CO11 ................86 D4
Hilton Rd IP3 .................18 C1
Hilton Way CO9 ..............75 E8
Hilton Wlk CO9 ...............75 F8
Hines Cl CO6 .................133 B8
Hintesham Ct IP4 .............18 F5
Hintlesham Dr IP11 .........221 B5
Hinxton Rd CB10 ..............3 A7
Hipkins CM23 ................145 E4
Hiskin Cl IP5 ...................18 F7
Hitch Common Rd CB11 .....66 F8
Hitcham Rd CO6 .............130 F3
Hitchcock Pl CO10 ...........15 E1
Hitchin Mews CM7 ..........155 B8
Hitherwood Rd CO2 ........135 C2
Hobart Cl CM1 ...............204 E5
Hobbs Dr CO4 .................83 A5
Hobbs La CO10 .................2 D2
Hoblongs Ind Est CM6 .....150 E6
Hockerill
Anglo-European Sch
CM23 .........................146 B7
Hockerill Ct **7** CM23 ......146 A7
Hockerill St CM23 ...........146 A7
Hockney Gdns IP3 ............38 A8
Hodges Holt CM8 ............195 A7
Hodgkinson Rd IP11 ........221 A3
Hoe Dr CO3 ..................135 A5
Hoe La Great Waltham CM3 .190 E6
Pentlow CO10 .................13 F8
Hoe Mill Rd CM9 ............208 E4
Hoffmans Way CM1 .........205 B4
Hog's La CB9 ..................19 D3
Hogarth Cl CO5 ..............201 D6
Hogarth Ct CM1 .............205 E6
Hogarth End CO13 ..........170 E7
Hogarth Rd IP3 ...............18 A1
Hogarth Sq IP3 ...............18 A1
Holborough Cl CO4 .........136 F7
Holbrook Cl CO16 ...........188 B4
Holbrook Cres IP11 .........221 B4
Holbrook High Sch IP9 ......62 D6
Holbrook Prim Sch IP9 ......62 D6
Holbrook Rd Harkstead IP9 ..63 A2
Haverhill CB9 ...................8 E6
Ipswich IP3 ...................17 F1
Stutton IP9 ....................62 A2
Holcombe Cres IP2 ..........16 D2
Holden Cl IP2 .................17 D3
Holden Rd CO4 ..............109 F2
Holdsworth Cl CO10 ..........2 B3
Holkham Cl IP4 ...............18 F5
Holland Haven Ctry Pk
CO15 .........................189 D8
Holland Haven Prim Sch
CO15 .........................189 E6
Holland Ho CO15 ...........189 A3
Holland Lodge CO15 ........188 F3
Holland Park Prim Sch
CO15 .........................189 B5
Holland Rd Clacton-on-S,
Clacton-on-S, Rush
Green CO15 ..................188 F2
Felixstowe IP11 ..............221 D3
Frinton-on-S CO13 ..........170 E3
Ipswich IP4 ...................17 F6
Kirby Cross CO13 ...........170 B6
Little Clacton CO16 .........168 E2
Hollands Rd CB9 ...............9 A6
Holledge Cres CO13 ........170 E6
Hollies Rd CM7 ..............129 C3
Holliland Croft CO6 .........132 C8
Hollingtons Gr CO2 .........161 A3
Hollis Lock CM2 .............206 A3
Holliwell Cl CO3 .............134 D6
Hollow La Broomfield CM1 ..204 E8
Bures CO8 .....................55 F3
Chelmondiston IP9 ...........63 F7
Hollow Rd Ashen CO10 ......11 E3
Braintree CM6 ................153 B4
Chrishall SG8 .................19 D2
Elmdon CB11 ..................20 C4
Kelvedon CO5 ...............157 F2
Washbrook IP8 ................35 D8
Widdington CB11 .............67 C3
Holloway Rd CM9 ...........210 A5
Holly Bush Cnr CO7 .........58 C5
Holly Cl CO2 .................135 C2
Holly Cl CM1 .................205 B2
Holly La Belstead IP8 ........36 C7
Great Horkesley CO6 .........82 C4
Stutton IP9 ....................61 E3
Holly Oaks CO6 ...............80 E4
Holly Rd Colchester CO3 ...134 C4
Ipswich IP1 ...................16 F7
Rushmere St A IP5 ...........18 F7
Holly Way
Chelmsford CM2 .............216 D7
Elmstead CO7 ................138 A6
Tiptree CO5 ..................179 C5

Holly Wlk CM8 ...............177 B5
Hollybank CM7 ..............176 F1
Hollybush Hill CO7 ..........166 E3
Hollyhock Rd CB10 ...........22 E2
Hollymead Cl CM4 ..........109 C3
Hollytree Ct CO2 ............109 F3
Hollyview Cl CO16 ..........140 F5
Hollywood Cl CM2 ..........216 E6
Holm Oak CO2 ...............136 A3
Holman Cres CO3 ...........135 A4
Holman Rd CO9 ..............103 E8
Holmans CM3 ................206 E8
Holmbrook Way CO13 ......170 E5
Holmes Rd CO9 .............103 E8
Holmoak IP9 ...................62 D6
Holmswood House
Prep Sch CO3 ...............134 D8
Holmwood Cl CO16 .........188 B6
Holmwood House Prep
Sch CO3 .....................134 D2
Holt Dr Blackheath CO2 ....163 A7
Wickham Bishops CM8 .....195 E5
Holt's Rd CO6 .................81 B3
Holy Family RC Prim
Sch CM8 .....................194 F8
Holy Trinity CE Prim Sch
CO9 ...........................76 H4
Holybread La CM3 ..........207 C4
Holyrood CO12 ...............90 F2
Holyrood Cl IP2 ..............16 F2
Holywells Cl IP3 ..............17 E4
Holywells High Sch IP3 .....18 C1
Holywells Rd IP3 ..............17 E3
Home Cl IP9 ...................27 C7
Home Farm Cty Prim Sch
CO3 ..........................134 F6
Home Farm La
Ardleigh CO7 .................112 A8
Dedham CO7 ...................85 A1
Home Mead
Galleywood CM2 .............216 C2
Writtle CM1 ..................204 A1
Homebridge CB10 .............47 A3
Homedale Cotts CO4 .........83 B6
Homefield IP9 .................35 B1
Homefield Cl CM1 ...........204 D5
Homefield Rd
Colchester CO2 ..............135 C1
Haverhill CB9 ...................8 F5
Witham CM8 .................177 A4
Homefield Way
Cressing CM7 ................155 D7
Earls Colne CO6 .............105 B7
Hadleigh IP7 .................127 A5
Homelands Cl CO14 .........171 A7
Homelye Chase CM6 ........124 B1
Homeorr Ho IP11 ...........221 F4
Homerton Cl CO15 ..........188 F8
Homestead CM1 .............205 B7
Homestead Sch CO4 .........83 E4
Honey Bridge Rd CO6 .......56 C8
Homing Rd CO16 ............168 C4
Honey Cl CM2 ...............216 D6
Honey La CB11 ................64 F3
Honeybourne CM23 .........145 E4
Honeypot La
Little Clacton CO16 .........168 A7
Tolleshunt Knights CM9 ....180 B1
Weeley Heath CO16 .........168 A4
Wix CO11 .....................114 F3
Honeypots CM2 ..............216 C6
Honeysuckle Cl CM23 ......145 C6
Honeysuckle Gdns CO16 ....16 E4
Honeysuckle Path **9**
CM1 ..........................205 F6
Honeysuckle Way
Colchester CO4 ..............136 E8
Thorrington CO7 .............166 A5
Witham CM8 .................176 D4
Honeywood Ave CO6 ........131 A3
Honeywood Rd CO9 .........77 A3
Honywood Cl CO10 .........132 C3
Honywood Rd CO3 ..........135 D6
Honywood Sch The CO6 ...131 A3
Honywood Way CO13 .......170 F7
Hood Gdns CM7 .............128 C4
Hood Rd IP3 ...................17 E1
Hop Gardens La CM9 .......208 F4
Hopgrounds The CM7 ........72 D6
Hopkin's La CO12 .............91 D6
Hopkins Cl
Chelmsford CM2 .............206 A3
Kirby Cross CO13 ...........170 F6
Hopkins Mead CM2 .........206 A2
Hopkirk Cl CM3 ..............218 F8
Hopping Jacks La CM3 .....218 F7
Hoppit Mead CM7 ...........127 F1
Hopton Rise CB9 ...............8 B8
Horace Eves Cl **1** CB9 ......8 F8
Hordle Pl CO12 ...............91 D4
Hordle St CO12 ...............91 D4
Horkesley Hill CO6 ...........82 A7
Horkesley Rd
Great Horkesley CO6 .......109 E8
Nayland CO6 ...................56 A1
Horley IP2 ....................16 A4
Horley Cl CO16 ..............188 C6
Horn Hill CO9 .................75 C5
Hornbeam Cl
Chelmsford CM2 .............216 A6
Colchester CO2 .............109 C2
Hornbeam CM8 ..............177 A4
Hornbeam Wlk CO16 .......140 F7
Horne Row CM3 .............218 D5
Horner Pl **4** CM8 ..........177 A2
Hornsea Villas CM6 .........124 D7
Horrocks Cl CO2 .............136 A4
Horse & Groom La CM2 ....216 A3
Horse Pond Cl CM9 ..........34 C4

Horseshoe Cl CB11 ..........20 B4
Horseshoe La CB9 .............8 E7
Horsey Rd CO13 .............170 C8
Horsham Ave IP3 .............18 D3
Horsley Ho IP11 .............221 F4
Hospital App CM1 ...........191 B3
Hospital Cl CO3 .............135 D6
Hospital Rd CO3 .............135 D6
Hossack Rd IP3 ...............38 A8
Houblon Dr CM2 .............216 C2
Houchin's La CO6 ...........113 E3
Houghton Pl IP4 ...............18 F5
House Martins The IP11 ....221 D6
Hove Ct CO15 ................189 F6
Howard Ave CO12 ...........90 F2
Howard Cl CM7 ..............128 C3
Howard Dr CM2 .............206 A2
Howard Rd
Holland-on-S CO15 ..........189 C4
Saffron Walden CB10 .........22 E2
Howard St IP4 .................18 B6
Howard Vyse Ct CO15 ......188 E5
Howards Cl CM3 .............206 E8
Howards Croft CO4 .........109 D5
Howbridge CE Jun Sch
CM8 ..........................194 F8
Howbridge Hall Rd
Witham CM8 ..................194 F6
Witham CM8 ..................194 F7
Howbridge Inf Sch The
CM8 ..........................194 F8
Howbridge Rd CM8 .........194 F8
Howe Ave IP3 .................18 C3
Howe Chase CO9 .............76 E4
Howe Cl CO4 .................136 D7
Howe Green House Sch
CM2 ..........................146 D2
Howe La CB10 .................47 A5
Howlets Terr IP9 ..............63 E7
Hoxter Way CM7 .............15 E2
Hoxton Cl CO16 .............188 D5
Hoynors CM3 ................219 A7
Hubbards Chase CO14 .....171 B8
Hubert Rd CO3 ..............135 B8
Hucklesbury Ave CO15 .....189 C7
Hudson Cl
Clacton-on-S CO16 .........188 C5
Harwich CO12 .................91 A1
Haverhill CB9 ...................9 C6
Hudson's Hill CM7 ...........73 D4
Hudsons La CO6 ..............57 B5
Hugh Dickson Rd CO4 ......109 E2
Hugh Villas CM23 ...........146 A5
Hughes Cnr CO7 ..............59 A4
Hughes Rd CO2 ..............135 A2
Hughes Stanton Way
CO11 ...........................86 B4
Hull La CM3 ..................175 A2
Hull's La CM2 ................217 E7
Hulton Cl CM3 ...............206 E8
Hulver Ct IP3 .................18 A1
Humber Ave CO15 ..........203 E6
Humber Doucy La IP4 ........18 D8
Humber Rd
Chelmsford CM1 .............205 C5
Witham CM8 ..................176 D2
Humphry's Farm La
CM3 ..........................190 C7
Humphry Rd CO10 ...........33 E8
Hundon Pl **8** CB9 ...........9 B8
Hundred La CO4 ..............83 C4
Hungerdown La CO11,CO7 ..85 E1
Hunnable Rd CM7 ...........127 E2
Hunt Ave CM9 ...............210 B5
Hunt Cl CO5 .................158 D4
Hunt Dr CO16 ...............188 D6
Hunt Rd CO6 .................105 A6
Hunt Way CO13 .............170 C6
Hunt's Cl CM1 ...............215 B8
Hunt's Dr CM1 ...............215 B8
Hunter Cl CM23 .............135 D5
Hunter Dr CO11 ..............86 A3
Hunter Rd CM7 ..............128 C2
Hunter's Chase CO7 .........84 E2
Hunters Cnr CO3 ............134 F5
Hunters Ridge CO4 .........110 B4
Hunters Way
Chelmsford CM1 .............205 F7
Saffron Walden CB11 .........43 D7
Hunting Gate CO1 ..........136 C7
Huntingdon Way CO15 .....188 E6
Hunts Farm Cl CM9 ........199 D2
Hunts Cl CM9 ................199 D2
Hunts Hill CO10 ................2 B4
Hunts La CB10 .................3 B7
Hunwicke Rd CO4 ...........136 E7
Hurnard Dr CO3 .............135 A7
Hurrell Down
Boreham CM3 ................192 F1
Highwoods CO4 ..............110 A4
Hurrells La CM3 .............206 F3
Hurst Cl
Bishop's Stortford CM23 ...145 E7
Brightlingsea CO7 ...........186 A6
Hurst Way CM2 ..............205 F2
Hutland Rd IP4 ...............17 F7
Huxtables La CO3 ...........108 A1
Hyacinth Cl
Clacton-on-S CO16 .........188 C4
Tollesbury CM9 ..............199 E1
Hyacinth Cl **4** CM1 ........205 F6
Hyam's La IP9 .................61 F1
Hyams La IP9 .................62 D5
Hyde Chase Danbury CM3 ..219 B4
Woodham Mortimer CM9 ..219 D4
Hyde Gn CM3 ................219 B3
Hyde La Maldon CM9 ........219 B6
Wethersfield CM7 .............74 B2

Hyde Rd CO10 ................
Hydewood Rd CO9 ...........
Hyem's La IP11 ...............
Hylands Cl CM6 ..............
Hylands Par CM2 ............2
Hyldon Ct IP11 ...............22
Hyll Cl CB10 ..................
Hyntle Cl IP2 ..................16
Hythe Cl Braintree CM7 ....127
Clacton-on-S CO15 ..........203
Hythe Gr CO7 ................165
Hythe Hill CO1 ..............136 C
Hythe Quay CO2 .............136 D
Hythe Sta CO2 ...............136 D
Hythe Station Rd CO2 ......136 D
Hythe The CM9 ..............210 B

## I

Iceni Way CO2 ................135 B
Ickleton Pl **5** CB9 ..........9 B
Ickleton Rd Elmdon CB11 ...20 A
Great Chesterford CB10 ......3 C
Hinxton CB10 ..................3 C
Icknield Cl CB10 ...............3 A
Ickworth Cres CM4 ..........18 F
Ickworth Ct IP11 ............221 A
Ilex Cl CO2 ...................135 D
Imogen Cl **4** CO4 ..........136 F
Imphal Cl CO2 ...............135 C
Ingarfield Rd CO10 ..........189 E
Ingelrica Ave CM3 ...........194 B
Ingestre St CO12 ..............91 D
Ingham Rd CB9 .................9 B
Inglenook CO15 ..............189 B
Ingleside Ct CB10 .............22 D
Inglis Rd CO3 ................135 D
Ingram Mews CM7 ...........155 B
Ingram's Piece CO7 .........111 E
Ingram's Well CO10 ..........33 F
Ingram's Well Rd CO10 ......33 F
Inkerman Row **3** CO10 ....33 E
Inkerpole Pl CM2 ............205 F
Innes End **4** IP8 .............16 C
Innham Hill CO9 ..............75 C
Inverness Cl CO1 ............136 A
Inworth La CO6 ................79 D
Inworth Wlk **5** CO2 ........136 A
Ipswich Airport IP3 ...........38 C
Ipswich High Sch IP9 ........38 C
Ipswich Hospl IP4 ...........18 C
Ipswich Mus IP1 ..............17 B
Ipswich Prep Sch IP1 ........17 B
Ipswich Rd Ardleigh CO7 ...83 F
Brantham CO11 ...............60 E
Colchester CO4 ..............110 C
Dedham CO7 ..................84 B
Harkstead IP9 .................63 B
Holbrook IP9 ..................62 E
Holland-on-S CO15 ..........189 D
Ipswich IP10 ...................38 F
Stratford St M CO7 ...........58 E
Ipswich Sch Ipswich IP1 ....17 B
Ipswich IP1 ...................17 C
Ipswich Sta IP1 ...............17 B
Ipswich Transport Mus
IP3 ...........................18 C
Ireland Rd IP3 .................18 C
Ireton Rd CO3 ................135 D
Iris Cl Chelmsford CM1 .....205 F
Ipswich IP2 ....................16 F
Irlam Rd IP2 ..................16 D
Iron Latch La CO3 ...........134 C
Irvine Rd CO3 ................135 C
Irving Cl CM23 ..............145 D
Isbourne Rd CO4 ............136 F
Ishams Chase CM8 .........195 C
Island La CO13 ...............143 A
Island Rd CO14 ..............143 E
Ivor Brown Cl CO4 ..........110 B
Ivry St IP1 ....................17 B
Ivy Cotts CM7 ...............123 B
Ivy La CO5 ...................185 B
Ivy Lodge Rd CO6 ...........109 C
Ivy Todd Hill CB11 ...........68 A
Ixworth Rd CB9 ................8 E

## J

Jacaranda Cl CM1 ...........206 A
Jack Andrews Ave CO4 .....110 C
Jack Branch Ct CO15 .......188 E
Jack Hatch Way CO7 ........137 A
Jack's La CM22 ................68 D
Jackson Pl CM2 .............216 D
Jackson Rd CO15 ...........188 D
Jackson Sq **10** CM23 ......145 F
Jackson Wlk CO2 ............136 F
Jackson's La CB10 .............3 C
Jackson's Sq CB10 ............3 C
Jacobs Ct CO7 ...............185 F
Jacquard Way CM7 ..........127 E
Jacqueline Ct CO3 ..........135 A
Jaggard's Rd CO6 ...........131 A
James Boden Cl IP11 .......221 C
James Carter Rd CO3 .......134 F
James Cl CM7 ................137 C
James Croft CO2 .............216 B
James Gdns CO16 ...........187 B
James Hatfield Ho CO2 .....17 E
James Rd CO15 ..............188 C
James St
Brightlingsea CO7 ...........185 F
Colchester CO1 ..............136 A
Jameson Pl CO10 ............33 B

................188 C3
................16 E2
................177 A3
................9 D6
................189 C4
................3 ........3
................135 F8
................204 F6
................207 D5
CM23 ........145 C6
CM7

Clacford CM1 ........205 E7
ilter CO4 ........136 E8
sh IP2 ........16 F3
ane Hay CO15 ........203 G7
ers Green CM7 ........100 E2
ayrest Ctr CO3 ........134 E4
ymar Ct CM7 ........77 F2
Jays La CO3 ........134 E6
Jays The CO4 ........110 C3
Jaywick La CO15 ........189 A3
................9 A8
Jeans La CM23 ........145 E7
Jeffcut Rd CM2 ........205 E2
Jefferies Rd IP4 ........17 E6
Jefferson Cl CO3 ........134 C5
jffery Rd CM2 ........217 A7
jffry Cl IP3 ........134 F5
Jeffrey Rd CM1 ........155 E6
Jekylls La CM7 ........48 D4
Jellicoe Way CM7 ........128 C4
Jenkins Dr CM23 ........21 E6
Jenkins La CM22 ........146 C6
Jenner Cl CM7 ........127 F1
Jenner Mead CM2 ........206 A3
Jennings Cl IP9 ........136 C6
Jermyns CI IP9 ........35 B2
Jersey Rd CM9 ........210 B1
Jersey Way CM7 ........127 D2
Jervis CI IP9 ........62 D5
Jervis Rd CM23 ........145 F6
Jessica Cl CO4 ........136 F7
Jimmy's La CU11 ........60 F2
Joes Rd CO10 ........34 F6
John Ball Wlk CO1 ........135 F7
John Bird Ct CO1 ........109 F1
John Brainston Sch &
Sixth Form Ctr The
CM8 ........176 F1
John Bunyan Cty Jun &
Inf Sch CM7 ........127 E4
John Dane Player Ct CO4
................22 E1
John English Ave CM7 ........127 E4
John Harper St CO1 ........135 E8
John Henry Keene
Meml Homes CM1 ........205 A4
jhy Kavanagh Cl IP1
................136 A6
John Kent Ave CM2 ........145 B2
John King Cl CO7 ........185 F6
John Raven Ct CO5 ........164 E5
John Ray Cty Jun & Inf
Schs CM7 ........154 F0
John Ray Green CM7 ........155 B5
John Ray St CM7 ........128 A3
John St CO7 ........185 F6
John Tibauld Ct CB9 ........27 B6
Johnson Cl Braintree CM7 ........155 A7
Ipswich IP2 ........17 C3
Johnson Rd
Great Baddow CM2 ........217 A5
St Osyth CO16 ........187 B4
Johnson's Dr CO7 ........138 A6
Johnsons Yd CB11 ........22 D2
Johnston Cl Halstead CO9 ........103 F8
Holland-on-S CO15 ........189 E5
Jollyhoys La CM6 ........152 C6
Jonathan Feedham Ct
CO7 ........137 B1
Jonquil Way CO4 ........109 C2
Joseph Gdns CM8 ........156 E4
Josse Lyns The IP11 ........221 A8
Josselin Cl CO6 ........105 B7
Joyce's Chase CM9 ........212 A8
Jubilee Ave
Broomfield CM1 ........191 B2
Clacton-on-S CO16 ........188 E8
Jubilee Cl CO12 ........90 E1
Jubilee Ct
Great Dunmow CM6 ........123 C1
Sible Hedingham CO9 ........75 E8
Walton-on-t-N CO14 ........171 C2
Jubilee End CO11 ........86 C5
Jubilee La CO7 ........111 C3
Jubilee Rd CO10 ........33 F8
Jubilee Rise CM3 ........219 A6
Jubilee Terr CM1 ........205 A4
Jubilee Wik CO4 ........170 F6
Jubilee Wlk CB9 ........9 D7
Julian Ave CO4 ........110 B6
Julian Cl Broomfield CM1 ........191 B1
Haverhill CB9 ........9 D7
Julian Court Rd CM7 ........128 A4
Jun Sch Folsted The
CM6 ........152 B5
Juniper Cl CO9 ........103 D8
Juniper Cres CM8 ........177 A4
Juniper Ct CM6 ........123 B1
Juniper Dr CM2 ........216 B6
Juniper Rd Boreham CM3 ........206 F8
Colchester CO3 ........134 D5
Juniper Way CO4 ........135 C1
Juno Mews CO2 ........135 C1
Jupes Hill CO7 ........79 D1

Jupes Hill CO7 ........85 C4
Jupiter Cl CB9 ........9 D6
Jupiter Rd IP4 ........18 B7
Justinian Cl CB9 ........9 D6
Juvina CM8 ........194 F7

## K

Kale Croft CO3 ........134 D5
Kangels The CB11 ........40 D2
Kate Daniels Ho CO16 ........140 F1
Kate's La CB10 ........24 C8
Katherine Semar Cty Inf
Sch CB11 ........43 E6
Katherine Semar Jun Sch
CB11 ........43 E6
Kay Cl CM3 ........174 A7
Kayla Ct CO3 ........135 E6
Keable Rd CO6 ........132 E3
Keating Cl IP11 ........86 B4
Keats Ave CM7 ........154 D8
Keats Rd CO3 ........134 F6
Kebbles CO10 ........7 B6
Keble Cl CO3 ........135 D0
Kedington Hill CO10 ........34 B2
Keeble Cl CO5 ........179 E6
Keeble Ct CO7 ........166 E7
Keeble Pk CM7 ........220 F8
Keeble Way CM7 ........128 A3
Keeble's Yd CB9 ........9 A8
Keelars La CO7 ........137 E2
Keelers Way CO6 ........109 B2
Keep Way CM9 ........216 B3
Kelly Rd IP2 ........8 E7
Keith Ct CO15 ........189 B8
Kelly Rd IP2 ........16 D8
Kelso Cl CO6 ........170 D7
Kelvedon Cl CM1 ........205 A4
Kelvedon Dr IP4 ........18 E5
Kelvedon Hall La CO5 ........178 E5
Kelvedon Rd
Coggeshall CO6 ........158 A8
Messing CO5 ........159 C2
Tiptree CO5 ........179 B7
Tolleshunt D'arcy CM9 ........198 C6
Wickham Bishops CM8 ........195 F5
Kelvedon Sta CO5 ........158 A3
Kelvin Ct CO13 ........170 F3
Kemball St IP4 ........18 A5
Kempe Rd CM7 ........72 D6
Kempson Dr CO10 ........34 C5
Kempsters The IP11 ........221 B7
Kempton Pk CO16 ........168 B5
Kemsley Rd
Farls Colne CO6 ........105 A6
Felixstowe IP11 ........221 D5
Ken Cooke Ct CO1 ........135 F7
Kendall CE Prim Sch
CO1 ........136 C4
Kendall Rd CO1 ........136 A6
Kendall's
Almshouses CO1 ........136 A6
Ailsworth CO10 ........142 A2
Rushley Rd CO15 ........189 E6
Kennedy Cl IP3 ........18 A6
Kennedy Way CM1 ........199 A5
Kennedy Rd IP11 ........221 A4
Kennel Cl CO7 ........185 F7
Kent Cl CO7 ........185 E7
Kent Cres CM7 ........145 E4
Kent Gdns CM7 ........128 B4
Kent Ho IP11 ........221 C6
Kent's Ave CO15 ........189 A6
Kentford Rd IP11 ........221 A4
Kentings The CM7 ........127 E2
Kentmere CO4 ........110 C2
Kents Grass CM9 ........199 D2
Kents Yd CB11 ........21 F4
Kentwell Cl IP4 ........18 E4
Kenworthy Rd CM7 ........127 F2
Kenyon Cl CO7 ........58 D1
Kenyon St IP2 ........17 C4
Kerby Rise CM2 ........205 F8
Kerridge's Cut CO11 ........87 A4
Kerry Ct CO1 ........136 C7
Kersey Ave CO10 ........34 B6
Kersey Ct CO2 ........135 C3
Kersey Dr CO16 ........188 D8
Kersey Rd IP11 ........221 B3
Kessler Ave CM7 ........73 D7
Kesteven Rd IP2 ........17 B4
Kestrel Gdns CM23 ........145 C8
Kestrel Rd Haverhill CB9 ........9 F7
Ipswich IP2 ........16 D3
Kestrel Way CO13 ........188 F6
Kestrel Wlk CM2 ........216 B5
Keswick Ave CO15 ........189 C6
Keswick Cl CO13 ........170 F7
Ketleys CM2 ........216 C3
Ketleys View CM7 ........127 A7
Kettlebaston Way IP4 ........17 D8
Kew La CO13 ........170 A4
Key Rd CO15 ........188 E3
Keys Dr IP4 ........17 F8
Keymer Way CO4 ........134 D4
Keynes Way CO2 ........90 F1
Khartoum Rd IP4 ........17 F7
Kidder Rd CM7 ........126 F4
Kilburn Gdns CO16 ........188 D5
Kildermorie Cl CO4 ........110 D3
Kilmaine Rd CO12 ........91 B5
Kiln Barn Ave CO15 ........188 F7
Kiln Cotts Danbury CM3 ........218 C6
Dedham CO7 ........84 F5

Kiln Dr CO10 ........34 B6
Kiln Field IP11 ........221 B5
Kilns Hill CO6 ........130 F5
Kimberley Cl CM23 ........146 A5
Kimberley Rd CO1 ........136 B5
Kincaid Rd CO16 ........187 A4
King Charles Rd CO5 ........201 D6
King Coel Rd CO3 ........134 D7
King Edward Ind Pk CO2 ........136 D5
King Edward IV's
Almshouses CB11 ........22 D1
King Edward Quay CO2 ........136 D5
King Edward Rd IP4 ........18 B3
King Edward VI Gram
Sch CM1 ........205 A3
King Edward Way CM8 ........194 E8
King George Rd CO2 ........135 F4
King George's Ave CO12 ........91 B4
King Harold Rd CO3 ........135 A4
King St
Bishop's Stortford CM23 ........145 F7
Bradfield CO11 ........114 C8
Castle Hedingham CO9 ........51 F4
Felixstowe IP11 ........221 C6
Ipswich IP1 ........17 C6
Maldon CM9 ........210 A1
Saffron Walden CB10 ........22 D1
Sudbury CO10 ........33 E7
King Stephen Rd CO1 ........136 B6
King Street Mews
CM23 ........145 F7
King's Cl CO15 ........187 A3
King's Cotts CM23 ........146 A6
King's Ct CM6 ........123 D1
King's Ford Cty Jun &
Inf Schs CO2 ........135 C3
King's Head St CO12 ........91 E6
King's La Elmdon CB11 ........20 A3
Long Melford CO10 ........15 F7
King's Quay St CO12 ........91 E6
King's Way
Clacton-on-S CO15 ........188 F3
Harwich CO12 ........91 D
King's Way IP3 ........18 C2
Kingfisher Ave IP2 ........16 E3
Kingfisher Cl
Colchester CO4 ........136 F8
Haverhill CB9 ........9 F7
Heybridge CM9 ........210 C5
Kingfisher Gate CM7 ........128 A5
Kingfisher Lodge CM2 ........216 F7
Kingfisher Way
Bishop's Stortford CM23 ........146 A7
Kelvedon CO5 ........158 C2
Kingfishers CO15 ........188 F6
Kings Acre CO6 ........130 F2
Kings Ave
Clacton-on-S CO15 ........189 D5
Ipswich IP4 ........17 E5
Kings Chase CM8 ........177 A1
Kings Cl CO1 ........86 C4
Kings Ct
Bishop's Stortford CM23 ........145 C8
Holland-on-S CO15 ........189 E5
Kings Fleet Rd IP11 ........221 C3
Kings Ford Ct CO2 ........135 E8
Kings Head Ct CM2 ........200 C2
Kings Hill CM8 ........155 F1
Kings La CO5 ........129 A8
Kings Mead CO9 ........77 A2
Kings Meadow CO10 ........33 F7
Kings Meadow Ct CO5 ........158 D4
Kings Meadow Rd CO1 ........135 E8
Kings Mews CO7 ........137 C4
Kings Par CO15 ........189 E5
Kings Prom CO15 ........203 J8
Kings Quay St CO12 ........91 E6
Kings Rd Braintree CM7 ........127 E4
Chelmsford CM1 ........204 F4
Glemsford CO10 ........2 B5
Great Totham CM9 ........196 D7
Halstead CO9 ........76 F1
Kings Reach CO14 ........144 A8
Kings Road Cty Jun &
Inf Sch CM1 ........204 F4
Kings Vale CO15 ........199 E1
Kingsbridge Cl CM7 ........127 F8
Kingsbridge Rd CM23 ........146 A4
Kingsbury Cl CO6 ........132 F3
Kingsbury Rd IP11 ........221 A7
Kingsdale Ind Est The
CM1 ........205 C3
Kingsfield Ave IP11 ........17 D8
Kingsgate Dr IP4 ........17 F8
Kingsland Beach CO5 ........201 C5
Kingsland Cl CO5 ........201 D6
Kingsland Rd CO5 ........201 D6
Kingsman Dr CO16 ........188 C5
Kingsmead Rd CM23 ........146 A8
Kingsmere Cl CO5 ........201 D7
Kingston Ave CM2 ........205 E3
Kingston Chase CM9 ........209 F5
Kingston Cres CM9 ........205 E3
Kingston Rd IP1 ........16 F8
Kingsway Harwich CO12 ........91 B4
Tiptree CO5 ........179 C6
Kingswode Hoe Specl
Sch CO3 ........135 A7
Kingswoud Rd CO4 ........109 F4
Kingwell Ave CO4 ........110 B4
Kinlett Cl CO7 ........110 B4
Kinloch Chase CM8 ........177 A4
Kino Rd CO14 ........171 D8

Kipling Cl CM1 ........205 A5
Kipling Way CM7 ........155 A8
Kirby Cl IP4 ........18 A7
Kirby Cross Sta CO13 ........170 B6
Kirby Hall Rd CO9 ........51 D5
Kirby Rd
Great Holland CO13 ........170 B5
Walton-on-t-N CO14 ........171 B8
Kirby St IP4 ........18 A7
Kirby-le-Soken Cty
Prim Sch CO13 ........170 B7
Kirk Pl CM2 ........205 F3
Kirkbare CO13 ........170 E6
Kirkham Cl IP2 ........17 A2
Kirkhurst Cl CO7 ........186 A6
Kirklees CM1 ........204 E4
Kirknans Rd CM23 ........216 D3
Kirkton Cl IP9 ........91 A8
Kirtling Pl IP2 ........9 B8
Kitchen Field CM7 ........128 D3
Kitchen Hill CO10 ........1 B6
Kitchener Rd IP11 ........16 F8
Kitchener Way IP9 ........91 A8
Kittiwake Cl IP2 ........16 E3
Kittiwake Dr CM9 ........210 C5
Knapton Cl CM1 ........205 D7
Knebworth Ct CM23 ........145 D6
Knight's Ct IP2 ........8 E7
Knights Cl
Bishop's Stortford CM23 ........145 C8
Lawford CO11 ........86 C4
ivgrove CO5 ........179 F3
Knights Rd
Braintree CM7 ........128 C3
Coggeshall CO6 ........130 F2
Knights Way CM6 ........202 D7
Knightsbridge Cl CO2 ........135 C2
Knightsbridge Ct CO15 ........189 B3
Knole La CB11 ........41 A7
Knowles Cl CO7 ........76 E1
Knox Cl CO15 ........188 E5
Knox Gdns CO15 ........188 E5
Knox Rd CO15 ........188 E5
Knutsford Cl CM8 ........16 C1
Kohima Rd CO2 ........135 B1
Knoswell Cl CO2 ........91 B2
Kynaston Pl CM8 ........177 B2
Kynaston Wy CM7 ........127 A7

## L

Laburnum CM3 ........194 A3
Laburnum Cl
Clacton-on-S CO15 ........188 A3
Great Bentley CO7 ........166 F8
Ipswich, Chantry IP8 ........16 C2
Ipswich, Warren Heath IP3 ........18 E2
Laburnum Cres CM7 ........128 C4
Laburnum Dr CM2 ........216 C6
Laburnum Gr CO16 ........168 D2
Laburnum Gr CO4 ........136 E6
Laburnum Way CM8 ........177 A5
Lacey St IP4 ........17 E6
Ladbrook Dr CO2 ........136 A3
Ladbrooke Rd CO16 ........188 D6
Ladell Cl CO5 ........134 E3
Lady D'Arcy Charity
Almhouses CO1 ........135 F6
Lady La Chelmsford CM2 ........205 C2
Ipswich IP1 ........17 B6
Ladygate CO9 ........8 E6
Ladysmith Ave CO7 ........185 E6
Ladysmith Cotts CM6 ........152 B4
Ladywell La CO9 ........217 B5
Lafenloud Rd IP4 ........18 C7
Laing Rd CO4 ........136 E6
Laings Ave CO15 ........180 C3
Lake Wlk IP2 ........188 C3
Lakes Mdw CO11 ........131 A2
Lakes Rd CM7 ........128 B2
Lakeside Cl IP2 ........16 C1
Lakeside Rd IP2 ........16 C1
Lakforth CO10 ........15 D8
Lamarsh Hill Bures CO8 ........55 E1
Lamarsh CO8 ........55 B6
Lamarsh Rd CO8 ........55 A4
Lamb La CO9 ........75 D7
Lambert Cross CB10 ........22 E3
Lambert's Rd CO6 ........105 F3
Lambeth Wlk CO15 ........188 F6
Lambourne Cl
Clacton-on-S CO15 ........188 F8
Colchester CO3 ........134 D4
Lambourne Gr CM9 ........210 E4
Lammas Way CO7 ........137 C2
Lancaster Gdns E CO15 ........189 A3
Lancaster Gdns W CO15 ........189 A3
Lancaster Ho IP11 ........221 C5
Lancaster Rd
Ipswich IP4 ........17 E6
Sudbury CO10 ........15 D2
Lancaster Way
Bishop's Stortford CM23 ........145 C8
Braintree CM7 ........127 E4
Lancing Ave IP4 ........18 A8
Land La CO1 ........136 A7
Landermere Rd CO16 ........168 A7
Landermere View CO16 ........142 A2
Landers Ct CM2 ........204 E5
Landisdale CM3 ........219 A7
Landscape View CB11 ........43 D6
Landsdown Rd CO10 ........34 A8
Landseer Rd IP3 ........18 A1

Landseer Ct
Clacton-on-S CO15 ........188 F2
Haverhill CB9 ........8 F6
Landseer Rd
Colchester CO3 ........135 B5
Ipswich IP3 ........17 E2
Lane Rd CO6 ........106 B7
Lane The Mistley CO11 ........86 F4
West Mersea CO5 ........201 A7
Lanercost Way IP2 ........17 A1
Langdale CM7 ........154 C7
Langdale Cl CO4 ........110 B4
Langdale Gdns CM2 ........216 D8
Langenhoe Cty Prim
Sch CO5 ........163 B2
Langenhoe Hall La CO5 ........183 C7
Langenhoe Pk CO5 ........163 B2
Langer Cty Prim Sch
IP11 ........221 C2
Langford Rd
Heybridge CM9 ........209 F6
Wickham Bishops CM8 ........195 C2
Langham Court Prim
Sch CO4 ........83 A4
Langham Dr CO16 ........188 B4
Langham La CO4 ........83 B2
Langham Rd CO4 ........82 F1
Langley Ave
Felixstowe IP11 ........221 C4
Wethersfield CM7 ........73 D7
Langley Cl Felixstowe IP11 ........221 C5
Harwich CO12 ........91 C3
Langley Hill CO8 ........106 C5
Langsion IP11 ........221 B7
Langton Ave CO4 ........204 E5
Languire Cl CO10 ........34 C6
Langwood CO5 ........90 F2
Lanham Green Rd CM7 ........156 A7
Lansdowne Cl CO15 ........179 C6
Lansdowne Rd
Felixstowe IP11 ........221 F6
Ipswich IP3 ........18 A5
Lanvalley Rd CO3 ........134 E6
Lanyards IP11 ........221 F4
Lapwing Dr
Heybridge CM9 ........210 C5
Kelvedon CO5 ........158 D2
Lapwing Rd IP2 ........16 D3
Larch Cl CO3 ........136 D8
Larch Gr Chelmsford CM2 ........216 C6
Nayland CO6 ........56 A1
Witham CM8 ........177 A5
Larch Ho IP11 ........221 B8
Larch Way CM6 ........123 B1
Larch Wlk CM9 ........210 C6
Larches The CM23 ........206 E8
Larchwood CM23 ........145 D5
Larchwood Cl IP2 ........16 C5
Lark Rise CO10 ........33 D5
Lark's La Broomfield CM1 ........191 A6
Great Waltham CM3 ........190 F5
Larkfield Rd CO7 ........139 D1
Larkhill Way IP11 ........221 B5
Larkrise Cty Prim Sch
CM2 ........216 E6
Larks Cl IP9 ........9 C7
Larksfield Cres CO12 ........91 B4
Larksfield Rd IP9 ........62 A2
Larkspur Cl
Bishop's Stortford CM23 ........145 D6
Witham CM8 ........176 E4
Larkspur Ct CM1 ........205 F6
Larkspur Rd IP2 ........16 F3
Larkswauy
Bishop's Stortford CM23 ........145 C6
Felixstowe IP11 ........221 B3
Larkway CO13 ........170 E7
Larman Ct CO4 ........86 C7
Laser, The CO13 ........170 E7
Latchingdon Rd CM3 ........182 B6
Lathcoates Cres CM2 ........216 E8
Lattice Ave IP4 ........18 C6
Laud's Cl CO12 ........90 F2
Laundry Gdns CO10 ........15 C7
Laurel Ave CO12 ........90 F2
Laurel Cl IP3 ........189 B7
Laurel Ct CO4 ........136 E8
Laurel Dr
Great Dunmow CM6 ........122 D1
Long Melford CO10 ........15 C7
Laurel Gr CM2 ........216 A8
Laurelhayes IP2 ........17 A3
Laurels The Braintree CM7 ........128 A3
Great Notley CM7 ........154 C8
Laurence Ave CM8 ........195 A8
Laurence Cl CO7 ........137 F6
Laurence Croft CM1 ........205 C3
Lavender Cl
Bishop's Stortford CM23 ........145 D6
Tiptree CO5 ........179 C4
Lavender Cl CM1 ........205 F5
Lavender Ct CM1 ........205 F5
Lavender Hill IP2 ........16 F4
Lavender Rd CM1 ........109 C2
Lavender Wlk CO15 ........203 G7
Lavenham Cl CO16 ........188 B4
Lavenham Ct CO2 ........135 C2
Lavenham Rd IP11 ........16 E5
Lawford CE Prim Sch
CO11 ........86 B2
Lawford La
Chelmsford CM1 ........204 D3
Writtle CM1 ........204 C1

Lawford Mead Cty Inf Sch CM1 ....204 D5
Lawford Mead Cty Jun Sch CM1 ....204 D5
Lawling Ave CM9 ....210 C5
Lawn Chase CM8 ....176 F1
Lawn La CM1 ....205 D6
Lawn Way IP11 ....221 C5
Lawns Cl CO5 ....201 C7
Lawns The
　Chelmsford CM1 ....205 D5
　Ipswich IP4 ....18 C8
Laws Cl CB11 ....43 D7
Lawshall's Hill CO6 ....78 D1
Laxton Ct CO3 ....135 A4
Laxton Gr CO13 ....170 A5
Laxton Rd CO7 ....165 B8
Lavender Field 7 CB10 ....22 E7
Layer Breton Hill CO2 ....161 B1
Layer Cross CO2 ....161 F5
Layer Ct CO2 ....135 D4
Layer Marney Tower CO5 ....180 D8
Layer Rd Abberton CO5 ....162 E4
　Abberton CO5 ....163 A3
　Colchester CO2 ....135 C3
　Great Wigborough CO5 ....181 E5
　Haverhill CB9 ....8 E7
Layer-de-la-Haye CE Prim Sch CO2 ....161 F5
Layzell Croft CO10 ....34 C4
Le Cateau Rd CO2 ....135 E6
Lea Cl
　Bishop's Stortford CM23 ....119 B1
　Braintree CM7 ....128 D1
Lea Gr
　Bishop's Stortford CM23 ....119 B1
　Hatfield Peverel CM9 ....194 F1
Lea La CM8 ....177 F2
Lea Side CO5 ....201 D6
Leach Cl CM2 ....217 B7
Leam Cl CM... ....136 F7
Leapingwell Cl CM2 ....206 A3
Leas La Clacton-on-S CO15 ....188 D2
　Colchester CO2 ....135 C1
Leas Sch The CO15 ....188 D2
Leas The CO13 ....171 B6
Leather La
　5 Braintree CM7 ....127 F3
　Great Yeldham CO9 ....30 A1
　Haverhill CB9 ....8 E7
Lee Ct CM2 ....216 E7
Lee Rd Harwich CO12 ....91 C3
　Ipswich IP3 ....17 F3
Lee Wick La CO16 ....186 D2
Leech's La CO4 ....109 D4
Leeward Ct IP11 ....221 E5
Leeway The CM2 ....218 F7
Leez La CM3 ....152 E2
Leez Priory CM3 ....153 A2
Legerton Cotts CO8 ....79 C1
Legg St CM1 ....205 B3
Legions Way CM23 ....146 A8
Leicester Cl
　Colchester CO1 ....136 A8
　Ipswich IP2 ....16 F1
　Jaywick CO15 ....187 F1
Leicester Ct CM8 ....156 D3
Leigh Dr Elsenham CM22 ....94 C1
　Wickham Bishops CM8 ....195 D5
Leigh Rd CM3 ....191 E6
Leighton Rd IP3 ....38 A8
Leighton Sq IP3 ....38 A8
Leiston Rd CB9 ....8 E7
Lely Rd IP3 ....37 F8
Lemons Hill IP9 ....61 D8
Leonard Mews CM7 ....155 B8
Leopold Gdns IP4 ....18 B8
Leopold Rd
　Felixstowe IP11 ....221 E4
　Ipswich IP4 ....18 A8
Les Bois CO2 ....162 A5
Leslie Rd IP3 ....18 D1
Lethe Gr Blackheath CO2 ....163 A8
　Colchester CO2 ....162 F8
Letton Cl IP9 ....35 A1
Levens Way CM7 ....154 C6
Levington Rd
　Felixstowe IP11 ....221 C1
　Ipswich IP3 ....18 A3
Lewes Cl IP3 ....18 E3
Lewin Pl CM1 ....206 E8
Lewis Dr CM2 ....216 B6
Lewis La IP9 ....61 E2
Lexden Ct CO3 ....135 C7
Lexden Cty Prim Sch CO3 ....134 C6
Lexden Gr CO3 ....134 F7
Lexden Mews CO3 ....134 C6
Lexden Park Ho CO3 ....135 A7
Lexden Rd Colchester CO3 ....135 B7
　West Bergholt CO6 ....108 D4
Lexden Springs Sch CO3 ....134 C7
Lexdon Pl CO3 ....134 C7
Ley Field Marks Tey CO6 ....132 E3
　Takeley CM22 ....148 C7
Ley The CM7 ....128 D1
Leybourne Dr CM1 ....205 E7
Leyfields CM7 ....126 F1
Leys Dr CO16 ....168 C1
Leys Rd CO7 ....137 C3
Leys The Chelmsford CM2 ....205 F5
　Wimbish CB10 ....45 C3
Leyside CM7 ....126 F2

Leyton Ct CO15 ....188 F8
Leywood Cl CM7 ....128 D2
Lichfield Cl
　Chelmsford CM1 ....204 E4
　Colchester CO1 ....136 A8
Lidgate Ct IP11 ....221 A4
Lichild Cl CM8 ....195 A7
Lilac Ave CO16 ....203 B6
Lilac Cl CM2 ....216 C6
Lilac Ct CO7 ....137 A2
Lilac Tree Ct CO4 ....136 E8
Lilley's La CO7 ....112 D4
Lillies The CM7 ....102 B1
Lilly Cnr CM1 ....27 B6
Lilly Cl CM1 ....205 F6
Limbourne Dr CM9 ....210 D5
Lime Ave Colchester CO4 ....136 D8
　Harwich CO12 ....91 B3
Lime Cl Clacton-on-S CO15 ....188 C3
　Witham CM8 ....177 A5
Lime Gr CO10 ....33 C5
Lime St CO7 ....185 F5
Lime Wlk CM2 ....216 C6
Limebrook Way CM9 ....220 E7
Limefields CB10 ....22 D4
Limekiln La CM24 ....119 C5
Limes Cres 4 CM24 ....146 A7
Limes The Ardleigh CO7 ....111 F8
　Clacton-on-S CO15 ....189 A3
　Galleywood CM2 ....216 B2
　Gosfield CO9 ....102 E7
　Long Melford CO10 ....15 C7
Limetree Dr IP3 ....18 D2
Lincoln Ave CO15 ....203 D6
Lincoln Cl CM23 ....145 D5
Lincoln La CO6 ....82 C1
Lincoln Terr IP11 ....221 D3
Lincoln Way CO1 ....136 A6
Lindbergh Rd IP3 ....18 C2
Linden Cl Chelmsford CM2 ....216 C7
　Colchester CO4 ....110 E1
　Lawford CO11 ....86 B3
Lindens The CO15 ....188 E7
Lindens The
　Bishop's Stortford CM23 ....145 F6
　Braintree CM7 ....128 A1
Lindisfarne Cl IP2 ....17 A1
Lindisfarne Cl CM9 ....220 E8
Lindsey Ave CO10 ....34 B6
Lindsey Cl CM23 ....118 F1
Lindsey Rd
　Bishop's Stortford CM23 ....118 F1
　Ipswich IP4 ....18 C7
Line Cotts CO4 ....83 A4
Linfold Cl CM7 ....128 D4
Linford Mews CM9 ....220 E8
Ling's La IP9 ....63 D5
Lingwood Cl CM3 ....218 E2
Link Cl CO4 ....109 E4
Link La IP9 ....60 D6
Link Rd
　Bishop's Stortford CM23 ....145 F8
　Brightlingsea CO7 ....186 A6
　Capel St M IP9 ....35 A1
　Clacton-on-S CO15 ....188 D2
　Halstead CO9 ....103 D8
Link The IP9 ....60 D6
Link Way CM23 ....145 E6
Links Ave IP11 ....221 A4
Links Bsns Ctr The CM23 ....146 C7
Links Dr CM2 ....215 F7
Links Rd Bradwell CM7 ....129 D1
　Cressing CM7 ....156 C7
　St Osyth CO16 ....204 B8
Linksfield IP5 ....18 E7
Linksfield Gdns IP5 ....18 F7
Linkside CO13 ....170 E3
Linley Gdns CO15 ....188 D2
Linnet Dr CM2 ....216 B6
Linnet Rd IP2 ....16 D4
Linnet Way CO7 ....166 D8
Linnets CO15 ....188 F6
Linnets The CO13 ....170 B6
Linnetts La CM9 ....10 A4
Linstead Cl CO16 ....168 C4
Linton Cl CB11 ....43 F8
Linton Pl 18 CM9 ....9 B8
Linton Rd CB1 ....5 B7
Lintons The CM2 ....217 D6
Lion Meadow CB9 ....27 B3
Lion Rd CO10 ....2 B3
Lion St IP1 ....17 C6
Lion Wlk 25 CO1 ....135 F7
Lionel Hurst Cl CO10 ....34 C5
Lionfield Terr CM1 ....205 D3
Lisle Ho CO3 ....135 A7
Lister Cl CO2 ....136 A5
List Ho CO10 ....15 C8
Lister Rd CM7 ....154 F8
Lister Tye CM2 ....216 C7
Listonhall Chase CO9 ....75 B5
Litchborough Pk CM3 ....218 F8
Litchfield CO12 ....90 E2
Litchfield Cl CO15 ....188 E5
Littell Tweed CM2 ....206 A3
Little Baddow Rd
　Danbury CM3 ....218 E2
　Woodham Walter CM9 ....208 C3
Little Bakers CO14 ....171 A7
Little Bentley Rd CO16 ....114 B1
Little Bradfords CM7 ....128 A4
Little Braxted La CM8 ....177 C3
Little Bromley Rd
　Ardleigh CO7 ....112 B7
　Great Bromley CO7 ....112 F3
　Little Bentley CO7 ....113 E1

Little Chishill Rd SG8 ....39 C8
Little Church St CO12 ....91 D6
Little Clacton Engaines Prim Sch CO15 ....168 C2
Little Clacton Rd
　Clacton-on-S CO16 ....188 B7
　Great Holland CO13 ....169 E2
Little Croft St IP3 ....17 C3
Little Dorrit CM1 ....204 E7
Little Fields CM3 ....219 A7
Little Gipping St 7 IP1 ....17 B6
Little Gr 8 IP9 ....35 A1
Little & Great Sir Hughes La CM2 ....217 B2
Little Gulls 8 IP9 ....35 A1
Little Harrods CO14 ....171 A7
Little Horkesley Rd CO6 ....81 D5
Little Hyde Cl CO9 ....30 A2
Little Hyde Rd CO9 ....30 A2
Little Larchmount CB11 ....43 D8
Little London Hill CM7 ....72 D8
Little London La CM9 ....208 D4
Little Meadow CM1 ....204 A1
Little Meadows CM9 ....219 E6
Little Nell CM1 ....204 E7
Little Oakley CE Inf Sch CO12 ....117 B7
Little Sq 6 CM7 ....127 F3
Little St Mary's CO10 ....15 C7
Little Stile CM1 ....215 A8
Little Stone Ct CO15 ....203 J8
Little Tey Rd CO5 ....158 F7
Little Totham Rd
　Goldhanger CM9 ....211 D8
　Little Totham CM9 ....197 C1
Little Tufts IP9 ....35 B1
Little Walden Rd CB10 ....22 E5
Little Waltham CE Prim Sch CM3 ....191 B7
Little Waltham Rd CM1 ....191 D1
Little Whip St 9 IP2 ....17 C4
Little Wood CO13 ....170 E6
Little Yeldham Rd CO9 ....30 C3
Little's Cres IP2 ....17 C4
Littlebury Gdns CO2 ....136 C4
Littlebury Green Rd CB11 ....21 D3
Littlecotes CO4 ....109 D4
Littlefield Rd CO2 ....135 C2
Livery Mews CM3 ....146 A1
Llewellyn Cl CM1 ....205 D3
Lloyd Rd IP9 ....91 A8
Lloyds Ave 7 IP1 ....17 C6
Loamy Hill Rd
　Great Braxted CO5 ....178 F1
　Tolleshunt Major CM9 ....197 A7
Loates Pasture CM24 ....119 D8
Lobelia Cl CM1 ....206 A6
Locarno Rd IP3 ....18 B3
Lock Rd CO9 ....103 E8
Lockhart Ave CO3 ....134 C5
Lockram La 8 CM8 ....177 A2
Lodge Ave CM2 ....216 F7
Lodge Cl
　Clacton-on-S CO15 ....188 E4
　Little Oakley CO12 ....117 B7
Lodge Cres CO15 ....206 E7
Lodge Cotts CO4 ....108 F4
Lodge Farm La CO16 ....187 D4
Lodge Farm Rd CO10 ....2 C3
Lodge La Abberton CO5 ....163 D1
　Ardleigh CO7 ....111 A6
　Ardleigh CO7 ....111 C6
　Brightlingsea CO7 ....185 E7
　Langham CO4 ....110 D8
　Peldon CO5 ....182 E7
　Purleigh CM3 ....220 C2
　Tendring CO16 ....140 F6
Lodge Rd Braintree CM7 ....127 F1
　Brightlingsea CO7 ....185 E8
　Hazeleigh CM3 ....220 B5
　Little Clacton CO16 ....169 A5
　Little Oakley CO12 ....117 C8
　Maldon CM9 ....209 F3
　Messing CO5 ....159 D3
　Thorpe-le-S CO16 ....168 F6
　Writtle CM1 ....215 B8
Lodge The CO15 ....189 F6
Loftin Way CM2 ....216 D7
Lombard Ct IP4 ....17 F7
Lombardy Pl CM1 ....205 B3
Lombardy Rd CO10 ....15 D2
London Hill CM8 ....88 A2
London Rd
　Chelmsford CM2 ....215 F2
　Galleywood CM2 ....216 C3
London Land Cotts CO6 ....80 C4
London Rd
　Bishop's Stortford CM23 ....146 A5
　Braintree CM7 ....127 E1
　Capel St M IP9 ....35 B1
　Chelmsford CM2 ....215 E6
　Clacton-on-S CO15 ....188 E7
　Colchester CO3 ....134 E6
　Copford CO6 ....133 D4
　Feering CO5 ....159 B7
　Great Chesterford CB10 ....3 D2
　Great Horkesley CO6 ....81 F2
　Great Notley CM7 ....154 C5
　Ipswich IP2 ....17 A2
　Ipswich IP1 ....16 F5
　Kelvedon CO5 ....158 B1
　Littlebury CB11 ....21 C2
　Maldon CM9 ....209 D3
　Marks Tey CO6 ....133 A3
　Newport CB11 ....67 A6
　Saffron Walden CB11 ....43 D8
　Washbrook IP8 ....35 E6

London Rd continued
　Wendens Ambo CB11 ....42 F4
　Wendens Ambo CB11 ....42 F7
Lone Barn Ct IP11 ....16 D8
Long Acres CO5 ....158 F6
Long Border Rd CM24 ....120 E1
Long Brandocks CM1 ....204 A1
Long Comm CM9 ....209 F5
Long Croft CM24 ....119 D8
Long Field IP11 ....221 B6
Long Gdns CO9 ....53 F5
Long Gn CM7 ....133 C8
Long Green La CM7 ....99 C2
Long Horse Croft CB11 ....43 E7
Long La Arkesden CB11 ....41 E5
　Great Holland CO13 ....170 C3
　Rayne CM7 ....153 F8
Long Ley CB11 ....40 D2
Long Meadow
　Bishop's Stortford CM23 ....145 D6
　Great Notley CM7 ....154 B5
Long Meadows CO12 ....90 F2
Long Melford Prim Sch CO10 ....15 C7
Long Pastures CO10 ....2 C3
Long Perry IP9 ....35 B1
Long Rd CO11 ....86 C3
Long Rd E CO7 ....185 D7
Long Rd W CO7 ....184 E3
Long St IP3 ....17 E5
Long Wyre St CO1 ....135 F7
Longacre Chelmsford CM1 ....215 E8
　Colchester CO4 ....109 E2
Longacre Rd CM7 ....155 E6
Longacres CM7 ....128 A1
Longcroft Felixstowe IP11 ....221 C6
　Hempstead CB10 ....46 E8
　Takeley CM22 ....148 C7
Longcroft Rd CO4 ....110 B4
Longedryve CO2 ....135 C4
Longfellow Rd CM9 ....210 A1
Longfield CM8 ....176 E5
Longfield Rd Capel St M IP9 ....35 B2
Longfields CO16 ....187 B4
Longhedges CB11 ....22 E1
Longleaf Dr CM7 ....155 A8
Longleat Cl CM1 ....204 F7
Longmead Ave CM2 ....216 D4
Longmeads CM8 ....195 C5
Longmeads Cl CM1 ....204 A1
Longmore Ave CM2 ....216 E8
Longridge CO4 ....136 F8
Longs La CM3 ....173 F1
Longship Way CM9 ....220 E8
Longshots Cl CM1 ....191 A1
Longstomps Ave CM2 ....216 A7
Longstraw Cl CO3 ....134 D6
Lonsdale 4 IP2 ....17 C4
Lonsdale Cl IP4 ....17 F7
Lonsdale Rd CO16 ....142 A2
Looe Rd IP11 ....221 F5
Loompits Way CB11 ....43 D7
Loraine Way IP8 ....16 A8
Lord Holland Rd CO2 ....135 F3
Lord's Croft La CB9 ....9 A8
Lords Ave CM23 ....145 B7
Lords Cl CB10 ....23 D1
Lordship Rd CM1 ....204 B3
Lordsland La CM7 ....103 C1
Lordswood Rd CO2 ....135 C2
Lorkin Way CO6 ....108 F4
Lorkin's La CO10 ....54 C4
Lott's Rd CO16 ....168 B4
Louise Cl CO14 ....144 E3
Louse La CO7 ....84 C6
Louvain Rd CO22 ....91 A1
Love La CO7 ....185 F8
Love Way CO16 ....188 C6
Loveday Cl SG8 ....19 D3
Lover's La CO7 ....167 A7
Lovers La IP9 ....62 A5
Loves Wlk CM1 ....204 B1
Lovibond Pl 4 CM2 ....205 F4
Low Lighthouse Maritime Mus CO12 ....91 E5
Low Rd CO12 ....90 E1
Low St CO10 ....2 C6
Lowe Chase CO14 ....171 B8
Lowefields CO6 ....105 D5
Lower Anchor St CM2 ....205 A1
Lower Brook St IP4 ....17 C5
Lower Cotts SG9 ....64 A2
Lower Dales Rd IP1 ....17 A8
Lower Dales View Rd 3 IP1 ....17 A8
Lower Downs Slade CB9 ....9 A8
Lower Farm Rd CO4, CO6 ....82 C7
Lower Green CM8 ....88 F1
Galleywood CM2 ....216 C2
Wakes Colne CO6 ....79 C1
Lower Harlings IP9 ....91 A8
Lower Holt St CO6 ....105 D5
Lower Houses Rd IP9 ....63 D2
Lower King CM7 ....128 D1
Lower Langley CO6 ....106 C1
Lower Marine Par CO12 ....91 E5
Lower Mill Field CM6 ....150 A7
Lower Orwell St IP4 ....17 C5
Lower Park Cres CM23 ....145 D5
Lower Park Rd CO7 ....185 E6
Lower Rd Birch CO2 ....161 A8
　Birch CO2 ....181 A8
　Borley CO10 ....15 B3
　Glemsford CO10 ....2 B2
　Peldon CO5 ....182 D5
　Wormingford CO5, CO6 ....80 B5
Lower St Cavendish CO10 ....1 D1

Lower St continued
　Sproughton IP8 ....
　Stanstead CO10 ....
　Stansted
　　Mountfitchet CM24 ....
　Stratford St M CO7 ....
　Stutton IP9 ....
Lowry Gdns IP2 ....
Luard Way Birch CO2 ....
　Witham CM8 ....
Lubberhedges La CM6 ....
Lucas Ave Chelmsford CM2 ....
　Fordham CO6 ....
Lucas Ho CO3 ....
Lucas Rd Colchester CO2 ....13◆
　Sudbury CO10 ....33◆
Lucas's La CO16 ....
Lucerne Rd CO7 ....138 A◆
Lucerne Way CM1 ....215 B8
Luces La CO9 ....51 F◆
Luck's La CM3 ....172 F2
Lucksfield Way CM2 ....216 F◆
Lucy Cl CO3 ....134 C◆
Lucy La N CO3 ....134 C◆
Lucy La S CO3 ....134 C◆
Ludgores La CM3 ....220 C◆
Ludham Hall La CM7 ....154 D◆
Ludlow Ave CM2 ....177 F◆
Lufkin Rd CO4 ....109 F◆
Lugar CO4 ....136 E◆
Lukin's Dr CM6 ....150 D◆
Lulworth Ave IP3 ....18 D◆
Lulworth Cl CO15 ....203 I8
Lulworth Dr CB9 ....8 E◆
Lumber Leys CO14 ....171 A◆
Lundy Cl CB9 ....9 D◆
Lunnish Hill CO12 ....89 F◆
Lupin Dr CM1 ....205 F◆
Lupin Mews 1 CM1 ....206 E◆
Lupin Rd IP2 ....16 E◆
Lupin Way CO16 ....188 C◆
Lushington Ave CO13 ....170 E◆
Lushington Rd CO11 ....86 C◆
Luther Rd IP2 ....17 C◆
Lutus Cl CO10 ....15 B◆
Lydgate Cl CO11 ....86 B4
Lydia Dr CO16 ....186 A◆
Lymington Ave CO15 ....189 A◆
Lyndhurst Ave IP4 ....18 D◆
Lyndhurst Dr CM1 ....205 F◆
Lyndhurst Rd CO15 ....189 C◆
Lynmouth Ave CM2 ....216 B◆
Lynmouth Gdns CM2 ....216 B◆
Lynne Cl CO13 ....170 E◆
Lynton Cl CO12 ....91 B◆
Lynton Ct CM23 ....145 E◆
Lynton Dr CM1 ....205 E◆
Lynwood Ave IP11 ....221 F◆
Lyon Cl Clacton-on-S CO15 ....189 A4
Galleywood CM2 ....216 B3
Lyons Hall Cty Prim Sch CM7 ....128 B◆
Lyons Hall Rd CM7 ....128 D◆
Lyster Ave CM7 ....217 A7

## M

Mabbitt Way CO4 ....110 B5
Maberly Ct CB10 ....22 D2
Macbeth Cl CO4 ....136 A4
Mace Wlk CM1 ....204 E7
Mackay Ct CO2 ....136 B3
Maclarens CM8 ....196 A6
Macmillan Cl 4 CM2 ....205 B3
Madeira Rd CO15 ....189 D4
Madeline Pl CM1 ....204 E6
Madgements Rd CM7 ....129 C8
Magazine Farm Way CO3 ....135 A6
Magdalen Cl CO15 ....188 E4
Magdalen Ct CO15 ....188 E4
Magdalen Gn
　Colchester CO1 ....136 B6
　Thaxted CM6 ....70 B2
Magdalen Rd CO15 ....188 E4
Magdalen St CO1 ....136 A6
Magdalene Cres CM8 ....156 D2
Magingley Cres IP5 ....18 F6
Magnaville Rd CM23 ....145 C4
Magnolia Cl
　Chelmsford CM2 ....216 B6
　Witham CM8 ....177 A5
Magnolia Dr CO4 ....136 F8
Magpie Cl IP8 ....16 C2
Magwitch Cl CM1 ....204 F7
Maidenburgh St CO1 ....135 F7
Maidenhall App CO ....17 B3
Maidenhall Gn IP2 ....17 B3
Maidment Cres CM8 ....194 F8
Maidstone Cty Inf Sch IP11 ....221 C5
Maidstone Rd IP11 ....221 C5
Mailers La CM23 ....92 F2
Main Rd Bicknacre CM3 ....218 F1
　Boreham CM3 ....192 B2
　Braintree CM3 ....153 D4
　Broomfield CM1 ....191 B2
　Chelmondiston IP9 ....63 D7
　Danbury CM3 ....218 A7
　Danbury CM3 ....218 E3
　Frating CO7 ....138 F3
　Great Holland CO13 ....170 A3
　Great Leighs CM3 ....173 F7
　Harwich, Bath Side CO12 ....91 B3
　Harwich, Dovercourt CO12 ....91 B3
　Rainsey CO12 ....90 A1

*continued*

...re St A IP5 .................18 F8
...e CM2 .......................217 F7
...rence CM0 ..................213 C1
...verstone IP9 ...............38 B2
...ingford C06 ................80 F4
... St CB1 ......................16 F2
... Ct IP2 ......................16 F2
...rtland Ct C013 .............170 F4
...rtland Rd CM24 .............119 E6
...ckemores CM7 ..............126 F2
...aillin IM1 C012 .............90 F5
...aldon Court B rh CM7 ......209 F3
Maldon Ct
  **U** Colchester C03 .........135 E6
  Great Dunmow CO10 ..........34 B/
**Maldon Cty Prim Sch**
CM9 ............................210 A2
**Maldon District Mus**
CM9 ............................210 B2
Maldon Rd Birch C02 .........160 E4
Bradwell Waterside CM0 ......214 F1
Colchester, Abbey Field
C03 ............................135 D5
Colchester, Stanway Green
C03 ............................134 D1
Danbury CM3 ..................219 B5
Danbury CM3 ..................219 B7
Goldhanger CM9 ..............217 E2
Great Baddow CM2 ............217 C7
Great Totham CM8 ............196 B4
Great Wigborough CU5 ........181 G2
Hatfield Peverel CM3 .........194 D3
Hatfield Peverel CM8 .........194 F5
Heybridge CM9 ................209 D6
Kelvedon C05 .................158 C1
Margaretting CM4 .............215 D1
Tiptree C05 ...................179 B3
Tolleshunt D'arcy CM9 ........198 C2
Witham CM8 ...................195 A6
Woodham Mortimer CM9 ......219 E6
Maldon Way CU16 .............188 B4
**Malin Cl** C09 ................19 C2
**Mallard Cl**
Great Notley CM7 ..............154 C5
Kelvedon C05 .................158 C3
Layer-de-l-H C02 .............162 A5
Tollesbury CM9 ...............199 D2
Mallard Ct IP2 ................16 F3
**Mallard Rd** CM2 .............216 A5
**Mallard Way**
Great Cornard CO10 ...........34 C5
Ipswich IP2 ...................16 E3
**Mallow Wlk** CM8 .............8 C8
**Mallowhayes Cl** IP2 ........17 B3
Mallows Field C09 ............76 F2
**Mallows Green Rd** CM23 ....92 D1
Mallows La C09 ...............49 F3
Malmesbury Ct IP7 ...........17 A1
**Maltese Rd** CM1 .............205 A4
**Malthouse Rd** C011 .........86 D4
Malting Farm La L07 .........84 D2
**Malting La** Clare CU10 .....12 B7
Kirby-le-S CO13 ..............143 C1
Malting Rd Colchester C02 ...135 C1
Peldon C05 ....................182 E6
**Malting Torr** IP7 ............17 D1
Malting Yd C07 ...............164 B8
Maltings Cl IP8 ...............18 F1
Maltings Ct CMR ..............194 F8
Maltings La CMR ..............194 F8
**Maltings Rd**
Brightlingsea CO7 .............165 E1
Great Baddow CM2 ............217 A5
**Maltings The**
Cavendish CO10 ...............1 D2
Great Dunmow CM6 ...........123 D1
Ramsey C012 ..................116 E8
Rayne CM7 ....................123 A2
Saffron Walden CB10 .........22 D1
Thaxted CM6 ..................70 A2
**Maltings View** CM7 .........128 A3
**Maltings Park Rd** C06 ......108 F4
**Malvern Cl**
Chelmsford CM1 ..............204 D6
Ipswich IP1 ...................18 B4
Rushmere St A IP5 ...........10 F7
Malvern Way C06 ..............109 B7
Malvon Rd I'M8 ...............194 F8
**Manchester Rd**
Holland-on-S C015 ............109 F6
Ipswich IP2 ...................16 D2
**Mandeville Rd**
Marks Tey C06 .................132 L3
Saffron Walden CB11 .........43 D8
**Mandeville Way**
Broomfield CM1 ...............191 B3
Kirby Cross C013 .............170 F6
**Mandy Cl** IP4 ...............18 A6
**Mandiefield Gdns** C016 ....187 B5
**Manning Rd** IP11 ...........221 D3
**Mannings Cl** CB11 ..........43 E7
**Mannings La** IP4 ...........38 A2
**Mannington Cl** IP4 .........18 F5
**Mannington Ct** CM7 ........136 F4
**Manningtree Rd**
Brantham C011 ................86 A8
Dedham CO7 ...................85 B6
East Bergholt C07 ............59 F1
Little Bentley CO7 ............139 F8
Stutton IP9 ....................61 F2
**Manningtree Sch** C011 .....86 A5
**Manor Cl** Cavendish CO10 ..1 C2
Great Horkesley C06 ..........109 C7
Manor Cres CM2 ..............191 B5
**Manor Dr** CM2 ..............216 F7

Manor Fields JMI Sch
CM23 ..........................145 D5
**Manor House Way** C07 .....185 E8
**Manor La**
Great Chesterford CB10 ......3 D2
Harwich C012 ................91 B2
Stutton IP9 ...................61 E2
**Manor Links** CM23 ..........146 C7
**Manor Rd**
Bishop's Stortford CM23 .....146 A7
Chelmsford CM2 ..............205 C1
Colchester C03 ...............135 E7
Felixstowe IP11 ..............221 C1
Great Holland C013 ..........170 A3
Harwich C012 ................91 B3
Hatfield Heverel CM3 .........194 C1
Haverhill CB9 .................9 E7
Ipswich IP4 ...................17 D8
Little Easton CM6 .............122 F5
Maldon CM9 ...................209 A4
Stansted
Mountfitchet CM24 ...........119 E5
Sudbury CO10 .................15 E1
West Bergholt C06 ............108 E5
Witham CM8 ...................177 A4
Wivenhoe C07 .................137 C1
Wrⁿdham Walker CM9 .........208 E5
**Manor St** CM7 ..............128 A3
**Manor Way** C015 ...........189 G6
**Manors** CM8 .................156 D4
**Manors Way** CMR ...........156 C4
**Mansard Ct** C015 ...........189 C5
Manse Chase C07 .............210 A1
Mansfield Twrs CU15 .........188 F2
Manston Dr CM23 .............119 B7
Manuden Cty Prim Sch
CM23 ..........................93 A2
**Manwick Rd** IP11 ...........221 D2
**Maple Ave**
Bishop's Stortford CM23 .....145 D8
Braintree CM7 .................127 D2
Heybridge CM9 ...............210 C6
**Maple Cl**
Bishop's Stortford CM23 .....145 D8
Clacton-on-S C015 ...........188 C3
Halstead C09 .................77 A2
Harwich C012 ................91 B3
Ipswich IP2 ...................17 A3
**Maple Dr**
Chelmsford CM2 ..............216 B6
Kirby Cross C013 .............170 D6
Witham CM8 ...................177 A5
Maple Gr CM23 ...............145 D8
Maple Ho IP11 ................221 C1
**Maple La** CB10 ..............45 C5
Maple Leaf C05 ...............179 C7
Maple Rd C010 ...............34 B5
**Maple Spring** CM23 ........145 D8
Maple Way C002 .............156 A4
Maples The IP4 ...............18 E8
Maplin Ct C015 ...............189 D4
**Maple Dr**
Chelmsford CM2 ..............216 B6
Kirby Cross C013 .............170 D6
Witham CM8 ...................177 A5
**Marasca Enrt** C02 ..........163 A7
**Maraschino Cres** C02 ......163 A7
**Marauder Way** C06 .........104 F7
Marconi Rd CM1 ..............205 D5
**Marconi Way** C015 .........189 B3
Marcus Cl IP9 .................9 D7
**Marennes Cres** C07 ........185 E7
**Mareth Rd** C02 .............135 C2
**Margaret Cl** C07 ............186 A6
Margaret Rd C01 .............135 F8
**Margaret St**
Felixstowe IP11 ..............221 C5
Fleeted CM6 ...................70 A3
**Margaret Way** CR10 ........22 D1
**Margaretting Rd**
Chelmsford CM2 ..............215 F1
Galleywood CM2 ..............216 A2
Writtle CM1 ...................215 A6
**Morgate Rd** CM3 ...........18 C3
**Margoya Gdns** CM23 .......145 E5
**Marguerite Way** CM23 .....145 C6
**Maria St** C012 ...............91 D5
**Marigold Ave**
Clacton-on-S C016 ...........188 C4
Ipswich IP2 ...................16 E3
**Marigold Cl**
Chelmsford CM1 ..............205 F6
Colchester C04 ...............136 E8
**Marina Gdns**
Clacton-on-S C015 ...........189 C5
Felixstowe IP11 ..............221 C2
**Marina Mews** ■ C014 ......171 C8
**Marina Point** C015 .........188 D1
**Marina Rd** C04 ..............194 A4
**Marine Ct**
Clacton-on-S C015 ...........188 E1
Frinton-on-S C013 ............170 F4
**Marine Par** C012 ...........91 D3
**Marine Par E** C015 .........189 B3
**Marion Ave** C015 ...........188 E6
**Maritime Ave** CM9 ..........210 E3
**Marlborough Cl**
Bishop's Stortford CM23 .....145 D8
Clacton-on-S C015 ...........188 C3
**Marlborough Rd**
Braintree CM7 .................128 A7
  **3** Chelmsford CM2 ........205 A1
Ipswich IP4 ...................18 A6
Marlowe Cl CM7 ...............155 A8
**Marlowe Rd**
Clacton-on-S C015 ...........203 G8
Jaywick C015 .................188 A1
**Marlowe Way** C03 ..........134 F6
**Marlpits Rd** CM3 .............219 E4
**Marna Rd** C02 ...............135 E4
**Marney Cl** CM2 ..............216 E8
**Marney Way** C013 ...........171 B6
Marquis Cl CM23 ..............145 E7
**Marram Cl** C03 ..............134 B6
**Marsden Ct** C03 .............134 E4
**Marsh Cres** C05 .............164 A8
Marsh Farm La C07 ..........166 D3
**Marsh Rd** C06, C07 .........57 E6
Marsh Way C07 ...............185 E6
**Marshall Cl** C05 .............158 D4
**Marshalls Piece** CM6 .......124 D6
**Marshalls Rd** CM7 ..........127 E1
**Marshbarns** CM23 ..........145 C8
**Marshy La** C06, C10 ........30 C7
**Marston Beck** CM7 .........206 A2
**Martello Rd** C014 ...........171 C8
**Marten's La** C06 .............56 F8
**Martens Mdw** CM7 .........128 D3
Martin End C02 ...............162 A5
**Martin Mews** CB9 ...........8 C8
Martin Rd IP2 .................17 C4
**Martin's Rd** C09 .............76 E1
**Martingale Dr** CM1 ..........205 F7
Martinsdale C015 ............188 F6
**Martyns Rise** C010 ..........15 C5
**Marvens** CM2 ................216 D3
**Mary La S** C02 ..............139 A8
**Mary La S** C02 ..............139 B6
**Mary McArthur Pl** CM24 ...119 F8
**Mary Park Gdns** CM23 .....145 F4
**Mary Warner Rd** C07 .......111 E7
**Maryborough Gr** C02 .......136 B2
**Maryland Ct** ■ C02 .........136 A3
**Maryon Rd** IP3 ..............18 B1
**Mascalls The** CM2 ...........216 E8
**Mascalls Way** CM2 ..........216 H8
**Masefield Dr** C013 ..........134 F6
**Masefield Rd** Ipswich IP4 ..18 D7
  **1D** Chelmsford CM2 ......205 C2
**Mashbury Rd** CM3 ...........190 B7
**Mashey Rd** C09 .............30 D5
**Mason Ct** C02 ...............136 B3
**Mason Rd**
Clacton-on-S C016 ...........188 B3
Colchester C01 ...............109 F1
**Masons Ct** CM23 ............145 E7
**Masterman Wharf**
  **B** Bishop's Stortford,
  Hockerill CM23 ..............146 A7
  **12** Bishop's Stortford, New
  Town CM23 ..................145 F7
**Matching La** CM23 ..........145 D8
**Matfield Cl** CM1 .............205 D7
**Mathams Dr** CM23 ..........145 D5
**Mather Way** IP2 .............17 A4
**Mathews Cl** Halstead C09 ..77 A3
  Stratford St M CO7 ..........58 C1
**Matlock Cl** ■ IP2 ...........18 A2
**Matson Rd** IP1 ..............16 F8
**Maudlyn Rd** C01, C04 .......136 A8
**May Rd** IP3 ..................18 C2
**May Wlk** Chelmsford CM2 ...216 C7
  Elsenham CM24 ..............94 A1
**Maybank Rd** C09 ............84 E4
**Mayberry Wlk** C02 ..........136 A3
**Maybury Cl** C06 .............132 F3
**Maybury Rd** IP3 .............18 B1
**Mayda Cl** C09 ...............76 D1
**Mayes Cl** CM23 ..............146 D6
**Mayes La** Danbury CM3 .....218 E6
  Harwich C012 ................90 C1
  Sandon CM2 ..................217 E5
**Mayes Pl** CM6 ...............97 A6
**Mayfield Ct** C04 .............163 B5
**Mayfield Pk** CM23 ...........145 D3
**Mayfield Rd** Ipswich IP4 ....18 D7
  Writtle CM1 ..................204 A2
**Mayflower Ave** C02 .........91 E5
**Mayflower Cl** C03 ...........134 B5
**Mayflower Cty Prim Sch**
  The C012 .....................91 B4
**Mayflower Gdns** CM23 .....145 B6
**Mayflower Ho** C012 .........91 D6
**Mayflower Way** C016 .......15 F2
**Mayford Way** C016 ..........188 B6

Mayland Cl CM9 ...............210 D4
**Mayland Rd** C08 .............177 A2
**Maylands Dr** CM7 ...........154 D8
**Maynard Cl** C04 .............123 D1
**Maynard Villas** CM6 ........122 F5
**Mayne Crest** CM1 ...........205 E6
**Maypole Cl** CM11 ...........43 C7
**Maypole Dr** C016 ...........187 B4
**Maypole Green Rd** C02 .....135 C1
**Maypole Rd** Tiptree C05 ....179 C6
  Wickham Bishops CM8 .......195 F2
**Maypole The** CM6 ...........69 F3
**Mays Ct** IP11 ................221 D3
**Maysent Ave** CM7 ...........127 F5
**Maytree Gdns** CM22 ........94 B3
**Maze Green Hts** CM23 ......145 C7
**Maze Green Rd** CM23 .......145 D7
**Mazers Cl** ■ CM7 ...........127 F2
**Mazoe Cl** CM23 ..............145 F5
**Mazoe Rd** CM23 .............145 F5
**Mead Cl** C015 ...............188 E3
**Mead Monks** CM3 ...........218 F2
**Mead Pastures** CM9 ........208 D3
**Mead Path** LM2 ..............215 F8
**Mead The**
  Great Cornard CO10 .........34 B4
  Great Dunmow ÖM6 .........123 C2
  Thaxted CM6 ..................70 A3
**Meadgate Ave** CM2 .........216 U8
**Meadgate Cty Prim Sch**
CM2 ............................216 E8
**Meadow Brown Cl** CM7 .....127 E1
**Meadow Cl**
  Chelmondiston IP9 ...........63 F7
  Clacton-on-S C015 ...........189 B7
  Elmstead C07 .................137 F6
  Great Bromley C07 ...........137 A6
  Halstead C09 .................103 F8
  Panfield CM7 .................127 A7
**Meadow Clays** CB11 ........21 F4
**Meadow Grass Cl** CM1 .....134 B6
**Meadow La** Sudbury C010 ..33 E7
  West Mersea C05 .............201 C5
**Meadow Rd**
  Bicknacre CM3 ...............218 E1
  Great Bardfield CM7 .........72 B2
  Kirby-le-S CO13 ..............143 D1
  Tiptree C05 ...................179 B5
**Meadow View Cl** C03 .......134 E5
**Meadow View Rd** C010 .....33 D5
**Meadow Way**
  Abberton C05 .................163 B2
  Black Notley CM7 ............155 C5
  Clacton-on-S C015 ...........203 G7
  Meadow Wlk CM7 ............127 D4
**Meadowbrook Ct** C01 .......136 B7
**Meadowcroft** CM4 ...........119 E7
**Meadowcroft Way** C013 ....170 F7
**Meadowford** CB11 ...........42 F1
**Meadowlands** CM23 ........119 A2
**Meadows Cl** C07 .............137 F6
**Meadows The**
  Bishop's Stortford CM23 ....145 E5
  **3** Chelmsford CM2 ........205 C2
**Meadowside**
  Braintree CM7 .................127 C5
  Chelmsford CM2 ..............205 C3
**Meadowside Ct** CM3 ........192 E1
**Meadowside Gdns** IP4 ......18 E8
**Meadowsweet Cl** CM3 ......205 F6
**Meadowvale Ct** CM4 .........119 E6
**Mead's Thⁿ** CM24 ...........119 F6
**Meadside** LM7 ...............73 B3
**Meadway** Gosfield CUV .....102 E8
  Lawford CU11 ................86 B0
  Maldon CM9 ..................210 B1
**Mearns Pl** ■ CM2 ...........205 H4
**Medⁿ Way** C07 ..............137 C3
**Medlar Cl** LMB ...............1/7 A4
**Medley Rd** CM7 ..............126 F2
**Medusa Cl** C015 .............189 E5
**Medway Ave** CM8 ...........176 D2
**Medway Cl** CM1 .............204 D4
**Medway Rd** IP3 ..............17 F2
**Meekings Rd** C010 ..........34 B8
**Meers The** C013 .............170 E6
**Meeson Meadows** CM9 .....220 E8
**Meeting Field** C010 .........15 C7
**Meeting La**
  East Mersea C05 ..............184 C1
  Ridgewell C09 ................29 B7
**Meeting Wlk** CB9 ............9 B7
**Megs Way** CM7 ..............128 B2
**Melba Ct** CM1 ...............204 D4
**Melbourne Ave** CM1 ........204 C5
**Melbourne Cty Prim Sch**
  CM1 ...........................204 B4
**Melbourne Park Cty**
  Prim Sch CM1 ...............204 F6
**Melbourne Rd**
  Clacton-on-S C015 ...........188 E4
  Ipswich IP4 ...................18 D7
**Melford Cl** IP4 ..............18 F5
**Melford Rd** Cavendish CO10 .1 E2
  Sudbury C010 ................15 D2
**Melford Way** IP11 ...........221 A3
**Mell Rd** CM9 .................199 C5
**Mellis Ct** IP11 ...............221 B5
**Melⁿr Chase** C003 ...........134 E1
**Melplash Cl** IP3 .............18 E4
**Melplash Rd** IP3 .............18 E4
**Melrose Gdns**
  Clacton-on-S C015 ...........189 C5

**Melrose Gdns** *continued*
  Ipswich IP1 ...................18 B8
**Melrose Rd** C05 .............206 D8
**Melton Cl** C014 .............188 A4
**Melville Rd** IP4 ..............17 F5
**Menai Cl** IP1 .................17 B7
**Mendip Dr** IP5 ..............18 F6
**Mendip Rd** CM1 .............204 D6
**Mendlesham Cl** C016 .......188 B4
**Menin Rd** C02 ...............135 D4
**Menish Way** CM2 ............206 A3
**Meon Cl** CM1 ................205 C6
**Meopham Ct** C010 ..........16 F6
**Mercantile Ho** ■ C01 .......135 F6
**Mercers Ave** CM23 ..........145 B4
**Mercers Row** CB10 ..........22 D1
**Mercers Way** ② C01 .......135 E8
**Mercia Cl** CM7 ...............217 A5
**Mercury Cl** C02 ..............135 A3
**Meredith Rd** C015 ...........188 E3
**Meres Cl** CM8 ................176 F1
**Meriden Ct** C015 ............189 A5
**Merivale** Cl C011 ...........86 B3
**Merivale Rd** C011 ...........86 B3
**Merlin End** C04 ..............110 F1
**Merlin Pl** CM1 ...............204 F5
**Merlⁿ IM'** IP7 ...............16 C3
**Merriam Cl** C01 .............86 D8
**Merrilees Cres** C015 ........189 D4
**Merrill Pl** ■ CM23 ..........145 E5
**Merrion Cl** ■ IP7 ...........16 C2
**Merrymount Gdns** C015 ....189 B5
**Mersea Ave** C05 .............201 B6
**Mersea Ct** C05 ..............201 B7
**Mersea Fleet Way** CM7 .....128 C1
**Mersea Mus** C05 ............201 B6
**Mersea Point Nature**
  Reserve C05 ..................185 C3
**Mersea Rd** Abberton C05 ...163 B5
  Colchester C02 ...............136 A3
  Peldon C05 ....................182 F5
**Mersea View** C016 ..........186 A3
**Mersey Rd** Ipswich IP3 .....17 F2
  Witham CM8 ..................177 A6
**Mersey Way** CM1 ...........204 C5
**Merstham Dr** C016 .........188 C6
**Merton Ct** C02 ..............163 A7
**Messines Rd** C02 ...........135 D5
**Messing-cum-Inworth**
  Cty Prim Sch C05 ...........159 C2
**Meteor Way** CM1 ............204 F2
**Mews Ct** CM2 ................205 B1
**Mews The**
  Bishop's Stortford CM22 ....146 A3
  Frinton-on-S C013 ...........171 AG
  Panfield CM7 .................126 A7
  Stansted
  Mountfitchet CM24 ..........119 F7
**Meyrick Cres** C02 ...........135 F5
**Micawber Way** CM1 .........204 D7
**Michaels Rd** CM23 ..........119 A2
**Michaelstowe Cl** C012 .....90 C2
**Michaelstowe Dr** C012 .....90 C2
**Mickfield Mews** IP11 ........221 B5
**Micklegate St** IP11 .........221 C1
**Middle Cl** C06 ...............79 C1
**Middle King** CM7 ...........129 D1
**Middle Mill Rd** C01 .........135 F8
**Middle Row** ■ CM23 ........145 F6
**Middle St** CB11 ..............65 C4
**Middle Way** C010 ...........15 D8
**Middleborough** C01 .........135 F8
**Middlefield** C09 .............76 F1
**Middlefield Rd** C011 ........87 A3
**Middleton Cl**
  Clacton-on-S C015 ...........188 D6
  Ipswich IP3 ...................16 D2
**Middleton Rd** C010 .........33 D5
**Middlewick Cl** ■ C02 .......124 A1
**Midguard Way** CM9 .........220 F8
**Midland Cl** C02 ..............135 F4
**Midway** C015 ................203 E6
**Midway Rd** C02 ..............135 C2
**Milburn Cres** C04 ...........204 D1
**Milch La** CM3 ................153 E6
**Milden Rd** IP2 ...............16 E5
**Mildenhall Pl** ■ CB9 ........9 B8
**Mildmay Cl** ■ CM2 .........205 B1
**Mildmay Cty Jun & Inf**
  Sch CM2 .....................216 e5
**Mildmay Rd**
  Chelmsford CM2 ..............205 B1
  Ipswich IP3 ...................18 B1
**Mildmays** CM3 ...............218 C7
**Mile End Rd** C04 ............109 E3
**Miles Cl** C03 .................134 C6
**Milestones The** CM3 ........194 A4
**Milford Cl** CM7 ..............137 D1
**Military Cl** ■ C01 ...........136 A6
**Military Rd** C01 .............136 A5
**Mill Chase** Halstead C09 ...76 F2
  Steeple Bumpstead CB9 .....27 C5
**Mill Cl** Elsenham CM22 .....94 C1
  Felixstowe IP11 ..............221 B5
  Great Bardfield CM7 .........72 B2
  Tiptree C05 ...................179 C6
**Mill Cotts** C02 ...............217 C8
**Mill Cswy** SG8 ...............19 C5
**Mill Ct** Braintree CM7 ......128 B2
  Takeley CM6 ..................149 B7
**Mill End** CM6 ................70 A2
**Mill Field** Barnston CM6 ....151 A4
  Chelmondiston IP9 ...........63 E8
**Mill Hill** Braintree CM7 .....128 B2
  Chelmsford CM2 ..............215 F2

**Mill Hill** continued
Farnham CM23 .............118 E5
Harwich CO12 ..............91 C3
Haverhill CB9 .................9 A7
Lawford CO11 ................85 D4
Manningtree CO11 ..........86 C4
Purleigh CM3 ...............220 C1
Stansted
Mountfitchet CM24 ........119 E6
Sudbury CO10 ................33 D7
Wormingford CO8 ..........80 E6
Mill House Cotts CO12 ...116 D4
**Mill La** Ardleigh CO7 ....112 B4
Birch CO2 ....................161 A3
Bradfield CO11 ...............87 D2
Broomfield CM1 ............191 C1
Cavendish CO10 .............13 B8
Coggeshall CO5 ............131 F1
Colne Engaine CO6 ........105 B8
Cressing CM7 ...............155 D5
Danbury CM3 ................219 A6
Dedham CO7 ..................84 F7
Felixstowe IP11 ............221 C4
Finchingfield CM7 ..........48 F3
Ford End CM3 ................172 D7
Great Dunmow CM6 .......123 D1
Great Holland CO13 ........169 E3
Great Leighs CM3 ..........174 B7
Great Maplestead CO9 .....76 E8
Harkstead SG9 ...............64 A5
Harwich CO12 .................91 D3
Hinxton CB10 ..................3 A7
Ickleton CB10 ..................2 B5
Layer-de-l-H CO2 ...........162 B5
Little Baddow CM3 .........207 E3
Little Yeldham CO9 ..........30 A3
Littlebury CB11 ...............21 F4
Maldon CM9 .................210 A3
Manningtree CO11 ..........86 D4
Pebmarsh CO9 ...............78 A7
Purleigh CM3 ...............220 C1
Rayne CM7 ...................153 E8
Saffron Walden CB10 ......22 F2
Salcott-cum-virley CM9 ..199 B8
Stebbing CM6 ...............124 E5
Stoke-by-N CO6 ..............56 D7
Sudbury CO10 ................33 D7
Terling CM3 ..................175 A3
Thorpe-le-S CO16 ..........141 F1
Tolleshunt Major CM9 ....197 E3
Walton-on-t-N CO14 .......171 C8
Washbrook IP8 ...............16 A1
Weeley Heath CO16 .......168 A6
Witham CM8 .................176 F1
**Mill Lane** CE CO16 ......168 A6
**Mill Park Dr** CM7 ........128 B1
**Mill Rd** Birdbrook CO9 ...10 E2
Boxted CO4 ....................82 F4
Clare CO10 .....................12 C7
Colchester CO4 .............109 F4
Debden CB11 ..................43 C8
East Bergholt CO7 ..........59 E2
Elder Street CB10 ...........45 B3
Felsted CM6 .................152 A4
Finchingfield CM7 ..........72 D5
Fordham CO6 .................14 C5
Foxearth CO10 ...............14 C5
Great Bardfield CM7 ........72 B2
Great Totham CM9 ........196 D7
Haverhill CB9 ...................9 A7
Helions Bumpstead CB9 ...26 C8
Henham CM22 .................66 F4
Ipswich IP3 ...................18 F1
Maldon CM9 .................210 B2
Marks Tey CO6 .............133 C4
North End CM6 ..............151 F2
Ridgewell CO9 ................29 B6
Stanbourne CO9 .............28 C3
West Mersea CO5 ..........201 D7
**Mill Rise** IP9 ................62 D5
**Mill Side** CM24 ...........119 E6
**Mill St**
Bishop's Stortford CM23 ..146 A5
Brightlingsea CO7 .........186 A6
Colchester CO1 .............136 A6
Nayland CO6 ..................56 B1
St Osyth CO16 ..............186 F4
Stoke-by-N CO6 ..............56 D8
**Mill Tye** CO10 ..............34 A4
**Mill Vale Lo** CM8 ........176 F2
**Mill View** CM7 ............129 D3
**Mill Vue Rd** CM2 ........205 F2
**Mill Wlk** CO5 .............179 C8
**Millars The** CM1 .........191 A3
**Millbridge Rd** CM8 .....176 F2
**Millcroft** CM23 ...........119 A1
**Milldene Cty Prim Sch**
The CO5 ......................179 D6
**Millenium Way** CM7 ....155 D8
**Miller's Barn Rd** CO15 ..188 A1
**Miller's Cl** CM6 ..........151 A4
**Millers Cl**
Bishop's Stortford CM23 ..145 C5
Braintree CM7 ..............128 A8
Colchester CO3 .............134 C6
Great Horkesley CO6 ......109 B7
**Millers Croft**
Great Baddow CM2 ........216 F6
Great Dunmow CM6 .......123 C1
**Millers La** CO3 ...........134 D6
**Millers Mead** CO5 .......158 E4
**Millers Row** CM7 ..........48 C6
**Millfield Gdns** IP4 ........18 A6
**Millfields** Stansted
Mountfitchet CM24 ........119 E6

**Millfields** continued
Writtle CM1 ..................204 A1
**Millfields Prim Sch** CO7 .137 D1
**Millfields Way** CB9 .........9 B8
**Millhouse Villas** CM6 ....151 A4
**Milligans Chase** CM2 ....216 B1
**Millmers Way** CM23 .....145 C4
**Mills La** CO10 ...............15 C4
**Mills Rd** CO10 ..............34 A8
**Mills The** IP8 ................18 E8
**Millside** CM23 .............146 A5
**Millson Bank** CM2 .......206 A4
**Millways** CM9 .............196 B4
**Millwrights** CO5 ..........179 C6
**Milner Rd** Sudbury CO10 ..34 B8
Sudbury CO10 ................34 B8
**Milner St** IP4 ...............17 E5
**Milnrow** IP2 .................16 C2
**Milton Ave** CM7 ..........155 A8
**Milton Cl** CO3 .............134 F6
**Milton Cl** CO15 ...........189 E6
**Milton Pl** CM1 .............205 A5
**Milton Rd** Harwich CO12 ..91 D4
Lawford CO11 ................86 B2
Witham CM8 .................176 F5
**Milton St** IP4 ...............18 B6
**Mimosa Cl** CM1 ..........205 F6
**Mimosa Ct** CO4 ..........136 E8
**Minden Rd** CO10 ..........33 F7
**Minerva Cl** Harwich CO12 ..90 F1
Haverhill CB9 ...................9 D6
**Minerva End** CO2 .........133 C2
**Minsmere Dr** CO16 ......188 C6
**Minsmere Way** CO10 .....34 C6
**Minster Way** CM9 .......220 E8
**Minters Cotts** CO11 .....115 C5
**Miranda Wlk** CO4 .........136 E7
**Mirosa Dr** CM9 ...........210 B1
**Mission La** CO7 .............60 B3
**Mistley Norman CE Prim**
Sch CO11 .....................87 A4
**Mistley Place Park** CO11 ..86 E4
**Mistley Sta** CO11 ..........86 E4
**Mistley Towers** CO11 .....86 F4
**Mitchell Ave** CO9 ..........76 E1
**Mitchell Circ** CM7 ..........73 C6
**Mitre Gdns** CM23 ........146 A4
**Mitton Vale** CM2 .........205 E2
**Moat Farm** CO9 ............28 B7
**Moat Farm Chase** CM8 ..176 F3
**Moat Farm Cl** IP4 ..........17 F8
**Moat Fields** CO7 ..........107 D6
**Moat La** CO8 .................55 A4
**Moat Rd** Birdbrook CO9 ..28 D7
Fordham CO6 ................107 D6
**Moat Wlk** CB9 ...............8 E8
**Modlen Rd** CO14 .........171 B7
**Moffat Ave** IP4 ...........18 B8
**Mole Hall La** CB11 .........67 F3
**Mole Hall Wildlife Pk**
CB11 .............................67 F3
**Molehill Green Cotts**
CM22 ..........................121 C6
**Molehill Green Rdbt**
CM22 ..........................121 C5
**Molrams La** CM2 ..........217 B6
**Monk's Cnr** CB10 ..........47 B4
**Monk's La** CO7 .............84 D4
**Monkdowns Rd** CO6 .....131 B3
**Monklands Ct** CO9 ........76 C1
**Monks Ct** CM8 .............176 E3
**Monks Gate** IP8 ...........18 A6
**Monks Hill** CB11 ...........43 F8
**Monks Lodge Rd** CO9 .....52 D2
**Monks Rd** CO5 ............105 E4
**Monks Wlk** CM9 ..........213 E8
**Monkswood Dr** CM23 ...145 D6
**Monkwick Ave** CO2 ......135 F1
**Monkwick Cty Jun &**
Schs CO2 .....................136 A2
**Monmouth Cl** IP2 ..........17 B1
**Mons Rd** CO2 ..............135 D4
**Montague Rd** IP11 .......221 F4
**Montbretia Cl** CO13 .....134 D6
**Montbretia Ct** CO16 .....188 C4
**Montfort Ct** CB9 ............8 F7
**Montgomery Cl**
Chelmsford CM1 ...........205 E7
Colchester CO2 .............136 B4
**Montgomery Cty Jun &**
Inf Sch CO2 .................135 D2
**Montgomery Rd** IP2 .......17 B1
**Monton Rise** IP2 ...........16 D2
**Montrose Ct** IP3 ...........17 F4
**Montrose Ho** CO4 .........135 F7
**Montrose Rd** CM2 ........206 A4
**Moor Hall La** CB9 ...........9 D4
**Moor Hall La** CB9 .........218 E2
**Moor Rd** Great Tey CO6 ..132 C8
Langham CO4 ................83 D4
**Moor's Farm Chase** CM9 .197 A3
**Moor's La** CO7 .............139 A2
**Moore Cl** CO15 ............158 E5
**Moorfield Cl** CM8 .........176 F1
**Moorhouse Gn** CO7 .....111 E8
**Moorings The** CM23 ......146 A5
**Moors Cl** CO7 ..............139 C1
**Moors La**
Little Dunmow CM6 .......151 D7
Rayne CM7 ...................126 D3
**Moors The** CM6 ...........151 D7
**Moorsfield** CO10 ...........34 B4
**Moorside** CO1 ..............136 B7
**Mope La** CM8 ..............195 D6
**Moran Ave** CM1 ...........205 B7
**Morant Rd** CO1 ...........136 B5
**Morebarn Rd** CO7 ........112 E2
**Morecambe Ct** IP4 ........18 A7

**Morella Cl** CO7 ............166 E8
**Morello Ct** CO2 ...........163 A7
**Moretons** CM2 .............216 B2
**Morland Ct** CO6 ...........82 B1
**Morland Prim Sch** IP3 ...38 A8
**Morland Rd** IP3 .............37 F8
**Morley Rd** Halstead CO9 ..76 F2
Tiptree CO5 ..................179 D4
**Morleys Rd** CO6 ...........203 E6
**Mornington Ave 2** IP1 ...17 A8
**Morris Harp** CB10 ..........22 E3
**Morris Rd** CM2 .............205 D2
**Morrow La** CO7 ............112 A6
**Mors End** CO7 ...............58 D2
**Morses La** CO7 ............135 E8
**Morten Rd** CO1 ...........135 E8
**Mortimer Rd** CM3 ........194 A4
**Morton Rd** CM9 ...........196 A4
**Morton Way** CO9 ..........77 A3
**Moss Path** CM2 ...........216 C3
**Moss Rd** Colchester CO3 .134 E4
Witham CM8 .................177 B3
**Moss Way** CO6 ............108 E3
**Mossfield Cl** CO13 ........135 C6
**Mott's La** CO6 .............132 D4
**Mottram Cl 9** IP2 ..........16 C2
**Motts Cl** CM7 ...............127 E4
**Motts La** CM8 ..............177 B4
**Motts Yd** CM6 .............124 E5
**Moules La** CB1 ...............5 C6
**Moulsham Chase** CM2 ..216 C8
**Moulsham Cty Jun & Inf**
Sch CM2 ......................216 B7
**Moulsham Dr** CM2 .......216 B8
**Moulsham Hall La**
Braintree CM3 ..............153 F2
Great Leighs CM3 ..........154 A1
**Moulsham High Sch**
CM2 ............................216 B7
**Moulsham St**
Chelmsford CM1 ...........205 B2
Chelmsford, Moulsham CM2 ..205 B2
**Moulsham Thrift** CM2 ...216 A6
**Mount Dr** Ipswich IP3 .....18 F1
Stansted
Mountfitchet CM24 ........119 E5
**Mount Hill** CO9 ..............76 D1
Felixstowe IP11 ............221 A4
**Mount Lodge Chase** CM9 .196 E6
**Mount Pleasant**
Halstead CO9 ................76 E1
Maldon CM9 .................209 F2
**Mount Pleasant Cotts**
CB11 .............................43 D8
**Mount Pleasant Est** CM9 .196 E6
**Mount Pleasant Rd** CB11 ..43 E8
**Mount Rd** Braintree CM7 ..128 C1
Coggeshall CO6 .............131 B2
Haverhill CB9 ...................9 B7
**Mount Rise 4** CO9 .........76 D1
**Mount The** Colchester CO3 .134 F6
Tollesbury CM9 .............199 D1
**Mountain Ash Cl** CM1 ...110 C2
**Mountain's Farm Rd**
CM6 ............................196 C7
**Mountains Rd** CM6 ......196 C7
**Mountbatten Cl** CO10 .....15 C2
**Mountbatten Ct 7** IP11 ..17 A7
**Mountbatten Dr** CO2 ....136 B4
**Mountbatten Rd**
Braintree CM7 ..............128 C4
Sudbury CO10 ...............15 C2
**Mountbatten Way** CM1 ..205 E7
**Mountfitchet Castle &**
Norman Village CM24 ...119 F6
**Mountfitchet High Sch**
The CM24 .....................119 F4
**Mountfitchet Rd** CM24 ..119 E5
**Mounthill Ave** CM2 ......205 D3
**Mountview Cres** CM0 ....213 C1
**Mountview Rd** CO15 .....189 A5
**Moverons La** CO7 .........165 C2
**Mowden Hall La** CM3 ...193 D1
**Mowlands** IP9 ...............35 B1
**Moy Rd** CO2 ................134 C4
**Moze Cross** CO12 .........116 D1
**Mulberries The** CM7 .....128 A2
**Mulberry Ave** CO4 .......136 A4
**Mulberry Ct** CM23 .......146 A5
**Mulberry Gdns** CM8 .....177 A4
**Mulberry Way** CM1 ......205 D4
**Mullins Rd** CM7 ...........127 F6
**Mumford Cl** CO6 ..........108 E4
**Mumford Rd** Ipswich IP1 ..16 E8
West Bergholt CO6 .........108 D4
**Mumfords La** CO13 ......170 A7
**Mundon Rd** Braintree CM7 .128 D1
Maldon CM9 .................210 A1
**Munnings Cl** IP3 ............38 B8
**Munnings Dr** CO16 .......188 D6
**Munnings Rd** CO3 ........135 A5
**Munnings Way** CO11 .....86 B5
**Munro Rd** CM6 ............176 F5
**Murchison Cl** CM1 ........204 E5
**Murray Cl** CM7 ............127 F6
**Murray Rd** IP3 ...............38 A3
**Murrayfield Prim Sch** IP3 .18 A2
**Murrell Lock** CM2 .........206 A4
**Murrills Rd** IP3 .............18 A1
**Murton Slade 6** CB9 ........9 A8
**Muscade Cl** CO5 ...........179 D6
**Museum St**
**15** Colchester CO1 .......135 F7
Ipswich IP1 ....................17 C6
Saffron Walden CB10 ......22 D2
**Musgrave Cl** CO12 ........90 F1
**Musk Cl** CO3 ...............134 D7

**Muswell Wlk** CO16 .......188 D5
**Mutlow Cl** CB11 .............42 F5
**Mutlow Hill** CB11 ..........42 F5
**Mychett Cl** CO16 ..........188 B6
**Myddylton Pl** CB10 ........22 D2
**Myland Cty Prim Sch**
CO4 ............................109 E4
**Myland Hall Chase** CO4 .110 A5
**Mynards Way** CM3 .......218 C2
**Myneer Pk** CO6 ............131 B2
**Myrtle Gr** CO2 .............136 B5
**Myrtle Rd** IP3 ...............17 E4

**N**

**Nabbott Rd** CM1 ...........204 E2
**Nabbotts Cty Jun & Inf**
Sch CM1 ......................205 E7
**Nacton Cres** IP3 ...........18 B2
**Nacton Rd** Felixstowe IP11 .221 C1
Ipswich, Racecourse IP3 ..18 B2
Ipswich, Rose Hill IP3 .....18 A3
**Nails La 13** CM23 .........145 F7
**Nalla Gdns** CM1 ...........205 A6
**Nancy Smith Cl** CO2 .....135 F5
**Nansen Rd**
Holland-on-S CO15 .......189 D6
Ipswich IP3 ...................18 B2
**Napier Ave** CO15 .........203 D6
**Napier Ct** CM1 .............204 E5
**Napier Rd** CO2 ............135 F6
**Narvik Cl** CM9 .............220 E8
**Nash Cl** Colchester CO3 ..135 B5
Lawford CO11 ...............86 B5
**Nash Dr** CM1 ...............191 A3
**Nash Gdns** IP3 ..............38 B8
**Nassau Rd** CO16 ..........187 B4
**Nathan Cl** CO2 .............163 B8
**Nathan's La** CM1 ..........215 A6
**Nats La** CB11 .................42 E6
**Navarre St 4** IP1 ...........17 C6
**Navigation Rd** CM2 ......204 B2
**Nayland Cty Prim Sch**
CO6 .............................56 A1
**Nayland Dr** CO16 .........188 B4
**Nayland Rd** Bures CO8 ...55 E8
Colchester CO6 .............109 D6
Felixstowe IP11 ............221 A4
Great Horkesley CO6 ......82 B4
Haverhill CB9 ...................8 E6
Little Horkesley CO6 .......81 F6
West Bergholt CO6 .........108 D7
**Nayling Rd** CM7 ...........127 C2
**Naze Nature Reserve**
The CO14 .....................144 D6
**Naze Nature Trail The**
CO14 ...........................144 E4
**Naze Park Rd** CO14 ......144 E2
**Neale Rd** CO9 ................76 E1
**Neale St** IP1 .................17 C6
**Neasden Ave** CO16 .......188 D5
**Neath Dr** IP2 .................17 A1
**Nelson Gdns** CM7 ........128 C4
**Nelson Gr** CM1 ............204 F3
**Nelson Rd**
Bishop's Stortford CM23 ..146 A5
Clacton-on-S CO15 ........188 E1
Colchester CO3 .............134 E6
Harwich CO12 ................91 D4
Ipswich IP4 ...................18 A6
**Nelson St** CO7 .............185 F6
**Neptune Ct 5** CO1 .......136 C6
**Ness Wlk** CM8 .............176 D2
**Nethaniah Home For The**
Aged 8 IP2 ....................17 C4
**Nether Ct** CO9 ...............77 A1
**Nether Hill** CO9 .............31 D3
**Nether Rd** CO10 .............43 D8
**Nethergate St** CO10 ......12 B7
**Netley Cl** IP2 .................16 B4
**Neville Rd** CB10 .............22 E2
**New Barn La** CM22 .......146 D1
**New Bowers Way** CM1 ..205 F6
**New Captains Rd** CO5 ...201 B6
**New Cardinal St** IP1 .......17 B5
**New Church Rd** CO6 .....133 D5
**New Cotts** Great Tey CO6 ..132 C8
Wakes Colne CO6 .........106 C6
**New Cut** Bures CO8 ........79 E8
Glemsford CO10 ..............2 B3
Great Bentley CO7 .........166 E8
Layer-de-l-H CO2 ..........161 F5
**New Cut E** IP2, IP3 ........17 D6
**New Cut W** IP2 ..............17 D6
**New Dukes Way** CM2 ....205 F4
**New England Cl** CM3 .....218 F1
**New Farm Lodge** CO3 ...134 D5
**New Farm Rd** CO3 ........134 D6
**New Hall Cotts** CO7 ........58 F7
**New Hall Vineyard** CM3 .220 D2
**New House La** CB10 ........24 C3
**New Kiln Rd** CO3 ..........135 C7
**New La** CO5 .................158 F5
**New Lodge Chase** CM3 .207 B2
**New London Rd** CM2 ....205 A1
**New Meadgate Terr**
CM2 ............................216 D8
**New Nabbotts Way** CM1 .205 F7
**New Orleans Flats** CO5 ..201 B5
**New Park Rd** CO5 .........201 F3
**New Park St** CO1 ..........135 F6
**New Pier St 7** CO14 ......171 C8
**New Pond La** CO3 ..........22 C2
**New Queens Rd** CO10 ....15 C1
**New Rd** Aldham CO6 .....107 B2
Broomfield CM1 ............191 B1
Colchester CO3 .............134 D6

**New Rd** continued
Elsenham CM22 ..............
Gosfield CO9 ...................
Great Baddow CM2 ..........
Hatfield Peverel CM3 .........1
Hinxton CB10 ...................
Holbrook IP9 ....................6
Kelvedon CO5 ................158
Long Melford CO10 ..........15
Messing CO5 ..................159
Mistley CO11 ...................86 e
Pharos Cl CM7 ................127 A
Saffron Walden CB10 ........22 E
Shudy Camps CB1 .............7 C
Terling CM3 ....................175 C
Tiptree CO5 ....................179 D
Tollesbury CM9 ..............199 D
**New Road Terr** CM7 ......126 F
**New St** Braintree CM7 ....127 F
Brightlingsea CO7 ..........185 F
Chelmsford CM1 .............205 B
Glemsford CO10 ...............2 C
Great Dunmow CM6 ........150 D
Halstead CO9 ..................76 E
**2** Ipswich IP4 .................17 D
Maldon CM9 ...................209 F
Sudbury CO10 ..................33 E
**New Street Fields** CM6 ..150 D
**New Thorpe Ave** CO16 ...142 A
**New Town Rd**
Colchester CO1 ..............136 A
Thorpe-le-S CO16 ...........141 F
**New Village** CO11 ..........86 C
**New Way** Ipswich IP2 ......16 F
Point Clear B CO16 ........185 F
**New Writtle St** CM2 ......205 B
**Newark Cl** IP4 ...............16 F
**Newbarn Rd** CO6 ..........106 B
**Newbiggen St** CM6 ........69 F
**Newbourne Gdns** IP11 ...221 B
**Newbridge Hill** CO6 ......108 D
**Newbridge Rd** Birch CO5 ..180 A
Tiptree CO5 ....................179 F
**Newbury Ho** IP4 ............18 B
**Newbury Rd** IP4 ............18 C
**Newby Dr** IP4 .................18 F
**Newcastle Ave** CO3 .......134 F
**Newcomen Way** CO4 ....110 C
**Newcourt Rd** CM2 .........205 B
**Newcroft 1** CB10 ...........22 E
**Newgate St 1** CO14 ......171 C
**Newhaven La** CO12 ........91 D
**Newhouse Rd** CO4 ........110 A
**Newington Gdns** CO15 ..188 F
**Newland Ave** CM7 .........72 B
**Newland Pl** CM8 ...........177 A
**Newland St** CM8 ...........177 A
**Newlands Dr** CM7 .........128 A
**Newlands La** CO6 ...........56 B
**Newlands Prec 8** CM8 ...177 A
**Newlands Spring Prim**
Sch CM1 .......................204 D
**Newman's Rd** CO10 ........33 F
**Newmarket Rd** CB10 .......3 C
**Newmill La** Brantham CO11 .61 A
Stutton CO11 ...................87 A
**Newnham Cl** CM7 .........127 E
**Newnham Ct** IP2 ...........16 E
**Newnham Gn** CM9 ........209 C
**Newpasture La** CM6 ......125 C
**Newport Cl**
Great Baddow CM2 ........217 B
Harwich CO12 ................91 A
**Newport Cty Prim Sch**
CB11 .............................66 F
**Newport Dr**
Clacton-on-S CO15 ........189 A
Rickling Green CB11 .........66 F
**Newport Free Gram Sch**
CB11 .............................42 F
**Newport Rd** CB11 ...........43 C
**Newport Sta** CB11 ..........67 A
**Newport Way** CO13 .......171 A
**Newpots Cl** CO5 ...........182 D
**Newpots La** CO5 ...........182 D
**Newquay Cl** IP5 .............18 F
**Newry Ave** IP11 ............221 D
**Newson Cl** IP1 ...............17 B
**Newton Cl 4** CM7 .........127 F
**Newton Croft** CO10 ........34 A
**Newton Gdns** CO16 .......187 A
**Newton Gn** CM6 ...........123 C
**Newton Pl 15** CB9 ..........9 B
**Newton Rd** Harwich CO12 ..91 A
Ipswich IP3 .....................18 A
Sudbury CO10 ..................34 A
**Newton St 10** CM9 .........17 D
**Newton Way** CO16 ........187 B
**Newtown Rd** CM23 .......145 F
**Nicholas Cl**
Chelmsford CM1 .............204 E
**2** Chelmsford,
Moulsham CM2 .............205 A
Witham CM8 .................176 E
**Nicholas Rd** IP11 ..........221 A
**Nicholls Cl** CM1 .............86 B
**Nichols Cnr** CO7 ...........112 A
**Nickleby Rd** CM1 ..........204 D
**Nickolsons Gr** CO10 ......136 A
**Nien-Oord** CO16 ...........188 C
**Nightingale Cl**
Clacton-on-S CO15 ........188 F
Colchester CO3 .............137 A
Harwich CO12 ................90 F
Witham CM8 .................194 E

Hill CO4 ....83 F6
. Mews 5 CB10 .22 F2
.e Rd IP3 ....38 A8
.le Sq IP3 ....38 A8
ale Way CO15 ....138 A5
.ges IP2 ....16 D5
.es CM7 ....128 A1
.ve CM24 ....120 B2
.s Ark La CO10 ....33 D7
.s Cross CM8 ....178 B2
.es Ave CM2 ....216 E6
.es Rd IP7 ....
.les The CM23 ....145 D6
.nsuch Meadow CO10 ..33 F7
.ok The CO7 ....164 C8
.ch CI CO10 ....132 F3
.rbury Rd IP4 ....18 B8
.ordic Lodge CM7 ....220 F8
.orfolk Ave
  Clacton-on-S CO15 ....189 E7
  West Mersea CO5 ....201 D7
.orfolk CI CM9 ....209 E1
.orfolk Cres CO10 ....110 B1
.orfolk Dr CM1 ....205 A7
.orfolk Gdns CM7 ....128 B4
.orfolk Rd Ipswich IP4 ....17 D6
  Maldon CM9 ....209 E1
.orfolk Way CM23 ....145 F5
.orman Way
  Colchester, Lexton CO3 ....135 B6
  Colchester, Shrub End CO3 ..135 B4
.oint Clear B CO16 ....185 F3
.orman's Way CM24 ....119 E7
.ormandy Ave CO8 ....79 E8
.ormandy Ave CO2 ....136 A3
.ormanhurst CO15 ....188 E1
.ormansfield CO6 ....
.orris CI
  Bishop's Stortford CM23 ....146 C7
  Great Notley CM7 ....128 C5
.orth Ave Chelmsford CM1 ..204 F5
  Haverhill CB9 ....8 E8
.orth CI IP4 ....17 E8
.orth Cres CB9 ....
.orth Cty Prim Sch CO1 ..135 E8
.orth Dell CM1 ....205 E7
.orth Dr CM2 ....216 F7
.orth End Rd
  Gestingthorpe CO9 ....31 C2
  Hinxton CB10 ....3 B8
.ittle Waldham CO9 ....30 E2
.orth Hill Rd CB11 ....67 A2
.orth Hill Colchester CO1 ..135 E7
  Little Baddow CM3 ....207 D5
.orth Hill Gdns 6 IP4 ....17 E6
.orth Hill Rd IP4 ....17 E6
.orth Ho CO13 ....170 F4
.orth La CO6 ....133 B5
.orth Lawn IP4 ....18 C8
.orth Mill PI CO9 ....76 E3
.orth Rd
  Belchamp Walter CO10 ....31 F6
  Brightlingsea CO7 ....
  Clacton-on-S CO15 ....188 F6
  Great Yeldham CO9 ....
  Takeley CM22 ....148 C8
  Tollesbury CM9 ....199 C2
.orth Rise CO10 ....34 A6
.orth St
4 Bishop's Stortford CM23 ..145 F7
  Great Dunmow CM6 ....123 D1
  Maldon CM9 ....210 B2
  Manningtree CO11 ....86 D4
  Steeple Bumpstead CB9 ....27 B7
  Sudbury CO10 ....33 E8
  Tolleshunt D'arcy CM9 ....198 E5
  Walton-on-t-N CO14 ....171 C8
.orth Station Rd CO1 ....135 E8
.orth Street Par 1 CO10 ..33 E7
.orth Terr 5 CM23 ....145 F8
.orth View Cotts CO6 ....109 E5
.orth Wall CO16 ....186 A3
.orthampton Mdw CM7 ....72 B2
.orthbourne Rd CO15 ....188 F4
.orthcroft CO7 ....33 E7
.orthfield CM7 ....72 B3
.orthfield Gdns CO4 ....110 A4
.orthfield Rd CB11 ....43 E8
.orthgate End CM23 ....145 F8
.orthgate JMI Sch CM23 ..145 E8
.orthgate St
  Colchester CO1 ....135 F8
  Ipswich IP1 ....17 C6
.ortholt Ave CM23 ....119 B1
.orthumberland CI CM7 ..128 B4
.orthumberland Ct 1
  CM2 ....205 F4
.orton Rd
  Chelmsford CM1 ....205 A3
  Haverhill CB9 ....8 E6
.orway Cres CO12 ....90 F3
.orwich CI
  Clacton-on-S CO16 ....188 E6
  Colchester CO3 ....136 A8
.orwich Ct 2 IP1 ....17 A7
.orwich Rd IP1 ....17 A7
.orwood Ave CO15 ....189 B5
.orwood Way CO14 ....171 A7
.otcutts CO7 ....59 E1

O

Oak Ave CO16 ....188 A2
Oak Bglws CM7 ....127 E3
Oak CI Felixstowe IP11 ....221 C4
  Rushmere St A IP4 ....18 E7
  Thorpe-le-S CO16 ....142 A1
  West Bergholt CO6 ....108 D4
Oak Cnr Beaumont CO16 ..141 F8
  Woodham Mortimer CM9 ..219 D6
Oak Cotts CM3 ....206 E8
Oak Fall CM7 ....177 A5
Oak Farm Rd CM9 ....208 E1
Oak Hall CM23 ....145 E8
Oak Haven CO12 ....90 F1
Oak Hill Beazley End CM7 ..101 A8
  Wethersfield CM7 ....73 F1
Oak Hill La IP2 ....17 B3
Oak Ho IP2 ....17 B3
Oak Lodge Tye CM1 ....206 A6
Oak Rd Chappel CO6 ....106 B3
  Great Cornard CO10 ....34 B6
  Halstead CO9 ....103 D7
  Heybridge CM7 ....210 B6
  Little Maplestead CO9 ....77 A8
  Pebmarsh CO9 ....77 F8
  Rivenhall CM8 ....177 C6
  Tiptree CO5 ....179 C7
Oak Ridge CO12 ....117 B7
Oak St CM73 ....145 F6
Oak Tree Cotts CM8 ....133 B8
Oak Tree Rd CO7 ....165 B8
Oak Wlk CO7 ....51 D2
Oak Yd CO9 ....76 E2
Oakapple CI CO12 ....135 D1
Oakfield La CM3 ....175 A2
Oakfield Rd Belstead IP8 ..36 A7
  Washbrook IP8 ....35 F6
Oakland Rd CO12 ....91 C3
Oaklands Ave CO3 ....134 E5
Oaklands CI
  Bishop's Stortford CM23 ..119 B2
  Great Notley CM7 ....154 D8
Oaklands Cres CM2 ....216 B8
Oaklands Cty Inf Sch
  CM2 ....216 B8
Oaklands Dr CM23 ....119 B2
Oaklands Pk CM23 ....119 B2
Oaklands Way CM23 ....207 E2
Oaklea IP2 ....17 A1
Oakleigh Rd CO15 ....188 F8
Oakley Cross CO12 ....117 B7
Oakley Rd Braintree CM7 ..127 F7
  Harwich CO12 ....90 D1
  Wix CO11 ....115 E5
Oakmead Rd CO16 ....186 B3
Oakroyd Ave CM6 ....150 E8
Oaks CI CO3 ....135 D7
Oaks Hospl The CO4 ....109 E3
Oaks PI CO4 ....109 C2
Oaks The CO13 ....170 F6
Oaksmere Gdns IP2 ....17 A2
Oakstead CI IP4 ....18 A6
Oaktree CI 14 CM23 ....145 F7
Oakview CO12 ....90 F1
Oakwood Ave
  Clacton-on-S CO15 ....189 E7
  West Mersea CO5 ....201 D7
Oakwood CI CO13 ....170 E6
Oakwood Cty Inf Sch
  The CO15 ....188 D2
Oakwood Dr CO5 ....201 D7
Oakwood Gdns CO5 ....201 D7
Oasis Ct CM1 ....205 F5
Oasthouse Ct CB10 ....22 D1
Oatfield CI CO3 ....134 D6
Oatlands CO7 ....137 F6
Oban St IP1 ....17 B7
Oberon CI CO4 ....136 F7
Obrey Way CM23 ....145 E3
Observation Ct IP1 ....17 B5
Observer Way CO5 ....158 C4
Ockelford Ave CM1 ....204 F5
Ockendon Way CO4 ....171 A8
Octavia Dr CM8 ....194 E2
Oddcroft CO7 ....77 F1
Odin Lodge CM9 ....220 F8
Office La CM9 ....197 A4

Old Barn Rd CO8 ....80 A6
Old Bell CI CM24 ....119 D6
Old Burylodge La CM24 ..120 A4
Old Cattle Market 5 IP4 ..17 C5
Old Chapel The CO6 ....106 D4
Old Church La Bulmer CO10 ..32 F2
  Bulmer CO10 ....32 F3
  West Bergholt CO6 ....108 D5
Old Clements La CB9 ....8 F7
Old Coach Rd CM7 ....136 B7
Old Coastguard Cotts
  CM8 ....214 E4
Old Court Rd CM2 ....205 D3
Old Ct CM2 ....205 D3
Old Forge CO7 ....137 C2
Old Forge Rd
  Boreham CM3 ....206 E8
  Layer-de-l-H CO2 ....161 F5
Old Foundry Rd IP4 ....17 D6
Old Hall CI CB9 ....27 C7
Old Hall La Capel St M IP9 ..35 F3
  Tolleshunt D'arcy CM9 ....199 C5
  Walton-on-t-N CO14 ....144 E3
Old Heath Rd CO1 ....136 C4
Old House La CO4 ....83 B2
Old House Rd CO6 ....109 A8
Old Ipswich Rd CO7 ....110 E7
Old London Rd
  Capel St M IP9 ....59 F7
  Woodham Walter CM9 ....208 E1
Old Maltings The 2
  CM23 ....146 A7
Old Market St 3 CO10 ....33 E7
Old Market PI 2 CO10 ....33 E7
Old Mead La CM22 ....94 D4
Old Mead Rd CM22 ....94 C5
Old Mill Chase CM7 ....73 C4
Old Mill La CO5 ....158 D7
Old Mill Rd Langham CO4 ..83 D5
  Saffron Walden CB11 ....43 E8
Old Parsonage
  Way CO13 ....170 F5
Old Pier St CO14 ....171 C8
Old Rd Clacton-on-S CO15 ..188 E4
  Coggeshall CO6 ....131 E1
  Frinton-on-S CO13 ....170 F4
  Chappel CM7 ....79 F3
  Wickham St P CO9 ....53 D5
Old River La CM23 ....145 F7
Old Rope Wlk CB9 ....8 E7
Old Rose Gdns CO4 ....109 D4
Old School La CO10 ....34 C1
Old School Ct CM3 ....194 B3
Old School Field CM1 ....205 E4
Old School Ho The
  Rowhedge CO5 ....164 A8
Shotley Gate CM7 ....91 B8
Old School Yard CB11 ....43 D8
Old Southend Rd CM2 ....217 D1
Old St The IP7 ....35 B1
Old Vicarage Rd CO12 ....91 C3
Old Vicarage The CM7 ....72 D6
Old Way CO13 ....170 F4
Oldbury Ave CM2 ....216 F8
Olde Forge CO5 ....165 E1
Oldfield Rd IP8 ....16 B1
Oldhouse Villas CM2 ....216 F8
Oline Gr CO2 ....135 D2
Oliver PI CM8 ....177 B2
Oliver Way CM1 ....204 F7
Olivers CI
  Clacton-on-S CO15 ....188 E4
  Long Melford CO10 ....15 D7
Olivers Cres CO15 ....188 E4
Olivers Dr CM8 ....195 A7
Olivers La CO2 ....135 A1
Olivers Rd CO15 ....188 E4
Oliveswood Rd CM6 ....150 D7
Ongar CI CO16 ....188 B4
Ongar Rd
  Great Dunmow CM6 ....150 D6
  Writtle CM1 ....204 A1
Ongar Road Trad Est
  CM6 ....204 B1
Ongark Rd CM1 ....204 B1
Onslow Cotts CO5 ....160 A7
Onslow Cres CO2 ....136 B3
Opal Ave IP1 ....16 D8
Ophir Rd CO7 ....185 F5
Orange St CM6 ....70 A2
Orange Tree CI CM7 ....216 C6
Orchard Ave CO9 ....76 D2
Orchard CI
  Chelmsford CM2 ....216 C6
  Clacton-on-S CO15 ....188 C5
  Copford CO6 ....133 D2
  Elmstead CO7 ....138 A6
  Great Oakley CO12 ....116 C3
  Hatfield Peverel CM3 ....194 A4
  Haverhill CB9 ....8 F7
  Maldon CM9 ....209 F2
  Newport CB11 ....66 F8
  Ramsey CO12 ....90 A2
  Ridgewell CO9 ....28 B3
  Saffron Walden CB11 ....43 D7
  Thaxted CM6 ....70 A3
  Tollesbury CM9 ....199 E1
  Writtle CM1 ....204 B1
Orchard Cotts
  Langham CO4 ....83 F3
  Little Horkesley CM6 ....81 E5
Orchard Ct CO3 ....135 C7
Orchard Dr
  Braintree CM7 ....128 A1
  Great Holland CO13 ....170 A4
Orchard Gate IP2 ....16 C5

Orchard Gdns CO4 ....136 B8
Orchard Gr IP5 ....18 F7
Orchard Lodge CO5 ....179 D4
Orchard Mews CO5 ....179 C4
Orchard Pightle CB1 ....5 C6
Orchard Rd Alresford CO7 ..165 B8
  Bishop's Stortford CM23 ..119 B1
3 Colchester CO1 ....135 E8
  Kelvedon CO5 ....158 C3
  Maldon CM9 ....209 F2
Orchard St
  Chelmsford CM2 ....205 B1
9 Ipswich IP4 ....17 D6
Orchard The CM6 ....152 C5
Orchard Way CO10 ....15 D6
Orchards CM8 ....176 F1
Orchid Ave CM6 ....176 E4
Orchid CI IP2 ....16 E4
Orford Cres CM1 ....205 D5
Orford Rd
  Felixstowe IP11 ....221 C1
  Haverhill CB9 ....8 F6
Orford St IP1 ....17 B7
Oriel CI CO10 ....34 B6
Oriole Way CM23 ....145 C6
Orion Way CM7 ....128 B4
Orkney CI CB9 ....9 D7
Orlando CI CO14 ....171 C8
Ormonde CI CO6 ....108 E4
Orpen CI CO6 ....108 E4
Orpen's Hill CO2 ....161 A5
Orplands Cotts CM9 ....214 F1
Orsino Wlk CO4 ....136 F7
Orvis La CO7 ....59 E1
Orwell CI CO4 ....110 E7
Orwell CI 4 IP11 ....17 D5
Orwell Gdns IP2 ....17 A3
Orwell High Sch IP11 ....221 C5
Orwell Ho IP11 ....221 A4
Orwell Hts IP11 ....16 E2
Orwell Jun Sch IP3 ....17 F1
Orwell PI
  Chelmondiston IP9 ....63 F7
2 Ipswich IP4 ....17 C5
Orwell Rd
  Clacton-on-S CO15 ....188 F2
  Felixstowe IP11 ....221 D3
  Harwich CO12 ....91 D4
  Ipswich IP3 ....18 A4
Orwell Ret Pk IP2 ....16 F5
Orwell Rise IP9 ....63 F8
Orwell Way CO16 ....188 D6
Orwell Wlk CM8 ....176 E3
Osbert Rd CM8 ....194 E8
Osborne CI CO15 ....189 A7
Osborne Rd Ipswich IP3 ....18 A4
  West Mersea CO5 ....135 F6
Osborne St CO2 ....135 F6
Osbourne Gdns 6 CM23 ..145 F5
Osbournes Ct CO7 ....185 F6
Osea Rd CM9 ....211 B3
Osea Way CM1 ....205 F5
Osier PI 3 CB9 ....8 F8
Osprey Rd CB9 ....9 C8
Osprey Way CM2 ....216 A5
Ospreys CO15 ....188 F6
Ostler CI CM23 ....145 C4
Othello CI CO4 ....136 F7
Otley CI IP11 ....221 B5
Otten Rd CO10 ....13 B1
Ottershaw Way CO16 ....188 B6
Oulton CI CO12 ....90 F3
Oulton Rd IP3 ....17 E2
Our Lady Immaculate
  RC Prim Sch CM2 ....205 A1
Ouse Chase CM8 ....176 D2
Outpart Eastward CO12 ....91 E6
Over Hall La CB10 ....6 D2
Overhall Hill CO4 ....78 C2
Overstone Ct CO2 ....135 C3
Ovington PI 8 IP4 ....17 F8
Owen Ward CI CO2 ....135 A3
Owl's Hill CM1 ....217 A3
Owls Retreat 1 CO4 ....136 F8
Ox Yd CO9 ....102 E7
Oxcroft CM23 ....145 F3
Oxenford CI CO12 ....90 F1
Oxford CI CO10 ....34 A6
Oxford Cres CO15 ....188 F4
Oxford Ct
  Chelmsford CM2 ....205 E4
  Colchester CO3 ....135 D6
  Earls Colne CO6 ....105 B6
Oxford La CO9 ....51 D2
Oxford Mdw CO9 ....105 B6
Oxford PI CO5 ....135 B6
Oxford Rd
  Clacton-on-S CO15 ....188 F4
  Colchester CO3 ....135 C6
  Frinton-on-S CO13 ....171 A5
  Halstead CO9 ....76 D1
  Ipswich IP4 ....17 E5
  Manningtree CO11 ....86 D4
Oxley Hill Abberton CO5 ..163 A3
  Tolleshunt D'arcy CM9 ....198 B8
  Tolleshunt Knights CM9 ..180 A1
Oxley Ho CM7 ....154 F3
Oxley Parker Sch The
  CO4 ....110 A6
Oxley Rd CM8 ....176 E4
Oxney Villas CM6 ....152 D6
Oyster CI CO5 ....201 C7
Oyster Pk CO7 ....136 D6
Oyster PI CM2 ....205 F4
Oyster Tank Rd CO7 ....186 A1
Ozier Ct CB11 ....43 E7
Oziers CM22 ....94 C2

P

Packard Ave IP3 ....18 B2
Packards La CO6 ....80 F1
Packe CI CO5 ....158 D4
Paddock CI CO12 ....91 C4
Paddock Dr CM1 ....205 E8
Paddock The CM23 ....145 D3
Paddock Way CO7 ....137 C3
Paddocks The Bures CO8 ....79 E8
  Great Notley CM7 ....196 A4
  West Mersea CO5 ....201 D6
  Witham CM8 ....177 A2
Page CI CM8 ....194 D8
Page Rd CO15 ....188 E3
Pages CI CM23 ....145 D5
Pages La CM9 ....198 F1
Paget Ct CM22 ....94 C1
Paget Rd Ipswich IP1 ....17 B7
  Rowhedge CO5 ....163 F8
Paignton Ave CM1 ....205 D5
Pakenham PI 8 CB9 ....9 B8
Palace Gdns CM23 ....145 E5
Palfrey Hights CO11 ....86 D8
Pallister Rd CO15 ....188 F2
Palm CI Chelmsford CM2 ....216 C6
  Witham CM8 ....177 A5
Palmers Croft CM7 ....206 A2
Palmers La
8 Bishop's Stortford CM23 ..145 F7
  Chrishall SG8 ....19 C3
Palmerston Lodge CM2 ....216 F7
Palmerston Rd Ipswich IP4 ..17 F6
  Thorpe-le-S CO16 ....142 A2
Pampas CI CO4 ....110 A4
Panfield La CM7 ....127 E5
Pannells Ash CO10 ....11 D1
Pannells CI CO10 ....2 B4
Pantile CI CM8 ....195 A7
Pantlings La CO5 ....158 A5
Panton Cres 7 CO4 ....136 E7
Panton Mews CM7 ....155 A5
Papermill Cotts CO9 ....76 E2
Papillon Rd CO3 ....135 A5
Parade Rd IP4 ....17 F7
Parade The
  Colchester CO2 ....136 A1
  Kirby Cross CO13 ....170 B6
  Walton-on-t-N CO14 ....171 C8
Paradise Rd CM1 ....215 B8
Pardoe PI IP4 ....18 E5
Park Ave
  Bishop's Stortford CM23 ..145 F3
  Chelmsford CM1 ....204 F3
  Felixstowe IP11 ....221 F5
Park Bvd CO15 ....189 E6
Park Chase CO16 ....187 C5
Park CI CO10 ....34 A8
Park Cotts Gosfield CO9 ....102 E8
  Manningtree CO11 ....86 D3
Park Ct Felixstowe IP11 ....221 D2
  Sible Hedingham CO9 ....51 D1
Park Dr Braintree CM7 ....155 A8
  Brightlingsea CO7 ....185 E7
  Halstead CO9 ....76 E1
  Maldon CM9 ....210 B1
Park Drive Par CO7 ....185 E7
Park Farm Ind Est SG8 ....39 C2
Park Farm La SG8 ....39 C2
Park Gate Cotts CM7 ....101 C6
Park Gate Rd CM7 ....157 B3
Park La
  Bishop's Stortford CM23 ..145 F4
  Bulmer CO10 ....32 F2
  Castle Camps CB1 ....7 F3
  Earls Colne CO6 ....105 B6
  Glemsford CO10 ....2 D4
  Gosfield CO9 ....102 F7
  Langham CO4 ....83 E3
  Langley CB11 ....40 A3
  Saffron Walden CB10 ....22 D1
  Tolleshunt Knights CM9 ..180 B3
  Toppesfield CO9 ....50 B7
Park North IP4 ....17 D8
Park PI CM23 ....111 B3
Park Rd Ardleigh CO7 ....111 B3
  Chelmsford CM1 ....205 B2
  Clacton-on-S CO15 ....188 D2
  Colchester CO3 ....135 C6
  East Bergholt CO7 ....60 B2
  Eisenham CM22 ....94 D1
  Ford End CM3 ....172 A3
  Great Chesterford CB10 ....3 E5
  Harwich CO12 ....91 D4
  Haverhill CB9 ....8 D8
  Ipswich IP1 ....17 C8
  Little Bentley CM7 ....139 D8
  Little Easton CM6 ....122 F3
  Little Horkesley CO6 ....82 B8
  Maldon CM9 ....209 F2
  Rivenhall CM8 ....157 A2
  Stansted
  Mountfitchet CM24 ....119 E6
  Stoke-by-N CO6 ....56 E4
  Sudbury CO10 ....34 A8
  Wivenhoe CO7 ....164 C8
Park CO4 ....137 A4
Park Side CM6 ....124 D6
Park Sq E
  Clacton-on-S CO15 ....203 G8
  Jaywick CO15 ....188 A1

**Park Sq W**
Clacton-on-S CO15 ....203 F8
Jaywick CO15 ...........187 F1
**Park St** Stoke-by-N CO6 ...56 D5
Thaxted CM6 ............70 A2
**Park Terr** Harwich CO12 ...91 D4
Long Melford CO10 .......15 C7
**Park The** CO11 ..........86 D3
**Park Vale** Cl CO9 ......51 E4
**Park View** CO10 ........12 C8
**Park View Cres** CM2 ...216 F5
**Park View Rd** IP1 ......17 B8
**Park Way** CO15 ........188 D1
**Park Wood La** CM9 .....197 A3
**Parkdale** CM7 ..........218 C2
**Parker Cl** CM0 .........214 F4
**Parker Rd** CM2 .........205 C1
**Parker Way** CO9 .......103 E8
**Parker's Way** CO6 ......56 A1
**Parkeston Rd**
Felixstowe IP11 ........221 B4
Harwich, Parkeston CO12 ...90 F4
Harwich, Upper
Dovercourt CO12 ........91 A4
**Parkfield St** CO5 .......163 F7
**Parkfields** CO9 .........51 D1
**Parkgate Cnr** CO16 ....169 A2
**Parkhall Rd**
Beazley End CM7 ........101 E2
Gosfield CO9 ...........102 B7
**Parklands** Cl CO1 .....136 C5
**Parklands** CM7 ........155 A8
**Parklands** Cl CO10 .....2 C5
**Parklands** Cl CO16 ....188 B3
**Parklands Dr** CM1 .....205 D3
**Parklands Way** CM2 ...216 C2
**Parkside** Haverhill CB9 ...8 F6
Saffron Walden CB10 ....22 C1
**Parkside Ave** IP4 ......17 D7
**Parkway**
Chelmsford CM1 CM2 ...205 B2
Shudy Camps CB1 ........7 C6
**Parkwood** IP1 ..........17 C7
**Parkwood Ave** CO7 ....137 B1
**Parkwood Dr** CO10 ....15 E2
**Parliament Rd** IP4 ....18 B5
**Parmenter Dr** CO10 ....34 C5
**Parnell** Cl CO2 ........136 A2
**Parnham PI** IP4 ........18 F5
**Parr Cl** CM7 ...........128 D4
**Parr Dr** CO3 ...........134 E4
**Parrington Way** CO11 ..86 A3
**Parry Dr** CO16 .........188 C5
**Parson's Field** CO7 ....85 A6
**Parson's Heath** CO10 ..110 E2
**Parson's Hill** CO3 .....135 A6
**Parsonage Cl**
Broomfield CM1 .........191 A1
Felixstowe IP11 ........221 B4
**Parsonage Farm Trad**
Est CM24 ...............119 F3
**Parsonage La** CB9 .......8 B7
**Parsonage Gr** CO8 ......79 E8
**Parsonage La**
Barnston CM6 ...........151 D3
Bishop's Stortford CM23 ...146 C8
Clavering CB11 ..........65 B3
Elder Street CB10 .......44 F3
Howe Street CM3 .......172 F2
Little Baddow CM3 .....207 D2
Stansted
Mountfitchet CM24 .....119 F4
Tendring CO16 .........140 E8
**Parsonage Rd** CM22 ...148 C8
**Parsonage St** CO9 ......76 F1
**Parsons Ct 4** CO9 .....76 F2
**Parsons Heath CE Prim**
Sch CO4 ...............110 E2
**Parsons Hill** CO10 .....138 F8
**Parsons La** CO1 .......136 C6
**Parsons Yd 6** CO11 ....86 D4
**Partridge Ave** CM1 ....204 F6
**Partridge Cl** CO12 ....116 D4
**Partridge Dr** CO6 .....107 D5
**Partridge Rd** IP2 ......16 E3
**Paschal Way** CM2 .....216 F8
**Pashlers Alley** CO10 ...12 B7
**Paske Ave** CB9 ..........8 F7
**Pasture High** CM3 .....207 D3
**Pastures The** IP4 ......18 F5
**Patching Hall La** CM1 ...205 A6
**Paternoster Row 6**
CO14 .................171 C8
**Path The** CO7 .........166 E8
**Pathfields Rd** CO15 ...188 D4
**Pathway The** CO13 ....170 E6
**Patmore Cl** CM23 ......145 C8
**Patmore Fields** CM22 ...93 E6
**Patmore Rd** CO4 .......110 D1
**Patricia Gdns** CM23 ...145 C5
**Patten Cl** CO6 ..........132 F3
**Pattern Bush Cl** CO11 ...86 D8
**Patteson Rd** IP3 ........17 E4
**Patticroft** CO10 .........2 B6
**Pattison Cl** CM8 ......195 A8
**Pattocks La** CO6 .......106 C2
**Patrick's La** CO12 ......91 C4
**Paul Spendlove** Cl CO4 ...110 E1
**Paul's Rd** IP2 ..........16 F5
**Pauline Cl** CO15 ......189 B6
**Pauline St 8** IP2 ......17 C4
**Pauls Cres** CO7 .......137 F6
**Pauls Way** CO15 ......188 A1
**Pavilion Ct** CB9 .........9 B7

**Pavitt Mdw** CM2 ......216 C2
**Pawle Cl** CM2 ..........217 A7
**Paxman Ave** CO2 ......135 A3
**Paxton Rd** CO15 ......189 B8
**Paycocke Way** CO6 ...131 A3
**Paycocke's House** CO6 ...130 F2
**Payne's La** CO11 ......113 C3
**Peace Rd** CO3 .........134 D7
**Peacock Cl** Braintree CM7 ...127 F1
**5** Ipswich IP8 ..........36 D6
**Peacocks** Cl CO10 ......1 C2
**Peacocks Rd** CO10 ......1 C2
**Peakes** Cl CO5 .........179 B4
**Peal Rd** CB11 ...........43 F7
**Pearce Manor** CM2 .....215 F8
**Pearce Rd** IP3 .........18 A5
**Pearl Rd** IP1 ...........16 D8
**Pearmain Way** CO3 ....134 C4
**Pearse Way** IP3 .......18 E1
**Pearson Rd** IP3 ........18 E1
**Pearsons** Cl CO10 .......2 A4
**Peartree Bsns Ctr** CO3 ...134 E4
**Peartree Cl** Braintree CM7 ...128 A1
Goldhanger CM9 .........211 E6
**Peartree Hill** Bures CO8 ...80 A4
Bures CO8 ..............80 B4
**Peartree La** CM3 ......218 F3
**Peartree Rd** CO3 ......134 E4
**Peartree Way** CO16 ...168 C2
**Peaslands Rd** CB11 .....43 E8
**Pebmarsh Cl** CO2 ......163 A8
**Pebmarsh Rd**
Alphamstone CO8 ........54 E2
Colne Engaine CO6 ......77 F2
**Pecockes** Cl CO10 .......43 C1
**Pedder's** Cl CO3 ......134 F3
**Pedlars Cl** CM3 ........219 A6
**Pedlars Path** CM3 .....219 A6
**Pedler"s Cnr** CO11 ....86 D2
**Peek's Cnr** CO6 .......105 D5
**Peel Cres** CM7 ........127 E7
**Peel Rd** CM2 ..........205 F4
**Peel St 3** IP1 ..........17 C6
**Peerswood Rd** CO2 ....135 D2
**Peewit Ct** IP11 .......221 B3
**Peewit Hill** IP11 ......221 B3
**Peewit Rd** IP2 .........16 C3
**Peg Millar's La** CM3 ...175 E5
**Pegasus Way**
Braintree CM7 ..........127 E5
**4** Colchester CO4 .....110 C1
**Peggotty Cl** CM1 .....204 F6
**Peggy's Wlk** CB11 ....204 F3
**Peldon Cres** CO5 ......182 E5
**Peldon Rd** Abberton CO5 ...182 E7
Great Wigborough CO5 ...182 A3
**Pelham Cl** CO12 ........90 F2
**Pelham Rd** CB11 ........65 C4
**Pelham's La 20** CO1 ...135 F7
**Pelican Cl** IP2 ..........16 E3
**Pelly Ave** CM8 .........195 A8
**Pembroke Ave** CM9 ...209 F1
**Pembroke Cl**
Colchester CO2 .........136 C3
Ipswich IP2 .............17 B3
**Pembroke Gdns** CO15 ...189 E6
**Pembroke Pl**
Chelmsford CM1 ........205 B7
Sudbury CO10 ...........15 D2
**Pen Wlk** CM1 .........204 D5
**Pendleton Rd** IP2 .....16 D1
**Penfold Rd**
Clacton-on-S CO15 .....188 E2
Felixstowe IP11 .......221 E4
**Penhaligon Ct 9** CM8 ...177 A2
**Penlan Hall La** CO6 ...107 B5
**Penn Cl** IP9 ............35 B2
**Penn Mews** CM7 .......155 A8
**Pennine Rd** CM1 ......204 D6
**Pennington La** CM24 ...93 D2
**Penningtons** CM23 .....145 C5
**Pennsylvania La** CO5 ...179 C5
**Penny Cnr** IP1 .........16 C8
**Penny La** IP3 ..........18 F1
**Penny Meadow** IP9 ....35 A1
**Penny Royal Rd** CM3 ...218 D6
**Pennyroyal Cres** CM8 ...176 E4
**Pennyroyal Gdns** IP2 ...16 E4
**Pennystone Rd** CB11 ...43 E8
**Penrice Ct** CO4 .......136 E6
**Penrose Mead** CM1 ....215 B8
**Penshurst Pl** CM7 .....154 B6
**Penshurst Rd** IP3 .....18 D4
**Penticton Rd** CM7 ....127 D2
**Pentland Ave** CM1 ....205 A6
**Pentlow Dr** CO10 ......1 E1
**Pentlow Hawke Cl** CM7 ...9 B7
**Pentlow Hill** CO10 ....14 A8
**Penzance Cl**
Chelmsford CM1 ........205 E5
Clacton-on-S CO15 .....203 J8
**Penzance Rd** IP5 ......18 F6
**Pepper's Rd** CO4 .......82 E1
**Peppercorn Cl** CO4 ...109 F2
**Peppercorn Way** IP2 ...17 D3
**Pepples La** Debden CB10 ...69 A8
Elder Street CB10 ......45 A1
**Pepys St** CO12 .........91 D5
**Percival Rd**
Kirby-le-S CO13 ........143 D1
Walton-on-t-N CO14 ....144 D2
**Peregrine Cl**
Bishop's Stortford CM23 ...145 D6
Clacton-on-S CO15 .....188 F7
**Peregrine Ct** CO4 .....136 F8
**Peregrine Dr** CM2 ....216 A4
**Perkins Way** IP3 .......17 F1
**Perriclose** CM1 .......205 D7

**Perrin Pl** CM2 ........205 A1
**Perry Hill** CM1 .......205 D3
**Perry La** CO4 ..........84 A4
**Perry Rd** Tiptree CO5 ...179 C5
Witham CM8 ............177 B1
**Perry Way** CM8 .......177 B1
**Perryfield** CO10 .......34 B4
**Perryfields Jun & Inf**
Sch CM1 ...............205 D6
**Persandi Ct** CO2 ......163 A7
**Pershore End** CO3 ....134 E5
**Perth Cl** CO2 .........136 A1
**Pertwee Cl** CO7 ......185 E8
**Pertwee Dr** CM2 .....216 F6
**Pertwee Way** CO5 ....163 B2
**Pesthouse La** CO12 ...116 D3
**Peter Bruff Ave** CO15 ...188 C5
**Peter Kirk Sch** CM24 ...119 F6
**Peter's Gr** IP9 ..........35 A1
**Peterfield's La** CO9 ...102 F5
**Peterhouse Cl** IP2 ....16 E2
**Peters Ho** CO5 .........158 C2
**Petersfield** CM1 ......205 B7
**Peto Ave** CO4 ..........109 F2
**Petrebrook** CM2 .......206 A3
**Petrel Way** CM2 ......216 C6
**Petrolea Cl** CO4 .......109 F1
**Pettit La** CM7 .........156 A4
**Petts La** CO10 ...........4 E1
**Petunia Cres** CM1 ....205 F6
**Petworth Cl**
Great Notley CM7 .......154 B7
Wivenhoe CO7 ..........164 C8
**Pevensey Dr** CO15 ....203 I8
**Peverel Ave** CM3 .....194 C1
**Peverells Rd** CB10 .....44 D1
**Pewterers Ave** CM23 ...145 C4
**Pharos La** CO5 .........201 C6
**Pheasant Rd** IP2 .......16 E3
**Pheasant Rise** IP8 .....35 F8
**Philip Ave** IP11 .......221 B3
**Philip Cl** CO15 ........171 A8
**Philip Morant Sch The**
CO3 ...................135 B5
**Philip Rd** Ipswich IP2 ...17 C4
Witham CM8 ...........194 E8
**Philips Cl** CM7 ........126 F2
**Philips Rd** CM7 .......126 F2
**Phillip Rd** CO7 ........164 B8
**Phillips Chase** CM7 ...128 A5
**Phillips Field Rd** CO10 ...34 A5
**Philpot End La** CM6 ...150 B4
**Phoenix Ct** CO2 ......136 D5
**Phoenix Gr** CM2 ......216 A8
**Phoenix Rd** IP4 ........18 A7
**Piccotts La** CM7 ......126 B8
**Pickers Way** CO15 ....189 E7
**Pickford Wlk** CO4 ....134 F7
**Pickpocket La** CM7 ...154 D6
**Pickwick Ave** CM1 ....204 D6
**Pickwick Rd** IP2 .......16 E5
**Pier App** CO14 ........171 C8
**Pier Gap** CO15 .......188 F2
**Pierce Glade** CO5 .....179 C5
**Pierrefitte Way** CM7 ...127 E3
**Pig La** CM22 ..........146 A3
**Pigeon's La** IP8 ........16 A3
**Piggots Way** CO13 ....170 D5
**Pightle The** Capel St M IP9 ...35 B2
Finchingfield CM7 ......72 D6
Haverhill CB9 ...........9 A8
**Pightle Way** CO14 ....171 A7
**Pilborough Way** CO3 ...134 E3
**Pilcox Hall La** CO16 ...140 D8
**Pilgrim Cl** CM7 ........127 F5
**Pilgrims Cl** CB10 .......3 D2
**Pimblett Row** CM2 ....94 F5
**Pimpernel Rd** IP2 .....16 F6
**Pin Mill Cl** IP2 .........16 C1
**Pincey Rd** CM24 ......120 F3
**Pincey Rdbt** CM24 ....121 A3
**Pinchpools Rd** CM23 ...93 A3
**Pine Ave**
Great Dunmow CM6 ....123 B1
Ipswich IP1 .............17 B8
**Pine Cl** Brantham CO11 ...86 D8
Great Bentley CO7 .....166 F8
**Pine Gr**
Bishop's Stortford CM23 ...146 B6
West Mersea CO5 ......201 B7
Witham CM8 ...........177 A5
**Pine Ho** IP11 .........221 C4
**Pine Tree Ct** CO4 ....136 E8
**Pine View Rd** IP1 .....17 A8
**Pinecroft Gdns** CO4 ...110 B3
**Pinecroft Rise** CO10 ...33 D5
**Pinelands** CM23 .......118 F1
**Pines Hill** CM24 ......119 D5
**Pines The** CM1 .......204 D5
**Pines The** CM3 ........194 A5
**Pinetree Ct** IP5 .......18 F7
**Pinewood Cl**
Clacton-on-S CO15 .....188 E7
Kirby Cross CO13 ......170 D6
**Pink La** CM3 ..........219 D5
**Pinkeneys Sch** CO5 ....179 D5
**Pinkham Dr** CM8 .....194 F8
**Pinkney Cl** CB10 .......44 E2
**Pinkuah La** CO10 ......13 B5
**Pinmill Rd** IP9 .........63 F8
**Pintail Cl** IP2 .........16 E3
**Pintail Cres** CM7 .....154 C6
**Pioneer Pl 8** CO1 ....136 A6
**Pipchin Rd** CM1 ......204 F6
**Piper Rd** CO3 .........135 B7
**Piper's Tye** CM2 ......216 D3
**Piperell Way** CB9 ......9 A5

**Pipers Cl** CB9 ..........9 C6
**Pippins The** Glemsford CO10 ...2 C4
Halstead CO9 ...........76 D2
**Pirie Rd** CO6 ..........108 E3
**Pit La** CO5 ............179 C6
**Pitcairn Rd** IP1 .......16 E8
**Pitmire La** CO8 .........55 B6
**Pitt Ave** CM8 .........195 A8
**Pitt Chase** CM2 ......216 E5
**Pitt Gn** CM8 ..........195 A8
**Pitt Rd** CO2 ..........136 D2
**Place Farm Cty Prim Sch**
CB9 ....................8 F8
**Plains Farm** Cl CO7 ...112 B6
**Plains Field** CM7 .....128 D1
**Plains Rd**
Great Totham CM9 .....196 F6
Little Totham CM9 .....197 A6
**Plaistow Green Rd** CO9 ...103 C5
**Plane Tree Cl** CM2 ...216 B6
**Plane View Cl** CO15 ...188 B2
**Plane View Cl** CO5 ...188 B2
**Plantation Cl** CB11 ....43 E6
**Plantation Rd** CM3 ...192 F1
**Planton Way** CO7 ....185 E6
**Platters Cl** IP3 .........38 B7
**Platters Rd** IP11 .....221 C2
**Plaw Hatch Cl** CM23 ...146 B8
**Plaw Hatch Cnr** CM23 ...146 B8
**Players Ct** CM6 .......152 C6
**Playfield Rd** IP9 .......35 B1
**Playford Ct 22** CO10 ...33 E8
**Playford Rd** IP4 .......18 E8
**Playle Chase** CM9 ....196 B4
**Pleasant Rd** CM23 ....145 E8
**Pleasant Row 12** CM7 ...17 D5
**Pleasant Valley** CB10 ...43 D7
**Pleasants Mews** CO5 ...201 C6
**Pleshey Rd** CM3 ......172 B5
**Plough Cnr** CO16 .....168 C4
**Plough Dr** CO3 .......135 A5
**Plough La** CO10 ......33 D2
**Plough Rd** CO7 .......166 E6
**Plough St** IP3 ..........17 E4
**Ploughmans La** CM23 ...145 C5
**Ploughmans**
Headland CO3 .........134 E5
**Plover Cl** CO13 .......170 E6
**Plover Rd** IP2 .........16 E2
**Plover Wlk** CM2 .....216 B5
**Plowright Ho 8** CO1 ...135 E8
**Plum St** CO10 ...........2 A6
**Plume Ave** Colchester CO3 ...135 A4
Maldon CM9 ...........209 F1
**Plume Sch (Lower Sch)**
The CM9 ...............210 A2
**Plume Sch (Upper Sch)**
The CM9 ...............209 F2
**Plummers Rd** CO6 ....107 E7
**Plumptre La** CM3 .....218 D5
**Plums La** CM7 .........99 E4
**Plumtree Ave** CM2 ...216 F6
**Plymouth Rd**
Chelmsford CM1 ........205 E5
Felixstowe IP11 .......221 D6
**Pochard Way** CM7 ....154 C5
**Pocklington Cl** CM2 ...206 A3
**Pods La** CM7 .........126 D2
**Point Clear Rd** CO16 ...186 D3
**Pointwell La** CO6 .....158 A8
**Pole Barn La** CO13 ...170 F5
**Pole La** CM8 .........155 C3
**Polecat Rd** CM7 ......155 F5
**Pollard Ct** IP2 ........16 D2
**Pollard Wlk** CO4 .....188 C5
**Pollard's Gn** CM2 ....205 F2
**Pollards Villas** CM7 ...99 D2
**Polley Cl** CO13 .......170 E7
**Polstead St** CO6 .......56 D5
**Polstead Way** CO16 ...188 B4
**Pond Chase** CO3 .....135 B4
**Pond Cl** IP11 .........221 B5
**Pond Cross Cotts** CB11 ...67 A8
**Pond Cross Farm** CB11 ...67 A8
**Pond Cross Way** CB11 ...67 A8
**Ponders Rd** CO6 .....107 C4
**Pondfield Rd** CO4 ....110 D1
**Pondholton Dr** CM8 ...194 F7
**Pondtail Cl** CM2 ......216 B1
**Pondtail Ct** CO13 ....170 C6
**Poney Chase** CM8 ....195 F5
**Pony's** CM8 ..........195 F5
**Pontisbright Cotts** CO6 ...106 C6
**Poole Cl** IP3 ..........18 D3
**Poole St** Cavendish CO10 ...1 C1
Great Yeldham CO9 .....51 B6
**Poore St** CB11 .......46 E8
**Pope's La** CO5 ........135 E7
**Pope's Rd** CO6 .......106 D4
**Poperinghe Rd** CO2 ...133 F4
**Popes Cl** CB9 ...........9 E5
**Poplar Ave** CO16 ......188 A2
**Poplar Chase** CM2 ...216 C6
Clacton-on-S CO15 .....188 B2
Great Yeldham CO9 ......30 A1
Halstead CO9 ..........107 B8
Witham CM8 ...........177 A5
**Poplar Cl** CO10 ........34 B7
**Poplar Grove Chase** CM8 ...210 B8
**Poplar Rd** CM8 ........177 A5
**Poplar Way** CO16 ....188 C6
**Poplar Way** CO13 .....170 D6
**Poplars Cl** CO7 .......165 B7
**Poplars The**
Brantham CO11 .........60 D2
Great Dunmow CM6 ....123 C2
Great Hallingbury CM22 ...146 F4

**Poppy Cl** IP2 ...........16
**Poppy Gdns** CO2 .......
**Pork La** CO13 ..........
**Port La**
Bishop's Stortford CM22 ...
**Port Of Felixstowe Rd**
IP11 ...................
**Portal Prec** CO1 .......
**Porter Rd** IP3 ........... 18
**Porter's Way** CO10 ....1
**Porter's Cl** CO13 ......10
**Porter's Cotts** CO3 ....107
**Porter's La** CO3 .......107
**Porters Brook Wlk** CO4 ...110
**Porters Pk** CM3 .......113
**Portland Ave** CO12 ....91
**Portland Cl** CM7 ......128
**Portland Cres** CO12 ...91
**Portland Ho** CO13 ....170
**Portland Pl 11** CM23 ...145
**Portland Rd**
Bishop's Stortford CM23 ...145
**15** Colchester CO2 ....135
**Portland Cl** CO11 ......87
**Portman Rd** IP1 ........17
**Portman Road (Ipswich**
Town FC)** IP1 .........17
**Portman's Wlk** IP1 ....17
**Portmans Walk Ind**
Ctr** IP1 ...............17
**Portobello Rd** CO14 ...171
**Portreath Pl** CM1 .....205
**Portsmouth Rd** CO15 ...203
**Pourway Ct** CO9 .......76
**Posford Ct** CO4 ........109
**Post Mill Cl** IP4 .......17
**Post Office Cnr** IP9 ....61
**Post Office La**
Glemsford CO10 ..........2
Little Totham CM9 .....197
**Post Office Rd**
Broomfield CM1 ........205
Woodham Mortimer CM9 ...219
**Pot Kiln Chase** CM3 ...31
**Pot Kiln Cty Prim**
Sch CO10 ..............34
**Pot Kiln Rd** CO10 .....34
**Pot Kilns The** CO10 ....34
**Potash Cotts** IP9 .......60
**Potash La** IP9 .........60
**Potter St**
Bishop's Stortford CM23 ...145
Sible Hedingham CO9 ...75
**Potters Cl** CM3 .......219
**Pottery La**
Castle Hedingham CO9 ...51
Chelmsford CM1 ........205
**Poulk Hall La** CM3 ...174
**Poulteney Rd** CM2 ....119
**Pound Farm Dr** CO12 ...91
**Pound Fields** CM1 ....215
**Pound Gate** CM6 .....124
**Pound La** Belstead IP8 ...36
Capel St M IP9 ..........59
Washbrook IP8 ..........35
**Pound Wlk** CO10 .......22
**Poundfield Cl** CO7 ....165
**Poundfield Ho** CO7 ...138
**Powers Hall Cty Inf**
Sch CM8 ...............176
**Powers Hall Cty Jun**
Sch CM8 ...............176
**Powling Rd** IP3 ........18
**Pownall Cres** CO2 ....135
**Poynter Pl** CO13 ......170
**Prail Ct** CO6 ..........130
**Pratt's La** IP9 ..........38
**Pratts Farm La** CM3 ...191
**Prentice Hall La** CM9 ...213
**President Rd** CO3 .....134
**Preston Rd** CO15 .....189
**Prestwick Dr** CM23 ...119
**Pretoria Rd** CO9 .......76
**Prettygate Jun & Inf**
Sch CO3 ...............135
**Prettygate Rd**
Colchester CO3 ........135
Colchester CO3 ........135
**Pretyman Rd**
Felixstowe IP11 .......221
Ipswich IP3 .............18
**Prime's Cl** CB10 ......22
**Primrose Cl** CM23 ....145
**Primrose Hill**
Chelmsford CM1 ........204
Haverhill CB9 ...........8
Holbrook IP9 ...........62
Ipswich IP4 ............18
**Primrose Wlk**
Colchester CO4 ........136
Maldon CM9 ...........210
**Primula Way** CM1 ....206
**Prince Albert Rd** CO5 ...201
**Prince Charles Cl**
Clacton-on-S CO15 .....188
Sudbury CO10 ..........33
**Prince Charles Rd** CO2 ...136
**Prince Of Wales Dr** IP2 ...17
**Prince Of Wales Rd** CM9 ...196

...lbt ...133 B4
...e CO15 ...188 C1
...v CO2 ...136 A1
...33 E8
...014 ...144 F2
...y ...84 F7
M23 ...145 C7
...e CM23 ...145 C7
...ans IP11 ...221 D4
...rd CM2 ...216 B7
Prior Cl CO5 ...103 D8
Prior Way CO4 ...109 E2
Prior's Hall Barn CB11 ...67 C7
Prior's Wood Rd CM22 ...148 C7
Priors ⑥ CM23 ...146 A7
Priors Way CO6 ...131 A3
Priory CM9 ...8 F7
Priory Cl Chelmsford CM3 ...194 B1
Hatfield Peverel CM3 ...194 B1
Ickleton CB10 ...3 A3
St Osyth CO16 ...203 A6
Priory Ct
Bishop's Stortford CM23 ...145 F7
Hatfield Peverel CM3 ...194 A4
Priory Cty Prim Sch The CM3 ...218 F2
Priory Dr CM24 ...119 E5
Priory Farm Rd CM3 ...194 B2
Priory Heath Prim Sch IP3 ...18 C1
Priory La CM3 ...218 F1
Priory Mews CM3 ...194 C2
Priory Rd Bicknacre CM3 ...218 E1
Chappel CO6 ...106 B3
Clacton-on-S CO15 ...188 E3
Sudbury CO10 ...15 D1
Tiptree CO5 ...178 F3
Priory St Colchester CO1 ...136 A7
Earls Colne CO6 ...105 B7
Priory The CM1 ...215 B8
Priory Wlk
⑥ Colchester CO1 ...135 F7
⑥ Haverhill CB9 ...8 E8
Priory Wood CO10 ...33 E7
Priory Wood Rdbt CM22 ...147 A8
Prittlewell IP2 ...16 F1
Proctor Cl CO5 ...163 B2
Proctor Way CO6 ...132 E3
Proctors Way CM23 ...146 A4
Progress Ct CM7 ...127 E3
Progress Way CO16 ...168 C1
Promenade
Clacton-on-S CO15 ...203 D6
Harwich CO12 ...91 C2
Promenade Way CO7 ...185 E5
Prospect Cl CM3 ...194 A3
Prospect Hill CO10 ...34 D3
Prospect Pl CB11 ...22 F1
Prospect Rd IP1 ...17 A7
Prospect St ⑥ IP1 ...17 A7
Prospero Cl CO4 ...136 F8
Provence Cl CO3 ...134 C7
Providence La IP1 ...17 A7
Providence Pl CO1 ...136 B6
Providence St ⑥ IP1 ...17 C6
Provident Sq CM2 ...205 C2
Prunus Ct CO7 ...163 A7
Prykes Dr CM1 ...205 A2
Pryor Cl CM8 ...177 A1
Pryors Ct CM23 ...146 A6
Pryors Rd CM2 ...216 D2
Pudding La CO2 ...161 B3
Puffinsdale CO15 ...188 F5
Pulford Pl CM6 ...124 D7
Pulpitfield Cl CO4 ...171 A8
Pump Hill
Great Baddow CM2 ...216 F6
Harkstead SG9 ...64 A2
St Osyth CO16 ...187 D4
Pump La Chelmsford CM1 ...205 E6
Danbury CM3 ...218 D5
Purleigh CM3 ...220 D1
Punchard Way IP11 ...221 A8
Punders Field CM7 ...128 D1
Purbeck Ct
⑥ Colchester CO1 ...136 D7
Great Baddow CM2 ...216 F6
Purcell Cl Colchester CO4 ...136 E6
Writtle CM1 ...204 A1
Purdis Ave IP3 ...18 F2
Purdis Farm La IP3 ...18 F2
Purleigh Cty Prim Sch CM3 ...220 D1
Purley Way CO16 ...188 B6
Purplett Ho IP2 ...17 D4
Purplett St IP2 ...17 D4
Purvis Way CO4 ...110 B5
Putticks La CO7 ...59 E3
Pye Cnr CO9 ...51 E4
Pyecat's Cnr CO7 ...137 C7
Pyefleet Cl
Brightlingsea CO7 ...185 E7
Fingringhoe CO5 ...164 C6

Pyefleet Ho CO5 ...201 D7
Pyefleet View CO5 ...163 B3
Pyesand CO13 ...170 C8
Pygot Pl CM7 ...127 E4
Pyms Rd CM2 ...216 B3
Pynchbek CM23 ...145 E3
Pynchon Mews CM1 ...205 D3
Pyne Gate CM2 ...216 B1

**Q**

QM Ind Pk IP3 ...18 C1
Quadling St IP1 ...17 C5
Quadrangle Ctr The IP3 ...18 C1
Quaker's La CB9 ...9 A2
Quale Rd CM2 ...206 B4
Quantock Cl IP5 ...18 F7
Quay Court Yd ❷ CO11 ...86 D4
Quay La Beaumont CO16 ...142 B5
Kirby-le-S CO13 ...143 D1
Sudbury CO10 ...33 E6
Quay St
❶ Manningtree CO11 ...86 D4
Wivenhoe CO7 ...164 B8
Quay The CO12 ...91 D6
Quay Theatre CO10 ...33 E6
Queech La IP9 ...87 C8
Queech The IP9 ...35 B2
Queen Anne Dr CO5 ...201 D6
Queen Anne Gdns CO5 ...201 D6
Queen Anne Rd CO5 ...201 D7
Queen Edith Dr CB9 ...27 B6
Queen Elizabeth Ave
CO15 ...188 C1
Queen Elizabeth Way
CO2 ...136 A2
Queen Mary Ave CO2 ...135 F4
Queen St
Brightlingsea CO7 ...185 F6
Castle Hedingham CO9 ...51 E3
Chelmsford CM2 ...205 A1
Coggeshall CO6 ...131 A2
Colchester CO1 ...135 F7
Felixstowe IP11 ...221 C6
Great Oakley CO12 ...116 C4
Queen Victoria Dr CO12 ...91 B8
Queen's Ave CM9 ...210 A1
Queen's Cotts CO6 ...105 B6
Queen's Ct
Clacton-on-S CO15 ...189 D4
❻ Haverhill CB9 ...8 E8
Queen's Gdns CM7 ...127 B7
Queen's Head Rd CO4 ...82 E3
Queen's Ho CO13 ...170 F4
Queen's Rd
Chelmsford CM2 ...205 D2
Clacton-on-S CO15 ...188 D1
Colchester CO3 ...135 C6
Earls Colne CO6 ...105 B7
Felixstowe IP11 ...221 E4
Frinton-on-S CO13 ...170 E6
Harwich CO12 ...91 A2
West Bergholt CO6 ...108 D3
Wivenhoe CO7 ...164 C8
Queen's Sq IP3 ...18 B2
Queen's Way IP3 ...18 B2
Queenborough La
Great Notley CM7 ...154 D8
Rayne CM7 ...154 B8
Queenbury Cl CO5 ...201 E6
Queens Cl Stansted
Mountfitchet CM24 ...119 E8
Sudbury CO10 ...33 E8
Queens Cnr CO5 ...201 D7
Queens Cres CM23 ...145 E5
Queens Mews CO5 ...201 D7
Queens Rd Braintree CM7 ...127 F5
Sudbury CO10 ...33 E8
Queens Sq ❺ CB9 ...9 A8
Queens St CB9 ...9 A8
Queens Terr CO10 ...34 A7
Queensberry Rd IP3 ...18 A1
Queensbury Ave CO4 ...133 D5
Queenscliffe Rd IP2 ...17 A3
Queensgate Dr IP4 ...17 F8
Queensland Cres CM1 ...204 E5
Queensland Dr CO2 ...136 A1
Queensway
Clacton-on-S CO15 ...189 D5
Great Cornard CO10 ...34 B5
Haverhill CB9 ...8 E8
Lawford CO11 ...86 C4
Tiptree CO5 ...179 C6
Quendon Pl ❼ CB9 ...9 A8
Quendon Way CO13 ...171 A6
Quentin Cl IP1 ...16 E8
Quickset Rd CM1 ...205 C5
Quicksie Hill CB11 ...41 E2
Quilp Dr CM1 ...204 F7
Quilter Dr IP8 ...16 C1
Quilter Rd IP11 ...221 F4
Quince Cl CO10 ...15 D4
Quinion Cl CM1 ...204 D7
Quinton Cnr CO7 ...59 D4
Quintons Rd CO7 ...59 D4

**R**

RA Butler Cty Prim & Inf
Sch CB11 ...22 E1
Rachael Ct ❶ CM2 ...205 B1

Rachael Gdns CM8 ...156 E4
Rachel Ct ❸ IP4 ...17 D6
Radcliffe Dr IP2 ...16 D2
Radiator Rd CO10 ...34 A5
Radwinter Rd Ashdon CB10 ...21 A5
Saffron Walden CB10 ...23 B1
Sewards End CB10 ...23 E6
Raeburn Cl CO13 ...170 F7
Raeburn Inf Sch IP3 ...17 F1
Raeburn Rd IP3 ...18 A1
Raeburn Rd S IP3 ...17 F1
Raglan Mews CO5 ...188 C3
Raglan Rd CO13 ...171 A5
Ragley Cl CM7 ...154 B6
Raile Wlk CO10 ...15 D8
Railey Rd CB11 ...43 E8
Railway App IP11 ...221 E5
Railway Cotts CB11 ...42 F5
Railway Sq CM1 ...205 A3
Railway St Braintree CM7 ...128 A3
Chelmsford CM1 ...205 A3
Manningtree CO11 ...86 D4
Railway Terr
Clacton-on-S CO15 ...188 F3
❿ Manningtree CO11 ...86 D4
Rainbow Mead CM3 ...194 A5
Rainbow Mews CM9 ...209 C5
Rainbow Rd CO5 ...201 D6
Rainbow Way CO6 ...77 F1
Rainham Way CO13 ...171 B6
Rainsborowe Rd CO2 ...135 C4
Rainsford Ave CM1 ...204 F3
Rainsford High Sch CM1 ...204 E4
Rainsford La CM1 ...204 F2
Rainsford Rd
Chelmsford CM1 ...204 F3
Stansted
Mountfitchet CM24 ...119 E8
Rambler Cl CO3 ...134 D7
Rampart Cotts CO6 ...109 D7
Ramparts Cl CO6 ...109 D7
Ramplings Ave CO15 ...188 E5
Ramsden Cl CO15 ...189 A5
Ramsey Cl Heybridge CM9 ...210 D4
Ipswich IP2 ...17 A1
Ramsey Cty Prim Sch
CO12 ...89 F1
Ramsey Mews CO2 ...136 A4
Ramsey Rd Halstead CO9 ...103 D8
Harwich CO12 ...90 C2
Ramsey Sch The
Halstead CO9 ...76 F2
Halstead CO9 ...77 A2
Ramsgate Dr IP3 ...18 B3
Ramshaw Dr CM2 ...205 F3
Rana Ct CM7 ...127 F4
Rana Dr CM7 ...127 F4
Randall Cl CM6 ...123 D1
Randolph Ave CM7 ...73 C6
Randolph Cl CM9 ...220 F8
Rands Way IP3 ...18 B2
Randulph Terr CM1 ...205 D3
Randwell Cl IP4 ...18 B1
Ranelagh Cr IP11 ...221 E4
Ranelagh Prim Sch IP2 ...16 F5
Ranelagh Rd
Felixstowe IP11 ...221 E4
Ipswich IP2 ...17 A5
Ranger Wlk CO2 ...162 A6
Rangoon Cl CO2 ...135 B1
Ransom Rd CO5 ...179 C5
Ransome Cl IP8 ...16 A6
Ransome Cres IP3 ...18 B3
Ransome Rd IP3 ...18 B3
Ransomes Europark IP3 ...38 E8
Ransomes Way
Chelmsford CM1 ...205 B4
Ipswich IP3 ...38 D8
Ranulph Way CM3 ...194 B3
Raphael Dr CM1 ...205 F7
Rapier St IP2 ...17 C3
Rat Hill IP9 ...63 F2
Ratcliffe Ct
Frinton-on-S CO13 ...170 F5
Ratcliffe Rd CO3 ...134 E6
Raven Way CO4 ...109 E4
Ravens Ave CO9 ...76 F1
Ravens Cres CM6 ...152 E6
Ravensbourne Dr CM1 ...204 E4
Ravenscroft Cty Prim
Sch CO16 ...188 B4
Ravensdale CO15 ...188 F6
Ravenswood ⑪ CO16 ...136 A6
Rawden Cl CO12 ...91 B4
Rawhedge Cl CO7 ...164 F8
Rawlings Cres CO4 ...110 B5
Rawstorn Rd CO3 ...135 E7
Ray Ave CO12 ...91 A3
Ray Ho CO5 ...201 D7
Ray La Harwich CO12 ...90 D5
Ray Mead CM3 ...190 F7
Ray The CM1 ...205 E5
Raycliff Ave CO15 ...188 D4
Raydon Way CO10 ...34 C6
Rayer's Wlk CO10 ...15 D4
Rayhaven CO12 ...90 D2
Rayleigh Cl Braintree CM7 ...128 A4
Colchester CO4 ...110 A4
Rayment's Bungalows
CB10 ...45 E3
Raymouth Ho CO2 ...216 D2
Rayne Cty Prim Sch CM7 ...126 F2
Rayne Rd CM7 ...127 D3
Rayner Rd CO2 ...135 B4
Rayner Way CO9 ...76 E1
Raynham Rd CM23 ...146 B8

Reaburn Ct CM1 ...205 E6
Reade Rd IP9 ...62 D5
Reader's Cnr CM2 ...216 E5
Readers Ct CM2 ...216 E6
Reading Rd IP4 ...18 B7
Rebecca Rd CM3 ...135 A5
Rebecca Gdns CM8 ...156 E4
Rebecca Meade CM6 ...122 F8
Rebow Rd Harwich CO12 ...91 A2
Wivenhoe CO7 ...164 B8
Rebow St CO1 ...136 B6
Reckitts Cl CO15 ...189 B4
Recreation Cl IP11 ...221 D6
Recreation Ground CM24 ...119 E6
Recreation La CM1 ...221 D6
Recreation Rd
Clacton-on-S CO15 ...188 F3
Colchester CO1 ...136 C5
Haverhill CB9 ...9 A7
Sible Hedingham CM7 ...75 D8
Recreation Way
Brightlingsea CO7 ...185 F7
Ipswich IP3 ...18 B2
Recreation Wlk CO10 ...34 B5
Rectory Cl
Bishop's Stortford CM23 ...145 D3
Colchester CO4 ...109 E2
Glemsford CO10 ...2 B5
Little Waltham CM3 ...191 C6
Littlebury CB11 ...21 F4
Rectory Field IP9 ...63 E7
Rectory Hill
East Bergholt CO7 ...59 C1
Stoke-by-N CO6 ...56 D7
Wivenhoe CO7 ...137 C1
Rectory La Abberton CO5 ...163 A3
Ashdon CB10 ...60 E1
Braintree CM7 ...127 F8
Chelmsford CM1 ...205 B4
Farnham CM23 ...118 D6
Great Leighs CM3 ...173 D7
Ramsey CO12 ...90 A1
Rivenhall CM8 ...177 A6
Wickham St P CO9 ...53 C6
Woodham Mortimer CM9 ...219 F6
Rectory Mdw CM7 ...129 C2
Rectory Rd Aldham CO6 ...132 F7
Copford CO6 ...133 E2
Frating CO7 ...138 F1
Great Henny CO10 ...33 E4
Great Holland CO13 ...170 A3
Harkstead IP9 ...63 C2
Ipswich IP2 ...17 C4
Langham CO4 ...83 F7
Little Bentley CO7 ...139 E8
Little Oakley CO12 ...117 A7
Rowhedge CO5 ...163 E8
Sible Hedingham CO9 ...51 D1
Stisted CM7 ...129 B7
Tiptree CO5 ...179 C5
Tolleshunt Knights CM9 ...180 C1
Weeley Heath CO16 ...167 F3
Wivenhoe CO7 ...137 C1
Woodham Walter CM9 ...208 D3
Wrabness CO11 ...89 A3
Writtle CM1 ...215 B8
Red Barn La CO12 ...118 B2
Red Barn Rd CO7 ...185 F8
Red House La CO10 ...34 A3
Red La IP9 ...60 A8
Red Lion Ct ❻ CM23 ...146 A7
Red Lion Yd ⑩ CO1 ...135 F7
Red Sleeve ❻ IP9 ...35 A1
Redan St IP1 ...17 B7
Redbridge Rd CO15 ...188 F8
Redcliffe Rd ❹ CM2 ...205 A1
Reddings Cl CO4 ...83 E8
Rede Way CO10 ...34 C6
Redgate La CM3 ...37 D5
Redgate La IP9 ...35 A1
Redgates Pl CM2 ...205 D4
Redhouse La
Great Horkesley CO4 ...82 D2
Sudbury CO10 ...33 E7
Redmayne Dr CM2 ...215 F8
Redmill CO3 ...135 A3
Redrose Wlk CO16 ...188 C4
Redruth Cl CM1 ...205 E5
Redshank Cl CB9 ...9 C7
Redshank Dr CM7 ...210 C5
Redvers Cl CM23 ...119 A2
Redwing Cl IP2 ...16 D3
Redwood Cl
Colchester CO4 ...110 C1
Witham CM8 ...177 A5
Redwood La ❷ CM23 ...146 E8
Redwood Dr CM1 ...204 A1
Reed Cl CO16 ...188 C5
Reed Hall Ave
Colchester CO2 ...136 C3
Colchester CO2 ...135 D3
Reedland Way CM3 ...221 B5
Reeds La CB9 ...7 C8
Refinery Rd CO12 ...90 E5
Regal Cl CM2 ...216 D2
Regency Cl
Bishop's Stortford CM23 ...145 E7
Chelmsford CM3 ...210 A5
Regency Ct CM9 ...210 A5
Regency Gn CO3 ...135 A3
Regency Lodge CO15 ...188 E5
Regent Cl CO7 ...163 A8
Regent Ct CO7 ...164 B8
Regent Rd CO7 ...185 F7
Regent St Ipswich IP4 ...17 C6
❻ Manningtree CO11 ...86 D4
Regents Cl CO4 ...110 C5

Regina Cl IP4 ...18 B5
Regina Rd CO3 ...205 C3
Reigate Ave CO16 ...168 A8
Reigate Cl IP3 ...18 B3
Rembrandt Gr CM1 ...205 E6
Rembrandt Way CO3 ...135 B5
Rembrow Rd IP3 ...35 A1
Remembrance Ave CM3 ...193 F4
Remercie Rd CO11 ...87 A4
Remus Cl CO4 ...109 F5
Rendlesham Ct ❽ IP1 ...17 A7
Rendlesham Rd
Felixstowe IP11 ...221 B5
Ipswich IP1 ...17 A6
Renoir Pl CM1 ...205 F7
Retreat The
West Bergholt CO6 ...108 D3
Witham CM8 ...177 A1
Reverdy Ho CO2 ...135 E2
Reydon Ho IP3 ...18 A2
Reymead Cl CO5 ...201 C6
Reynard Copse CM23 ...118 F1
Reynard Ct CM2 ...216 B2
Reynards Cl CO13 ...170 D6
Reynards Copse CO4 ...110 A3
Reynolds Ave
Colchester CO3 ...135 B5
Ipswich IP3 ...38 A8
Reynolds Rd IP3 ...18 A1
Rhodes Ave CM23 ...145 F5
Rhodes Meml Mus &
Commonwealth Ctr
CM23 ...146 A6
Riby Rd IP11 ...221 D3
Rice Bridge Ind Est CO16 ...169 A7
Rich Cl CM3 ...173 F7
Richard Avanue CO7 ...137 C3
Richard Ave CO7 ...185 F6
Richard de Clare Cty
Prim Sch CO9 ...76 F1
Richard Wittington JMI
Sch CM23 ...145 E4
Richards Wlk CO15 ...188 E6
Richardson La IP9 ...63 D8
Richardson Rd CO7 ...59 D3
Richardson Wlk
Colchester CO3 ...134 F5
Witham CM8 ...177 B2
Richardsons La IP9 ...63 D8
Riche Cl CM6 ...152 B5
Richmond Cl CM23 ...145 C7
Richmond Cres CO12 ...91 B2
Richmond Dr CO15 ...188 A1
Richmond Ho ❻ IP4 ...17 D5
Richmond Rd
Chelmsford CM2 ...206 A4
Ipswich IP1 ...16 F8
West Mersea CO5 ...201 D6
Rickling CE Prim Sch
CB11 ...93 E8
Rickling Green Rd
Quendon CB11 ...66 E1
Rickling Green CB11 ...93 E8
Rickling Rd CB11 ...66 B6
Rickstones Rd CM8 ...177 A6
Rickstones Sch The CM8 ...176 F6
Riddiford Dr CM1 ...204 F4
Riddles Dr CO4 ...109 F2
Ridge The
Little Baddow CM3 ...207 E2
Walton-on-t-N CO14 ...171 B8
Ridgeway CO14 ...110 A4
Ridgeway The
Braintree CM7 ...128 A1
Colchester CO1 ...91 B3
Ridgewell Ave CM1 ...204 F4
Ridgewell CE Prim Sch
CO9 ...29 B6
Ridgewell Rd
Birdbrook CO9 ...10 E2
Great Yeldham CO9 ...29 E3
Ridgewell Way CO2 ...135 F1
Ridings The
Bishop's Stortford CM23 ...145 D4
Great Baddow CM2 ...216 E2
Ridlands Cl CM7 ...155 E6
Ridley Gdns CM2 ...94 C2
Ridley Rd CM1 ...205 B8
Riffhams Chase CM3 ...207 D2
Riffhams Ct CM2 ...217 A7
Riffhams La Danbury CM3 ...218 C8
Little Baddow CM3 ...207 C1
Rifle Hill CM7 ...127 F1
Rifle Hill Works CM7 ...127 F1
Rigby Ave CO11 ...87 A3
Rignal's La CM2 ...216 D3
Riley Ave CO15 ...203 E6
Rimini Cl CO2 ...135 C3
Ringham Rd IP4 ...18 A6
Ripley Cl CO16 ...188 B6
Ripple Way CO4 ...110 B4
Risby Cl Clacton-on-S CO16 ...188 A4
Ipswich IP4 ...18 F7
Rise The CM4 ...134 A8
Ritabrook Rd IP2 ...16 E1
Rivenhall CE Prim Sch
CM8 ...177 B8
River Cl CO9 ...76 F1
River Cotts CM3 ...206 F8
River Hill CM3 ...175 B3
River Mead CM7 ...128 A5
River View Braintree CM7 ...127 F1
Holbrook IP9 ...62 D5

**River View** continued
Manningtree CO11 ..........86 C4
Witham CM8 .................195 A8
**River View Rd** IP9 ..........63 B2
**Riverbank Cl** CO10 ..........12 C7
**Riverdale Ct** IP11 ..........221 D3
**Rivermead Gate** CM1 .....205 B4
**Rivermead Ind Est** CM1 ...205 B4
**Rivers Ho** CO14 ...........144 D2
**Rivers St** IP4 .............17 F7
**Riverside**
 Bishop's Stortford CM23 ...145 F7
 Bradwell CM7 ...............129 D3
 Chelmsford CM1 ............205 C3
 Great Dunmow CM6 ..........123 E1
**Riverside Ave E** CO11 ......86 C5
**Riverside Ave W** CO11 .....86 C5
**Riverside Cotts** CO11 ......86 C4
**Riverside Ind Pk** IP2 ......17 D3
**Riverside Pk** CO5 ..........205 C3
**Riverside Rd** IP1 ..........16 F7
**Riverside Way** CO5 .........158 C2
**Riverside Wlk**
 16 Bishop's Stortford CM23 ..145 F7
 Colchester CO1 .............135 E8
**Riverton Dr** CM4 ...........213 B1
**Rivish La** CO10 .............15 C7
**Roach Vale** CO4 ............110 E1
**Roach Vale Cty Prim**
 **Sch** CO4 .................110 E1
**Robeck Rd** IP3 .............17 F1
**Robert Cl** CM2 .............205 F4
**Robert Wallace Cl** CM23 ...118 F1
**Robert's Hill** CO6 ..........79 F3
**Robertus Ct** CM2 ...........216 E7
**Roberts Rd** CO1, CO2 .......136 A5
**Robin Cl**
 Great Bentley CO7 ...........166 D8
 Haverhill CB9 ...............9 C7
**Robin Dr** IP2 ..............16 D3
**Robin Hood Rd** CM22 ........94 C1
**Robin Way**
 Chelmsford CM2 .............216 B5
 Sudbury CO10 ...............33 C5
**Robina Cl** 4 CO4 ...........136 E7
**Robinsbridge Rd** CO6 .......130 F2
**Robinsdale** CO15 ...........188 F6
**Robinson Cl** CM23 ..........145 F5
**Robinson Rd** CO7 ...........186 A7
**Robjohns Rd** CM1 ...........215 E8
**Robletts Way** CO6 ..........80 E4
**Rochdale Way** CO4 ..........136 E6
**Rochelle Cl** CM6 ............70 A3
**Rochester Cl** CM7 ..........128 D4
**Rochester Ct** 6 CB10 .......22 F2
**Rochester Way** CO10 ........15 D2
**Rochford Cl** CM4 ...........119 E5
**Rochford Rd**
 Bishop's Stortford CM23 .....119 C1
 Chelmsford CM2 .............205 C1
 St Osyth CO16 ..............187 B4
**Rochford Way**
 Frinton-on-S CO13 ..........170 F7
 Walton-on-t-N CO14 .........171 A7
**Rockall Cl** IP9 .............9 D7
**Rockhampton Wlk** 10
 CO2 .......................136 A1
**Rockingham Cl** CO4 .........110 D3
**Rodbridge Hill** CO10 ........15 B5
**Roddam Cl** CO3 .............135 C6
**Roding Ct** CM7 .............128 D1
**Rodney Gdns** CM7 ...........128 C4
**Rodney Way** CM1 ............215 E7
**Rogation Cl** CO3 ...........134 D6
**Rogers Cl** IP11 ............221 D6
**Rokell Way** CO13 ...........170 F4
**Rolands Cl** CM1 .............205 B7
**Rollerworld** CO2 ...........136 B7
**Rolley La** CO5 ..............158 C2
**Rolph CE Prim Sch** CO16 ....141 F1
**Rolph Ct** CM1 ..............142 A2
**Roman Ct** Braintree CM7 ....128 C1
 Saffron Walden CB11 .........43 E7
**Roman Ho** 3 CM2 ...........205 B1
**Roman Rd** Colchester CO1 ...136 A7
 Little Waltham CM3 ..........191 B5
**Roman Way** Haverhill CB9 ....9 D7
 Lifford Melford CO10 ........15 C6
 Point Clear B CO16 .........186 A3
**Romans Pl** CM1 .............204 B1
**Romans Way** CM1 ...........204 B1
**Romford Cl** CO4 ............110 D4
**Romney Cl** Braintree CM7 ...127 E6
 Brightlingsea CO7 ...........165 E1
 Clacton-on-S CO16 ..........188 D5
 Kirby Cross CO13 ...........170 E7
**Romney Rd** IP3 .............38 A8
**Romulus Ct** CO4 ............109 F5
**Ronald Rd** CO9 .............103 E8
**Rook End La** CB11 ...........69 B5
**Rookeries The** CO6 .........133 B4
**Rookery Chase** CO7 ..........84 E2
**Rookery Cl**
 Great Chesterford CB10 ......3 D3
 Hatfield Peverel CM3 ........194 A5
**Rookery La**
 Great Totham CM9 ...........196 E7
 Tiptree CO5 ................179 C7
 Wendens Ambo CB11 ..........42 E4
**Rookery The** Lawford CO11 ...86 F8
 Stansted
 Mountfitchet CM24 ..........119 E8
**Rookes** CB10 ...............22 D3
**Rookwood Cl** CO15 ..........188 D7

**Rookwood Way** CB9 ..........9 A6
**Roos Hill Debden Rd** CB11 ..43 E5
**Roosevelt Way** CO2 .........136 B4
**Roothings The** CM9 .........210 B5
**Roots La** CM8 ..............195 E5
**Rope Wlk** Ipswich IP4 ......17 F5
 Maldon CM9 .................210 A1
**Roper Ct** IP4 ..............18 C5
**Roper's Chase** CM1 .........215 A7
**Ropers La** CO10 ............15 B5
**Rosabelle Ave** CO7 .........137 B1
**Rosalind Cl** CO4 ...........136 F7
**Rose Acre** CO7 .............58 F6
**Rose Ave** CO3 .............134 C4
**Rose Cotts** SG9 ............64 A5
**Rose Cres** CO4 .............134 C4
**Rose & Crown Wlk** CB10 .....22 D2
**Rose Gdns** Braintree CM7 ...128 A2
 St Osyth CO16 ..............203 B6
**Rose Glen** CM2 .............216 C7
**Rose Hill** CM7 .............128 A2
**Rose Hill Cty Prim Sch**
 IP3 .......................18 A4
**Rose Ho** 12 CO11 ...........136 A6
**Rose La**
 Great Chesterford CB10 ......3 E2
 Ipswich IP1, IP4 ...........17 C5
 Salcott-cum-virley CM9 ......199 B8
 Wivenhoe CO7 ...............164 B7
**Rose Wlk** CO9 ..............29 B6
**Roseacres** CM22 ............148 C7
**Rosebank** CO12 ............91 A2
**Rosebank Ct** CO15 .........189 A3
**Rosebank Rd** CO5 ..........201 B6
**Rosebay Cl** CM8 ............176 D3
**Rosebery** CO8 .............146 C6
**Rosebery Ave** CO1 .........136 A7
**Rosebery Rd**
 Chelmsford CM2 .............216 B8
 Felixstowe IP11 ............221 F4
 Ipswich IP4 ................17 F5
**Rosecroft Cl** CO15 .........188 E6
**Rosedale Cotts** CO3 ........133 F5
**Rosefinch Cl** CB9 ...........9 C7
**Rosehill Cres** IP3 ..........17 F4
**Rosehill Rd** IP3 ............17 F4
**Rosemary Ave**
 Braintree CM7 ..............127 F4
 Felixstowe IP11 ............221 F6
**Rosemary Cl**
 Great Dunmow CM6 ...........123 C1
 Tiptree CO5 ................179 C5
**Rosemary Cotts** CM3 ........192 E1
**Rosemary Cres**
 Clacton-on-S CO15 ..........188 F2
 Great Dunmow CM6 ...........123 C1
 Tiptree CO5 ................179 C5
**Rosemary Ct** 2 CO4 ........136 D8
**Rosemary Gdns** CO10 ........15 F2
**Rosemount Ct** IP11 .........221 F4
**Rosery Mews** CO13 .........170 D4
**Rosewood Cl** CO4 ...........110 A4
**Roslings Cl** CM1 ...........204 D5
**Ross Cl** Haverhill CB9 ......9 D7
 Saffron Walden CB11 ........43 E6
**Rossendale** CM1 ............204 E1
**Rossendale Cl** CO4 .........110 D3
**Rossetta Cl** CO7 ...........137 B2
**Rossland Ct** CO15 ..........188 F3
**Rosslyn Terr** CO5 ..........158 C3
**Rothbury Rd** CM1 ...........204 D1
**Rothesay Ave** CM2 ..........216 A8
**Rothmans Ave** CM2 .........216 E6
**Roughtons** CM2 .............216 C3
**Round Cl** CO13 .............135 B7
**Round Coppice Rd**
 Great Hallingbury CM24 .....147 A8
 Stansted
 Mountfitchet CM24 ..........120 B1
**Roundacre** CO9 ............103 E8
**Roundbush Cnr**
 Birch CO5 ..................160 D3
 Great Dunmow CM6 ...........196 D6
**Roundbush Rd** CO5 ..........160 D2
**Roundridge Rd** IP9 .........35 B2
**Roundwood Rd** CM1 .........18 A7
**Rous Chase** CM2 ............216 B1
**Routh Ave** IP3 .............18 F1
**Rover Ave** CO15 ............203 E6
**Row The** CO7 ..............58 C2
**Rowallan Cl** CO3 ...........135 A3
**Rowan Chase** CO5 ..........179 C6
**Rowan Cl**
 Clacton-on-S CO15 ..........188 C3
 Colchester CO3 .............134 D4
 Great Bentley CO7 ..........166 F8
 Harwich CO12 ...............91 B3
 Ipswich IP9 ................18 D2
 Rowan Dr CM9 ...............210 C5
**Rowan Way**
 Hatfield Peverel CM3 .......194 A3
 Witham CM8 .................177 A5
**Rowanhayes Cl** IP2 .........17 B3
**Rowhedge Ferry Rd** CO7 ....164 A8
**Rowhedge Rd** CO2, CO5 .....136 E1
**Rowherns La**
 Great Bentley CO7 ..........139 E4
 Great Bentley CO7 ..........139 F4
**Rowland Ho** IP11 ...........221 B5

**Rowland's Yd** CO12 .........90 E2
**Rowley Cl** CO11 ............86 D8
**Rowley Ct** CB9 .............9 E5
**Rowley Hill** CB9 ...........9 E5
**Rowney Ave** CB10 ...........44 E2
**Rowntree Way** CB11 .........43 D7
**Roxborough Cl** CO4 ........132 E3
**Roxburghe Rd** CO16 ........167 F6
**Roxwell Ave** CM1 ...........204 D3
**Roxwell Rd**
 Chelmsford CM1 .............204 C4
 Writtle CM1 ................204 A4
**Roy Ave** IP3 ...............18 B5
**Royal Ct** Colchester CO4 ...110 E1
 Maldon CM9 .................210 A1
**Royal Oak Gdns** 6 CM23 ....145 F6
**Royal Sq** CO7 ..............84 F7
**Roydon Way** CO13 ..........170 F6
**Royston Dr** IP2 ............16 D2
**Royston La** CB11 ...........20 C6
**Royston Rd** CB11 ..........42 C5
**Ruaton Dr** CO16 ...........188 C8
**Rubens Gate** CM1 ..........205 F7
**Rubens Rd** IP3 ............18 A1
**Rudkin Rd** CO4 ............109 F5
**Rudlands** IP8 .............16 C1
**Rudsdale Way** CO3 .........134 F5
**Rue de Jeunes** 8 CM7 ......127 F2
**Ruffels Field** CM6 .........124 E4
**Rugby Rd** CO10 ............34 B4
**Rugosa Cl** CO3 ............134 C7
**Rumsey Fields** CM3 ........218 F7
**Runnacles St** CM8 .........136 C8
**Runnacles Way** IP11 .......221 B5
**Running Mare La** CM2 ......216 A3
**Runsell Cl** CM3 ...........218 F7
**Runsell La** CM3 ...........218 F8
**Runsell View** CM3 .........219 A7
**Rurik Ct** CM9 .............220 E8
**Rush Green Rd** CO16 .......188 B2
**Rush La** CM22 .............94 C1
**Rushbury Cl** IP4 ..........18 B8
**Rushes Ct** CM23 ...........146 A5
**Rushleigh Gn** CM23 ........145 D4
**Rushleydale** CM1 ..........205 E5
**Rushmere Cl** CO5 ..........201 D6
**Rushmere Rd**
 Ipswich IP4, IP5 ...........18 E8
 Rushmere St A IP5 .........18 E8
**Ruskin Cl** CO13 ...........170 E7
**Ruskin Rd** Chelmsford CM2 .205 E2
 Ipswich IP4 ................17 F5
**Ruskins The** CM7 ..........126 F1
**Russell Cl** Colchester CO2 ..136 B4
 Felixstowe IP11 ............221 C1
**Russell Gdns** CM2 .........216 A4
**Russell Rd**
 Clacton-on-S CO15 ..........189 A3
 Ipswich IP2 ................221 D2
 Ipswich IP11 ...............17 B5
**Russell Way** CM1 ..........215 E7
**Russell's Rd** Gosfield CO9 ..76 A1
 Halstead CO9 ...............103 B8
**Russet Way** CO3 ...........134 D6
**Russets** CM2 ..............216 D3
**Rutherfords** CM1 ..........191 B1
**Rutland Ave** CO2 ..........135 B3
**Rutland Ct** 11 CB9 ........8 E7
**Rutland Gdns** CM7 .........128 A4
**Rutland Pl** CM7 ...........128 A4
**Rutland Rd** CM1 ...........205 A7
**Rydal Way** CM7 ............154 C6
**Ryde Field The** CM3 .......207 B3
**Rye Hills** CO9 ............103 F8
**Ryde Ave** CO15 ............189 A8
**Rye Cl** Brightlingsea CO7 ...165 E1
 Colchester CO3 .............134 E5
 Hatfield Peverel CM3 .......194 A3
 Ipswich IP3 ................18 D4
**Rye Ct** 3 CB9 .............8 E7
**Rye Field The** CM3 ........207 B3
**Rye Hills** CO9 ............103 F8
**Rye La** CO2 ...............162 A4
**Rye Mill La** CO5 ..........158 D4
**Rye St** CM23 ..............118 F1
**Ryes La** CO10 .............35 A2
**Rygate Rd** CO1 ............135 F7
**Rylands** IP7 ..............35 A2
**Ryle The** CM1 .............215 A8
**Rylstone Way** CB11 ........43 F8
**Rysley** CM3 ...............207 D4

**S**

**Sackville Cl** CM1 ..........204 E3
**Sackville Way** CO6 .........108 E3
**Saddle Mews** CO3 ..........134 E6
**Saddle Rise** CM1 ..........205 E8
**Saddlers Cl** CM23 .........145 C4
**Sadds Yd** CO15 ............188 F3
**Sadler Cl** CO2 ............136 B4
**Sadlers Cl** CO13 ..........170 C6
**Saffron Bsns Ctr** 1 CB10 ..22 F2
**Saffron Ct** CM7 ...........73 C3
**Saffron Gdns** CM7 .........73 C3
**Saffron Walden Cty High**
 **Sch** CB11 .................43 D8
**Saffron Walden Mus** CB10 ..22 D2
**Saffron Walden Hospl**
 CB10, CB11 .................23 A2
**Saffron Wlk** CM7 ..........73 B3
**Sage Rd** CO2 ..............136 A2
**Sage Wlk** CO5 .............179 C4
**Sages** CM22 ...............94 F5
**Sages End Rd** CB9 .........26 B8
**St Agnes Way** IP5 .........18 E1

**St Alban's Cath Sec Sch**
 IP4 .......................18 C7
**St Alban's Rd**
 Clacton-on-S CO15 ..........189 A3
 Colchester CO3 .............135 D7
**St Andrew's Ave** CO4 ......137 A5
**St Andrew's Ave**
 (Colchester By-Pass
 Rd) CO4 ...................136 D7
**St Andrew's CE Jun Sch**
 & Hatfield Peverel Cty
 Inf Sch** CM3 ..............194 B3
**St Andrew's CE Prim Sch**
 Bulmer CO10 ................32 E4
 Great Yeldham CO9 ..........29 F2
 Halstead CO9 ...............7 A3
 Wormingford CO6 ...........80 E5
**St Andrew's Cotts** CM3 .....194 B3
**St Andrew's Cty Jun &**
 **Inf Schs** CO4 .............136 D7
**St Andrew's Dr** IP9 ........63 E7
**St Andrew's Prim Sch**
 CO6 .......................132 E3
**St Andrew's Rd**
 Clacton-on-S CO15 ..........188 E3
 Felixstowe IP11 ............221 E5
 Hatfield Peverel CM3 .......194 A4
 Weeley CO16 ................140 F1
**St Andrew's Rise** CO10 .....32 E5
**St Andrews**
 Alresford CO7 ..............165 B7
 Ipswich IP4 ................18 D5
**St Andrews Cl** 3 CO4 ......136 C8
**St Andrews Gdns** CO4 ......136 C8
**St Andrews Pl** CO7 ........165 C1
**St Andrews Rd**
 Boreham CM3 ...............192 F1
 Great Cornard CO10 ........34 A6
 Halstead CO9 ...............76 F1
**St Anne's Cty Prim Sch**
 CO4 .......................110 C1
**St Anne's Prep Sch** CM2 ...205 A1
**St Annes Cl** CO4 ...........136 C8
**St Annes Cl** CO6 ...........131 B2
**St Annes Ct** CM1 ..........205 C3
**St Ann's Rd** CO15 .........188 E4
**St Anthony's Dr** CM2 ......216 C7
**St Aubins Ct** CO15 .........189 B4
**St Aubyns Rd** IP4 .........18 A5
**St Augustine Mews** CO1 ....136 A7
**St Augustine Rd** IP3 .......18 D4
**St Augustine's Gdns** IP3 ...18 C3
**St Austell Rd** CO4 .........110 D2
**St Austin's La** CO12 .......91 E6
**St Barbara's Rd** CO2 ......135 D4
**St Bartholomew Cl** CO14 ...110 D3
**St Bartholomews La** CO10 ..15 D2
**St Benedict RC Coll** CO3 ...136 B6
**St Bernard Rd** CO4 ........110 D2
**St Botolph's Pl** 4 CB9 .....8 E7
**St Botolph's Church Wlk** 7
 CO2 .......................135 F6
**St Botolph's St** 6 CO2 .....135 F6
**St Botolph's Sta** CO1 ......136 A6
**St Botolph's Terr** 11
 CO13 ......................171 C8
**St Botolph's Way** CB9 .....8 F8
**St Brelades Ct** CO15 .......189 B5
**St Bride Ct** CO4 ..........110 C2
**St Bridewells Ind Est**
 CO6 .......................12 C8
**St Catherine's Ct** IP2 .....16 E1
**St Catherine's Rd**
 Chelmsford CM1 .............204 E2
 Long Melford CO10 ..........15 E3
**St Catherines Cl** CO2 ......135 D1
**St Catherines St** CM23 .....145 E7
**St Cedd's Sch** CM1 .........205 A3
**St Christopher Ct** CO4 .....110 D2
**St Christopher Rd** CO4 .....110 D2
**St Christophers Way**
 CO15 ......................189 B4
**St Clair Cl** CO15 ..........188 F8
**St Clair's Dr** CO16 .........187 B5
**St Clair's Rd** CO16 ........187 B5
**St Clare Dr** CO3 ...........135 A7
**St Clare Rd** CO3 ...........135 A6
**St Clare's RC Prim Sch**
 CO16 ......................188 B4
**St Clement Rd** CO4 ........110 D2
**St Clement's Church La**
 IP4 .......................17 D5
**St Clement's Cl** CO4 .......110 D2
**St Clements** CM6 ...........70 A2
**St Clements Hospl** IP3 .....18 B4
**St Cleres Hall La** CO16 ....187 B3
**St Cleres Way** CM3 .........218 D7
**St Columb Ct** CO4 .........110 C2
**St Cyrus Rd** CO4 ..........110 C2
**St David's Rd** IP3 ........18 B3
**St Davids Cl** CO4 ..........110 C2
**St Denis Cl** CO12 ..........91 A1
**St Dominic Rd** CO4 ........110 D2
**St Edmund's Cl** CO4 .......110 D2
**St Edmund's Hill** CO8 ......55 D6
**St Edmund's Pl** IP1 .......17 C8
**St Edmund's Rd**
 Felixstowe IP11 ............221 D2
 Ipswich IP1 ................17 B8
**St Edmunds Cl** CO12 .......91 A1
**St Edmunds Croft** CM6 .....123 E2
**St Edmunds Fields** CM6 ....123 E2
**St Edmunds La** Bures CO8 ..55 F1
 Great Dunmow CM6 ..........123 E1
**St Edmundsbury Ho** IP4 ....17 E6
**St Fabian's Dr** CM1 ........204 E4
**St Faith Rd** CO4 ...........110 D2

**St Felix RC Prim Sch**
**St Fillan Rd** CO4 ..........
**St Francis RC Prim**
 Braintree CM7 ..............
 Maldon CM9 .................
**St George's Ave** CO12 .....
**St George's CE Prim**
 **Sch** CO7 ..................
**St George's Inf Sch** CO2 ..
**St George's Jun**
 **Sch** CO2 ..................
**St George's St** IP1 ........
**St Giles CE Prim Sch** CO9 ..
**St Giles Cl**
 Great Maplestead CO9 .......
**St Giles Cotts** CO9 .......209
**St Giles Cres** CM9 ........209 A1
**St Gregory Prim**
 **Sch** CO10 .................33 D7
**St Gregory's Ct** CO10 .....33 D8
**St Helen's Church La** 5
 IP4 .......................17 E6
**St Helen's Gn** CO12 ........91 E5
**St Helen's La** 8 CO1 .......135 F7
**St Helen's Prim Sch** IP4 ...17 E6
**St Helen's St** IP4 .........17 D6
**St Helena Mews** CO3 .......135 D5
**St Helena Rd** CO3 .........135 D5
**St Helena Sch** CO3 ........135 D6
**St Helens Ave** CO15 .......189 A8
**St Helier Cl** CO15 .........189 B4
**St Ives Cl** CO16 ...........188 B2
**St Ives Rd** CO5 ...........158 D3
**St James' CE Prim Sch**
 CO1 .......................136 B7
**St James Cl**
 Brightlingsea CO7 ..........185 E6
 Clacton-on-S CO15 ..........188 E3
 Haverhill CB9 ...............8 E8
**St James Pk** CM1 ..........204 D4
**St James Rd** CM7 ..........127 F5
**St James's Way** CM23 ......145 C3
**St James's Sr**
 Castle Hedingham CO9 ......51 F4
 Castle Hedingham CO9 ......52 C2
**St John Payne RC**
 **Comp Sch** CM1 .............205 A6
**St John The Baptist CE**
 **Sch** CO9 ..................78 B8
**St John's Ave**
 Chelmsford CM2 .............216 B8
 12 Colchester CO2 ..........135 F6
**St John's CE Prim Sch**
 Colchester CO4 .............110 A7
 Ipswich IP4 ................18 A7
 St John's Cres CM24 ........119 E7
 St John's Ct Ipswich IP4 ....18 A7
 Tollesbury CM9 .............199 C3
**St John's Danbury CE**
 **Prim Sch** CM3 .............218 F7
 St John's Gn CM ............204 B3
**St John's Green Cty**
 **Prim Sch** CO2 .............135 F6
**St John's Hospl** CM2 .......205 F7
**St John's La** CM24 .........119 E7
**St John's Pl** 14 CO2 .......135 F6
**St John's Rd**
 Chelmsford CM2 .............216 B8
 Clacton-on-S CO16 ..........188 C5
 Colchester CO4 .............110 D3
 Ipswich IP4 ................18 A6
 Stansted
 Mountfitchet CM24 ..........119 E7
 Wivenhoe CO7 ..............164 C8
 Writtle CM1 ................204 B1
**St John's St**
 Colchester CO2 .............135 F6
 Tollesbury CM9 .............199 C3
**St John's Terr** CM7 ........72 B2
**St Johns Ave** CO4 .........135 F8
**St Johns Cl** CB11 ..........43 D7
**St Johns Ct** IP11 ..........221 D7
**St Joseph Rd** CO4 .........110 C3
**St Joseph Sch** IP2 ........17 A3
**St Joseph's Jun Sch** IP7 ...17 B3
**St Joseph's Prim Sch**
 CO10 ......................33 D8
**St Joseph's RC JMI Sch**
 CM23 ......................145 E6
**St Joseph's RC Prim Sch**
 CO12 ......................91 B2
**St Jude Gdns** CO4 .........110 E2
**St Judes Cl** CO4 ..........110 C2
**St Julian Gr** CO1 ..........136 A6
**St Lawrence Ct** 3 CM7 .....127 F5
**St Lawrence Dr** CM0 .......213 B3
**St Lawrence Rd** CO4 .......110 C2
**St Lawrence St** 11 IP1 .....17 C6
**St Leonard's Hospl** CO10 ...33 F7
**St Leonard's Rd** CO1 .......136 C6
**St Leonards Cl** CB11 .......43 A2
**St Leonards Rd** IP3 ........18 A1
**St Leonards School Ho**
 CO1 .......................136 C6
**St Leonards Terr** CO11 .....86 D7
**St Luke's Chase** CO5 .......179 D5
**St Luke's Church Sch**
 CO4 .......................110 D2
**St Margaret's CE Prim**
 **Sch** Ipswich IP4 ..........17 C6
 Toppesfield CO9 ............50 C2
**St Margaret's Ct** CO10 .....188 C4
**St Margaret's Gn** 2 IP4 ....17 D6

ret's Plain 🔟
...................17 D6
St Margaret's Rd CM2 ....205 E3
St Margaret's St IP4 .........17 D6
St Mark k Dr CM4 ...........110 C2
St Marks RC Prim Sch IP2 .16 F3
St Marks Rd CO15 ..........188 E4
St Martins CI CO15 ........188 E4
St Mary Magdalen Ho
................136 B6
St Mary's Art Ctr CI1 ......135 E7
St Mary's Cath CM1 ........205 B2
St Mary's CE Prim Sch
Ardleigh CO7 ..............111 E7
Kelvedon CO5 .............158 C2
Stansted
Mountfitchet CM24 ........119 E7
St Mary's CI
Great Baddow CM2 ........216 F6
Great Bentley CO7 .........166 F5
Panfield CM7 ..............127 B7
St Mary's Convent Sch
CO1 .....................136 B7
St Mary's Cres IP11 .......221 D6
St Mary's Dr CM24 ........119 F5
St Mary's Hospl
Salcombe Rd CM7 .........135 E7
Tattingstone IP9 ...........61 D7
St Mary's La LM9 ..........210 R2
St Mary's Pl CM6 ..........151 D7
St Mary's Prim Sch CB10 ..22 U2
St Mary's RC Prim Sch
IP4 ......................17 F7
St Mary's RC Sch CM2 ....145 E7
St Mary's Rd
Braintree CM7 .............128 B3
Clacton-on-S CO15 .......188 E4
Friston-on-S CO13 ........171 A5
Great Bentley CO7 .........166 F6
Kelvedon CO5 .............158 C2
Rivenhall CM8 .............177 B7
St Mary's Sch
Colchester CO3 ...........135 C7
Copford CO3 ..............133 F5
St Mary's Sq CO5 .........158 B1
St Mary's Villas CM7 .......72 B1
St Mary's Wlk CB9 .........27 B6
St Marys Mead CM1 .......191 A1
St Marys Mews
Friston-on-S CO13 ........171 A5
Tollesbury CM9 ...........199 D2
St Mathew's Ho ▲ IP1 ....17 B6
St Matthew's CE Prim
Sch IP1 ..................17 B6
St Matthew's St ⁊ .........17 B6
St Michael's CE Prim
Sch
Bishops Stortford CM23 ...145 F7
Braintree CM7 .............127 D2
St. Michael's Chase CO6 ..133 D2
St Michael's Ct ▲ CM2 ....127 F2
St Michael's Cty Prim
Sch CO2 .................135 C1
St Michael's Hospl CM7 ...127 E3
St Michael's La ▲ LM7 ....127 F2
St Michael's Prim Sch
CM23 ...................145 E7
St Michael's Rd
Braintree CM7 .............127 F2
Chelmsford CM2 ...........216 B8
Harwich CO12 .............91 D2
Thorpe-le-S CO16 .........141 F2
St Michaels Ct ⁊ CO1 .....86 D4
St Michaels Rd CO2 .......135 D1
St Michaels Wlk CM7 ......216 C2
St Mildreds Rd CM2 .......216 B8
St Monance Way CO4 ......110 U2
St Nazaire Rd CM1 ........204 E6
St Neots CI CM4 ...........110 D2
St Nicholas Cl CM8 ........176 F4
St Nicholas Ct CM4 ........91 D6
St Nicholas Field CM23 ....92 B8
St Nicholas' Gdns CM7 ....127 F8
St Nicholas Pas 🔟 CO1 ...135 F7
St Nicholas Rd CM4 .......176 F4
St Nicholas St
⁊ Colchester CO1 .........135 F7
Ipswich IP1 ...............17 C5
St Osyth CE Prim Sch
CO16 ...................187 B4
St Osyth CE Sch CO15 ....188 E3
St Osyth CI IP2 ...........36 F8
St Osyth Priory CO4 ......187 A4
St Osyth Rd Alresford CO7 .165 D7
Clacton-on-S CO15 .......168 B8
Little Clacton CO16 .......168 B1
St Osyth Rd E CO16 ......168 C2
St Osyth Rd W CO16 ......168 C1
St Paul's Ave
Clacton-on-S CO15 .......189 A3
Ipswich IP1 ...............1₃1 F9
St Peter's Ave CM7 ........209 F2
St Peter's CE Prim Sch
Coggeshall CM7 ...........131 B2
Sible Hedingham CO9 .....75 D8
St Peter's CI CM7 .........127 F4
St Peter's Hospl CM9 ....209 F2
St Peter's Rd
Braintree CM7 .............127 F4
Chelmsford CM2 ...........204 E2
Coggeshall CO6 ...........131 B2
West Mersea CO5 ........201 B6
St Peter's Wlk CM7 .......127 F3

St Peter's-in-the-Fields
CM7 .....................127 F4
St Peters Ct
Clacton-on-S CO15 .......189 B5
Clare CO10 ...............12 B7
Colchester CO1 ...........135 E8
🔟 Sudbury CO10 .........33 E7
St Philip's Priory Sch
CM2 .....................216 A8
St Philomena's Sch CO13 .170 F5
St Pius X RC Prim Sch
CM1 .....................204 F6
St Runwald St 🔟 CO1 .....135 F7
St Saviour CI CO4 .........110 D2
St Stephens La 🔟 IP1 .....17 C6
St Swithins Cotts LM7 .....217 C3
St Teresa's RC Prim
Sch CO3 .................134 E5
St Thomas CI CO4 .........110 E2
St Thomas More RC Prim
Sch CB11 ................43 E8
St Valery CM22 ............148 C7
St Vincent Chase CM7 ....128 B5
St Vincent Rd CO15 .......188 E1
St Vincents Rd CM2 .......216 B8
Sainty CI CO7 .............164 C8
Salary CI CO4 .............140 F1
Salcombe Rd CM7 .........128 C1
Salcott Creek Ct CM7 .....128 D1
Salcott St CM9 ...........199 C8
Salehurst Rd IP3 ..........18 E3
Salerno Cres CO2 .........135 F2
Salerno Way CM1 .........204 E6
Saling Hall Gardens CM7 ..126 A8
Salisbury Ave CO3 ........135 E6
Salisbury CI CM23 ........145 F6
Salisbury Ct
Clacton-on-S CO15 .......189 D5
⁊ Haverhill CB9 ..........8 F7
Salisbury Rd
Clacton-on-S CO15 .......189 D5
Ipswich IP3 ...............18 A4
Salisbury Terr 🔟 CO10 ....33 E8
Sallows CI IP1 ............17 A2
Salmon CI CO3 ............134 E4
Salmon Parr CM1 .........205 B3
Salmon's La CO6 ..........132 A4
Salmons CI CM6 ..........151 A5
Saltcote Maltings CM9 ....210 E8
Salter Pl CM2 .............205 F2
Salter's Mdw CM9 .........198 D4
Salters CI CO3 ............145 C4
Salters Hall Mews CO10 ...33 D7
Salthouse St 🔟 IP4 .......17 D6
Salvia CI CO10 ............188 C4
Sanford CI IP9 ............62 D7
Samford Pl IP8 ............16 B6
Samphire CI CM8 .........176 D3
Sampson's La CO5 ........182 F3
Samson's CI CO7 .........165 D1
Samson's Rd CO7 ........165 E1
Samsons CI CO7 .........185 E8
Samuel Ct ⁊ IP4 ..........17 D6
Samuel Manor CM2 .......205 F3
Sunderling Gdns CM9 ....199 D3
Sanders Gn CO5 ..........135 B7
Sanderson Mews ⁊ CM2 ..135 F7
Sandford CI CO7 ..........164 C8
Sandford Mill Rd
Great Baddow CM2 ........206 B2
Sandford Rd CM2 .........205 E3
Sandhurst Ave IP3 .........17 F4
Sandle Rd CM23 ..........146 A7
Sandling Cres IP4 ........18 F5
Sandlings The IP3 .........18 E3
Sandon CI CO6 ...........109 C7
Sandon Hall
Bridleway CM2 ............217 D4
Sandon Hall CM2 ..........172 A6
Sandon Sch The CM2 .....217 B6
Sandown CI CO15 .........189 A0
Sandpiper CI
Colchester CO4 ...........137 A8
Haverhill CB9 .............9 C8
Heybridge CM9 ...........33 E2
Sandpiper Rd IP2 .........16 E2
Sandpiper Wlk CM2 .......216 C6
Sandpit CI IP4 ............18 F5
Sandpit La 🔟 CM7 ........127 F3
Sandringham CI IP2 .......16 F2
Sandringham Ct CO10 ....34 A7
Sandringham Dr CO7 .....136 A4
Sandringham Gdns 🔟
CM23 ...................145 E7
Sandringham Pl LM2 .....205 C2
Sandwich CI CM7 .........127 E6
Sandwich Rd
Brightlingsea CO7 .........185 E8
Clacton-on-S CO15 .......203 J8
Sandy Hill CO8 ...........80 C6
Sandy La Bulmer CO10 ....32 F5
⁊ Bury CO10 .............33 B5
Sandyhill La IP3 , , .......18 E5
Sapling Pl IP4 , , .........18 E5
Saran Ct CO7 .............13⁊ ₄7
Sarcel CM7 ...............12⁊ Fₒ
Sargeant Ct CO2 .........136 B3
Sarre Way CO7 ...........185 E8
Sassoon Way CM1 .........210 A1
Saul's Ave CM6 ...........195 A8
Sauls Bridge CI CM8 .....195 A8
Saunders Ave CM7 .......127 E3
Saunders Ct CM2 .........94 C1
Savernake Rd CM1 .......204 E1
Savill Rd CO2 .............136 C2
Saville CI CB11 ...........65 C4

Saville St CO14 ...........144 C1
Sawkins Ave CM2 .........216 D6
Sawkins CI Abberton CO5 .163 B2
Chelmsford CM2 ..........216 D6
Sawkins Gdns CM2 .......216 D6
Sawney Brook CM1 .......204 A1
Sawpit La CM23 ..........202 F2
Sawston Ct IP7 ...........17 A2
Sawyer's Rd CM9 .........197 C5
Sawyers CI ⁊ IP9 .........35 A1
Saxmundham Way CO16 ..188 A3
Saxon Bank CM7 .........128 B2
Saxon CI Colchester CO3 ..134 E6
Halstead CO9 .............76 F2
Saxon Ct CM9 ............210 A4
Saxon Dr CM8 ............176 E3
Saxon La IP8 .............35 D7
Saxon Way
Broomfield CM1 ...........205 B7
Holland-on-S CU15 .......189 F6
Maldon CM9 ..............21ₒ A1
Point Clear B CO16 .......185 F5
Saffron Walden CM1 ......22 C1
Saxstead Dr CO16 ........188 A4
Saywell Brook CM2 .......206 A2
Scarfe Way CO4 ..........136 E6
Scarfe's Cnr CM6 ........172 E8
Scarletts CI CM6 .........195 A7
Scarletts Rd CO1 .........136 C4
Sceptre CI CM9 ..........199 D2
School Barn Cotts CO10 ..13 F7
School Chase CO9 ........103 E8
School CI CM9 ............35 A1
School CI CO12 ...........91 C6
School Hill Birch LO2 .....161 A4
Washbrook IP8 ............35 F8
School Ho
🔟 Colchester CO1 .......126 A6
Shafford CM7 .............100 E5
School La Birch CO2 ......161 A3
Brantham CO11 ...........60 D1
Broomfield CM1 ...........191 A1
Chelmsford CM1 ..........204 F8
Dedham CO7 .............84 F7
Duddenhoe End CB11 ....41 A7
East Bergholt CO7 ........59 B3
Great Bentley CO7 ........166 A8
Great Horkesley CO6 .....81 D5
Great Horkesley CO6 .....82 A2
Great Leighs CM3 ........173 F8
Great Wigborough CO5 ...181 F3
Haverhill CB9 .............18 A8
Henham CM22 ............94 F5
Lawford CO11 ............86 A2
Mistley CO11 .............86 F4
Newport CB11 ............42 F7
Stratford St M CO7 .......58 D2
Takeley CM22 ............121 D6
West Bergholt CO6 .......106 A4
School Mews CO6 ........130 F2
School Rd Colchester CO2 .136 A2
Copford CO6 .............133 D3
Elmstead CO7 ............138 A4
Friston-on-S CO13 ........170 E5
Great Oakley CO12 .......116 C3
Great Totham LM9 ........196 B3
Langham CO4 ............83 E4
Little Horkesley CO6 ......81 U4
Little Maplestead CO9 ....97 R3
Little Totham CM9 ........30 D3
Messing CO5 ............159 U2
Pentlow LO10 ...........117 A2
Rayne CM7 ..............153 E8
Shotley Gate IP9 .........91 R8
Sible Hedingham CO9 ....75 D8
Silver End CM8 ...........156 E3
Tattingstone IP9 .........36 D1
Tendring LO16 ...........140 E6
Wickham Bishops CM8 ...195 E5
Wickham St P CO9 .......53 C5
School St Foxearth CO10 ..14 D6
Great Chesterford CB10 ..3 D2
Stoke-by-N LO6 .........56 D5
Sudbury CO10 ...........33 E7
School View Rd CM1 .....204 F7
School Villas
Great Eastnn CM6 ........123 A8
Henham CM6 .............95 F2
Lindsell CM6 .............97 F4
Takeley CM22 ...........121 C6
School Wlk CM7 ..........127 F3
Schoolfield CO10 .........2 B5
Schreiber Rd IP4 .........18 B7
Scofield Ct CO10 .........34 A6
Scotland St CO6 .........56 E6
Scott Ave CM7 ...........73 D6
Scott CI CM7 .............155 A8
Scott Dr CO3 .............134 E6
Scott Rd
Bishops Stortford CM23 ..145 E6
Ipswich IP3 ...............18 B1
Scotts Wlk CM1 ..........204 D5
Scraley Rd CM9 ..........210 E6
Scrip's Rd CO6 ...........158 A7
Scrivener Dr IP2 ..........16 C2
Scurry Hall La CM3 .......173 C1
Scythe CI CM9 ...........210 C6
Scythe Way CM7 .........134 F4
Sea Cornflower Way
CO15 ...................⁊₀7 D7
Sea Cres CO15 ...........203 G7
Sea Flowers Way CO15 ...203 G7
Sea Glebe Way CO15 .....203 G7
Sea Holly Way CO15 ......203 G6
Sea King Cres CO15 ......110 B4
Sea Lavender Way CO15 ..203 G7
Sea Pink Way CO15 .......203 G6

Sea Rd IP11 ..............221 D2
Sea Rosemary Way CO15 .203 G7
Sea Shell Way CO15 ......203 G6
Sea Thistle Way CO15 ....203 G7
Sea View Par CM0 ........213 C1
Sea View Prom CM0 ......213 B1
Sea Way CO15 ...........203 F6
Seabrook Gdns CM3 .....192 F1
Seabrook Rd CM2 ........217 A6
Seafield Ave CO11 ........87 B4
Seafield Rd CO12 .........91 B2
Seafields Gdns CO15 .....189 C5
Seafields Rd CO15 .......189 C5
Seagers CM9 .............196 B4
Searle Way CO6 ..........108 B1
Seaton CI CO11 ..........86 B3
Seaton Rd IP11 ..........221 D5
Seaview Ave
Little Oakley CO12 ........117 C7
West Mersea CO5 .......201 E6
Seaview Hts CO14 .......171 C7
Seaview Rd
Brightlingsea CO7 ........185 F7
St Osyth CO16 ...........203 B7
Seaview Terr CO16 .......186 A3
Seawick Rd CO16 ........203 B6
Sebastian CI CO4 ........136 F7
Seckford CI IP4 ..........18 F5
Second Ave
Chelmsford CM1 .........205 B5
Clacton-on-S CO15 ......189 B4
Frinton-on-S CO13 .......170 E3
Glemsford CO10 ..........2 C5
Halstead CO9 ............77 B1
Harwich CO12 ............91 C3
St Osyth CO16 ...........203 C6
Stansted
Mountfitchet CM24 .......120 B2
Sudbury CO10 ...........15 F1
Trimley St M IP11 ........221 A7
Walton-on-t-N CU14 .....144 E3
Weeley CO16 ............167 F8
Seden CI CO15 ...........169 B1
Sedgefield Way CM7 .....128 B1
Sedop CI CB11 ..........43 D7
Seebeod Ctr CO4 ........110 C6
Selby CI CO2 .............135 D1
Seldon Rd CO5 ..........179 D5
Selhurst Ct CO14 ........170 F7
Selkirk Rd IP4 ...........18 B8
Selsey Ave CO15 .........203 J8
Selvale Way IP11 .........221 C4
Selwyn CI IP2 ............17 C4
Serpentine Rd IP3 .......18 C2
Serpentine Wlk CO1 ......109 E1
Servite Ho IP4 ...........17 F6
Seven Ash Gn CM1 ......205 C5
Seven Devils La CB11 ....43 D6
Seventh Ave
Chelmsford CM1 .........205 B6
Stansted
Mountfitchet CM24 .......120 B2
Severalls Hospl CO4 .....109 E5
Severalls La CO4 .........110 B6
Severn Rd
Clacton-on-S CO15 ......188 F5
Ipswich IP3 ...............17 F3
Sewell's La CO10 .........13 B1
Sexton CI CO2 ...........163 B8
Sextons La CM2 ..........178 A1
Seymour Rd Ipswich IP2 ..17 C4
Jaywick CO15 ............18⁊ F1
Seymour St CM2 .........204 A1
Shackleton CI CO12 ......90 F1
Shackleton CI IP3 ........18 B3
Shackleton St ⁊ IP3 ......18 B3
Shaftenbue End Rd SG8 ..39 B8
Shaftesbury Ave CM2 ....91 B4
Shaftesbury St 🔟 CB9 ...9 F7
Shaftesbury Sq 🔟 IP4 ...17 D7
Shafto Rd IP1 ............16 F8
Shair La CO16 ...........140 B2
Shakespeare CI CM7 .....155 A7
Shakespeare Dr LM9 .....210 A1
Shakespeare Rd CO3 ....134 F6
Shakeston CI CM1 .......215 B8
Shalford Cty Prim Sch
CM7 .....................100 E5
Shalford Lodge CM1 .....205 B8
Shalford Rd CM7 .........126 A3
Shamrock Ave CM7 ......116 E6
Shamrock CI CM9 ........199 D2
Shamrock Ho CM23 ......203 J8
Shangani Rd CO10 .......145 F5
Shanklin CI CO15 ........189 A8
Shannon CI CM7 .........127 E6
Shannon Rd IP3 .........38 A8
Sharlands Row CM9 ......199 A8
Sharpington CI CM2 .....216 C3
Shatters Rd CO2 .........161 A1
Shaw CI CO13 ...........170 E7
Shaw Dr CM0 ............73 D7
Shaw Rd Long Melford CO10 .15 D8
Witham CM8 .............176 F5
Shawlands Ave CO10 ....34 B7
Shearers The CM3 .......145 C4
Shearers Way CM3 ......192 F1
Shearman Ct 🔟 CB9 .....9 A7
Shears CI CO15 ..........201 D5
Shears Ct CO15 .........201 D5
Sheds La CB10 ..........22 E2
Sheepcotes La CM9 .....196 F2
Sheepcote Rd IP9 .......51 F3
Sheepcote La
Little Waltham CM3 ......191 C⁊
Silver End CM8 ..........156 E5
Sheepen Pl CO3 .........135 D7

Sheepen Rd CO3 .........135 D8
Sheepshead Hill CO10 ....34 C6
Sheering Wlk CO2 .......135 F2
Sheerwater Mews CO4 ...137 A8
Sheldrake Dr IP2 .........16 E2
Shellcroft CO6 ...........77 F1
Shellduck Cres CM7 .....154 C5
Shelley Ave CO10 ........34 B6
Shelley La CO16 .........168 F2
Shelley Rd
Chelmsford CM2 .........205 D2
Colchester CO3 ..........134 F6
Shelley St 🔟 IP2 ........17 C4
Shenley Rd IP3 ..........18 B1
Shepherd Dr IP8 .........16 C2
Shepherds CI CM23 .....145 C4
Shepherds Croft CO3 ....134 D5
Shepherds Ct 🔟 CO9 ....8 E7
Shepherds La CO16 ......22 A6
Shepherds Way CO10 ....22 F2
Sheppard CI CO16 .......188 D6
Sheppard Dr CM2 ........206 A4
Sherborne Rd CM1 ......205 D5
Sherborne Ct CO13 .....170 F7
Sherbourne Rd CO9 .....136 F7
Sheriffs Way CO15 .......180 E7
Sherrington Rd IP1 ......17 A0
Sherwood CI CO4 ........136 D7
Sherwood Ct 🔟 CM23 ...145 F7
Sherwood Dr
Chelmsford CM1 .........204 D1
Clacton-on-S CO15 ......188 E6
Sherwood Way CO5 .....158 D4
Shetland CI IP4 ..........9 D8
Shetland Rd CB9 .........9 D8
Shillito CI CO3 ...........134 F3
Ship La CO11 ............87 E3
Ship Launch Rd IP3 ......17 E3
Shipyard Pst CO7 ........185 F5
Shire CI CM1 .............205 F7
Shire CI ⁊ CB9 ..........8 E7
Shire Hall Yd 🔟 IP4 ......17 D5
Shire Hill CB11 ..........22 F1
Shire Hill La CB10 .......44 A8
Shire La CO6 .............108 C6
Shirley Ct CO15 .........188 A1
Shoebridge's Hill CO7 ...84 E6
Shop La CO5 .............184 F3
Shop Rd CO11 ...........113 B6
Shops The CM8 .........156 D4
Shore La Bradfield CO11 ..87 E3
Harkstead IP9 ...........63 A2
Shoreham Rd CO15 ......203 J8
Short Cut Rd CO11 ......135 E7
Short Wyre St ⁊ CO1 ....135 F7
Shortcroft CM23 .........16 D1
Shortlands IP8 ...........16 D1
Shortlands Pl CM23 .....145 F8
Shortridge Ct CM8 ......194 F8
Shotley CI
Clacton-on-S CO15 ......188 A1
Felixstowe IP11 ..........221 B4
Ipswich IP2 ..............16 C2
Shropshire CI CM2 .......216 F5
Shrub End Rd CO2 .......135 B4
Shrubland CI CO15 ......189 B5
Shrubland Ct IP4 ........18 F5
Shrubland Rd
⁊ Colchester CO2 .......136 A6
New Mistley CO11 .......87 A3
Shrublands CO10 ........22 E3
Shums Hill CO13 ........170 C8
Shut La CO6 .............105 B6
Siam Pl CO10 ............33 E7
Sidegate Ave IP4 ........18 A8
Sidegate La IP4 ..........18 A8
Sidegate Prim Sch IP4 ...18 A8
Sidmouth Rd CM1 .......205 E6
Sidney Terr CM23 .......145 F6
Siena Mews CO2 ........136 B4
Siggin's La CB1 ..........10 C2
Silcock CI CO4 ...........110 C2
Silcott St CO7 ...........185 E6
Silent St ⁊ IP1 ..........17 C5
Silk Factory Row CO10 ...2 B6
Silk Mus CM7 ...........127 F2
Silke Way CM7 ..........127 F2
Sillett CI CO16 ...........188 D6
Silvanus CI CO3 .........135 D6
Silver End Cty Prim Sch
CM8 .....................156 E3
Silver Leys IP9 ...........60 E6
Silver Row CB11 .........42 F5
Silver St Maldon CM9 ....209 F3
Silver End CM8 ..........156 D4
Stansted
Mountfitchet CM24 .......1₊9 D6
Wethersfield CM7 ........73 B3
Silverdale CI CO15 ......189 B5
Silverthorne CI CO2 .....136 A3
Silvester Way CM3 ......218 F8
Simons La CO1 ..........136 B6
Simpson CI IP3 ..........17 F1
Simpsons La CO5 ........17⁊ A3
Sims CI CO6 .............105 B7
Sinclair CI CO4 ..........109 F2
Sinclair Dr IP2 ...........17 C3
Singer Ave CO15 ........202 F8
Singleton CI CO4 ........34 A5
Sinnington End CO4 .....110 C4
Sioux CI CO4 ............110 C4
Sir Charles Lucas Sch
CO4 .....................136 E8
Sir Isaac's Wlk CO1 .....135 F7

**Sir John Payne RC**
Comp Sch CM1 . . . . . . . . . . 204 F6
**Sirdar Rd** IP1 . . . . . . . . . . . . . .17 A7
**Siskin Cl** CO4 . . . . . . . . . . . . 136 F8
**Sittang Cl** CO2 . . . . . . . . . . . 135 C1
**Sitwell Cl** CO11 . . . . . . . . . . . .86 B4
**Siward Rd** CM8 . . . . . . . . . . . 194 D8
**Six Bells Ct** CM7 . . . . . . . . . 127 F5
**Sixth Ave** Chelmsford CM1 . .205 B6
Stansted
 Mountfitchet CM24 . . . . . . .120 C3
**Sixth Form Coll The** CO1 . .135 E7
**Skate's Hill** CO10 . . . . . . . . . . .2 B2
**Skeins Way** CB11 . . . . . . . . . .65 C4
**Skelmersdale Rd** CO15 . . . . .188 F3
**Skelton Cl** CO11 . . . . . . . . . . .86 C4
**Skerry Rise** CM1 . . . . . . . . . .205 B7
**Skiddaw Cl** CM7 . . . . . . . . . .154 D7
**Skinner's La** CM2 . . . . . . . . .216 B3
**Skinners St** CM23 . . . . . . . . .145 C4
**Skipper Cl** CM7 . . . . . . . . . . .154 F8
**Skitts Hill** CM7 . . . . . . . . . . .128 A1
**Skitts Hill Ind Est** CM7 . . . .128 B1
**Skreens Ct** CM1 . . . . . . . . . .204 D4
**Sky Hall Hill** CO4 . . . . . . . . . .83 D7
**Skylark La** IP8 . . . . . . . . . . . .16 C2
**Skylark Wlk** CM2 . . . . . . . . .216 B5
**Skyrmans Fee** CO13 . . . . . . .170 E6
**Sladbury's La** CO15 . . . . . . .189 C6
**Sladburys La** CO15 . . . . . . . .189 D8
**Slade Rd** CO15 . . . . . . . . . . .189 C6
**Slade St** 1 IP4 . . . . . . . . . . . .17 D5
**Slade The** CB10 . . . . . . . . . . .22 F7
**Slade's La** CM2 . . . . . . . . . . .216 A3
**Slades Cl** CO10 . . . . . . . . . . . .2 C5
**Slate** CO9 . . . . . . . . . . . . . . . .76 F1
**Slaters Cl** CO13 . . . . . . . . . . .170 E6
**Sleaford Cl** IP2 . . . . . . . . . . . .17 A3
**Slippers The** CM9 . . . . . . . . .199 D1
**Sloe Hill** CO9 . . . . . . . . . . . . .76 C2
**Slough Farm Rd** CO9 . . . . . . .76 D2
**Slough House Cl** CM7 . . . . . .128 D1
**Slough La** Ardleigh CO7 . . . .111 D4
 Elmstead CO7 . . . . . . . . . . . . .137 A6
 Purleigh CM3 . . . . . . . . . . . . .219 D3
**Slough Rd** Danbury CM3 . . . .219 C3
 East Bergholt CO7 . . . . . . . . . .60 D2
**Slushy La** IP9 . . . . . . . . . . . . .63 B3
**Smaley La** CO10 . . . . . . . . . . .15 C8
**Smallbridge Entry** CO8 . . . . .80 D8
**Smallwood Rd** CO2 . . . . . . . .135 B3
**Smart St** 11 IP4 . . . . . . . . . . .17 D5
**Smeaton Cl** CO4 . . . . . . . . . .110 A6
**Smeetham Hall La** CO10 . . . .32 E6
**Smith's End La** SG8 . . . . . . . . .39 A8
**Smith's Cl** IP9 . . . . . . . . . . . . .35 A1
**Smithers Dr** CM2 . . . . . . . . .217 A6
**Smiths Cotts** CM22 . . . . . . . .93 E4
**Smiths Field**
 Colchester CO1 . . . . . . . . . . .136 C5
 Rayne CM7 . . . . . . . . . . . . . .126 F2
**Smythe Cl** CO16 . . . . . . . . . .188 C6
**Smythies Ave** CO1 . . . . . . . . .136 A7
**Snakes La**
 Stansted Mountfitchet CM24 . .93 F2
 Ugley CM22 . . . . . . . . . . . . . . .94 A2
**Snape Cl** CO16 . . . . . . . . . . . .188 A4
**Snape Way** CO13 . . . . . . . . .170 F7
**Sneating Hall La** CO13 . . . . .169 E8
**Snelling Gr** CM2 . . . . . . . . . .216 F6
**Sniveller's La** CO5 . . . . . . . . .157 D3
**Snow Hill La** CO6 . . . . . . . . . .57 D5
**Snowberry Ct** CM7 . . . . . . . .128 D4
**Snowberry Gr** CO2 . . . . . . . .136 A3
**Snowcroft** IP9 . . . . . . . . . . . . .35 A1
**Snowdon Cl** 5 CB9 . . . . . . . . .8 E6
**Snowdon Rd** IP2 . . . . . . . . . . .17 A2
**Snowdrop Cl**
 Bishop's Stortford CM23 . . . .145 C6
 Chelmsford CM1 . . . . . . . . . .205 E7
 Witham CM8 . . . . . . . . . . . . .176 E4
**Snowley Par** CM23 . . . . . . . .119 B1
**Snows Way** CO11 . . . . . . . . . .86 D8
**Soane St** IP4 . . . . . . . . . . . . . .17 D6
**Soft Rd** CO10 . . . . . . . . . . . . .31 F5
**Soils The** CO12 . . . . . . . . . . .116 E5
**Solway Ct** 3 CO4 . . . . . . . . .136 E8
**Somers Rd** CO3 . . . . . . . . . . .135 A4
**Somerset Cl** CO2 . . . . . . . . . .135 B3
**Somerset Ct** 9 CB9 . . . . . . . . .8 E7
**Somerset Pl** CM1 . . . . . . . . .205 A7
**Somerset Rd** CM7 . . . . . . . . .17 F8
**Somerset Way** CO15 . . . . . . .187 F1
**Somerton Ct** IP11 . . . . . . . . .221 F4
**Somme Rd** CO2 . . . . . . . . . . .135 E4
**Sonell Ct** CM7 . . . . . . . . . . . .137 B2
**Songers Cotts** CO4 . . . . . . . .83 F8
**Sorrel Cl** Colchester CO4 . . . .109 C2
 Ipswich IP2 . . . . . . . . . . . . . . .16 F3
**Sorrel Horse Mews** 22
 IP4 . . . . . . . . . . . . . . . . . . . . . .17 D5
**Sorrell Cl**
 Goldhanger CM9 . . . . . . . . . .211 E7
 Little Waltham CM3 . . . . . . . .191 B6
**South Area** IP1 . . . . . . . . . . . .16 C7
**South Cl** Halstead CO9 . . . . .103 E8
 Ipswich IP4 . . . . . . . . . . . . . . .17 E5
 St Osyth CO16 . . . . . . . . . . . .187 B4
**South Gn** CB11 . . . . . . . . . . . .67 D4
**South Green Rd** CO5 . . . . . . .163 F3
**South Heath Rd** CO7 . . . . . . .166 F3
**South Hill** IP11 . . . . . . . . . . . .221 D3
**South Hill Cl** CO13 . . . . . . . .218 D6
**South Ho** CO13 . . . . . . . . . . .170 F4
**South Primrose Hill** CM1 . .204 F3

**South Rd**
 Bishop's Stortford CM23 . . . .146 A5
 Saffron Walden CB11 . . . . . . .22 E1
 Takeley CM22 . . . . . . . . . . . .148 C8
**South St**
 Bishop's Stortford CM23 . . . .145 F6
 Braintree CM7 . . . . . . . . . . . .127 F2
 Colchester CO2 . . . . . . . . . . .135 E6
 Great Chesterford CB10 . . . . . .3 D2
 Great Waltham CM3 . . . . . . . .191 A8
 Ipswich IP1 . . . . . . . . . . . . . . .17 B7
 Manningtree CO11 . . . . . . . . .86 D4
 Tolleshunt D'arcy CM9 . . . . . .198 D4
**South St Commercial
 Ctr** 1 CM23 . . . . . . . . . . . . .145 F6
**South Strand** CO11 . . . . . . . . .86 C5
**South Suffolk Bsns Pk**
 CO10 . . . . . . . . . . . . . . . . . . . .34 A7
**South View** CM6 . . . . . . . . . .150 C8
**South View Gn** IP9 . . . . . . . . .60 E6
**Southborough Rd** CM2 . . . . .216 A8
**Southcliff** CO14 . . . . . . . . . . .171 C7
**Southcliff Ct** CO15 . . . . . . . .189 B4
**Southcliff Hall** CO15 . . . . . . .188 F2
**Southcliff Pk** CO15 . . . . . . . .189 A4
**Southcliff Prom** CO14 . . . . . .171 C7
**Southcote Rd** CM6 . . . . . . . .176 F4
**Southcroft Cl** CO13 . . . . . . . .170 C6
**Southend Rd**
 Great Baddow CM2 . . . . . . . .217 B4
 Howe Green CM2 . . . . . . . . . .217 D2
 Woodham Mortimer CM9 . . . .219 C5
**Southey Cl** CM9 . . . . . . . . . . .210 C4
**Southfield** CO13 . . . . . . . . . . . .3 A3
**Southfields** CO7 . . . . . . . . . . .84 F6
**Southgate Gdns** CO10 . . . . . .15 C6
**Southgate St** IP9 . . . . . . . . . .16 B1
**Southgate St** CO10 . . . . . . . .15 C6
**Southgates Ind Pk** CB10 . . . .43 F7
**Southgreen Gdns** CO16 . . . .188 C4
**Southland Cl** CO4 . . . . . . . . .110 C1
**Southlands Chase** CM2 . . . . .217 E2
**Southmill Rd** CM23 . . . . . . . .146 A5
**Southmill Trad Ctr** CM23 . . .146 A6
**Southview Dr**
 Holland-on-S CO15 . . . . . . . .189 F6
 Walton-on-t-N CO14 . . . . . . .171 C7
**Southview Rd** CM3 . . . . . . . .218 D6
**Southview Terr** CM3 . . . . . . .218 D6
**Southway**
 Brightlingsea CO7 . . . . . . . . .185 F7
 Colchester CO1, CO3 . . . . . . .135 E6
**Southwark Cl** CO16 . . . . . . . .188 A5
**Southwood Chase** CM3 . . . . .219 A4
**Sovereign Cl** CM7 . . . . . . . . .128 D4
**Sovereign Cres** CO3 . . . . . . .135 C6
**Sovereign Ctr** IP1 . . . . . . . . . .16 C7
**Sowerberry Cl** CM1 . . . . . . . .204 F7
**Spa Dr** CM0 . . . . . . . . . . . . . .213 B1
**Spa Rd** Feering CO5 . . . . . . . .158 E4
 Witham CM8 . . . . . . . . . . . . .176 E2
**Spalding Ave** CM1 . . . . . . . . .204 E5
**Spalding Cl** CM7 . . . . . . . . . .127 E4
**Spalding Way** CM2 . . . . . . . .216 F8
**Spanbies Rd** CO7 . . . . . . . . . .58 D2
**Spansey Ct** 1 CO9 . . . . . . . . .76 D1
**Sparepenny La** N CB10 . . . . .47 A4
**Sparepenny La S** CB10 . . . . .47 B4
**Sparkey Cl** CM8 . . . . . . . . . . .195 A7
**Sparks La** CO9 . . . . . . . . . . . .29 A4
**Sparling Cl** CO2 . . . . . . . . . . .135 C2
**Sparlings The** CO13 . . . . . . .170 C8
**Sparrow Cl** CO9 . . . . . . . . . . .75 D8
**Sparrow Rd** CO10 . . . . . . . . . .34 B6
**Sparrows Herne** CO15 . . . . .188 F6
**Sparrowsend Cotts** CB11 . . . .43 A4
**Sparrowsend Hill** CB11 . . . . .43 A5
**Speckled Wood Ct** CM7 . . . .154 E8
**Speedwell Cl** CM8 . . . . . . . . .176 D4
**Speedwell Rd**
 Colchester CO2 . . . . . . . . . . .136 D2
 Ipswich IP2 . . . . . . . . . . . . . . .16 F4
**Spencer Cl** Elsenham CM22 . .94 C3
 Stansted
 Mountfitchet CM24 . . . . . . . .119 E6
**Spencer Rd**
 Great Chesterford CB10 . . . . . .3 D3
 Thorpe-le-S CO16 . . . . . . . . .142 A2
**Spencer Sq** CM7 . . . . . . . . . .127 F8
**Spencers Piece** CO4 . . . . . . . .83 E4
**Spendells Cl** CO14 . . . . . . . .144 D2
**Spending Dr** CM1 . . . . . . . . .204 D7
**Spennells The** CO16 . . . . . . .142 A2
**Spenser Way** CO15 . . . . . . . .187 F1
**Spicers La** CO10 . . . . . . . . . . .15 C8
**Spindle Rd** CB9 . . . . . . . . . . . .8 D8
**Spindle Wood** CO4 . . . . . . . .110 B4
**Spinks La** CM8 . . . . . . . . . . .176 F1
**Spinnaker Cl** CO15 . . . . . . . .203 J8
**Spinnaker Dr** CM9 . . . . . . . .210 E3
**Spinnel's Hill** CO11 . . . . . . . .88 B1
**Spinnel's La** Wix CO11 . . . . .115 D7
 Wrabness CO11 . . . . . . . . . . . .88 C1
**Spinner Cl** IP1 . . . . . . . . . . . .16 D8
**Spinney The**
 Braintree CM7 . . . . . . . . . . . .128 C1
 Earls Colne CO6 . . . . . . . . . . .105 A6
 Newport CB11 . . . . . . . . . . . . .67 A7
 Rushmere St A IP4 . . . . . . . . . .18 F4
 Stansted
 Mountfitchet CM24 . . . . . . . .119 E6
**Spinneyfields** CO5 . . . . . . . .179 D6
**Spires The** CM2 . . . . . . . . . . .216 F6
**Spital Rd** Maldon CM9 . . . . .209 F2
 Maldon CM9 . . . . . . . . . . . . .220 D7
**Sporehams La**
 Danbury CM3 . . . . . . . . . . . .218 C4
 Howe Green CM2, CM3 . . . . .217 F4

**Sportsman La** CM3 . . . . . . . .194 A2
**Sportsway** CO1 . . . . . . . . . . .135 F8
**Spots Wlk** CM2 . . . . . . . . . . .216 D3
**Spout La** CO10 . . . . . . . . . . . .55 D7
**Spratts La** CO11 . . . . . . . . . .113 B4
**Spring Chase**
 Brightlingsea CO7 . . . . . . . . .185 E7
 Wivenhoe CO7 . . . . . . . . . . .137 B2
**Spring Cl**
 Clacton-on-S CO16 . . . . . . . .188 C5
 Colchester CO4 . . . . . . . . . . .110 C3
 Little Baddow CM3 . . . . . . . .207 D5
**Spring Elms La** CM3 . . . . . . .207 F3
**Spring Gardens Rd** CO6 . . . .106 E6
**Spring Hill** CB11 . . . . . . . . . . .22 A1
**Spring La** Colchester CO3 . . .135 A7
 Colchester CO3 . . . . . . . . . . .135 A8
 Eight Ash G CO3 . . . . . . . . . .108 B1
 Great Totham CM9 . . . . . . . .196 D7
 Hatfield Peverel CM3 . . . . . . .194 F2
 Sproughton CO3 . . . . . . . . . .134 C8
 West Bergholt CO6 . . . . . . . .108 E3
 Witham CM8 . . . . . . . . . . . . .195 A7
 Wivenhoe CO7 . . . . . . . . . . .137 B2
**Spring Lane Rdbt** CO3 . . . . .135 A7
**Spring Meadow** CO10 . . . . . . .2 B6
**Spring Meadow Prim
 Sch** CO12 . . . . . . . . . . . . . . .91 A3
**Spring Pond Cl** CM2 . . . . . . .216 E8
**Spring Rd**
 Brightlingsea CO7 . . . . . . . . .185 F7
 Ipswich IP4 . . . . . . . . . . . . . . .18 A6
 St Osyth CO16 . . . . . . . . . . . .187 A3
 Tiptree CO5 . . . . . . . . . . . . . .179 C4
**Spring Rise** CM2 . . . . . . . . . .216 C2
**Spring Sedge Cl** CO3 . . . . . .134 C7
**Spring Way** CO9 . . . . . . . . . . .51 E1
**Springbank Ave** CO11 . . . . . . .86 B3
**Springbok Ho** CM2 . . . . . . . .216 F5
**Springett's Hill** CO8 . . . . . . . .55 D2
**Springfield Ave** IP11 . . . . . . .221 E5
**Springfield Cotts** CM9 . . . . .210 B5
**Springfield Ct** CM23 . . . . . . .145 E8
**Springfield Gn** CM1 . . . . . . . .205 E4
**Springfield Inf Sch** IP1 . . . . . .16 F8
**Springfield Jun Sch** IP1 . . . . .16 F8
**Springfield La** IP1 . . . . . . . . . .16 F8
**Springfield Park Ave**
 CM2 . . . . . . . . . . . . . . . . . . . .205 E2
**Springfield Park Hill**
 CM2 . . . . . . . . . . . . . . . . . . . .205 D2
**Springfield Park La** CM2 . . .205 E2
**Springfield Park Par**
 CM2 . . . . . . . . . . . . . . . . . . . .205 D2
**Springfield Park Rd** CM2 . . .205 E2
**Springfield Pl** CM1 . . . . . . . .205 E5
**Springfield Rd**
 Chelmsford CM1 . . . . . . . . . .205 E4
 Colchester CO1 . . . . . . . . . . . .15 E1
**Springfield Terr** CO10 . . . . . .33 F8
**Springfields**
 Brightlingsea CO7 . . . . . . . . .185 F7
 Great Dunmow CM6 . . . . . . .150 D8
 Frinton-on-S CO13 . . . . . . . .170 F5
 Springfield CM7 . . . . . . . . . .127 C2
 Springfield CM1 . . . . . . . . . .205 D3
**Springhill Cl** CO7 . . . . . . . . .138 E8
**Springhill Rd** CB11 . . . . . . . . .43 D8
**Springhurst Cl** CM4 . . . . . . . .17 F6
**Springland Cl** IP4 . . . . . . . . . .18 A6
**Springlands Way** CO10 . . . . .15 F2
**Springmead** CM7 . . . . . . . . . .154 D7
**Springvalley La** CO7 . . . . . . .111 C4
**Springwell Rd** CB10 . . . . . . . .22 A5
**Springwood Cr** CM7 . . . . . . .127 D3
**Springwood Dr** CM7 . . . . . . .127 C2
**Springwood Ind Est** CM7 . . .127 D3
**Sprites End** IP11 . . . . . . . . . .221 B7
**Sprites Jun & Inf Sch** IP2 . . .16 C2
**Sprites La** IP8, IP2 . . . . . . . . .16 C2
**Spriteshall La** IP11 . . . . . . . .221 B7
**Sproughton Bsns Pk** IP1 . . . .16 C8
**Sproughton CE Prim Sch**
 IP8 . . . . . . . . . . . . . . . . . . . . . .16 B6
**Sproughton La** IP8 . . . . . . . . .16 A6
**Sproughton Rd** IP1 . . . . . . . . .16 D7
**Spruce Ave** CO4 . . . . . . . . . .136 E8
**Spruce Cl**
 West Mersea CO5 . . . . . . . . .201 B7
 Witham CM8 . . . . . . . . . . . . .177 A4
**Spurgeon Cl** CO9 . . . . . . . . . .51 E1
**Spurgeon Pl** CO5 . . . . . . . . .158 C2
**Spurgeon St** CO1 . . . . . . . . .136 C6
**Square The**
 Colchester CO3 . . . . . . . . . . .135 B3
 West Mersea CO5 . . . . . . . . .201 B6
**Squire's Ct** 11 CB9 . . . . . . . . .8 F7
**Squires Cl** CM23 . . . . . . . . . .145 C8
**Squirrells Cl** CM1 . . . . . . . . .204 F5
**Squirrels Cl** 2 CM23 . . . . . . .145 F8
**Squirrels Field** CO4 . . . . . . .109 F5
**Squirrels The** IP9 . . . . . . . . . .35 A2
**Stable Cl** Colchester CO4 . . .136 D4
**Stable Mews** CO5 . . . . . . . . .201 E7
**Stablecroft** CM1 . . . . . . . . . .205 E8
**Stablefield Rd** CO14 . . . . . . .171 A7
**Stacey Cl** CM23 . . . . . . . . . . .145 F6
**Stackyard The** CB10 . . . . . . . .3 A3
**Staff Ho** CM1 . . . . . . . . . . . . .190 F4
**Stafford Cl** CO13 . . . . . . . . . .170 E6
**Stafford Cres** CM7 . . . . . . . .128 D4
**Stafford Rd** CO13 . . . . . . . . .145 F5
**Stalin Rd** CO2 . . . . . . . . . . . .136 B4
**Stallards Cres** CO13 . . . . . . .170 E6
**Stambourne Rd**
 Great Yeldham CO9 . . . . . . . . .29 D3
 Ridgewell CO9 . . . . . . . . . . . .28 F5
 Toppesfield CO9 . . . . . . . . . . .50 B7

**Stambridge Rd** CO15 . . . . . .188 C4
**Stamford Cl** IP2 . . . . . . . . . . . .36 FB
**Stammers Rd** CO4 . . . . . . . . .109 F4
**Standard Ave** CO15 . . . . . . . .203 D6
**Standard Rd** 9 CO1 . . . . . . . .136 C6
**Standing Rd** CO14 . . . . . . . . .144 D1
**Standrums** CM6 . . . . . . . . . . .150 D8
**Stane Cl** CM23 . . . . . . . . . . .118 F1
**Stane Field** CO6 . . . . . . . . . .132 E3
**Stanes Rd** CM7 . . . . . . . . . . .127 F6
**Stanfield Cl** CO3 . . . . . . . . . .134 E3
**Stanfield Mdw** CM8 . . . . . . .155 F1
**Stanley Ave**
 Brightlingsea CO7 . . . . . . . . .186 A7
 Ipswich IP3 . . . . . . . . . . . . . . .18 A4
**Stanley Rd**
 Clacton-on-S CO15 . . . . . . . .188 C2
 Felixstowe IP11 . . . . . . . . . . .221 E3
 Great Chesterford CB10 . . . . . .3 E3
 Halstead CO9 . . . . . . . . . . . . .76 D2
 Sudbury CO10 . . . . . . . . . . . . .33 E8
 Wivenhoe CO7 . . . . . . . . . . .137 C1
**Stanley Rise** CM2 . . . . . . . . .205 F3
**Stanley Wood Ave** CO10 . . . .15 F1
**Stanley Wooster Way**
 CO4 . . . . . . . . . . . . . . . . . . . .136 E7
**Stanleys Farm Rd** CB11 . . . . .43 F8
**Stanmore Cl** CO16 . . . . . . . .188 D5
**Stanmore Way** CO16 . . . . . .187 B4
**Stannard Way** CO10 . . . . . . . .34 A6
**Stanstead Rd** CO9 . . . . . . . . .103 F8
**Stansted Airport Sta**
 CM24 . . . . . . . . . . . . . . . . . . .121 B4
**Stansted Cl** CM1 . . . . . . . . . .204 E1
**Stansted Mountfitchet
 Sta** CM24 . . . . . . . . . . . . . . .119 E6
**Stansted Rd**
 Birchanger CM23 . . . . . . . . . .119 C4
 Bishop's Stortford CM23 . . . .119 B2
 Colchester CO2 . . . . . . . . . . .136 A1
 Elsenham CM22 . . . . . . . . . . .94 C1
**Stansted Way** CO13 . . . . . . .171 A6
**Stansrete Field** CM7 . . . . . . .154 B5
**Stanton Pl** 5 CB9 . . . . . . . . . . .9 B8
**Stanway Cl** CO10 . . . . . . . . . . .2 C5
**Stanway Cty Prim Sch**
 CO3 . . . . . . . . . . . . . . . . . . . .134 C6
**Stanway Fiveways Cty
 Prim Sch** CO3 . . . . . . . . . . .134 C5
**Stanway Sch** CO3 . . . . . . . . .134 D5
**Stanwell St** 9 CO2 . . . . . . . . .135 F6
**Stanwyn Ave** CO15 . . . . . . . .188 E3
**Stapleford Cl** CM2 . . . . . . . . .205 A1
**Staplers Cl** CM9 . . . . . . . . . .196 B4
**Staplers Heath** CM9 . . . . . . .196 B4
**Staplers Wlk** CM9 . . . . . . . . .196 B4
**Star La** Great Dunmow CM6 . .123 D1
 Ipswich IP4 . . . . . . . . . . . . . . .17 D5
**Star Mead** CM6 . . . . . . . . . . . .72 A8
**Starfield Cl** CM4 . . . . . . . . . . .18 B6
**Starling's Hill** CO9 . . . . . . . . .75 E4
**Starr Rd** CM22 . . . . . . . . . . . .94 F5
**Station App** Braintree CM7 . .128 A2
 Frinton-on-S CO13 . . . . . . . .170 F5
**Station Cotts** CO6 . . . . . . . . .133 D2
**Station Hill** CO6 . . . . . . . . . . .79 E8
**Station La** CO12 . . . . . . . . . . .91 C4
**Station Rd** Alresford CO7 . . .165 A8
 Ardleigh CO7 . . . . . . . . . . . . .111 E7
 Bentley IP9 . . . . . . . . . . . . . . .60 E6
 Birdbrook CO9 . . . . . . . . . . . .10 D1
 Bishop's Stortford CM23 . . . .146 A7
 Bradfield CO11 . . . . . . . . . . . .87 E3
 Braintree CM7 . . . . . . . . . . . .127 F2
 Brightlingsea CO7 . . . . . . . . .185 E6
 Clacton-on-S CO15 . . . . . . . .188 F3
 Clare CO10 . . . . . . . . . . . . . . .12 C7
 Colne Engaine CO6 . . . . . . . . .77 F1
 Cressing CM8 . . . . . . . . . . . .156 A3
 Earls Colne CO6 . . . . . . . . . .105 A7
 Elsenham CM22 . . . . . . . . . . .94 D2
 Felsted CM6 . . . . . . . . . . . . .151 F6
 Great Bentley CO7 . . . . . . . . .166 A8
 Great Bentley CO7 . . . . . . . . .166 E8
 Great Dunmow CM6 . . . . . . .150 D8
 Harwich, Bath Side CO12 . . . .91 E5
 Harwich, Dovercourt CO12 . . .91 D4
 Harwich, Parkeston CO12 . . . .90 F5
 Hatfield Peverel CM3 . . . . . . .193 F5
 Haverhill CB9 . . . . . . . . . . . . . .9 A8
 Kelvedon CO5 . . . . . . . . . . . .158 C3
 Kirby Cross CO13 . . . . . . . . .170 B6
 Long Melford CO10 . . . . . . . .15 C5
 Maldon CM9 . . . . . . . . . . . . .210 A3
 Manningtree CO11 . . . . . . . . .86 C5
 Marks Tey CO6 . . . . . . . . . . .133 B4
 Newport CB11 . . . . . . . . . . . .67 A8
 Rayne CM7 . . . . . . . . . . . . . .126 F1
 Saffron Walden CB11 . . . . . . .22 D1
 Sible Hedingham CO9 . . . . . . .51 E2
 Stansted
 Mountfitchet CM24 . . . . . . . .119 E6
 Sudbury CO10 . . . . . . . . . . . . .33 E7
 Takeley CM22 . . . . . . . . . . . .148 C7
 Thorpe-le-S CO16 . . . . . . . . .168 F8
 Thorrington CO7 . . . . . . . . . .166 A6
 Tiptree CO5 . . . . . . . . . . . . . .179 C4
 Tollesbury CM9 . . . . . . . . . . .199 D2
 Tolleshunt D'arcy CM9 . . . . . .198 E5
 Trimley St M IP11 . . . . . . . . .221 A7
 Wakes Colne CO6 . . . . . . . . .106 D6
 Wendens Ambo CB11 . . . . . . .42 F5
 White Colne CO6 . . . . . . . . . .105 E8
 White Notley CM8 . . . . . . . . .155 F2
 Wickham Bishops CM8 . . . . . .195 C4
 Witham CM8 . . . . . . . . . . . . .177 A3
 Wivenhoe CO7 . . . . . . . . . . .164 B8
 Wrabness CO11 . . . . . . . . . . .88 F3

**Station Road Ind Est**
 CM6 . . . . . . . . . . . . . . . . . . . . . .
**Station St** Ipswich IP2 . . . . . . .
 Saffron Walden CB11 . . . . . . . .
 Walton-on-t-N CO14 . . . . . . . .
**Station Villas** CM3 . . . . . . . . . .1
**Station Way** CO1 . . . . . . . . . . . .1
**Station Yd** IP2 . . . . . . . . . . . . . .1
**Steam Mill Rd** CO11 . . . . . . . .
**Steamer Terr** 2 CM2 . . . . . . .205
**Stebbing Cty Prim Sch**
 CM6 . . . . . . . . . . . . . . . . . . . . . .
**Stebbing Rd** CM6 . . . . . . . . . .152 B.
**Steeds Meadow** CO10 . . . . . .15 C8
**Steele Cl** CO6 . . . . . . . . . . . . .132 F3
**Steele Ho** CO12 . . . . . . . . . . . .91 C3
**Steeple Bumpstead Cty
 Prim Sch** CB9 . . . . . . . . . . . . .
**Steeple Bumpstead Rd**
 CB9 . . . . . . . . . . . . . . . . . . . . .26 E7
**Steeple Cl** CM9 . . . . . . . . . . .210 D5
**Steeple View** CM23 . . . . . . . .145 F8
**Steerforth Cl** CM1 . . . . . . . . .204 D7
**Stella Maris** IP2 . . . . . . . . . . .16 D5
**Stepfield** CM8 . . . . . . . . . . . . .177 B2
**Stephen Cl** Haverhill CB9 . . . . .8 F8
 Long Melford CO10 . . . . . . . .15 B5
**Stephen Cranfield Cl**
 CO5 . . . . . . . . . . . . . . . . . . . . .164 A7
**Stephen Marshall Ave**
 CM7 . . . . . . . . . . . . . . . . . . . . .72 C6
**Stephen Neville Ct** CB11 . . . .43 D8
**Stephen's Ct** IP4 . . . . . . . . . . .18 B6
**Stephenson Rd**
 Braintree CM7 . . . . . . . . . . . .128 A1
 Clacton-on-S CO15 . . . . . . . .189 B8
 Colchester CO4 . . . . . . . . . . .110 D6
**Stephenson Rd W** CO15 . . . .169 A1
**Sterling Cl** CO3 . . . . . . . . . . .134 E5
**Sterling Complex** IP1 . . . . . .16 D7
**Stevens La** CM6 . . . . . . . . . . .152 F6
**Stevens Rd** CM8 . . . . . . . . . .176 E1
**Stevens Wlk** CO4 . . . . . . . . . .136 F7
**Stevenson Rd** IP1 . . . . . . . . . .17 B6
**Stewards Cl** CO13 . . . . . . . . .170 F7
**Stewart Rd** CM2 . . . . . . . . . .216 A6
**Stewarts The** CM23 . . . . . . . .145 E6
**Stewarts Way** CM23 . . . . . . . .92 F2
**Stilemans Wood** CM7 . . . . . .128 D1
**Stiles The** CM3 . . . . . . . . . . . .210 E3
**Stirling Dr** CB9 . . . . . . . . . . . . .8 E8
**Stirrup Cl** CM1 . . . . . . . . . . . .205 E7
**Stirrup Mews** CO3 . . . . . . . . .134 E6
**Stisted CE Prim Sch** CM7 . . .129 B6
**Stivvy's Rd** CM9 . . . . . . . . . .208 C3
**Stock Chase** CM9 . . . . . . . . .210 B5
**Stock Rd** CM2 . . . . . . . . . . . .216 B2
**Stock Terr** CM9 . . . . . . . . . . .210 B5
**Stockhouse Cl** CM9 . . . . . . . .180 B2
**Stockhouse Rd** CO5 . . . . . . .180 B7
**Stocking La** SG8 . . . . . . . . . . .39 C1
**Stockley Cl** CB9 . . . . . . . . . . . .9 F7
**Stockmen Field** CM23 . . . . . .145 C8
**Stockmers End** 1 IP9 . . . . . . .35 A1
**Stockwell** 8 CO1 . . . . . . . . . .135 F7
**Stoke Coll** CO10 . . . . . . . . . . .11 C3
**Stoke Hall Rd** IP2 . . . . . . . . . .17 C4
**Stoke High Sch** IP2 . . . . . . . . .17 C2
**Stoke High Sch** IP2 . . . . . . . . .17 C2
**Stoke Park Dr** IP2 . . . . . . . . . .17 A1
**Stoke Rd** Clare CO10 . . . . . . .12 A6
 Nayland CO6 . . . . . . . . . . . . .56 B2
**Stoke St** IP2 . . . . . . . . . . . . . .17 C4
**Stoke-by-Nayland Mid
 Sch** CO6 . . . . . . . . . . . . . . . .56 C6
**Stoke-by-Nayland Prim
 Sch** CO6 . . . . . . . . . . . . . . . .56 C6
**Stokeash Cl** CO16 . . . . . . . . .188 A3
**Stokebridge Maltings** 1
 IP2 . . . . . . . . . . . . . . . . . . . . . .17 C4
**Stokes The** CO14 . . . . . . . . . .171 B8
**Stone La** Tiptree CO5 . . . . . . .179 C4
 Wrabness CO11 . . . . . . . . . . . .88 E5
**Stone Lodge La** CO3 . . . . . . .17 A3
**Stone Lodge La W** IP2 . . . . .17 A3
**Stone Lodge Wlk** IP2 . . . . . . .17 B3
**Stone Path Dr** CM3 . . . . . . . .193 F3
**Stone Rd** CO7 . . . . . . . . . . . .113 B1
**Stone's Green Rd** CO12 . . . .115 E2
**Stonebridge Hill** CO6 . . . . . .104 E7
**Stonechat Rd** IP2 . . . . . . . . . .16 D2
**Stonecrop** CO4 . . . . . . . . . . .109 C2
**Stonegrove Rd** IP11 . . . . . . .221 B1
**Stonehall** CO10 . . . . . . . . . . . .12 B7
**Stonehall Dr** CO16 . . . . . . . .168 D1
**Stonehall La** CO12 . . . . . . . .115 B1
**Stoneham St** CO6 . . . . . . . . .130 F2
**Stonehill Way** CO5 . . . . . . . .201 A6
**Stoneleigh Pk** CO3 . . . . . . . .134 F4
**Stoney Comm** CM24 . . . . . . .119 E5
**Stoney Common Rd**
 CM24 . . . . . . . . . . . . . . . . . . .119 D5
**Stoney La** CO10 . . . . . . . . . . .186 A8
**Stoney Pl** CM24 . . . . . . . . . . .119 E5
**Stoneyfield Dr** CM24 . . . . . . .119 E6
**Stonham Ave** CO16 . . . . . . . .188 A4
**Stony La** CM6 . . . . . . . . . . . . .70 A2
**Stopford Ct** 2 IP1 . . . . . . . . .17 A6
**Stores Rd** CO5 . . . . . . . . . . . .179 C6
**Storms Way** CM2 . . . . . . . . .206 B2
**Stort Lodge** CM23 . . . . . . . . .145 D8
**Stort Rd** CM23 . . . . . . . . . . . .145 F6
**Stortford Hall Ind
 Pk** CM23 . . . . . . . . . . . . . . . .146 B7
**Stortford Hall Pk** CM23 . . . .146 B8
**Stortford Hall Rd** 3
 CM23 . . . . . . . . . . . . . . . . . . .146 B8
**Stortford Rd**
 Clavering CB11 . . . . . . . . . . . .65 C4

...rd Rd continued
...y CM6 .........123 C1
...y Ave IP11 ........221 C3
...r CI Glemsford CO10 .....2 C2
...wich CO12 .........90 D2
...r CM7 .........128 D1
...ur Gdns CO10 .........34 B4
...ur Rd CO10 .........12 B6
...ur Rd CO12 .........91 D5
...tour St Cavendish CO10 .....13 C8
Manningtree CO11 ........86 D4
Sudbury CO10 ........33 E7
Stour Vale Clare CO10 .....12 A6
Stoke by C CO10 ........10 D7
Stour Valley Rd IP9 .....9 B7
Stour Vw CO12 ........91 D5
Stour Wlk CO4 ........110 E2
Stour Wood Nature
Reserve ........89 C3
Stourdale CI CO11 ........86 A3
Stourside IP9 ........91 A8
Stourton Rd CM8 ........176 E3
Stourview Ave CO11 .......87 A4
Stourview CI CO11 .......87 B4
Stow Ct CO4 ........109 F5
Stradbroke Rd IP4 ........18 A/
Straight Rd Boxted CO4 .....82 F2
Bradfield CO11 ........87 C1
Colchester CO3 ........134 I-3
Great Bentley CO7 .......167 A4
Straight Way CO2 ........161 A2
Strand The IP2 ........37 C8
Strasbourg Sq 6 CO9 .....9 B8
Stratford PI 4 CO14 .....171 C8
Stratford Rd
Clacton-on-S CO15 ........189 D6
Dedham CO7 ........84 D7
Stratford St Mary Prim
Sch CO7 ........58 C1
Straw La CO10 ........33 D7
Strawberry CI CM7 ........128 A1
Strawberry Fields CO9 .....8 D7
Strawberry La CO5 ........179 A1
Strawbrook Hill CM3 .....173 E4
Street The Ardleigh CO7 ....111 E8
Ashen CO10 ........11 D1
Belchamp Walter CO10 .....31 C8
Belstead IP8 ........36 C6
Berden CM23 ........92 B8
Birdbrook CO9 ........28 B7
Bradfield CO11 ........87 E1
Bradwell CM7 ........129 D3
Brantham CO11 ........61 A1
Bulmer CO10 ........32 A6
Capel St M IP9 ........35 A1
Chappel CO6 ........106 D5
Crossarg CM7 ........156 A6
East Bergholt CO7 ........59 B2
Fearing CO5 ........179 B6
Foxearth CO10 ........14 C6
Galleywood CM2 ........216 B2
Gosfield CO9 ........102 E7
Great Hallingbury CM22 ....147 B4
Great Henny CO10 ........33 C3
Great Ivy CO5 ........132 C8
Harkstead IP9 ........63 B2
Hatfield Peverel CM3 .....193 F4
Holbrook IPv ........62 D6
Kirby-le-S CO13 ........143 B1
Little Clacton CO16 ........168 C4
Little Dunmow CM6 .......151 D7
Little Horsham CM7 ........197 B5
Little Waltham CM3 ........191 B6
Manuden CM23 ........92 F2
Messing CO5 ........160 A2
Pebmarsh CO9 ........78 A8
Pentlow CO10 ........14 A8
Purleigh CM3 ........220 E1
Ramsey CO12 ........90 A1
Rayne CM7 ........126 F2
Salcott-cum-virley CM9 ....199 B8
Sisted CM7 ........129 C6
Stoke by C CO10 ........11 B3
Tendring CO16 ........140 E5
Terling CM3 ........175 C2
Toppesfield CO9 ........50 B7
Washbrook IP8 ........35 F8
Weeley CO16 ........140 F1
White Notley CM8 ........155 E1
Wickham Bishops CM8 ....195 F5
Woodham Walter CM9 ....208 D2
Stretford Ct CM3 ........156 D3
Strethall Rd CB11 ........21 C4
Strickmere CO7 ........58 D2
Strood Ct CO5 ........201 B7
Strood Dr CO5 ........183 C3
Strudwick CI 10 CM7 ....127 F2
Strutt CI CM3 ........194 A4
Stuart CI
Great Baddow CM2 ........217 B6
Ipswich IP4 ........17 F7
Stuart Pawsey Ct CO7 ....13 C1
Stuart's Way CM7 ........128 B2
Stubbs CI Ipswich IP3 .....18 A1
Kirby Cross CO13 ........170 E7
Lawford CO11 ........86 B4
Stubbs La CM7 ........155 A8
Studd's La CO4 ........109 D4
Stump Cross CB10 ........3 C5
Stump La CM1 ........205 D4
Sturdee Ave IP3 ........18 B3
Sturmer CI 10 CO12 ....136 A1
Sturmer Rd Haverhill CB9 ....9 C6
Haverhill, Calford Green CB9 ....9 F7
Sturrick La CO7 ........139 D1
Stutton CI IP9 ........62 A2

Stutton Gn IP9 ........62 C1
Stutton La IP9 ........61 C5
Stutton Rd CO11 ........61 A2
Stylemans La CM22 ......146 B5
Styles CM7 ........71 D2
Sub-Station Rd IP11 .....221 B2
Subbourne Ave CO16 .....168 C4
Sudbourne Rd IP11 .......221 B5
Sudbury Rd Bulmer CO10 ....32 F6
Bures CO8 ........55 F1
Castle Hedingham CO9 .....52 B4
Felixstowe IP11 ........221 A4
Gestingthorpe CO9 ........31 F2
Great Cornard CO10 ........34 F7
Great Maplestead CO9 .....53 C2
Halstead CO9 ........76 F3
Long Melford CO10 ........13 C5
Stoke-by-N CO6 ........56 C6
Sudbury Sta CO10 ........33 F7
Sudbury Upper Sch CO10 ....15 F1
Sue Ryder Mus CO10 ........1 D1
Suffolk Ave CO5 ........201 D7
Suffolk CI
Clacton-on-S CO15 ........189 E7
Colchester CO4 ........110 B1
Suffolk Cres CO9 ........209 E1
Suffolk Dr CM2 ........206 A4
Suffolk Ent Pk IP1 ........17 B5
Suffolk Knowle CO10 .....65 F1
Suffolk Rd Ipswich IP4 ....17 D7
Maldon CM9 ........209 E1
Sudbury CO10 ........33 E8
Suffolk Ent Pk IP1 ........17 A6
Suffolk Ski Ctr IP2 ........37 A8
Suffolk Sq CO10 ........33 E8
Suffolk St CO14 ........171 C8
Sugar La CO9 ........74 E7
Sulleys Hill IP7 ........58 B8
Sullivan CI CO4 ........136 E1
Summer Garden Ct CO9 ....51 E1
Summer Hill Rd CB11 .....43 D8
Summercroft Jun & Inf
Schs CM23 ........146 C8
Summerfield CI IP4 ........18 D8
Summerfield CI IP4 ........18 D8
Summerfields CO9 ........51 E1
Sun Lido Square Gdns
CM7 ........127 C2
Sunbank CM6 ........150 C7
Sunbeam Ave CO15 .......203 E6
Sunbury Way CM9 ........220 F8
Sundale CI CO15 ........189 F6
Sunfield CI IP4 ........18 A6
Sunflower CI 5 CM1 .....205 F6
Sunningdale CM23 ........145 E6
Sunningdale Ave IP4 .....18 D5
Sunningdale Dr IP11 .....221 F6
Sunningdale Fall CM3 ....194 B4
Sunningdale Rd CM1 .....204 E4
Sunningdale Way CO13 ....170 C7
Sunny Point CO14 ........144 E3
Sunnyfields Rd CM7 ......102 D2
Sunnyside Brightrae LM7 ....127 E3
Stansted
Mountfitchet CM24 ........119 E6
Sunnyside Rd CO6 ........107 D5
Sunnyside Way CO16 .....168 C1
Sunnyways Cotts CM3 ....218 E3
Sunray Ave IP11 ........221 F6
Sunrise Ave CM1 ........205 A5
Surbiton Rd IP1 ........16 F8
Surrey Ct CO15 ........169 A2
Surrey La CO5 ........179 C4
Surrey Rd Felixstowe IP11 ....221 A4
Ipswich IP1 ........17 A6
Sussex CI CMU ........200 C7
Sussex Gdns CO15 ........189 E6
Sussex Rd CO3 ........135 C7
Sutherland Ho CM1 ......205 A4
Sutor Ct CM8 ........176 E1
Sutton CE Prim Sch IP9 ....62 A2
Sutton Mead CM2 ........206 A4
Sutton Park Ave CO3 ....135 A1
Swallow CI CO2 ........162 A5
Swallow Field CO6 .......105 B6
Swallow Path CM2 ........216 B5
Swallow Rd IP2 ........16 C3
Swallow's Row CO7 .......140 B1
Swallowdale
Clacton-on-S CO15 .......188 F6
Colchester CO2 ........136 C3
Swan Chase CO9 ........77 D8
Swan CI Colchester CO1 ....135 F7
Maldon CM9 ........210 B4
New Mistley CO11 ........87 A3
Sible Hedingham CO9 ....75 E8
Swan Dale CO15 ........188 F6
Swan Farm Mews IP8 ....16 C4
Swan Gr CO6 ........106 C5
Swan Hill IP8 ........16 A2
Swan La Haverhill CB9 ....9 A8
Long Melford CO10 ........15 C7
Margaretting CM4 ........215 D3
Swan Pas 11 CO1 ........135 D7
Swan Rd CO16 ........141 D5
Swan Side CM7 ........127 F3
Swan St Chappel CO6 ....106 C5
Kelvedon CO5 ........158 D3
Sible Hedingham CO9 ....75 E8
Swan Yd CM6 ........131 A2
Swanfield CO10 ........15 C7
Swanscomb Rd CO6 .....105 F5
Swansea Ave IP2 ........17 B1

Swatchway CI IP3 ........38 B8
Swaynes CO7 ........55 C2
Sweden CI CO12 ........90 F4
Sweden CI CO11 ........115 B5
Sweet Briar CM23 ........145 B6
Sweet Briar Rd CO3 .....134 C7
Sweet Mead CB10 ........22 E3
Swift Ave CO15 ........203 F6
Swift CI CM7 ........155 A7
Swinbourne Dr CM7 ......127 D3
Swinton CI IP2 ........16 D1
Swiss Ave CM1 ........205 A4
Sworders Yd 8 CM23 ....145 F7
Sycamore CI Ipswich IP8 ....16 C1
Takeley CM22 ........148 C7
Witham CM8 ........177 A5
Sycamore Gr CM7 ........127 E1
Sycamore PI CO7 ........166 E8
Sycamore Rd
Colchester CO4 ........136 D8
Great Cornard CO10 ........34 B7
Heybridge CM9 ........210 C8
Sycamore Way
Brantham CO11 ........60 D1
Chelmsford CM2 ........216 C6
Clacton-on-S CO15 ........188 C3
Kirby Cross CO13 ........170 D6
Sycamores The CM7 .....145 B6
Sydner CI CM2 ........217 A5
Sydney St
Brightlingsea CO7 ........185 F6
Colchester CO2 ........136 B3
Syers Field CM7 ........74 B2
Sylvan CI CM2 ........216 B6
Symmons CI CM7 ........126 F1
Syringa CI 6 CO4 ........136 E7

# T

Tabor PI CM8 ........177 B3
Tabor Ave CM7 ........127 E3
Tabor CI CO7 ........137 D4
Tabor High (Mid) Sch
CM7 ........127 E3
Tabor High (Upper
Sch) The CM7 ........127 D4
Tabor Rd CO1 ........136 C7
Tabor's Hill CM2 ........216 B8
Tabors Ave CM2 ........216 F8
Tacket St IP4 ........17 D5
Tacon CI IP11 ........221 C1
Tacon Rd IP11 ........221 C1
Tailors CM23 ........145 B5
Talbot Ave CO5 ........203 F6
Talbot Rd
Little Clacton CO16 .......168 C4
Sudbury CO10 ........33 C7
Talbot St CO12 ........91 D5
Talbots IP11 ........221 D3
Talcott Rd CO2 ........136 A2
Talisman CI CO5 ........179 D6
Talisman Wlk CO5 ........179 D6
Tall Trees CO9 ........109 E3
Tally Ho CO4 ........110 B4
Tallyho Cnr CO7 ........58 D1
Tamar Rise CM1 ........205 C4
Tamarisk Way
Clacton-on-S CO15 .......203 F6
Colchester CO4 ........136 E8
Tambour CI CO6 ........132 C8
Tamdown Way CM7 ......127 C4
Tamworth Chase CO2 ....164 A2
Tan La CO16 ........168 F4
Tangerine CI CO4 ........136 D6
Tanners Mdw CM7 ........128 D2
Tanners Way CB10 ........22 C1
Tanyard The CM6 ........70 A2
Tapestry Ct CO4 ........110 E2
Tapestry Wlk CM7 ........128 D2
Tapley Rd CM1 ........205 F6
Tapworth CI CO16 ........188 D5
Tapwoods CO3 ........135 A7
Tara CI CO4 ........110 D1
Tarragon CI CO5 ........179 D4
Tarragona Mews CO2 ....136 B4
Tasman CI CM1 ........204 E5
Tasman Rd CB9 ........9 C7
Tasmania Rd IP4 ........18 D6
Tattersall Way CM1 .....215 E7
Tattingstone CE Prim
Sch IP9 ........61 D7
Taunton Rd
Chelmsford CM1 ........205 E5
Felixstowe IP11 ........221 E5
Tavern St IP1 ........17 C5
Taverners Wlk CM8 ......176 F4
Tavistock Rd CM1 ........205 E5
Tawney CI IP7 ........3b A1
Tawneys Ride ........80 A8
Taylor Ave CM1 ........204 E5
Taylor Ct CO1 ........135 F7
Taylor Dr CM1 ........86 C4
Taylor's Rd CO5 ........163 F8
Tayspill Ct CO2 ........135 B3
Teak Wlk CM8 ........177 A4
Teal CI Colchester CO4 ....137 A8
Great Notley CM7 ........154 B5
Thistledown CO4 ........110 B3
Teal Way CO5 ........158 D2
Teapot Cnr IP7 ........57 E8
Tedder CI CO2 ........136 A4
Tees CI CM8 ........176 E3
Tees Rd CM1 ........205 C4
Teign Dr CM8 ........176 D2
Telford Rd Braintree CM7 ...128 A1
Clacton-on-S CO15 ........189 C8

Telford Way CO4 ........110 D6
Temperance Yd CO6 .....105 B6
Templar Rd CM7 ........128 D2
Templar's Ct CB9 ........8 E7
Templars CI CM8 ........176 F4
Templars Cty Inf Sch
CM8 ........176 F5
Templars Cty Jun Sch
CM8 ........176 F5
Temple CI CO13 ........171 A6
Temple Ct CO4 ........110 D2
Temple La CM8 ........156 C3
Temple Pattle CO11 ......86 C7
Temple Rd
Colchester CO2 ........135 A2
Ipswich IP3 ........18 C4
Templemead CM8 ........176 F3
Templewood Rd
CO4 ........110 E1
Ten Acre App CM9 ........209 F5
Tenby Rd IP2 ........17 B1
Tendring Cty Prim Sch
CO16 ........140 F6
Tendring Rd
Little Bentley CO7 ........140 A8
Tendring CO12 ........114 D7
Thorpe-le-S CO16 ........141 D4
Tendring Tech Coll
CO16 ........142 A1
Tendring Tech & Sixth
Form Coll CO14 ........171 A7
Tennyson CI CM7 ........154 F8
Tennyson Rd
Chelmsford CM1 ........204 F5
Ipswich IP4 ........17 F5
Maldon CM9 ........210 A1
Tenpenny Hill CO7 ........165 E5
Tenter CI CM7 ........127 F5
Tenter Field CO7 ........58 F1
Tenterfield CO4 ........150 E8
Tenterfield Rd CM9 ......210 A2
Tenterfields CB11 ........42 F1
Tenth Ave CM24 ........120 C2
Terling CE Prim Sch
CM3 ........175 C3
Terling CI CO2 ........136 A1
Terling Hall Rd
Hatfield Peverel CM3 ....193 C7
Terling CM3 ........174 F1
Terling Rd
Hatfield Peverel CM3 ....193 F6
Witham CM8 ........176 B3
Terminal Rd N CM24 ....121 B4
Terminal Rd S CM22 ....121 B4
Termitts Chase CM3 .....194 A7
Tern CI
Haverhill CB9 ........9 C7
Kelvedon CO5 ........158 D3
Tern Rd IP2 ........16 E2
Terndale CO15 ........188 F6
Terra Cotta PI CO10 ......2 E8
Terrace Hall Chase
CO6 ........109 D6
Terrace The CO10 ........1 D1
Terrace The CM6 ........152 B5
Terraces The CM23 ......194 B5
Tewkesbury Rd CO15 ....188 F4
Tey Rd
Aldham CO6 ........106 E1
Coggeshall CO6 ........131 C4
Earls Colne CO6 ........105 D4
Tey Road CI CO6 ........105 D6
Thackeray CI CM7 ........155 A8
Thames Ave CM1 ........204 D4
Thames Rd CM1 ........128 D1
Thanet Rd IP4 ........18 E1
Thatchers Dr CO7 ........137 F6
Thatchers The CM23 .....145 C5
Thaxted Prim Sch
CM6 ........70 A2
Thaxted Rd
Debden CB11 ........68 C6
Elder Street CB10 ........44 C4
Saffron Walden CB10 .....43 F8
Thaxted CB10 ........69 E8
Thaxted Wlk CO4 ........163 A8
Thebarton Rd CM1 .......18 B1
Thelsford Wlk CO4 .......136 F7
Thetford CI CM1 ........204 C1
Thetford Rd 1 IP1 ........17 A7
Thheves' Cnr CM1 ........204 A4
Third Ave
Chelmsford CM1 ........205 B5
Clacton-on-S CO15 .......189 C4
Frinton-on-S CO13 .......170 E4
Glemsford CO10 ........2 E8
Halstead CO9 ........77 B1
Harwich CO12 ........91 C3
St Osyth CO16 ........203 B6
Stansted
Mountfitchet CM24 ......120 B2
Walton-on-n-N CO14 ....144 E3
Thirlmere CI CM7 ........154 D7
Thirslet Dr CM9 ........210 C4
Thirstieth St CM24 ........120 F3
Thistle CI IP2 ........16 F4
Thistle CI CO4 ........188 D6
Thistle Down CM7 ........127 A7
Thistledown CO4 ........110 B3
Thistley CI CM8 ........211 E6
Thistley Cres CB11 ........66 E1
Thistley Green Rd CM7 ....128 B7
Thomas Ave IP11 ........221 A6
Thomas Bell Rd CO6 ....105 A6
Thomas Dr CM2 ........205 F3
Thomas Heskin Ct 11
CM23 ........146 A7

Thomas, Lord Audley
Sch CO2 ........135 F2
Thomas Rd CO15 ........188 D4
Thomas St CO7 ........185 F6
Thomas Wakley CI CO4 ....109 F5
Thompson Ave CO3 ......134 F6
Thompson Rd IP1 ........16 F8
Thorley Cnr CM23 ........145 D4
Thorley High CM23 ........145 F2
Thorley Hill CM23 ........145 F5
Thorley Hill JMI Sch
CM23 ........145 F4
Thorley La
Bishop's Stortford CM23 ....145 B4
Bishop's Stortford CM23 ....145 D3
Bishop's Stortford CM23 ....145 F3
Thorley Park Rd CM23 ....145 F4
Thorn Gr CM23 ........146 B6
Thorn Grove JMI Sch
CM23 ........146 B6
Thorn Way IP11 ........221 C4
Thornbera CI CM23 ......145 F4
Thornbera Gdns CM23 ....145 F4
Thornberry CM23 ........145 F4
Thornberry Avp t CO1 ....145 F3
Thornbury Rd CO15 ......189 F4
Thornbush La IP8 ........16 A8
Thorncroft CB10 ........22 F2
Thorndon CI CO16 ........188 A4
Thorne Rd CO5 ........158 B2
Thorney Rd IP9 ........35 A1
Thornfield Ct CO2 ........136 D2
Thornfield Rd CM23 .....145 E8
Thornhayes CI IP2 ........17 A3
Thornhill ........220 D1
Thornhill CO13 ........170 F7
Thornley Dr IP4 ........18 C8
Thorns Way CO14 ........171 A8
Thornton Dr CO4 ........109 F2
Thornton Rd CM6 ........148 F7
Thornwood CO4 ........109 F4
Thornwood CI CO5 .......201 D6
Thoroughfare IP1 ........17 C6
Thoroughgood Rd LO15 ....188 F3
Thorpe Cross CO16 ......169 D8
Thorpe Park La CO16 ....169 D7
Thorpe Rd Beaumont CO16 ....141 B5
Clacton-on-S CO15 ........188 F7
Kirby Cross CO13 ........169 E7
Weeley CO16 ........141 A2
Thorpe Wlk CO4 ........136 F7
Thorpe-le-Soken Sta
CO16 ........168 F7
Thorrington Cross CO7 ....165 F5
Thorrington Rd
Great Bentley CO7 ........166 C8
Little Clacton CO16 ......168 C4
Thorrington Tide Mill
CO7 ........165 E3
Thracian CI CO2 ........135 A3
Threadneedle St
2 Chelmsford CM1 ......205 B2
Dedham CO7 ........84 F7
Three Acres CO16 ........187 A4
Three Crowns Rd CO4 ....109 C2
Three Gates CI CO4 ......103 D8
Three Mile Hill CM4 .....215 C2
Thremhall Ave
Bishop's Stortford CM23 ....146 F8
Great Hallingbury CM24 ....147 C8
Takeley CM24 ........121 A2
Thresher CI CM23 ........145 C5
Threshers End CO3 ......134 D5
Thrift Wood CM3 ........218 F1
Thriftwood Sch The CM2 ....216 B3
Thrushdale CO15 ........188 F6
Thurlow PI 10 CB9 ........9 B8
Thurlston CI CO4 ........110 D1
Thurstable Rd CM9 ......199 C2
Thurstable Rd CM9 ......199v B2
Thurstable Sch CO5 .....179 D6
Thurstable Way CM9 ....199 F2
Thurstun CI IP11 ........221 A3
Tibbetts CI CM8 ........176 E3
Tiberius Gdns CM8 ......194 E8
Tiburius CI CB9 ........9 u7
Tiberius CI CM8 ........176 D3
Tiberius Gdns CM8 ......194 E8
Tiburius Gdns CM8 ......128 D4
Tidings Hill CO9 ........103 E8
Tilbury Rd
Great Yeldham CO9 ........30 A3
Ridgewell CO9 ........29 C2
Tile Barn La CO11 ........85 C2
Tile House Rd CO6 ........105 B8
Tilley Rd CO6 ........130 F3
Tillwicks Cl CO4 ........105 A7
Timber Hill CO1 ........136 C6
Timbers CI CM7 ........154 B7
Timsons La CM2 ........205 E4
Tinabrook CI IP2 ........16 F2
TinsIgl Sq 8 CM1 ........205 B2
Tindal St CM1 ........205 B2
Tindon End Rd CB10 ......46 D7
Tinker Ave CM7 ........73 C4
Tinker St CO12 ........116 D8
Tinnocks La CM8 ........213 B1
Tintagel Way CM9 ........220 E0
Tintern CI IP2 ........17 A2
Tippett CI CO4 ........136 E6
Tiptree Hall La CO5 .....179 B2
Tiptree Heath Cty Prim
Sch CO5 ........179 B3
Tiptree Rd
Great Braxted CM8 ........196 B8
Wickham Bishops CM8 ....195 F6

Titania Cl CO4 .............136 F7
Tithe Cl CM8 ...............176 E3
Titus Way CO14 ...........110 B6
Tobruk Rd
  Chelmsford CM1 ........204 F6
  Colchester CO2 .........135 D3
Tofts Chase CM3 ...........207 E5
Tofts Wlk 2 CM7 .........127 F3
Tog La Great Horkesley CO6 .82 A3
  Little Horkesley CO6 .....81 F3
Toga Cl CO2 ................135 A2
Tokely Rd CO7 .............139 A3
Tokio Rd IP4 ...............18 A6
Toll Gate Rd IP9 ...........35 A1
Toller Rd IP3 ..............17 E3
Tollesbury Cty Prim Sch
  CM9 ....................199 D1
Tollesbury Rd CM9 ........198 F3
Tollesbury D'arcy Prim
  Sch CM9 ...............198 D4
Tolleshunt D'arcy
  Rd CM9 ................197 F3
Tollgate Ct CO3 ...........134 C6
Tollgate Dr CO3 ...........134 C6
Tollgate E CO3 ............134 C6
Tollgate Rd CO3 ..........134 C5
Tollgate Rdbt CO3 ........134 C6
Tollgate W CO3 ...........134 B5
Tolliday Cl CO7 ...........137 A2
Tolworth Rd IP4 ..........18 A6
Tom Davies Ho 8 CM7 ...127 F2
Tom Tit La CM9 ...........219 E7
Tom's La CM7 .............72 A6
Tomline Rd
  Felixstowe IP11 .........221 E4
  Ipswich IP3 .............18 A4
Tony Webb Cl CO4 ........110 C4
Tooley's Ct
  (Almshouses) 9 IP4 ....17 D5
Top Rd
  Tolleshunt Knights CM9 ..180 A2
  Wimbish CB10 ..........45 E3
  Woodham Walter CM9 ..208 D2
Toppesfield Rd CO9 .......50 F8
Torquay Rd CM1 ..........205 D5
Torrington Cl CM1 ........205 E5
Tortoiseshell Way CM7 ...127 E1
Tortosa Cl CO2 ...........136 B4
Torver Cl CM7 ............154 C6
Tot La CM23 ..............119 D4
Totham Hill Gn CM9 ......196 E6
Totlands Dr CO15 .........189 A7
Totnes Wlk CM1 ..........205 E6
Totteridge Cl CO16 ......188 D5
Touchells Way CO15 ......188 F6
Toulmin Rd CM3 ..........194 A4
Tovell's Way IP4 ..........17 F6
Tower Ave CM1 ...........204 F4
Tower Ct 4 CB9 ...........8 E7
Tower Cut CO7 ............185 F6
Tower Est CO16 ..........185 E4
Tower Hill Redoubt
  Fort CO12 ..............91 E5
Tower Mill Rd IP1 ........18 F7
Tower Ramparts IP1 .....17 C6
Tower RampartsCtr
  8 IP1 ..................17 C6
Tower Rd
  Clacton-on-S CO15 ......188 E1
  Felixstowe IP11 .........221 D3
  Wivenhoe CO7 .........137 B2
Tower St Brightlingsea CO7 185 F6
  Ipswich IP1 ............17 C6
Towers Rd CM9 ..........210 C5
Town Croft CM1 ..........205 A5
Town End Field CM8 .....194 F8
Town St CM6 .............70 A2
Townfield St CM1 .........205 B3
Townsend Rd CO15 ......179 C7
Towse Cl CO16 ...........188 C5
Traddles Ct CM1 .........204 F6
Trafalgar Cl CM4 .........17 F6
Trafalgar Cotts CO12 ....90 F3
Trafalgar Ct CM7 ........128 B4
Trafalgar Rd
  Clacton-on-S CO15 ......188 A1
  Colchester CO3 .........134 E6
Trafalgar Way CM7 ......128 B4
Trajan Cl CO4 ............110 B6
Tree Cl CO15 .............188 F7
Treetops IP11 ............221 C6
Treetops Ct CO4 ..........109 F5
Trefoil Cl IP2 .............16 F4
Trefoil Ct 4 CB9 .........8 E7
Trelawn CM3 .............206 E8
Trenchard Cres CM1 .....205 D8
Trenchard Lodge CM1 ...205 D7
Trent Rd Chelmsford CM1 .200 D5
  Ipswich IP3 ............17 F2
  Witham CM8 ...........176 E2
Trevose IP11 .............221 F4
Trews Gdns CO5 .........158 C3
Triangle Sh Ctr CO14 ....170 F7
Trickett Ct CO7 ..........137 B1
Trimley Cl CO16 .........188 B4
Trimley St Mary Cty
  Prim Sch IP11 .........221 A7
Trimley Sta IP11 .........221 A7
Trinity Ave IP11 .........221 A4
Trinity Cl

Trinity Ct CO9 ............76 E2
Trinity Farm Ct 11 CO11 .86 D4
Trinity Mews CO5 ........201 C7
Trinity Rd Chelmsford CM2 .205 D2
  Halstead CO9 ..........76 D1
  Manningtree CO11 .....86 D3
Trinity Road Cty Prim
  Sch ....................205 D2
Trinity Sq 21 CO1 .......135 F7
Trinity St
  Bishop's Stortford CM23 .145 F6
  Colchester CO1 ........135 F7
  Halstead CO9 ..........76 D2
  Ipswich IP3 ............17 E4
Trinity Terr 3 CO9 .......76 D1
Trinity Way CM23 .......145 F6
Triumph Ave CO15 ......203 E7
Troon Gdns IP4 .........18 B8
Trotters Field CM7 ......128 B3
Trotwood Cl CM1 ........204 E7
Troys Chase CM3 ........175 C6
Trunette Rd CO15 .......188 C3
Trusses Rd CM0 ........214 F3
Truswell Terr CO11 .....86 D7
Tryon Ct 6 CO9 .........76 D1
Tucker Dr CM8 ..........176 F1
Tucker's Row 4 CM23 ..145 F6
Tuddenham Ave IP4 .....17 E7
Tuddenham Rd IP4 .....17 E8
Tudor Cl Brightlingsea CO7 .185 E8
  Jaywick CO15 .........188 A4
  Sudbury CO10 .........15 E1
  Walton-on-t-N CO14 ...144 D2
  Witham CM8 ...........176 F1
Tudor Ct CO5 ...........201 C7
Tudor Gn
  Clacton-on-S CO15 .....203 F8
  Jaywick CO15 .........187 F1
  Sudbury CO10 .........15 E2
Tudor House Mus CM7 ..128 A5
Tudor Par CO15 .........203 G8
Tudor Pl 11 IP4 .........17 D6
Tudor Prim Sch CO10 ...15 F1
Tudor Rd CO10 ..........15 E1
Tudor Rose Cl CO3 .....134 C7
Tudor Works 12 IP4 ....17 C5
Tudwick Rd CO5 .........197 B6
Tufnell Way CM4 ........109 D2
Tufted Cl CM7 ..........154 C5
Tugby Pl CM1 ...........204 E6
Tukes Way CB11 ........43 F7
Tulip Cl CM1 ...........205 E7
Tulip Way CO16 ........188 C4
Tulip Wlk CO4 ..........136 D7
Tumulus Way CO2 ......134 F2
Tunstall Cl CO16 .......187 B5
Tupman Cl CM1 ........204 D6
Turin St IP2 .............17 C4
Turkentine Cl CO10 .....34 D5
Turkey Cock La CO3 ....133 E7
Turkey Oaks CM1 ......205 D3
Turner Ave CO11 .......86 B5
Turner Cl CO7 ..........137 C1
Turner Rd Colchester CO4 .109 F3
  Ipswich IP3 ...........38 A8
Turner Village Hospl
  CO4 ...................109 F3
Turners Cres CM23 .....145 C4
Turnpike Cl CO7 ........110 E8
Turnstone End 8 CO4 ..136 F8
Turpins Ave CO15 ......189 C5
Turpins Cl CO15 ........189 C5
Turpins Ct CO15 ........189 C5
Turpins La
  Kirby Cross CO13 ......170 E7
  Kirby-le-S CO13 .......170 E8
Turret Green Ct 7 IP1 ..17 C5
Turret La IP4 ...........17 C5
Turstan Rd CM8 .........194 E8
Tusser Cl CM8 ..........177 B2
Tusser Ct CM2 ..........216 D8
Tusset Mews CO3 .......134 E7
Tweed Cl CO9 ..........103 D8
Twelve Acres CM7 ......128 D3
Twentyfirst St CM24 ....120 F3
Twin Oaks CM2 ........206 A4
Twining Rd CO3 ........134 E4
Twitten La CM2 .........216 B2
Twitty Fee CM3 .........219 A8
Two Acres IP9 ..........35 B2
Twyford Bsns Ctr The
  CM23 .................146 A4
Twyford Bury La CM22 .146 A4
Twyford Cl CM23 .......146 A5
Twyford Gdns CM23 ...145 F4
Twyford Mill CM22 .....146 A3
Twyford Rd CM23 ......146 A5
Tyburn Hill CO6 ........106 A6
Tydeman Cl CO3 ........134 C4
Tye Gn CO10 ...........2 B5
Tye Green Rd CM22 ...120 D6
Tye La CO7 ............137 E3
Tye Rd CO7 ............137 E7
Tye Rd The CO7 ........167 B7
Tyehurst Cres CO4 .....110 C2
Tyler Ave CO16 ........188 B3
Tyler St Harwich CO12 ..90 F5
  Ipswich IP2 ...........17 D4
Tylers CB10 ............23 E1
Tylers Cl CM2 ..........216 B6
Tylers Gn IP11 ..........221 A7
Tylneys Rd CO9 ........77 A3
Tymperley Ct CO1 ......136 A6
Tymperleys Clock Mus
  CO1 ...................135 F7
Tyndale Dr CO15 .......188 A1
Tyndales La CM3 .......219 B5
Tyne Way CM1 .........204 D5

Tynedale Ct CO4 ........110 B4
Tynedale Sq CO4 .......110 B4
Tyrells Cl CM2 ..........205 E4
Tyrells Way CM2 .......216 F7
Tyrells Cty Prim Sch
  The CM1 ..............205 E5
Tyssen Mead CM3 ......206 E8
Tythe Cl CM1 ..........205 E8
Tythings The CO9 ......103 D8

**U**

Ufford Pl 8 CB9 ........9 B8
Ullswater Cl CM7 .......154 C6
Ulting Hall Rd CM9 .....208 E7
Ulting La CM9 ..........208 E6
Ulting Rd CM3 .........194 C2
Una Rd CO12 ..........90 F5
Undercliff Rd W IP11 ...221 D3
Union Rd CO15 .........203 G8
Union St 11 IP4 ........17 D6
Unity Cl CO2 ...........136 B4
Unity St IP3 ............17 E4
Univ Coll Suffolk IP4 ....17 E5
Univ of Essex CO4 .....136 H4
Upland Cres CO5 .......201 C7
Upland Dr CO4 .........110 C2
Upland Rd Ipswich IP4 ..18 A6
  West Mersea CO5 ......201 C7
Uplands Cres CO10 .....15 F1
Uplands Cres CO15 ....188 D1
Uplands Dr CM1 .......205 D7
Uplands Mid Sch CO10 .15 F1
Uplands Rd
  Clacton-on-S CO15 .....188 D1
  Sudbury CO10 .........15 E1
Upper Acres CM8 ......176 F5
Upper Barclay St 12 IP4 .17 D6
Upper Branston Rd CO15 188 D4
Upper Bridge Rd CM2 ..205 A1
Upper Brook St IP4 ....17 C5
Upper Cavendish St IP3 .18 A5
Upper Chapel St CO9 ...76 E2
Upper Chase 2 CM2 ...216 A8
Upper East St CO10 ....33 F8
Upper Farm Rd CO10 ..29 D8
Upper Fenn Rd CO9 ....77 A2
Upper Fourth Ave CO13 .170 F5
Upper High St 11 IP1 ...17 C6
Upper Holt St CO6 .....105 C6
Upper Mill Field CM6 ..150 E7
Upper Moors CM3 .....190 F7
Upper Second St IP4 ...17 D5
Upper Park Rd
  Brightlingsea CO7 ......185 E7
  Clacton-on-S CO15 .....188 D3
Upper Rd CO10 ........55 E8
Upper Roman Rd CM2 ..205 B1
Upper Second Ave CO13 .170 E5
Upper St Stanstead CO10 ..2 E8
  Stratford St M CO7 ....58 D1
Upper Third Ave CO13 ..170 E5
Upper Trinity Rd CO9 ...76 E1
Upperfield Dr IP11 .....221 F6
Upsheres CB11 .........43 F8
Upton Cl Ipswich IP4 ...17 E6
  West Bergholt CO6 ....108 D4
Urban Rd CM23 ........146 B7
Usterdale Rd CB10 .....22 E3
Uxbridge Cres IP3 .....18 C1

**V**

Valance Rd CB11 .......65 A6
Vale Cl CO4 ............110 E2
Vale End CM2 ..........216 C3
Vale La IP9 ............61 B4
Valentine Cl CM7 .......154 C6
Valentine Way CM8 ....156 D3
Valentines Dr CO4 .....110 C1
Valfreda Way CO7 .....137 B2
Valkyrie Cl CM7 .......199 D2
Valletta Cl CM1 .......205 B2
Valley Bridge CM1 .....205 B6
Valley Cl Branfham CO11 ..60 D1
  Colchester CO3 .......134 E3
Valley Cres CO6 .......108 E3
Valley La Tattingstone IP9 .36 F4
  West Bergholt CO6 ....108 D4
Valley Rd Braintree CM7 .128 A4
  Clacton-on-S CO15 .....189 A5
  Colchester CO4 .......136 F4
  Harwich CO12 .........90 D2
  Ipswich IP1 ..........17 B8
  Sudbury CO10 .........34 F8
  Wivenhoe CO7 ........164 C8
Valley View
  Finchingfield CM7 .....72 D6
  Stanstead CO10 ......2 C3
  West Bergholt CO6 ....108 E3
Valleybridge Rd CO15 ..189 A5
Valleyview Dr IP4 ......18 F4
Van Dieman's La CM2 ..216 C8
Van Dieman's Rd CM2 ..216 C8
Van Dyck Rd CO3 ......135 B5
Vandenburg Circ CM7 ..73 D6
Vandyck Rd IP3 ........38 A8
Vane Ct CM8 ..........177 A5
Vane La CO6 ..........131 A2
Vanessa Dr CO7 .......137 B1
Vange Pl 7 CB9 ........9 B8
Vanguard Way CM7 ...128 B4
Vanners Rd CB9 .......9 A7
Vansittart St CO12 ....91 D5

Vineway The CO12 ......
Vineyard Gate 4 CO2 ...
Vineyard St CO2 ........1
Vineyards The
  Braintree CM7 .........15
  Great Baddow CM2 ....21
Vinnicombe Ct 3 IP2 ...16
Vint Cres CO3 ..........135
Viola Wlk CO4 .........135
Violet Cl Chelmsford CM1 .205 E
  Ipswich IP2 ...........16 F
Virgil Rd CM8 ..........176 F5
Virginia Cl CO15 .......188 A1
Virley Cl CM9 ..........210 D4
Viscount Dr CO4 .......110 C5
Vista Ave CO13 ........143 D1
Vista Rd CO15 .........189 A3
Vitlus Cl CO4 ..........110 B6
Vivian Ct CO14 ........171 C8

**W**

Waddesdon Rd CO12 ...91 D4
Wade Rd CO15 ........189 B8
Wade Reach CO14 .....171 B8
Wadgate Rd IP11 ......221 C4
Wadhurst Rd IP3 ......18 D3
Wagtail Dr CM9 ........210 C5
Wainsfield Villas CM6 ..70 B2
Wakefield Cl
  Colchester CO1 ........136 A8
  Great Chesterford CB10 ..3 D3
Wakelin Way CM8 .....177 B2
Wakes St CO6 .........106 C6
Wakeshall La CO10 ....30 C8
Waldeck Ct CB11 ......43 D7
Waldegrave Cl CO11 ...86 B3
Waldegrave Rd CO11 ..86 C3
Waldegrave Rd CO11 ..86 B3
Waldegraves La CO5 ...201 G7
Waldegraves The CO8 ..79 F8
Walden Ave CO10 .....44 E2
Walden Castle CB10 ...22 D2
Walden Cl CM9 ........196 A4
Walden Ho CO13 ......170 F4
Walden House Rd CM9 .196 A4
Walden Rd Ashdon CB10 .22 D2
  Finchingfield CM7 .....73 A2
  Great Chesterford CB10 ..3 E3
  Hadstock CB1 .........5 B6
  Littlebury CB10 ......21 F4
  Radwinter CB10 ......45 D7
  Sewards End CB10 ...23 D1
  Thaxted CM6 .........69 F5
  Wendens Ambo CB11 ..42 F6
  Wendons Ambo CB11 ..43 A4
Walden Way CO13 ....171 A6
Waldgrooms CM6 ....123 C1
Waldingfield Rd CO10 ..33 F8
Walford Pl CM2 ........205 F2
Walford Way CO6 .....131 A2
Walk The Eight Ash G CO6 ..134 A8
  Felixstowe IP11 .......221 C5
  8 Ipswich IP1 ........17 C6
Walker Cl IP1 ..........18 C5
Walkers Cl CM1 .......205 D7
Wall Ct 6 CM7 ........127 F1
Wall La CO11 ..........88 D4
Wall St CO16 ..........202 D6
Wallace Binder Cl CM9 .209 F1
Wallace Cres CM2 .....216 D8
Wallace La CM3 .......172 B7
Wallace Rd IP1 ........16 E8
Wallace's La CM3 .....192 F4
Wallasea Gdns CM1 ...205 F5
Waller's Gr IP2 ........16 F4
Wallflower Ct 11 CM1 ..205 F5
Wallis Ct CO3 .........134 E3
Walls The CO11 .......86 D4
Walnut Dr
  Bishop's Stortford CM23 .145 D3
  Witham CM8 ..........177 A4
Walnut Gr CM7 ........127 E2
Walnut Tree Cotts CM3 .190 E5
Walnut Tree La
  Farnham CM23 ........118 E4
  Harkstead IP9 .........63 B2
  Sudbury CO10 ........33 D7
Walnut Tree Way
  Colchester CO2 ........135 B3
  Tiptree CO5 ..........179 C7
Walnut Way
  Brightlingsea CO7 .....185 E7
  Clacton-on-S CO15 .....188 C2
Walnuttree Hospl CO10 .33 D7
Walsingham Cl CO10 ...34 C5
Walsingham Rd CO2 ...135 F6
Walter Porter Ct CO4 ..110 D1
Walter Radcliffe Way
  CO7 ...................137 B1
Walter Way CM8 ......156 D4
Walters Cl CM2 .......216 C3
Walters Yd 8 CO1 .....135 F7
Waltham Cl IP2 ........17 A2
Waltham Glen CM2 ....216 C7
Waltham Rd
  Boreham CM3 .........193 A3
  Terling CM3 ..........175 A2
Waltham Way CO13 ...171 A6
Walton Ave IP11 ......221 A2
Walton Cl Colchester CO7 .134 F6
  Felixstowe IP11 .......221 D6
Walton Ho 4 Ipswich IP1 .17 A6
  Walton-on-t-N CO14 ...144 D1
Walton Maritme Mus
  CO14 .................144 D1
Walton Prim Sch CO14 .144 D1

**Walton Rd**
Clacton-on-S CO15 .......... 189 A3
Frinton-on-S CO13 .......... 170 F6
Kirby-le-S CO13 .......... 143 A1
Kirby-le-S CO13 .......... 170 E8
Thorpe-le-S CO16 .......... 142 D2
Walton-on-t-N CO13 .......... 171 B7

**Walton-on-Naze Sta**
CO14 .......... 171 C7
Wantz Chase CM9 .......... 210 A3
Wantz Haven CM9 .......... 210 A2
Wantz Rd CM9 .......... 210 A2
Wapping La CO7 .......... 165 B2
Warburton Ave CO9 .......... 75 D8
Ward Cres CM23 .......... 145 E6
Ward Rd IP8 .......... 16 B2
Warde Chase CO4 .......... 171 B8
Wardle Way CM1 .......... 204 E7
Wardley Cl IP2 .......... 16 D1
Wards Croft CB11 .......... 43 D7
Warehouse Rd CM6 .......... 124 D3
Warehouse Rd CM6 .......... 124 B4
Warehouse Villas CM6 .......... 125 A4
Wargrave Rd CO15 .......... 188 D4
Warham Rd CO12 .......... 90 F1
Warley Cl CM7 .......... 128 C3
Warley Way CO13 .......... 171 B6
Warner Cl CM7 .......... 126 F1
Warner Dr CM7 .......... 127 D4
Warner Way CO10 .......... 34 A8
Warners CM6 .......... 150 D8
Warnham Cl CO16 .......... 188 C5
Warren Cl Broomfield CM1 .......... 191 R3
Takeley CM22 .......... 148 D7
Warren Ct 1 CB9 .......... 8 E7
Warren Heath Ave IP3 .......... 18 D2
Warren Heath Rd IP3 .......... 18 D2
Warren La CO3 .......... 134 C2
Warren Rd Braintree CM7 .......... 128 C2
Halstead CO9 .......... 76 D1

**Warrens The**
Kirby Cross CO13 .......... 170 E6
Little Totham CM9 .......... 195 F5
Warrenside CM7 .......... 155 A8
Warrington Rd IP1 .......... 17 B7
Warwick Bailey Cl CO4 .......... 109 D2
Warwick Cl Braintree CM7 .......... 128 B4
Little Easton CM6 .......... 122 F5
Maldon CM9 .......... 210 A1

**Warwick Cres**
Clacton-on-S CO15 .......... 188 E3
Maldon CM9 .......... 210 A1
Warwick Ct 2 CB9 .......... 8 E8
Warwick Dr CM9 .......... 210 A1

**Warwick Rd**
Bishop's Stortford CM23 .......... 146 B6
Clacton-on-S CO15 .......... 188 E3
Ipswich IP4 .......... 17 E6
Warwick Sq CM1 .......... 204 F4
Wash Cnr CO7 .......... 107 C3

**Wash La**
Clacton-on-S CO15 .......... 188 D1
Little Totham CM9 .......... 211 B7
Washford Gdns CO15 .......... 188 D2
Washington Cl CM9 .......... 209 E1

**Washington Ct**
Colchester CO3 .......... 134 E5
Maldon CM9 .......... 209 E1

**Washington Rd**
Harwich CO12 .......... 91 A2
Maldon CM9 .......... 209 F1
Wasses Cnr CO16 .......... 141 D5
Wat Tyler Wlk 1 CM1 .......... 135 F7
Watch House Rd CM6 .......... 124 F5
Watchouse Rd CM2 .......... 216 C3
Water Hall La CM7 .......... 100 F6

**Water La**
Bishop's Stortford CM23 .......... 145 F8
Bures CO8 .......... 55 C1
Cavendish CO10 .......... 1 D2
Colchester CO3 .......... 135 D8
Debden CB11 .......... 44 B1
Great Easton CM6 .......... 122 C7
Helions Bumpstead CB9 .......... 26 D0
Little Horkesley CO6 .......... 81 F8
Newport CB11 .......... 43 A1
Pebmarsh CO9 .......... 78 A7
Radwinter CB10 .......... 45 E8
Sisalford CM7 .......... 100 F3

**Water La continued**
Stansted
Mountfitchet CM24 .......... 119 E6
Steeple Bumpstead CM9 .......... 27 B6
Stisted CM7 .......... 129 C5
Stoke-by-N CO6 .......... 56 E8
Sturmer CO9 .......... 9 F5
Waterleap Pk CO15 .......... 188 C2

**Waterhouse La**
Ardleigh CO7 .......... 112 B5
Chelmsford CM1 .......... 204 F1
Waterhouse St CM1 .......... 204 F1
Waterloo La CM1 .......... 204 F1
Waterloo Rd IP1 .......... 17 A7
Watermill Rd CO5 .......... 158 E4

**Waterside**
Brightlingsea CO7 .......... 185 F5
Stansted
Mountfitchet CM24 .......... 119 E6
Waterside Rd CM0 .......... 214 F3
Waterson Vale CM2 .......... 216 C8
Waterville Mews CO2 .......... 136 B3
Waterwick Hill CB11 .......... 40 A1
Waterworks Cl CO2 .......... 162 B6
Waterworks Dr CO16 .......... 188 B5
Waterworks St 6 IP4 .......... 17 D5
Watery La Bradwell CM7 .......... 129 F1
Coggeshall CO6 .......... 130 A1
Great Dunmow CM6 .......... 150 A2

**Watery La continued**
Manuden CM23 .......... 92 C1
Watling La CM6 .......... 69 F3
Watling St CM6 .......... 70 A3
Watson Rd CO15 .......... 188 E3
Watson's Cl CB10 .......... 47 B4
Watts Cl CM1 .......... 205 D8
Watts Rd CO2 .......... 135 B2
Watts Yd CM23 .......... 93 A2
Wave Bridge Ct CM9 .......... 210 B5
Wavell Ave CO2 .......... 135 C4
Wavell Cl CM1 .......... 205 D8
Waveney Dr CM1 .......... 205 C6

**Waveney Rd**
Felixstowe IP11 .......... 221 C3
Ipswich IP1 .......... 16 E8
Waveney Terr CB9 .......... 9 A7
Wavring Ave CO13 .......... 170 E7
Way Bank La CO10 .......... 10 E7
Wayback The CB10 .......... 22 E2
Wayside CM3 .......... 218 E8
Waytemore Rd CM23 .......... 145 E6
Waytmore Castle CM21 .......... 146 A7
Wear Dr CM1 .......... 205 B6
Weathervane Cotts CM7 .......... 72 B1
Weaver Cl IP1 .......... 16 D8
Weaver St CM23 .......... 145 C4
Weaverhead Cl CM6 .......... 70 A3
Weaverhead La CM6 .......... 70 A3
Weavers Cl Braintree CM7 .......... 127 F3
Colchester CO3 .......... 134 F5
Weavers Ct Halstead CO9 .......... 76 E1
Sudbury CO10 .......... 33 E7
Weavers Dr CO10 .......... 2 B4
Weavers Gn CO6 .......... 107 D6
Weavers La CO10 .......... 33 E7
Weavers Row CO9 .......... 76 E1
Weavers Terr 7 CO10 .......... 33 E7
Weaversfield CM8 .......... 156 C5
Webb St IP2 .......... 17 C3
Webster Cl CO9 .......... 75 D8
Weddell Rd CM7 .......... 9 C6
Wedgewood Dr CO4 .......... 109 E2
Wedow Rd CM6 .......... 70 A3
Weeley By-Pass Rd
CO16 .......... 140 E1
Weeley CE Prim Sch
CO16 .......... 167 F8

**Weeley Rd**
Great Bentley CO7 .......... 166 F5
Great Bentley CO7 .......... 166 F8
Little Clacton CO16 .......... 168 C4
Weeley Sta CO16 .......... 167 F8
Weggs Willow CO4 .......... 136 C7
Weighbridge Ct CB11 .......... 43 D8
Weight Rd CM2 .......... 205 D2
Weir La CO2,CO5 .......... 163 C7
Welhams Way CO10 .......... 86 D8
Weir Field Halstead CO9 .......... 103 F8
Writtle CM1 .......... 204 A1
Well La Danbury CM3 .......... 12 B7
Danbury CM3 .......... 218 C7
Easthorpe CO5 .......... 160 A6
Galleywood CM2 .......... 216 A4
Well Side CO6 .......... 132 E3
Well St CO7 .......... 185 E7
Well Terr CM7 .......... 210 B5
Well's St 1 CM1 .......... 205 A3
Well-Green Cl CB11 .......... 43 F2
Welland Ave CM1 .......... 204 C5
Wellands CM8 .......... 195 E5
Wellands Cl CM8 .......... 195 D5
Weller Gr CM1 .......... 204 E7
Wellesley Ho 7 CO3 .......... 135 E6

**Wellesley Rd**
Clacton-on-S CO15 .......... 188 E4
Colchester CO3 .......... 135 E6
Ipswich IP4 .......... 17 E5
Wellfield Way CO13 .......... 170 D7

**Wellington Cl**
Braintree CM7 .......... 128 C4
Chelmsford CM1 .......... 204 D5
Wellington Ct 5 IP1 .......... 17 A7

**Wellington Rd**
Maldon CM7 .......... 91 F6
Maldon CM9 .......... 209 F2
Wellington St
Brightlingsea CO7 .......... 185 F6
Colchester CO3 .......... 135 E6
Ipswich IP1 .......... 17 A5
Wellington Terr 7 CB9 .......... 8 E7
Wellmeads CM7 .......... 216 B8
Wells Cl 4 IP4 .......... 17 C6
Wells Ct Chelmsford CM1 .......... 205 D5
Great Dunmow CM6 .......... 123 C1
Wells Hall Cty Prim Sch
CO10 .......... 34 B5
Wells Hall Rd CO10 .......... 34 C4
Wells Mead CB11 .......... 67 D4
Wells Rd CO11 .......... 136 B8
Wellum Cl 8 CB9 .......... 8 E7
Welshwood Park Rd CO4 .......... 110 F2
Wenden Rd CB11 .......... 43 B8
Wendy Cl IP9 .......... 63 F7
Wenham La CO7 .......... 59 D6
Wenham Rd IP8 .......... 35 C7
Wenlock Rd CO16 .......... 167 F6
Wents Cl CO7 .......... 139 C8
Wentworth Cl CM3 .......... 194 B4
Wentworth Cres CM7 .......... 128 B1
Wentworth Cty Prim
Sch CM9 .......... 209 F1
Wentworth Dr
Bishop's Stortford CM23 .......... 145 D6
Ipswich IP2 .......... 16 C2
Wentworth
Meadows CM9 .......... 209 F2
Wentworth Terr 5 CB9 .......... 8 E8

**Wesel Ave** IP11 .......... 221 B3
Wesley Ave CO4 .......... 136 C8
Wesley End Rd CO9 .......... 28 D4
West Acre Ct CO3 .......... 135 B7
West Area IP1 .......... 16 C7
West Ave Chelmsford CM1 .......... 204 F5
Clacton-on-S CO15 .......... 188 E2

**West Bank Ferry
Terminal** IP2 .......... 17 C2
West Belvedere CM3 .......... 218 F7
West Bowers Rd CM9 .......... 208 C4
West Chase CM9 .......... 209 F3
West Ct CO3 .......... 134 F7
West Dock Rd CO12 .......... 90 E5
West Dr CM7 .......... 73 C3
West End La CO12 .......... 91 B1
West End Rd Ipswich IP1 .......... 17 A5
Tiptree CO5 .......... 179 A3
West Fields CB11 .......... 43 E8
West Green Cotts CO11 .......... 86 A7

**West Hanningfield Rd**
CM2 .......... 217 A3

**West Lawn**
Galleywood CM2 .......... 216 C2
Ipswich IP4 .......... 18 C8
West Lodge Rd CO3 .......... 135 D6
West Mersea Cty Prim
Sch CO5 .......... 201 C6
West Mill Gn IP9 .......... 60 E6

**West Rd**
Bishop's Stortford CM23 .......... 145 E6
Clacton-on-S CO15 .......... 203 H8
Halstead CO9 .......... 76 E1
Ipswich IP3 .......... 38 E8
Saffron Walden CB11 .......... 43 D8
Stansted
Mountfitchet CM24 .......... 119 E6
West Sq 6 .......... 
Chelmsford CM1 .......... 205 B2
Maldon CM9 .......... 209 F3
West St Coggeshall CO6 .......... 130 E1
Colchester CO2 .......... 135 E6
Harwich CO12 .......... 91 D6
Rowhedge CO5 .......... 163 F8
Tollesbury CM9 .......... 199 C1
Walton-on-t-N CO14 .......... 171 C4
Wivenhoe CO7 .......... 164 B8

**West Station Ind Est**
CM9 .......... 220 E8
West Station Yd CM9 .......... 209 E1
West Stockwell St CO1 .......... 135 F7
West View CM22 .......... 148 C8
West View Cl CO4 .......... 110 B3
West Wood Hill CO4 .......... 109 B7
West Wy CO4 .......... 103 E8
Westbourne Ct 1 CB9 .......... 9 A8
Westbourne Gr CM2 .......... 216 D7
Westbourne Rd IP1 .......... 16 F8
Westbury Cl CO6 .......... 133 D5

**Westbury Rd**
Great Holland CO13 .......... 170 A5
Ipswich IP4 .......... 18 B8
Westcliff Ct CO15 .......... 188 E1
Westcott Cl CO16 .......... 188 D6
Westerdale CM1 .......... 205 D7
Westerfield Cir IP4 .......... 17 D7
Westerfield Rd IP4 .......... 17 D8

**Westergreen Meadow**
CM7 .......... 127 E1
Westerings Danbury CM3 .......... 217 A7
Purleigh CM3 .......... 220 D1
Westerings The CM2 .......... 216 F5
Westerlings The CM7 .......... 155 E6

**Western Cl**
Rushmere St A IP4 .......... 18 F4
Silver End CM8 .......... 156 E3
Western Ho CO5 .......... 158 C2
Western La CM8 .......... 156 E3
Western Prom CO16 .......... 185 E5

**Western Rd**
Brightlingsea CO7 .......... 185 E6
Silver End CM8 .......... 156 F3
Western's End CO11 .......... 86 D8
Westfield CO10 .......... 12 A6
Westfield Ave CM1 .......... 205 A4
Westfield Cl CM23 .......... 145 E8
Westfield Cty Prim Sch
CB9 .......... 9 F7
Westfield Dr CO6 .......... 131 A3
Westfield Rd CM23 .......... 145 E8
Westgate St IP1 .......... 17 C6
Westholme Rd IP1 .......... 17 A8
Westlake Cres CO7 .......... 137 A2
Westlands Cty Inf Sch
CM1 .......... 204 F2
Westlands Prim Sch
CM1 .......... 204 E2
Westleton Way IP11 .......... 221 B5
Westley La CB10 .......... 22 D5
Westminster Cl IP4 .......... 18 B5
Westminster Ct
Clacton-on-S CO15 .......... 189 B3
Colchester CO2 .......... 136 C4
Westminster Gdns CM7 .......... 128 B4
Westmorland Cl CO11 .......... 87 B3
Weston Rd CM1 .......... 204 B4
Westridge Rd CO15 .......... 189 A6
Westropps CO10 .......... 15 C5
Westside Ctr CO3 .......... 134 A5

**Westway**
Chelmsford CM1 .......... 215 E8
Clacton-on-S CO15 .......... 135 C8
Westwood Ave CM1 .......... 217 A8
Westwood Dr CO15 .......... 201 E6
Wet La CO4 .......... 82 E6
Wetherfield CM24 .......... 119 D7
Wetherfield CE Prim
Sch CM7 .......... 73 C3

**Wethersfield Rd**
Blackheath CO2 .......... 163 A8
Sible Hedingham CO9 .......... 51 C1
Wetzlar Cl CO2 .......... 136 B4
Weymouth Cl CO15 .......... 203 J8

**Weymouth Rd**
Chelmsford CM1 .......... 205 E6
Ipswich IP4 .......... 17 F6
Whalebone Cnr CO4 .......... 83 F7
Whaley Rd CO4 .......... 136 C7
Wharf La CO6 .......... 79 F8
Wharf St CM23 .......... 
Bishop's Stortford CM23 .......... 145 F6
Chelmsford CM2 .......... 205 C2
Heybridge Basin CM9 .......... 210 F4
Wharfe Cl CM6 .......... 176 E2
Wheat Croft CM23 .......... 145 E4
Wheater Ind Est CM8 .......... 177 B1
Wheatfield Rd CO3 .......... 134 D5
Wheatfield Way CM1 .......... 204 F3
Wheatlands CO7 .......... 137 F6
Wheatley Ave CM7 .......... 128 C3
Wheaton Rd CM8 .......... 177 B2
Wheatsheaf Cl CO11 .......... 88 D3
Wheatsheaf La CM8 .......... 136 A6
Wheatsheaf La CO11 .......... 88 D3
Wheeler's Hill CM3 .......... 191 D6
Wheelwrights CM7 .......... 145 C4
Wheelwrights The IP11 .......... 221 A6
Wherry La IP4 .......... 17 D5
Wherstead Rd Ipswich IP2 .......... 17 C2
Ipswich IP2 .......... 17 C3
Whinchat Cl IP2 .......... 16 D3
Whinfield Ave CO12 .......... 90 F1

**Whitbreads Farm La**
CM3 .......... 173 D4
Whitby Rd IP4 .......... 17 F8
White Arch Pl CO4 .......... 83 B6
White Barns CM3 .......... 172 B6
White Bear LM24 .......... 119 E8
White Cotts CM3 .......... 174 E5

**White Court Cty Prim**
Sch CM7 .......... 154 C6
White Elm Rd CM8 .......... 219 A2
White Elm St IP3 .......... 17 E4

**White Hart La**
Colchester CO4 .......... 205 F8
West Bergholt CO6 .......... 108 E5
White Horse Ave CO8 .......... 103 D8
White Horse Hill IP9 .......... 36 D1

**White Horse La**
Maldon CM9 .......... 209 F2
Newport CB11 .......... 43 A1
Witham CM8 .......... 176 F3
White Horse Rd
Capel St M IP9 .......... 35 B1
East Bergholt CO7 .......... 59 E1
White Lodge Cres CO16 .......... 142 C1
White Mead CM1 .......... 191 B2

**White Notley CE Prim**
Sch CM8 .......... 155 F1
White Notley Sta CM8 .......... 155 F2
White St CM6 .......... 150 D8
Whiteditch La CM24 .......... 215 F7
Whiteditch La CB11 .......... 42 F2
Whitefriars Way CO3 .......... 135 A5
Whitegate Rd CO7 .......... 186 A6
Whitegates CM6 .......... 97 F4
Whitehall Cl CO2 .......... 136 C4
Whitehall Gn 1 CO2 .......... 118 E1
Whitehall Ct CM2 .......... 177 A2
Whitehall Ind Est CO2 .......... 136 D4

**Whitehall La**
Bishop's Stortford CM23 .......... 118 E1
Thorpe-le-S CO16 .......... 141 C3

**Whitehall Rd**
Bishop's Stortford CM23 .......... 118 E1
Colchester CO2 .......... 136 D4
Whitehart Cl CO12 .......... 91 D6
Whitehouse Cres CM2 .......... 216 D8
Whitehouse Hill CM9 .......... 199 A2
Whitehouse La
Belchamp St P CO10 .......... 13 B7
West Bergholt CO6 .......... 108 D3
Whitehouse Rd CM6 .......... 124 F5
Whites Field CO7 .......... 59 B3
Whites La CM3 .......... 173 E6
Whitesbridge La CM4 .......... 215 D3
Whiteshot Way CB10 .......... 22 F2
Whitethorn Gdns CM2 .......... 216 C7
Whitethorn Rd IP3 .......... 18 F1
Whiteways CB10 .......... 3 C2
Whiteways CM8 .......... 176 E3
Whitewell Rd 10 CO2 .......... 135 F6
Whitland Cl IP2 .......... 16 D1
Whitlands CO10 .......... 2 B6
Whitlock Dr CO9 .......... 29 F1
Whitlock Gr CO9 .......... 30 A1
Whittaker Way CO5 .......... 201 B7
Whittington Way CM23 .......... 145 F3
Whittle Rd IP2 .......... 16 B1
Whitworth Cl IP2 .......... 16 D7
Whybrews 4 CM4 .......... 136 C8
Whyverne Cl CM1 .......... 205 E6
Wick La Ardleigh CO7 .......... 111 B8
Fingringhoe CO5 .......... 164 C3
Harwich CO12 .......... 91 B2
St Osyth CO7,CO16 .......... 167 C3
Wick Rd Colchester CO2 .......... 167 B5
Great Bentley CO7 .......... 167 B5
Langham CO4 .......... 83 F3
Thorington Street CO4, CO6 .......... 57 D2
Wicken Rd Arkesden CB11 .......... 41 F1
Newport CB11 .......... 66 F8
Wickfield Ash CM1 .......... 204 D6

**Wickham Bishop Rd**
CM3 .......... 194 D4

Wickham Hall La CM8 .......... 195 D3

**Wickham Rd**
Colchester CO3 .......... 135 D6
Witham CM8 .......... 194 F8
Wickham's Chase CM3 .......... 219 C2
Wickhambrook Ct IP11 .......... 221 A4
Wickhay Cotts CM3 .......... 207 D5
Wicklow Ave CM1 .......... 204 D6
Wicks Cl CM7 .......... 127 C4
Widford Chase CM2 .......... 215 F7
Widford Cl CM2 .......... 215 F7
Widford Gr CM2 .......... 215 F7
Widford Ind Est CM1 .......... 215 E8

**Widford Lodge Boys
Prep Sch** CM2 .......... 215 F7
Widford Park Pl CM2 .......... 215 F7
Widford Rd CM2 .......... 215 F7
Widgeon Cl IP2 .......... 16 F3
Widgeon Pl CO5 .......... 158 C2
Widleybrook CM7 .......... 74 A3

**Widleybrook La**
Wethersfield CM7 .......... 73 F3
Wethersfield CM7 .......... 74 A2
Wigboro Wick La CO16 .......... 186 F2
Wigborough Rd
Layer-de-l-H CO2 .......... 161 L1
Peldon CO5 .......... 182 C5
Wigeon Cl CM7 .......... 154 C5
Wigmore Cl IP2 .......... 16 F1
Wignall St CO11 .......... 85 F3
Wilberforce St IP1 .......... 17 A6
Wilbye Cl CO4 .......... 135 B4
Wilbye Ho CO3 .......... 135 A7
Wilding Rd IP8 .......... 16 B1
Wildwood Cl CO4 .......... 135 A4
Wilkinsons Mead CM2 .......... 206 A4
Will's Ayley La CB1u .......... 23 F2
Willats Pond CO7 .......... 59 E1
Willatt Rd CO2 .......... 135 B3
Willetts Field CB10 .......... 47 A3
William Booth Way IP1 .......... 221 B5
William Boys Cl 1 CM3 .......... 136 D8
William Cl CO7 .......... 137 C4
William Dr CO15 .......... 188 D2
William Groom Ave CO12 .......... 91 A2
William Ho 9 CM2 .......... 17 A6

**William Julien
Courtauld Hospl** CM7 .......... 127 E2

**William Paul Housing
Trust 3** IP1 .......... 17 C4
William Sparrow Ct CO7 .......... 137 C2
William St 8 IP1 .......... 17 A4
William's Wlk 9 CO1 .......... 135 F7
Williams Rd CM1 .......... 191 B1
Williamson Ho 2 CO1 .......... 136 A6
Willinghale Rd CM7 .......... 128 D4
Willingham Way CO4 .......... 136 E7
Willoughby Ave CO5 .......... 201 D6
Willoughby Dr CM2 .......... 205 E2
Willoughby Rd IP2 .......... 17 B4
Willoughby's La CM7 .......... 128 C8
Willow Ave
Kirby Cross CO13 .......... 170 D6
St Osyth CO16 .......... 203 B6
Willow Cl Ardleigh CO7 .......... 110 D6
Bishop's Stortford CM23 .......... 145 E8
Brightlingsea CO7 .......... 185 D6
Broomfield CM1 .......... 191 B1
Willow Cres CM3 .......... 194 A3
Willow Hall La CO11 .......... 115 D8
Willow Mdws CO9 .......... 75 F8
Willow Pk CO6 .......... 133 D7
Willow Rise CM8 .......... 177 A5
Willow Springs CM23 .......... 145 D8
Willow Tree Cl 1 CM4 .......... 136 F8
Willow Tree Way CO6 .......... 105 B6
Willow Way
Clacton-on-S CO15 .......... 203 G2
Halstead CO9 .......... 76 D1
Harwich CO12 .......... 90 F2
Willow Wlk Tiptree CO5 .......... 179 C7
Weeley CO16 .......... 167 F8
Willowbank CM2 .......... 216 D3
Willowdene CO7 .......... 51 D2
Willows The Boreham CM3 .......... 206 F8
Colchester CO3 .......... 136 A3
Frinton on-S CO13 .......... 170 F5
Great Cestreforu CB10 .......... 3 D5
Wills Gn CO5 .......... 158 F6
Wilmington Rd CO4 .......... 110 C2
Wilmslow Dr IP2 .......... 16 C2
Wilshire Ave CM2 .......... 205 F3
Wilson Cl
Bishop's Stortford CM23 .......... 145 F5
Wivenhoe CO7 .......... 137 A2
Wilson Ct CO15 .......... 189 B8
Wilson Marriage Rd CO4 .......... 110 C1
Wilson Rd IP3 .......... 16 B1
Wilson's Ct CM9 .......... 210 B2
Wilson's La CO6 .......... 132 E3
Wilton Cl CM23 .......... 146 B7
Wimbish Wlk CB10 .......... 44 E2
Wimborne Ave IP3 .......... 18 E4
Wimbourne Gdns CO13 .......... 170 F7
Wimpole Ct IP5 .......... 18 F6
Wimpole Rd CO1 .......... 136 C5
Wimsey Ct CM8 .......... 176 E3
Wincelow Hall Rd CB10 .......... 25 E2
Winchelsea Dr CM2 .......... 216 E7
Winchelsea Pl CO7 .......... 185 F8
Winchester Cl CM23 .......... 145 D4
Winchester Ct
Colchester CO2 .......... 136 B5
Frinton-on-S CO13 .......... 171 A5
Winchester Way IP2 .......... 36 F8

Winckford Cl CM3 . . . . . . . .191 B6
Windermere Cl IP3 . . . . . . . . .38 B8
Windermere Ct CO15 . . . . . .189 A3
Windermere Dr CM7 . . . . . .154 C6
Windermere Rd
  Clacton-on-S CO15 . . . . . . .189 C6
  Great Notley CM7 . . . . . . . .154 C7
  Sudbury CO10 . . . . . . . . . . .34 A8
Windham Rd CO10 . . . . . . . .34 B8
Windhill CM23 . . . . . . . . . .145 E7
Windhill Old Rd CM23 . . . . .145 E7
Winding Piece IP9 . . . . . . . . .35 A1
Windmill Cl Boxted CO4 . . . . .82 F4
  Great Dunmow CM6 . . . . . .123 E1
  Ramsey CO12 . . . . . . . . . . .89 F1
Windmill Ct
  Clacton-on-S CO15 . . . . . . .188 F5
  Colchester CO4 . . . . . . . . . .109 E4
  Copford CO6 . . . . . . . . . . .133 D4
Windmill Fields CO6 . . . . . .130 F3
Windmill Gdns CM7 . . . . . . .128 A8
Windmill Hill CB10 . . . . . . . .22 B3
Windmill Pk CO15 . . . . . . . .188 F5
Windmill Rd Bradfield CO11 . .87 C1
  Halstead CO9 . . . . . . . . . . . .76 D1
Windmill Row CO10 . . . . . . . .2 C5
Windmill View CO5 . . . . . . .179 C6
Windmills CO6 . . . . . . . . . .106 C1
Windmills The CM1 . . . . . . .191 B3
Windrush Dr CM1 . . . . . . . .205 C6
Windsor Ave CO15 . . . . . . . .188 D3
Windsor Cl CO2 . . . . . . . . . .136 A2
Windsor Ct
  Brightlingsea CO7 . . . . . . . .185 F6
  **[6]** Colchester CO1 . . . . . . .136 C6
Windsor Gdns
  Bishop's Stortford CM23 . . .145 C7
  Braintree CM7 . . . . . . . . . .128 B4
Windsor Ho CO5 . . . . . . . . .201 D7
Windsor Pl CO10 . . . . . . . . .34 A7
Windsor Rd
  Clacton-on-S CO15 . . . . . . .188 D3
  Felixstowe IP11 . . . . . . . . . .221 C3
  Ipswich IP1 . . . . . . . . . . . . . .8 E6
  West Mersea CO5 . . . . . . . .201 D7
Windsor Sch CO15 . . . . . . . .189 B4
Windsor Terr CB9 . . . . . . . . . .8 E8
Windsor Way CM1 . . . . . . . .204 E1
Winfield Terr CO14 . . . . . . .144 D2
Winfrith Rd IP3 . . . . . . . . . . .18 D4
Wingate Cl CM7 . . . . . . . . . .127 E5
Wingfield St IP4 . . . . . . . . . .17 D5
Wingrove Ct CM1 . . . . . . . .205 A6
Winnock Rd CO1 . . . . . . . . .136 A6
Winnock's
  Almshouses CO1 . . . . . . . . .136 A6
Winnocks **[5]** CO1 . . . . . . . .136 A6
Winsey Chase CM7 . . . . . . . .72 C6
Winsford Way CM2 . . . . . . .206 C6
Winsgate Ho **[6]** IP1 . . . . . . . .17 A7
Winsley Rd CO1 . . . . . . . . . .136 B4
Winsley Sq CO1 . . . . . . . . . .136 B4
Winstanley Rd CB11 . . . . . . .43 E7
Winston Ave
  Colchester CO3 . . . . . . . . . .135 B4
  Ipswich IP4 . . . . . . . . . . . . .18 C8
  Tiptree CO5 . . . . . . . . . . . .179 E5
Winston Cl Braintree CM7 . .127 E6
  Felixstowe IP11 . . . . . . . . . .221 B5

Winston Ct CO13 . . . . . . . . .170 F4
Winston Way CO9 . . . . . . . . .77 A3
Winstree Ct CO3 . . . . . . . . . .134 C4
Winstree Rd CO3 . . . . . . . . .134 D5
Winstreet Cl CO2 . . . . . . . . .161 F5
Winter's Hill CO2 . . . . . . . . .160 F1
Winter's Rd CO5 . . . . . . . . . .160 E1
Winterbournes CO14 . . . . . .171 A7
Wisdoms Gn CO6 . . . . . . . . .131 B3
Wistaria Ct **[3]** CO4 . . . . . . .136 E7
Wistaria Pl CO16 . . . . . . . . .188 C5
Wisteria Lodge **[7]** CM1 . . .205 F6
Wiston Rd CO6 . . . . . . . . . . .81 D8
Witch Elm CO12 . . . . . . . . . .90 F2
Witch La CO6 . . . . . . . . . . .131 B8
Witchtree La CB10 . . . . . . . .25 F3
Witham Lodge CM8 . . . . . . .194 D7
Witham Rd
  Black Notley CM7 . . . . . . . .155 B5
  Cressing CM7 . . . . . . . . . . .156 B3
  Heybridge CM9 . . . . . . . . . .209 D7
  Terling CM3 . . . . . . . . . . . .175 E2
  Tolleshunt Major CM9 . . . . .197 D5
  Wickham Bishops CM8 . . . . .195 E6
Witham Sta CM8 . . . . . . . . .177 B2
Withersfield Rd CB9 . . . . . . . .8 F8
Withipoll St IP4 . . . . . . . . . . .17 D6
Withrick Wlk CO16 . . . . . . .187 A5
Witting Cl CO16 . . . . . . . . . .188 D5
Witton Wood Rd CO13 . . . .170 E5
Wivenhoe Cross CO7 . . . . . .137 C2
Wivenhoe Rd
  Alresford CO7 . . . . . . . . . . .165 B7
  Colchester CO7 . . . . . . . . . .111 C1
Wivenhoe Sta CO7 . . . . . . .164 B8
Wix By-Pass CO11 . . . . . . . .115 C6
Wix Cty Prim Sch CO11 . . . .115 B5
Wix Rd Beaumont CO16 . . . .141 E8
  Bradfield CO11 . . . . . . . . . . .87 E1
  Great Oakley CO12 . . . . . . .116 B3
  Ramsey CO12 . . . . . . . . . . .89 F1
  Tendring CO11 . . . . . . . . . .114 F8
  Wix CO11 . . . . . . . . . . . . . .115 C3
Woburn Ave
  Bishop's Stortford CM23 . . .145 C7
  Kirby Cross CO13 . . . . . . . .170 D7
Woburn Ct **[1]** CM2 . . . . . . .205 A1
Wolfe Ave CO1, CO2 . . . . . .136 A5
Wolmers Hey CM3 . . . . . . . .190 F7
Wolseley Ave CO15 . . . . . . .203 E6
Wolseley Rd CM2 . . . . . . . . .205 A1
Wolsey Art Gall IP4 . . . . . . . .17 D6
Wolsey Ct IP11 . . . . . . . . . . .221 E3
Wolsey Gdns IP11 . . . . . . . .221 E3
Wolsey St **[8]** IP1 . . . . . . . . .17 C5
Wolton Rd CO2 . . . . . . . . . .135 B2
Wolves Hall La CO16 . . . . . .114 F1
Wood Barn La CO11 . . . . . . .85 D1
Wood Cnr CM9 . . . . . . . . . .209 B2
Wood Dale CM2 . . . . . . . . . .216 E6
Wood End CB11 . . . . . . . . . .67 D3
Wood Field End CO2 . . . . . .162 A5
Wood La
  Birchanger CM23 . . . . . . . .119 C2
  Fordham Heath CO3 . . . . . .107 F1
  Harkstead SG9 . . . . . . . . . . .64 A6
  Heybridge CM9 . . . . . . . . . .210 A5
Wood Rd CM9 . . . . . . . . . . .210 B6
Wood St CM2 . . . . . . . . . . .216 A7
Wood Way CM7 . . . . . . . . . .154 B6
Woodberry Way CO14 . . . . .171 C7
Woodbridge Gr CO16 . . . . .188 A4

Woodbridge Rd
  Ipswich IP4 . . . . . . . . . . . . .17 E6
  Ipswich, California IP5 . . . . .18 B7
  Rushmere St A IP5 . . . . . . . .18 E7
Woodbridge Rd E IP4 . . . . . .18 D7
Woodcock Cl
  Colchester CO4 . . . . . . . . . .136 E6
  Haverhill CB9 . . . . . . . . . . . . .9 C7
Woodcock Rd IP2 . . . . . . . . .16 E2
Woodfield Cl Stansted
  Mountfitchet CM24 . . . . . . .119 E6
  Walton-on-t-N CO14 . . . . . .171 A7
Woodfield Cotts CM9 . . . . . .210 C6
Woodfield Dr CO5 . . . . . . . .201 B7
Woodfield La IP9 . . . . . . . . . .61 E3
Woodfield Rd CM7 . . . . . . . .128 A3
Woodfield Terr CM24 . . . . . .119 E6
Woodfield Way CM3 . . . . . . .194 A4
Woodfields CM24 . . . . . . . . .119 E6
Woodford Cl CO15 . . . . . . . .188 F8
Woodgates IP11 . . . . . . . . . .221 B6
Woodgates Rd CO7 . . . . . . . .59 D5
Woodhall Bsns Pk CO10 . . . .15 F2
Woodhall Cl CO10 . . . . . . . . .15 E1
Woodhall Cty Prim
  Sch CO10 . . . . . . . . . . . . . . .15 F2
Woodhall Gr CM23 . . . . . . . .145 D6
Woodhall Hill CM1 . . . . . . . .190 C2
Woodhall Par CM1 . . . . . . . .205 A7
Woodhall Rd
  Chelmsford CM1 . . . . . . . . .205 A7
  Sudbury CO10 . . . . . . . . . . .15 E1
Woodham Dr CM3 . . . . . . . .194 B4
Woodham Mortimer Rd
  CM9 . . . . . . . . . . . . . . . . . .219 E8
Woodham Walter Prim
  Sch CM9 . . . . . . . . . . . . . .208 D3
Woodhill Rd Danbury CM3 . .218 B6
  Sandon CM2 . . . . . . . . . . . .217 E6
Woodhouse La CM3 . . . . . . .191 A4
Woodhouse Sq **[5]** IP4 . . . .17 D5
Woodland Chase CO3 . . . . . .107 F1
Woodland Cl CM3 . . . . . . . .194 A5
Woodland Dr CO3 . . . . . . . .134 F5
Woodland Rd CM1 . . . . . . . .205 A4
Woodland Way
  Gosfield CO9 . . . . . . . . . . . .102 E8
  Wivenhoe CO7 . . . . . . . . . .137 B1
Woodlands
  Bishop's Stortford CM23 . . .146 C8
  Braintree CM7 . . . . . . . . . .128 C3
  Broomfield CM1 . . . . . . . . .191 A4
  Chelmondiston IP9 . . . . . . . .63 E7
  Colchester CO4 . . . . . . . . . .110 F2
  Great Oakley CO12 . . . . . . .116 B2
  Ipswich IP8 . . . . . . . . . . . . .16 C1
  Jaywick CO16 . . . . . . . . . . .188 A1
Woodlands Cl CO15 . . . . . . .189 A8
Woodlands Park Dr CM6 . . .123 B1
Woodlands Rd IP9 . . . . . . . . .62 D7
Woodlands Rise CO16 . . . . .140 F1
Woodlands Sch CM1 . . . . . .204 F6
Woodlands The CO7 . . . . . . .185 E8
Woodlands Wlk CM6 . . . . . .123 B1
Woodlark Cl IP2 . . . . . . . . . . .16 E1
Woodlyn Ct CO15 . . . . . . . .189 E6
Woodpecker Cl
  **[2]** Bishop's Stortford CM23 . .145 C6
  **[2]** Colchester CO4 . . . . . .136 F8
Woodpecker Rd IP2 . . . . . . .16 D3
Woodroffe Cl CM2 . . . . . . . .206 A3
Woodrolfe Farm La CM9 . . .199 E1

Woodrolfe Pk CM9 . . . . . . .199 F2
Woodrolfe Rd CM9 . . . . . . .199 E2
Woodrose Lodge **[6]** CM1 . .205 F6
Woodrow Way CO4 . . . . . . .136 E7
Woodrows La CO16 . . . . . . .188 B5
Woodrush End CO3 . . . . . . .134 B6
Woodrush Rd IP3 . . . . . . . . .18 E2
Woods Rd CM3 . . . . . . . . . .172 B6
Woodside
  Bishop's Stortford CM23 . . .146 D8
  Great Totham CM9 . . . . . . .196 B3
  Little Baddow CM3 . . . . . . .207 F1
  Walton-on-t-N CO14 . . . . . .171 B7
Woodside Cl CO4 . . . . . . . . .110 E1
Woodside Way CM6 . . . . . . .123 A1
Woodspring Cl **[2]** IP2 . . . .17 A2
Woodstock CO5 . . . . . . . . . .201 C7
Woodview Cl CO4 . . . . . . . .110 D4
Woodview Cotts CO5 . . . . . .180 C8
Woodview Dr CM3 . . . . . . . .174 A7
Woodview Rd CM6 . . . . . . . .150 D8
Woodville Rd IP4 . . . . . . . . . .17 F5
Woodyards CM0 . . . . . . . . . .214 F3
Woollards Cl IP11 . . . . . . . . . .17 A6
Woollards Gdns CO10 . . . . . .15 C8
Woolner Rd CO16 . . . . . . . .188 D6
Woolnough Cl CB9 . . . . . . . . .27 B6
Woolpack La CM7 . . . . . . . .127 F5
Woolpit Downs CO6 . . . . . . .79 E8
Woolpit's Rd CM7 . . . . . . . . .99 E1
Woolverstone Cl IP2 . . . . . . .16 C1
Woolwich Rd CO16 . . . . . . .188 C5
Worcester Cl CM7 . . . . . . . .128 A1
Worcester Cres CO7 . . . . . . .165 B8
Worcester Ct
  Clacton-on-S CO15 . . . . . . .188 E1
  Great Baddow CM2 . . . . . . .217 A5
Worcester Rd
  Colchester CO1 . . . . . . . . . .136 A8
  Ipswich IP3 . . . . . . . . . . . . .38 B8
Wordsworth Ct CM1 . . . . . .205 A5
Wordsworth Rd
  Braintree CM7 . . . . . . . . . .127 F7
  Colchester CO3 . . . . . . . . . .134 F6
Workhouse Corner CO2 . . . .116 C3
Workhouse Hill CO4 . . . . . . .82 E5
Workhouse Rd CO6 . . . . . . . .81 C2
Worlds End Ct CO5 . . . . . . .158 D3
Worsdell Way CO4 . . . . . . . .110 B6
Worsley Cl IP2 . . . . . . . . . . . .16 D2
Wortham Pl CM9 . . . . . . . . . .9 A8
Worthing Mews CO15 . . . . .203 I8
Worthington Way CO3 . . . . .134 F4
Wrabness Local Nature
  Reserve CO11 . . . . . . . . . . .88 D4
Wrabness Rd Ramsey CO12 . .89 D3
  Ramsey CO12 . . . . . . . . . . .90 A2
Wrabness Sta CO11 . . . . . . .89 A4
Wraglins The CM23 . . . . . . .146 B5
Wratting Rd CB9 . . . . . . . . . . .9 A8
Wren Ave IP2 . . . . . . . . . . . .16 D3
Wren Cl CO7 . . . . . . . . . . . .139 D1
Wrenbrook Rd CM23 . . . . . .145 F6
Wrendale CO15 . . . . . . . . . .188 E6
Wright Ct **[2]** CM7 . . . . . . .127 F3
Wright Rd IP3 . . . . . . . . . . . .18 C2
Wright's Ave CM7 . . . . . . . .155 E6
Wright's Piece CM22 . . . . . . .95 A6
Writtle Cl CO16 . . . . . . . . . .188 B4
Writtle Coll CM1 . . . . . . . . .204 B3
Writtle Cty Jun & Inf
  Schs CM1 . . . . . . . . . . . . . .215 A8

Writtle Rd CM1 . . . . . . . . . .215 E8
Wroxham Cl CO3 . . . . . . . . .135 B6
Wroxham Rd IP3 . . . . . . . . . .17 F3
Wryneck Cl CO4 . . . . . . . . .109 F3
Wulvesford CM8 . . . . . . . . . .194 D8
Wyatts La CO10 . . . . . . . . . . .55 D8
Wych Elm CO2 . . . . . . . . . .136 A3
Wycke Hill CM9 . . . . . . . . . .220 D8
Wycke Hill Bsns Pk CM9 . . .220 E8
Wycke La CM9 . . . . . . . . . . .213 E8
Wycliffe Gr CO11 . . . . . . . . .109 E1
Wye Rd IP3 . . . . . . . . . . . . . .18 A3
Wykeham Rd CM1 . . . . . . . .204 B1
Wykes Bishop St IP3 . . . . . . .17 E4
Wyncolls Rd CO4 . . . . . . . . .110 C6
Wyndham Cl CO2 . . . . . . . .163 B8
Wyndham Cres CO15 . . . . . .189 A5
Wynterton Cl IP3 . . . . . . . . . .18 B1
Wynyard Rd CB10 . . . . . . . . .22 E2
Wyseman Pl CO11 . . . . . . . .86 C7
Wyvern Ct CO7 . . . . . . . . . .137 B1
Wyverne CM6 . . . . . . . . . . .151 A5

**Y**

Yale Mews CO4 . . . . . . . . . .110 B4
Yardley Hall La CM6 . . . . . . .69 D6
Yare Ave CM8 . . . . . . . . . . .176 D2
Yarmouth Cl CO16 . . . . . . . .188 E6
Yarmouth Pl CB9 . . . . . . . . . .9 A8
Yarmouth Rd IP1 . . . . . . . . . .17 A6
Yarwood Rd CM2 . . . . . . . . .205 E2
Yeldham Lock CM2 . . . . . . .206 A2
Yeldham Pl CB9 . . . . . . . . . . .9 A8
Yeldham Rd CO9 . . . . . . . . . .51 D3
Yeoman Rd IP11 . . . . . . . . .221 B3
Yeomans Cl CM23 . . . . . . . .145 D6
Yerril Garden CB9 . . . . . . . . .8 E7
Yew Cl CM8 . . . . . . . . . . . .177 B5
Yew Ct IP2 . . . . . . . . . . . . . .17 B3
Yew Tree Cl
  Colchester CO4 . . . . . . . . . .136 E8
  Hatfield Peverel CM3 . . . . . .194 A5
Yew Tree Gdns CM2 . . . . . .216 C6
Yew Tree Pl CM23 . . . . . . . .145 F8
Yew Way CO15 . . . . . . . . . .203 F7
Yewtree Gr IP5 . . . . . . . . . . .18 F7
Yewtree Rise IP8 . . . . . . . . . .16 C1
Yorick Ave CO5 . . . . . . . . . .201 C6
Yorick Rd CO5 . . . . . . . . . . .201 C6
York Cl CO10 . . . . . . . . . . . . .33 E8
York Gdns CM7 . . . . . . . . . .128 B4
York Mans CO15 . . . . . . . . .189 E5
York Pl CO1 . . . . . . . . . . . . .136 A8
York Rd
  Brightlingsea CO7 . . . . . . . .185 E6
  Chelmsford CM2 . . . . . . . . .216 A8
  Clacton-on-S CO15 . . . . . . .189 E6
  Earls Colne CO6 . . . . . . . . .105 B6
  Felixstowe IP11 . . . . . . . . . .221 E4
  Haverhill CB9 . . . . . . . . . . . . .8 E7
  Ipswich IP3 . . . . . . . . . . . . .18 A4
  Sudbury CO10 . . . . . . . . . . .33 E8
York St **[6]** CO11 . . . . . . . .86 D4
Young Cl CO16 . . . . . . . . . .188 C5
Ypres Rd CO2 . . . . . . . . . . .135 E4

**Z**

Zambesi Rd CM23 . . . . . . . .145 F5